ALSO BY GIDEON ROSE

Understanding the War on Terror
(edited with James F. Hoge, Jr.)

America and the World:
Debating the New Shape of International Politics
(edited with James F. Hoge, Jr.)

How Did This Happen?
Terrorism and the New War
(edited with James F. Hoge, Jr.)

A History of American Intervention from World War I to Afghanistan

HOW WARS END

WHY WE ALWAYS FIGHT THE LAST BATTLE

GIDEON ROSE

SIMON & SCHUSTER

NEW YORK LONDON TORONTO SYDNEY

A COUNCIL ON FOREIGN RELATIONS BOOK

Simon & Schuster
1230 Avenue of the Americas
New York, NY 10020

First Simon & Schuster hardcover edition October 2010

Designed by Ruth Lee-Mui

Manufactured in the United States of America

10 9 8 7 6 5 4 3 2

Library of Congress Cataloging-in-Publication Data

Rose, Gideon.
How wars end : why we always fight the last battle / Gideon Rose.—1st Simon & Schuster hardcover ed.
p. cm.
Includes bibliographical references.
1. United States—History, Military—20th century. 2. United States—History, Military—21st century. 3. United States—Military policy. 4. Military planning—United States. 5. Politics and war—United States. 6. War—Termination. 7. Disengagement (Military science) I. Title.
E181.R677 2010
355.00973—dc22 2010034817

ISBN 978-1-4165-9053-8
ISBN 978-1-4165-9382-9 (ebook)

The Council on Foreign Relations (CFR) is an independent, nonpartisan membership organization, think tank, and publisher dedicated to being a resource for its members, government officials, business executives, journalists, educators and students, civic and religious leaders, and other interested citizens in order to help them better understand the world and the foreign policy choices facing the United States and other countries. Founded in 1921, CFR carries out its mission by maintaining a diverse membership, with special programs to promote interest and develop expertise in the next generation of foreign policy leaders; convening meetings at its headquarters in New York and in Washington, DC, and other cities where senior government officials, members of Congress, global leaders, and prominent thinkers come together with CFR members to discuss and debate major international issues; supporting a Studies Program that fosters independent research, enabling CFR scholars to produce articles, reports, and books and hold roundtables that analyze foreign policy issues and make concrete policy recommendations; publishing *Foreign Affairs,* the preeminent journal on international affairs and U.S. foreign policy; sponsoring Independent Task Forces that produce reports with both findings and policy prescriptions on the most important foreign policy topics; and providing up-to-date information and analysis about world events and American foreign policy on its website, www.cfr.org.

To the victims of bad planning

No one starts a war—or rather, no one in his senses ought to do so—without first being clear in his mind what he intends to achieve by that war and how he intends to conduct it.

Carl von Clausewitz, *On War*

CONTENTS

How Wars End

1

THE CLAUSEWITZIAN CHALLENGE

In late March 2003, the United States and a few allies invaded Iraq. Some of the war's architects thought things would go relatively smoothly once the enemy was beaten. As National Security Adviser Condoleezza Rice put it in early April, "We fundamentally believe that when the grip of terror that Saddam Hussein's regime has wreaked on its own people is finally broken and Iraqis have an opportunity to build a better future, that you are going to see people who want to build a better future—not blow it up."[1]

Others involved in the operation were more apprehensive. Lieutenant Colonel Steven Peterson was on the military staff that planned the ground campaign. He noted afterward:

> Over a month before the war began, the Phase IV planning group concluded that the campaign would produce conditions at odds with meeting strategic objectives. They realized that the joint campaign was specifically designed to break all control mechanisms of the [Iraqi] regime and that there would be a period following regime collapse in which we would face the greatest danger to our strategic objectives. This assessment described the risk of an influx of terrorists to Iraq, the rise of

> criminal activity, the probable actions of former regime members, and the loss of control of WMD that was believed to exist. It . . . identif[ied] a need to take some specific actions including: planning to control the borders, analyzing what key areas and infrastructure should be immediately protected, and allocating adequate resources to quickly re-establish post-war control throughout Iraq.

These concerns and recommendations were brought to the attention of senior military leaders, "but the planners failed to persuade the Commanding General and dropped these issues with little resistance."

In retrospect, this episode seems mystifying. It is bad enough not to see trouble coming. But to see it coming and then not do anything about it might be even less forgivable. How could such crucial, and ultimately prescient, concerns have been dismissed and abandoned so cavalierly? "Because," Peterson continued,

> both the planners and the commander had been schooled to see fighting as the realm of war and thus attached lesser importance to post-war issues. No officer in the headquarters was prepared to argue for actions that would siphon resources from the war fighting effort, when the fighting had not yet begun. . . . Who could blame them? The business of the military is war and war is fighting. The war was not yet started, let alone finished, when these issues were being raised. Only a fool would propose hurting the war fighting effort to address post-war conditions that might or might not occur.[2]

Lieutenant General James Conway, the commander of the 1st Marine Expeditionary Force, which helped capture Baghdad, was even more succinct. Asked whether postwar planning inevitably gets short shrift compared to planning for combat, he replied, "You know, you shoot the wolf closer to the sled."[3]

The Iraq War will long be remembered as a striking example of such attitudes and their unfortunate consequences, but it is hardly the only one. In fact, the notion of war-as-combat is deeply ingrained in the thinking of both the American military and the country at large. Wars, we believe, are like street fights on a grand scale, with the central strategic challenge being how to beat up the bad guys. This view captures some basic truths: America's enemies over the years have been very bad indeed, and winning wars has required beating them up. But such a perspective is misleading because it tells only half the story.

Wars actually have two equally important aspects. One is negative, or coercive; this is the part about fighting, about beating up the bad guys. The other is positive, or constructive, and is all about politics. And this is the part that, as in Iraq, is usually overlooked or misunderstood.

The coercive aspect of war involves fending off the enemy's blows while delivering your own, eventually convincing your opponent to give up and just do what you want. This is why Carl von Clausewitz, the great Prussian military theorist, defined war as "an act of force to compel our enemy to do our will." The constructive aspect involves figuring out what it is that you actually want and how to get it. This is why Clausewitz also defined war as "an act of policy . . . simply a continuation of political intercourse, with the addition of other means."[4]

Keeping this dual nature of war fully in mind at all times is difficult. It means recognizing that every act in war has to be judged by two distinct sets of criteria—political and military—and perhaps even by two distinct institutional sources of authority. This is messy, and nobody likes a mess. So there is a great temptation for governments to clean up matters by creating a clear division of responsibility. Civilians should deal with political matters, in this view, and military leaders should deal with military matters, and control should be handed off from the politicians and diplomats to the generals at the start of a conflict and then back to the politicians and diplomats at the end. As U.S. Central Command (Centcom) commander Tommy Franks put it to the deputy secretary of defense on the eve of the Iraq War, "*You pay attention to the day* after, *I'll pay attention to the day* of."[5]

Unfortunately, the clear-division-of-labor approach is inherently flawed, because political issues can permeate every aspect of war. The flaws can sometimes be obscured during the early and middle stages of a conflict, as each side tries to defeat the other on the battlefield. But at some point, every war enters what might be called its endgame, and then any political questions that may have been ignored come rushing back with a vengeance. "The main lines along which military events progress," Clausewitz observed, "are political lines that continue throughout the war into the subsequent peace. . . . To bring a war, or one of its campaigns, to a successful close requires a thorough grasp of national policy. On that level strategy and policy coalesce: the commander-in-chief is simultaneously a statesman."[6]

With the war's general outcome starting to become clear, the endgame is best thought of as a discussion over what the details of the final settlement will be and what will happen after the shooting stops. The problem is that this discussion, whether implicit or explicit, takes place under extremely trying circumstances. At least some officials on both sides may now be considering sheathing their swords, but they are doing so against the backdrop of the fighting itself: the triumphs and disasters experienced, the blood and treasure spent, the hopes and passions raised. By this point, moreover, leaders and publics have usually gotten so caught up in beating the enemy that they find it hard to switch gears and think clearly about constructing a stable and desirable political settlement. So they rarely handle endgame challenges well and usually find themselves at the mercy of events rather than in control of them.

Americans have fared on average no better than others in these situations, and sometimes worse. The country's leaders have rarely if ever closed out military conflicts smoothly and effectively. Trapped in the fog of war, they have repeatedly stumbled across the finish line without a clear sense of what would come next or how to advance American interests amid all the chaos. They have always been surprised by what is happening and have had to improvise furiously as they pick their way through an unfamiliar and unfriendly landscape.

For all endgames' drama and historical importance, however, they have received far less attention than other phases of war. A few books look at the ends of individual wars, and there is a small academic literature on what political scientists call war termination.[7] But in general, endgames have been as neglected by scholars as they have been by policymakers. This book is intended to help fix that problem. It tells the stories of the ends of American wars over the last century, exploring how the country's political and military leaders have handled the Clausewitzian challenge of making force serve politics in each major conflict from World War I to Iraq.

From one angle, therefore, this is a book about American history. Drawing on a broad range of primary and secondary sources, as well as extensive original interviews with participants in the more recent conflicts, I have tried to re-create the endgame choices that presidents and their advisers confronted during each war. The goal is to put readers inside the room with U.S. officials as they make decisions that affect millions of lives and shape the modern world—seeing what they saw, hearing what they heard, feeling what they felt.

From another angle, though, this is a book about how to think about war, foreign policy, and international relations more generally. Marx once noted, "Men make their own history, but they do not make it as they please," and in this, at least, he was exactly right. The agency that American leaders have displayed—their freedom of action to choose one course over another—has been constrained by various kinds of structures, aspects of their environment that nudged them toward some courses rather than others. To explain endgame decisionmaking properly, therefore, you have to focus not on agency or structure alone, but on how they interact.

As for which kinds of constraints on policymakers matter most, this is a matter of intense debate inside the academy. Followers of "realist" theories argue that a country's foreign policy is concerned above all with the pursuit of its security and material interests. Look to power politics and the country's external environment, they say, and you can predict how its leaders will behave. Critics of realism, in contrast, argue that foreign policy is driven primarily by internal factors, such as domestic politics, political ideology, or bureaucratic maneuvering. And followers of psychological theories, finally, argue that foreign policy is shaped by the cognitive structures inside leaders' minds—such as the lessons they have drawn from the country's last war. Throughout the book, I weigh the relative merits of these different approaches in accounting for what happened in each war. My conclusion is that all of them help explain at least some things some of the time, but a surprisingly large amount of the picture can be sketched out by looking at power and lessons alone. (The technical term for the theoretical approach I follow here—one that begins with power factors but then layers on other variables to gain greater insight—is "neoclassical realism."[8])

From a third angle, finally, this is a book about future policy and strategy. The specific mix of factors that led to chaos in Iraq after Baghdad fell are not going to come together again, but that doesn't mean similar mistakes won't be repeated. Time and again throughout history, political and military leaders have ignored the need for careful postwar planning or approached the task with visions of sugarplums dancing in their heads—and have been brought up short as a result. But there is simply no reason this process has to play itself out over and over, and if officials can manage to learn a few general lessons from past failures, perhaps it won't.

THE AMERICAN EXPERIENCE

For two and a half years, Woodrow Wilson kept the United States aloof from formal participation in World War I, entering in early 1917 only in response to Germany's unrestricted submarine attacks. While neutral, Wilson had tried to end the conflict through negotiations and a "peace without victory." He eventually added a grand international organization to his postwar wish list, an institutional arrangement that would oversee a liberal global order and help the world transcend the evils of war and the balance of power. When the United States finally joined the war, these objectives did not change; rather, Wilson and the nation came to identify German militarism as the main obstacle to achieving them. But since the Allies never really bought into Wilson's idealistic vision, they too presented an obstacle that had to be overcome.

During 1918, American intervention made German defeat inevitable, setting up an intricate triangular dance during the war's endgame. Germany sought to get off as easy as possible. The Allies sought the opposite, trying to recoup their losses and more at German expense. And Wilson, in the middle, pushed for "regime change" in Germany while trying to play both sides off against each another and usher in a new and better world. This delicate balancing act would probably have collapsed even if a master manipulator such as Bismarck were in charge—and the stiff-necked, high-minded Wilson was no Bismarck.

As a neutral, the United States had been unable to get the settlement it wanted because the two evenly matched European coalitions were determined to fight the war to a finish. By becoming a belligerent, Wilson gained a seat at the peace table, but only by helping one side win, paving the way for just the sort of illiberal peace he was desperate to avoid. With no reason to take American concerns seriously once the fighting was done, the Allies simply did what they wanted. And so the tragedy of Versailles—of hapless American attempts to forestall Allied impositions on a prostrate German Republic—is best understood as the working out of the tensions inherent in the war's final acts.

A generation later, the United States was back battling the Germans once again. The American effort in World War II was partly a fight *against* the Axis: the Roosevelt administration chose to seek total victory over its enemies and then achieved it. But the American effort was also a fight *for* a certain vision of international political and economic order. Even before the Japanese attacked, American leaders had hoped for a postwar settlement that would provide the United States and the world with lasting peace and prosperity.

The negative and positive fights occurred simultaneously, but American policymakers did not link them very well. In particular, they failed to recognize that even the total defeat of the Axis powers would be only a necessary but not a sufficient condition for the emergence of their desired postwar order. Washington had to ally with Stalin to destroy Hitler, and the price of that alliance was giving the Soviets control of half of Europe after the war. The reality of this Faustian bargain took a while to sink in, however, and so the endgame of the positive fight continued long after VE Day—until the emergence of NATO and the postwar settlement in the late 1940s and early '50s.

The Cold War, in other words, is best understood not as some new struggle, but rather as a continuation of the positive fight America had already been pursuing for several years. Given the Soviet Union's different vision for the world, such a clash was probably inevitable; only one side's abdication of the field could have prevented it. But the disillusionment and hysteria accompanying its onset was not inevitable, and stemmed in part from the failure of the Western allies to acknowledge the gap between their political and military policies during the first half of the decade.

As late as the beginning of 1945, Washington expected fighting in the Pacific to continue long after it had stopped in Europe. But the endgame in the east began in earnest in late spring that year, and Japan's capitulation followed a few months after Germany's. In the Pacific, three new factors came into play. Unlike the Nazis, Japanese leaders actually tried to negotiate and end the war short of total defeat. The divergence of long-term interests between the United States and the Soviet Union grew increasingly obvious. And the atomic bomb became available for use. During the summer of 1945, accordingly, U.S. officials actively debated which war-termination policies in the Pacific would best promote American interests. In dealing with Japan, as with Germany, they looked more to the lessons of the past and national ideology than to the calculations of Realpolitik. But beneath American decisions, underwriting policymakers' extraordinary ambition in both theaters, was the strongest relative power position the modern world had ever seen.

That strength remained largely intact several years later, and helps explain one of the most puzzling episodes in American military and diplomatic history—the final stages of the Korean War. Once North

Korean troops surged across the 38th Parallel in late June 1950, the fortunes of war shifted back and forth until both sides agreed to begin armistice negotiations the following summer. Six months of haggling dispensed with routine military matters such as the armistice line and postwar security requirements, and by the end of 1951 a settlement seemed imminent. But then an extremely unusual issue rose to the top of the agenda—the question of whether Communist prisoners in UN hands would be forced to go home against their will at the end of the conflict or instead be allowed to refuse repatriation.

Still smarting from having to accept a stalemate and feeling guilty about having forced the return of Soviet POWs to Stalin's tender mercies back in 1945, Harry S. Truman and Secretary of State Dean Acheson decided that there was no reason they had to witness such heart-rending scenes this time around, so they made the principle of voluntary repatriation official U.S. policy. Yet thanks to poor planning and extraordinary bureaucratic incompetence on the ground in Korea, the repatriation stance kept the fighting going for close to another year and a half.

More than 124,000 UN casualties, including nine thousand American dead, came during the period when prisoner repatriation was the sole contested issue at the armistice talks, and the policy cost tens of billions of dollars. Yet rather than end the war by reverting to the routine historical practice of an all-for-all prisoner swap, two successive American administrations chose to continue fighting, and one of them even seriously mulled the possibility of escalation to nuclear war. The only way to make sense of this behavior is to look at the lessons policymakers had drawn from the previous war along with the mid-century hegemony that gave the U.S. leaders extraordinary freedom of action to do pretty much whatever they wanted.

A decade further on, American officials believed that the fall of South Vietnam to communism would have terrible consequences at home and abroad, so they decided to do what was necessary to prevent such an outcome. During the Kennedy and Johnson administrations, the toughest question—whether to accept the true costs of victory or defeat—was kicked down the road. By gradually increasing the scale of the American effort, officials hoped, the United States could persuade the enemy to cease and desist. Once the patience of the American public wore thin, however, such an approach was no longer feasible. By 1968, the war was causing such domestic turmoil and costing so much blood and treasure that finding a way out became just as important as avoiding a loss.

Richard Nixon's first Vietnam strategy stemmed from the lessons policymakers had drawn from the endgame of the Korean War—that negotiations with Communists could be successful if you continued military operations and threatened radical escalation. When that strategy didn't work, the White House opted for what seemed to be a politically palatable middle path between staying the course and withdrawing quickly. It started withdrawing troops and reduced the U.S. role in ground combat while holding off a South Vietnamese collapse. In the end, the twists and turns of policy and negotiations yielded an agreement that permitted the United States to walk out, get its prisoners back, and not formally betray an ally. That same agreement, nevertheless—together with a changed domestic context in the United States—paved the way for the fall of South Vietnam two years later.

The lessons of Vietnam were very much on the minds of policymakers in the George H. W. Bush administration as they responded to Saddam Hussein's invasion of Kuwait in August 1990. Those lessons, officials believed, argued for a quick, decisive use of force to achieve carefully limited political objectives—something that the military campaign in the Persian Gulf accomplished by pushing Iraqi forces out of Kuwait within weeks.

But while undoing the invasion of Kuwait was the Bush administration's chief war aim, it was not the only one, since Washington also wanted to deal with the ongoing threat Iraq posed to the security of the Gulf region. And here the lessons of recent wars were problematic. Both a Korean-style solution (garrison Kuwait forever) and a Vietnam-like approach (get deeply entangled in nation-building in Iraq) seemed unattractive. So Washington convinced itself that it could have its cake and eat it, too—that Saddam was bound to be dispatched by one of his minions following a humiliating defeat, something that would make the problem go away without direct or ongoing American intervention in Iraqi politics or the Gulf more generally.

In the end, however, Saddam managed to retain control over his regime's security apparatus and use the reconstituted remnants of Iraq's armed forces to suppress popular uprisings against him by Shiites in the south and Kurds in the north. Days after celebrating their quick and relatively easy triumph, American officials found themselves watching their defeated enemy rise from the ashes and savage the very people

Washington had called on to revolt. Just when Bush thought he was out, therefore, Iraq pulled him back in, as the administration wound up permitting Saddam to reestablish his control over the country while backing into the Korean-style containment it had tried so hard to avoid.

Over the course of the next decade, Washington continued to contain Iraq while hoping for Saddam to fall—less because officials thought this policy was a good one than because they thought the alternatives were even worse. Then came the terrorist attacks of September 11, 2001, which convinced the administration of a different George Bush that the Middle East status quo was unacceptable. Afghanistan was the first front in Washington's subsequent "war on terror," but within days of the fall of Kabul the president ordered planning to start for what would become a second front in Iraq.

Previous administrations had shied away from toppling Saddam because they did not want to take responsibility for what would happen in Iraq afterward. The second Bush team got around such concerns by convincing itself that American commitments in a postwar Iraq could be limited without ill effect. Conventional wisdom about the need for extensive nation-building was misguided, senior officials believed; a light footprint on the ground and a quick handoff to friendly locals was all that was required to get things on track and allow the United States to move on to the next security challenge.

When this theory was put to the test, however, it failed spectacularly, and having toppled Saddam the United States was left presiding over a country rapidly spinning out of control, with officials having no plans or resources for what to do next. Liberation turned into occupation; local ambivalence into insurgency and then civil war. Four years later, a new and better-resourced American strategy managed to build on some positive local trends and stabilize the situation, so that by the end of the decade Iraq had pulled back from the brink and gained a chance at a better future. But even then nothing was guaranteed.

For all the attention devoted to the second Bush administration's distinctive ideas about national security policy, what made its approach to Iraq possible was its unfettered power. International primacy removed limits on American foreign policy imposed by the world at large, and the 9/11 attacks swept away limits imposed by the domestic political system. The administration's leading figures thus found themselves with extraordinary freedom of action and decided to use it to the fullest. Ironically, the mistakes they made had the effect of squandering the surplus capital they had inherited and leaving their successors constrained once again.

THE FIRE NEXT TIME

In early 2009, the Obama administration assumed responsibility for the still-unfinished wars in Iraq and Afghanistan. Some of the new president's supporters were surprised and dismayed when the administration failed to dramatically change U.S. policy toward either conflict and even increased U.S. involvement in the latter. They should not have been: wars are difficult to close out even when they are started well, and mistakes at the beginning complicate the job exponentially, no matter who is in charge later on. The crucial test for Barack Obama and his successors, accordingly, will be not simply whether they can muddle through the struggles they were bequeathed, but whether they can avoid making major mistakes themselves in the wars that will inevitably follow down the road.

When future American leaders tackle the Clausewitzian challenge, they will still possess great power and will have the advantage of knowing what their predecessors did and how they fared. As this book shows, lessons from previous wars can serve as cognitive blinders, narrowing the way officials think about the situations they face, and power can be a trap, underwriting hubris and folly. But lessons can also guide and power can create opportunities. So if new generations of wartime policymakers fail to think clearly about what they are doing and stumble badly once again, they will have nobody to blame but themselves.

2

WORLD WAR I

As dawn broke on Saturday, November 9, 1918, Matthias Erzberger paced up and down a railroad car in a forest near the village of Compiègne, France. The leader of the Center Party in the Reichstag, he had been sent out to negotiate the terms of an armistice ending the war between Imperial Germany and the Allies. Crossing the French border, he had noted in his diary: "Three weeks ago I traveled to [the officers' school in] Karlsruhe to the death-bed of my only son. . . . My feelings on the journey . . . which any father can readily understand, were no more depressed and painful than my feelings at the present moment." [1]

When Erzberger and his delegation had arrived at their destination on Friday morning and heard the conditions being imposed—the return of all territories occupied by Germany, the occupation of key positions in the German homeland by the Allies, the gutting of the German military machine, and a continuation of the Allied naval blockade—they had struggled to contain their shock and despair. Erzberger tried to get the terms softened and the seventy-two-hour signing deadline extended, but France's Marshall Ferdinand Foch, in charge on the Allied side, would not budge. Erzberger was allowed to send a message back home, and that was it. He did so, explaining the situation and asking for authority to sign. After working through the night on some further arguments for leniency, by Saturday morning the German delegation had little to do but wait.

Back in Berlin, Prince Max of Baden, the imperial chancellor, was getting desperate. He had sent Erzberger on his mission knowing that events were rapidly coming to a head—that Germany was threatened not only by military pressure abroad but also by political chaos at home. A moderate trying to end the war while preserving as much of the old regime as possible, Max had put matters bluntly to his cousin the Kaiser in a telephone call Friday evening:

> Your abdication has become necessary to save Germany from civil war. . . . The great majority of the people believe you to be responsible for the present situation. The belief is false, but there it is. If civil war and worse can now be prevented through your abdication, your name will be blessed by future generations. . . . [W]hatever step is decided on, it must be taken with the greatest possible speed. This sacrifice, if made after blood has once flowed, will have lost all its power for good. . . .

The Kaiser had coldly dismissed the suggestion, then denied Max's request to resign: "You sent out the armistice offer; you will also have to accept the conditions."[2]

Now, on Saturday morning, Max knew there was no time left. The mainstream Social Democratic leaders Friedrich Ebert and Philipp Scheidemann, recognizing that they themselves had only a brief moment to try to ride the political whirlwind before losing control of the situation, were demanding immediate abdication as a condition of their party's continued support of the government. Scheidemann called the Chancellery before 7 A.M. threatening to resign from the cabinet if Wilhelm did not abdicate within the hour. It would happen very soon, he was told. At 9 A.M. he called back and heard that the abdication would come "perhaps at noon." Not good enough, Scheidemann replied, and resigned right then.

At the headquarters of the Supreme Command in Spa, Germany's military leadership was also in turmoil. Field Marshall Paul von Hindenburg and First Quartermaster General Wilhelm Groener, the chief and deputy chief of the Imperial General Staff, had finally accepted the inevitable and went to meet with the Kaiser at 10 A.M. Tears running down his cheeks, Hindenburg could only beg to resign. It was up to Groener, a Wurtemberger less constrained by feudal loyalties than his Prussian colleagues, to break the news: the situation of the army was desperate, revolution was imminent, and an immediate armistice was an absolute necessity—with all that required. The Kaiser refused to believe it, proposing to lead the army himself back to Germany to quell the troubles. Groener burst his bubble: "Sire, you no longer have an army. . . . The army will march home in peace and order under its leaders and commanding generals, but not under the command of Your Majesty, for it no longer stands behind Your Majesty."[3]

Furious and incredulous, the monarch demanded written confirmation of this from all his generals. Since Wilhelm had raised similar issues the day before, on Friday evening Hindenburg and Groener had sent orders for the senior German field commanders to assemble at Spa immediately for consultations. Traveling through the night, thirty-nine of them had arrived by Saturday morning, when they were assembled in a separate room and asked two questions: would their troops fight to reconquer the homeland under the Kaiser's personal leadership, and would the troops fight against Bolshevism in a domestic civil war? Just before 1 P.M., a military aide brought in word of the officers' answers: essentially, no and no. After some more discussion, the Kaiser gave in and started to dictate a message for Prince Max that "he was prepared to renounce the Imperial Crown, if thereby alone general civil war in Germany were to be avoided, but that he remained King of Prussia and would not leave the army." An aide noted that such a momentous decision should really have some formal record, so the group decided to break for lunch and draw one up afterward.[4] "That silent gathering, in that cheerful, well-lit room, where, round a table decorated with freshly cut flowers, there was gathered nothing but anxiety, misery and despair, will always remain one of my saddest memories," Crown Prince Rupprecht wrote later.[5]

As the morning passed without a definitive answer from Spa, however, Prince Max grew tired of waiting and decided to take matters into his own hands. At 11:30 A.M. he issued a statement to the Wolff Telegraph Agency: "The Kaiser and King has resolved to renounce the throne. The Imperial Chancellor will remain at his post until decisions have been made on questions connected with the Kaiser's abdication, the Crown Prince's renunciation of the Imperial and Prussian thrones, and the creation of a regency." Max and other senior officials then met with the leaders of the Social Democrats and offered Ebert the chancellorship, which he accepted.

Soon afterward, when Ebert and Scheidemann were having lunch at the Reichstag, some workers and soldiers broke in to say that a crowd had gathered outside expecting a speech. As Scheidemann went out to the balcony, he was told that Karl Liebknecht, a more radical socialist leader, was speaking right then to another crowd from another balcony not far away. Determined not to be beaten to the punch, Scheidemann shouted to the cheering throng, "The old and the rotten, the monarchy, has collapsed! Long live the new! Long live the German Republic!" Then he went back to his potato soup.[6]

Out in Spa, the Kaiser and his advisers reconvened after their own meal to review the formal statement of abdication. Just after 2 P.M., they called Berlin to give officials there the text—at which point the undersecretary of state interrupted to tell them that the Kaiser's abdication had already been announced, and his renunciation of the Prussian throne, too. Dumbfounded and appalled, Wilhelm raged against such "barefaced, outrageous treason," but there was little he could do. Later that night he was packed off on a train to Holland.

Near 4 P.M., still haranguing his crowd in Berlin, Liebknecht shouted, "The day of liberty has dawned! . . . I proclaim the free Socialist Republic of Germany, which shall comprise all Germans. . . . We extend our hands to them and call on them to complete the world revolution." Two hours late and several crowds short, however, the insurrection never had much of a chance, and a couple of months later, their revolution stalled, Liebknecht and his colleague Rosa Luxemburg would be killed by right-wing militias in a government-sponsored crackdown against radicalism.

At dusk, Prince Max came to say good-bye to Ebert. The Social Democrat asked the aristocrat to stay in Berlin and help administer the new regime, but Max declined. "Herr Ebert," he said, "I commit the German Empire to your keeping." "I have already given it two sons," the new chancellor replied sadly. Later that evening, a telephone on Ebert's desk rang. Picking it up, he discovered it was a direct line to Supreme Command headquarters and that Groener was on the other end. Was the new government willing to maintain order and protect Germany from anarchy, the general wanted to know? Yes, Ebert responded. "Then the Supreme Command will maintain discipline in the army and bring it peacefully home."[7]

The following evening, still waiting in his railroad car in Compiègne, Erzberger finally received instructions from Berlin authorizing him to agree to the armistice terms. After some additional haggling, the document was signed just after 5 A.M. on Monday, to take effect six hours later. After it was done, Erzberger read out a short statement protesting the harshness of the agreement. It concluded: "A nation of seventy millions suffers but it does not die." For playing his part in Germany's humiliation, Erzberger himself was assassinated by right-wing radicals three years later.

Despite their extraordinary drama, the final moments of the Great War have received far less attention than the conflict's origins or diplomatic aftermath. But it was precisely in the fires of that fall that the outlines of the ultimate settlement were forged, along with the next, even bloodier war. The gap between the reality and the perception of Germany's military position, the gap between Woodrow Wilson's idealistic rhetoric and postwar German suffering, and the fact that the armistice was signed by a new, civilian leadership rather than the officials who had actually lost the war all combined to hobble the Weimar Republic from birth and pave the way for the rise of its Nazi successor.

The sheer scale of the war made turmoil and recriminations afterward inevitable. But the amount and nature of that turmoil, and the targets of those recriminations, were driven in part by the choices made by key actors during the conflict's final stages. It was then, for example, that Wilson, controlling the richest and least-bloodied state in the winning coalition, was forced to answer two questions that had been simmering in his consciousness for months: exactly what to demand of the Central Powers (principally Germany and Austria-Hungary) and what of the Allies (principally Britain, France, and Italy).

When war had broken out in Europe in August 1914, Wilson's assertion of American neutrality was automatic; any other course would have been unthinkable. And for two and a half years, he kept the United States aloof from formal participation, until Germany's unrestricted submarine attacks triggered America's entry. Absent territorial ambitions in Europe, seeking international stability and a harmonious liberal trading order, Wilson's America had tried while neutral to end the conflict through negotiations and a "peace without victory." Eventually a grand international organization was added to Wilson's wish list, an institutional arrangement that would permit all nations to transcend the evils of war and the balance of power. These American goals did not change when the United States joined the war in 1917; rather, Wilson and the nation came to identify German militarism as the main threat to this vision, a threat that had to be eliminated so that their original war aims could be achieved. The Allies, however, did not seem to share America's high-minded purposes, and therefore they too represented a threat to Wilson's vision—something the president made clear from the beginning by joining their coalition only as an "associate."

As American strength tipped the military balance during 1918 and made German defeat inevitable, the stage was set for triangular diplomacy during the war's endgame. Germany would naturally try to escape with as soft a punishment as possible. The Allies would seek the opposite result, trying to satisfy their own passions, greed, and fear. And Wilson, holding the whip hand, would try to reform Germany while playing both sides off against each other and midwifing a new world.

But in geopolitics, unlike geometry, triangles are the least stable of all configurations. The United States could not bring about its desired settlement from 1914 to 1917 because the two evenly matched coalitions were determined to fight the war to a finish. By joining the contest, Washington gained a seat at the peace table—but only by enabling one side to triumph, creating irresistible temptations for just the kind of illiberal peace Wilson wanted to avoid.

Others recognized what the Americans never did; as the French foreign minister commented to a colleague two weeks before the armistice, "Wilson cannot be a belligerent and an arbitrator at the same time."[8] Moreover, Wilson failed to understand just how difficult it was going to be to achieve any of his ambitious goals, let alone all of them simultaneously. He put his differences with the Allies to one side during the fighting rather than trying to hammer out a unified stance; he paid little attention to unifying his own country behind his controversial agenda; and he didn't bother to think through in advance what crucial concepts such as "democratization" would mean in practice.

As a consequence, the diplomatic flurries of October–November 1918 that began with such hope ended in chaos, with the capitulation of a defeated and barely democratized Germany, coupled with token Allied promises to keep Wilson's program in mind when drawing up the final settlement. The tragedy of Versailles—where the Allies brushed off American attempts to promote a generous peace—was merely the final working out of the tensions inherent in the war's final acts.

1914–1917: NEUTRALITY AND BELLIGERENCY

The outbreak of war in 1914 caught Americans by surprise, and their president with them. The policy response seemed so obvious as not to require discussion: remain uninvolved. And had the war not settled into a lengthy stalemate, that is precisely what would have happened. But when neither side proved able to force a decision on the battlefield, the conflict became a war of attrition, with each coalition striving to mobilize its own resources while preventing the other from doing the same. In this situation, given how economically powerful the United States had become, American "noninvolvement" was impossible—because *any* substantial commercial and financial relations with Europe were bound to affect the balance of resources somehow.[9] Three economic flows were particularly important: U.S. trade with the Central Powers and other continental nations, financing for the Allied war effort by private U.S. institutions, and U.S. trade with the Allies. British suppression of the first would cause frictions; the second would permit the Allies to remain in the war while tarnishing American neutrality in German eyes; and German attacks on the third would bring Washington into the conflict for real.

The logic of war usually leads belligerents to fight with whatever tools are at hand. For Britain, this meant using control of the seas to cut off German access to the outside world. At the start of the war, American trade with the continent was not insignificant and would have increased as the conflict wore on, so British efforts to isolate Germany led directly to tensions with the United States. By 1916, these had grown so great that Congress and the president both seriously considered major retaliatory action. There was no rupture in U.S.-Allied relations, however, for three reasons. First, British leaders realized that such a break would be disastrous for them, and carefully avoided provoking an impasse.[10] Second, at the same time that American trade with the Central Powers and their commercial partners was being curtailed, American trade with the Allies was booming, so any retaliatory measures against Britain would necessarily have hurt U.S. economic interests as well.[11] Third and most important, most Americans found Germany's actions even more distressing than the Allies': "In the glorious annals of German achievements," wrote the British ambassador in Washington, "nothing is so remarkable as the fact that Germany has almost made England popular in America."[12]

Apart from its other depredations, Germany sought through its submarine warfare to do to Britain what Britain was doing to Germany through the blockade: cut the enemy off from the outside world. The problem for Berlin was that this required sinking commercial shipping and thus killing civilians directly (rather than indirectly, as the British did). Even worse, it involved killing neutral citizens, including Americans who happened to be on board the ships in question.

The German strategy had a certain brutal logic, but it lacked the British strategy's outstanding quality of prudence. Wilson was personally sympathetic to the Allied cause, but he tried hard to keep the United States out of the war.[13] The president nonetheless made it clear that he would not restrict American commerce, that he considered the lives of Americans sacrosanct, and that he would respond harshly to unrestricted submarine warfare. German diplomats realized the danger, but could not get their military colleagues to take it seriously. And so at the end of 1916, when the war's continued stalemate seemed to offer Germany no choice other than a compromise peace or a gamble for outright victory, Berlin bet on its submarines and precipitated American intervention.

During the period of American neutrality, Wilson had reflected on international relations and decided that after the war things had to change. The fix he settled on was an ambitious international organization that would keep the peace once the war ended with no clear winner. That Wilson tried hard to achieve such an outcome shows that he initially thought Wilhelmine Germany could be a tolerable component of his new order—that "regime change," as we might put it today, was not necessary.[14] But German actions changed his mind; they "served to convince" him, as he told Congress in April 1917, "that the Prussian autocracy was not and could never be our friend." Unrestricted submarine warfare struck at both American interests and American ideals; those who could perpetrate such acts had to be both countered and reformed. "I have exactly the same things in mind now," Wilson declared, "that I had in mind" a few months earlier (when he delivered his "peace without victory" speech). What was new, however, was his conviction that "a steadfast concert for peace can never be maintained except by a partnership of democratic nations. No autocratic government could be trusted to keep faith within it or observe its covenants."[15]

The United States, in short, entered an illiberal war in order to achieve a generous peace and usher in a liberal world full of liberal nations. The contradictions inherent in this posture would come to the fore in the fall of 1918.

THE AMERICAN WAR

Wilson knew and cared little about military affairs, and so had not thought much beforehand about how the United States would achieve its war aims. American mobilization started practically from scratch in 1917, and was handled at first by men with little aptitude for the job. As a result, for more than a year after entering the conflict the United States contributed few soldiers and little materiel to the Allied war effort.

Where U.S. aid was crucial, however, was in averting an economic catastrophe for the Allied cause. As British foreign secretary Arthur Balfour wrote bluntly to Wilson's confidant Colonel Edward House at the end of June 1917, "we seem on the verge of a financial disaster which would be worse than defeat in the field."[16] Lord Northcliffe, chief of the British War Mission, badgered House again a few weeks later: "Unless the United States government can meet in full our expenses in America, including exchange, the whole financial fabric of the alliance will collapse. This conclusion will not be a matter of months but of days."[17] These financial pressures led eventually to the development of inter-Allied economic and administrative coordination, which channeled U.S. help where it was needed. As one of the key French participants in this network would later write: "Without means of payment in dollars . . . the Allies would have been beaten before the end of 1917. America's entry into the war saved them. Before the American soldier, the American dollar turned the tide."[18]

Thanks to slow mobilization and the decision to form a separate U.S. army rather than feed American soldiers piecemeal into existing Allied units, it was well into 1918 before American troops entered battle in significant numbers, and at that point the war was practically over. As Russia withdrew, the Germans decided to make a final attempt at victory in the west as well as the east. A series of offensives in early 1918 achieved initial success but ultimately failed to break the Allied line, and by summer, with the Americans coming in droves, the tide of the war had turned irreversibly against the Central Powers.

On August 8, powerful Allied attacks sent German defenders reeling; it was "the black day of the German Army in the history of this war," wrote Erich von Ludendorff, Groener's predecessor and the true master of the German military machine.[19] At a conference a week later, Hindenburg told the Kaiser and the civilian leadership, "we can no longer hope to break down the fighting spirit of our enemies by military action, and . . . we must set as the object of our campaign that of gradually wearing down the enemy's fighting spirit by a strategic defensive." The meeting concluded: "Diplomatic feelers must be thrown out at an opportune moment preparatory to an understanding with the enemy. Such a moment might present itself after the next successes in the west."[20] By stubbornly refusing to seek peace until every hope of victory had been extinguished, however, the Germans had long since passed the point where such a strategy might have worked. There would be no more "successes in the west"; there was no room left to maneuver.

WILSON AND THE GERMANS

German leaders actually faced a double dilemma, because military defeat brought their domestic troubles to a boil as well. Much of the Prussian military aristocracy that had provided the social support for the Kaiserreich was killed off early in the war; as Arthur Rosenberg put it, "the old Bismarckian Germany was destroyed on the battlefield of the Marne."[21] Since 1916, the nation had been run by Hindenburg and Ludendorff, with the Kaiser increasingly detached and acquiescent in a de facto military dictatorship. Despite growing restiveness within some political parties, meanwhile, the Reichstag went with the flow also, as did a succession of imperial chancellors of little consequence. The bristling front Germany presented to the world concealed a social and political vacuum; when that front gave way, the Kaiserreich was set to implode.

After deciding in early August that the war was unwinnable, German leaders dithered for a few more weeks. The other members of the Central Powers, however, were in even worse shape, and in the end it was their collapse that forced Germany's hand. In mid-September, Austria publicly appealed to the Allies for an end to the war, and days later Bulgaria capitulated outright. Both actions made the German people realize the direness of the situation and prodded the Reichstag parties out of their slumber; the collapse of Bulgaria also dealt Germany a massive military blow by opening a gap in its defenses and cutting the link to

Turkey. On the western front, moreover, Allied tanks and the dearth of German reserves combined to force continual German retreat.

These pressures came to a head at the end of the month. On September 28, Hindenburg and Ludendorff decided they had to stop the fighting immediately in order to protect the German army from being routed. When they told this the next day to Paul von Hintze, the secretary of state for foreign affairs, he suggested three possible courses of action: unify the country under an absolute dictatorship and fight to the end; proclaim democratic reforms to channel and co-opt domestic political unrest; or appeal for an armistice directly to Wilson, whose Fourteen Points promised a generous peace settlement. The generals agreed to a combination of the second and third courses, and the three men went to see the Kaiser. He agreed that the first option was out of the question, and accepted the moves to "canalize" the revolutionary upheaval and ask for an end to the fighting.[22]

When told of the decision, the aged chancellor Georg Graf von Hertling resigned his post rather than preside over the old elite's loss of power. Ludendorff was now desperate both to get a cease-fire and to shirk responsibility for defeat, and on October 1 he told fellow officers he wanted Social Democrats in the new government so that they would be the ones "to make the peace which now has to be made. They should now eat the soup which they have prepared!"[23] On October 3, a new government headed by Prince Max was bullied by military leaders into sending out a prewritten peace note requesting Wilson's help in "bring[ing] about the immediate conclusion of an armistice on land, on water, and in the air," with the Fourteen Points and subsequent pronouncements serving "as a basis for the peace negotiations."[24]

The German note reached the United States on October 6 and set off a frenzy of speculation. The British and French immediately suspected a German move to cheat them of victory and were determined to prevent such an occurrence at all costs. Many in the United States felt the same way. But Wilson, wanting more than just Germany's defeat and feeling uncertain about future military and political trends, was less decisive. His first draft of a reply was almost polite, insisting that the prerequisites for discussion of an armistice were outright acceptance of the Fourteen Points, withdrawal of German troops to prewar boundaries, and abandonment of a "scorched earth" policy during retreats.[25] The final result was tighter and cooler: it kept the demands for acceptance of Wilson's program and evacuation from occupied territories but added a clause asking "whether the Imperial Chancellor is speaking merely for the constituted authorities of the Empire who have so far conducted the war."[26]

To prepare himself for dealing with Wilson's response, on October 8 Max did something German leaders had failed to do for several years: he demanded from his generals an immediate account of the nation's politico-military position. Ludendorff was asked how long his army could hold out, whether the situation was likely to improve, and whether the government could afford to resist a demand for evacuation from all occupied territories.[27] Wilson's note arrived in the middle of this internal discussion, and the contradictions in the high command's arguments now began to emerge: military leaders, the cabinet was told, wanted "to save the Army, so that we can use it as a means of pressure during the peace negotiations"—but they could not offer any strategy for doing so and accepted the necessity of evacuation to German borders.[28] On October 12, therefore, the government agreed to Wilson's conditions.

Word of the German response reached the United States on the evening of October 13; when Wilson attended the opera soon afterward, the crowd cheered him enthusiastically. As the conflicting demands of the Allies, American public opinion, and his own ideals became clearer, however, the president was once again uncertain how to respond. House noted in his diary: "I never saw [Wilson] more disturbed. He said he did not know where to make the entrance in order to reach the heart of things. He wanted to make his reply final so there would be no exchange of notes. It reminded him, he said, of a maze. If one went in at the right entrance, he reached the center, but if one took the wrong turning, it was necessary to go out again and do it over."[29]

The resulting diplomatic note, composed during a day of discussions between Wilson and his advisers, contained three new elements. First, it told the Germans bluntly that "no [armistice] arrangement can be accepted by the government of the United States which does not provide absolutely satisfactory safeguards and guarantees of the maintenance of the present military supremacy of the armies of the United States and of the Allies in the field." Second, raising the point about "scorched earth" policies and referring to recent victims of unrestricted submarine warfare, it declared that an armistice would not even be "consider[ed] . . . so long as the armed forces of Germany continue the illegal and inhumane practices which they still persist in." Finally, it reminded the Germans of Wilson's earlier call for "the destruction of every arbitrary power . . . that can . . . disturb the peace of the world; or . . . at least its reduction to virtual impotency." "The power which has hitherto controlled the German nation is of the sort here described," Wilson wrote; the "choice of the German nation to alter it" was a "condition precedent to peace."[30]

This note drove home to the Germans that they had lost the war and that any favorable treatment in the final settlement would come from the kindness of the Allies rather than residual German strength. The military leadership, shocked and disbelieving, demanded the government reject Wilson's conditions and risk breaking off the negotiations. As one officer told the cabinet on October 17, "When the Supreme Army Command decided to make peace proposals, it acted on the supposition that an honorable peace can be concluded. Now for the first time it is evident that it is to be a case of 'to be or not to be.' " If Wilson persisted in offering "dishonorable terms," the government should "accept a fight to the end," summoning the German people to a final, purifying Götterdämmerung.[31] The civilian leadership, in contrast, saw little choice but to comply, especially after Ludendorff's unsatisfactory answers to a second questionnaire about the prospects for successful resistance. Exchanges between the two factions were bitter:

> IMPERIAL CHANCELLOR: So [you are saying that] the situation is no longer the same as it was . . . when we were persuaded to make a peace offer to Wilson.
>
> GENERAL LUDENDORFF: I am under the impression that before accepting the conditions of this note, which are too severe, we should say to the enemy: Win such terms by fighting for them.
>
> IMPERIAL CHANCELLOR: And when they have won them, will they not impose worse conditions?
>
> GENERAL LUDENDORFF: There can be no worse conditions.
>
> IMPERIAL CHANCELLOR: Oh, yes, they can invade Germany and lay waste the country.
>
> GENERAL LUDENDORFF: Things have not gone that far yet.[32]

Ultimately the government decided to overrule the army's opposition to the note's first demand (the guarantee of Allied military superiority) and the navy's opposition to its second (the restriction of submarine warfare). This still left the note's third demand, the abolition of "arbitrary power." No one was sure exactly what Wilson had in mind, although most felt he was asking for the abdication of the Kaiser.[33] Before pushing for such a dramatic step, however, the government decided to placate Wilson (and bolster its own position) by institutionalizing the democratic reforms that had recently occurred. The third German note of October 20 thus included, along with diplomatically phrased concessions regarding the military conditions of the armistice and submarine warfare, the following statement:

> Hitherto the representation of the people in the German Empire has not been endowed with an influence on the formation of the government. . . . These conditions have just now undergone a fundamental change. The new government has been formed in complete accord with the wishes of the representation of the people. . . . In future no government can take or continue in office without possessing the confidence of the majority of the Reichstag. The responsibility of the Chancellor of the Empire to the representation of the people is being legally developed and safeguarded. The first act of the new government has been to lay before the Reichstag a bill to alter the Constitution of the Empire so that the consent of the representation of the people is required for decisions on war and peace.[34]

Germany's third note, like its second, made American leaders ponder just what to do next. "Long conference at White House," noted Secretary of the Navy Josephus Daniels in his diary for October 21. "General opinion that Germany has accepted W.W.'s demands. Was she in good faith."[35] Wilson explicitly rejected "hard" alternatives such as demanding unconditional surrender, prolonging negotiations further, or consulting with the British and French. He also rejected, implicitly, the "softest" option of accepting the German position completely. His response, sent on October 23, informed the Germans that as a result of their concessions he was passing the correspondence on to the Allies and thus putting his weight behind a quick armistice, acceptance of which would entitle Germany to a peace based on the Fourteen Points. Yet the note also pressed for further political reforms:

> Significant and important as the [recent] constitutional changes seem to be . . . it does not appear that the principle of a government responsible to the German people has yet been fully worked out. . . . It may be that future wars have been brought under the control of the German peo-

> ple, but the present war has not been. . . . [T]he German people have no means of commanding the acquiescence of the military authorities of the Empire in the popular will. . . . [T]he United States cannot deal with any but veritable representatives of the German people who have been assured of a genuine constitutional standing as the real rulers of Germany. If it must deal with the military masters and the monarchical autocrats of Germany now, or if it is likely to have to deal with them later . . . it must demand, not peace negotiations, but surrender.[36]

The German government responded with a fourth note on October 27 to tell Wilson that it awaited concrete armistice proposals, emphasizing once again the reforms that had been made. Wilson remained silent. As the German government persisted on its diplomatic course, Ludendorff resigned, and momentum grew within Germany to force the Kaiser's resignation and end the war quickly.[37] A note from Wilson on November 5 instructed the Germans that armistice conditions were ready for them to sign, and informed them that the Allies too accepted the Fourteen Points as a basis for the final settlement, albeit with two reservations. As Germany descended into political chaos, Prince Max's government dispatched Erzberger's delegation to France. Within days the Kaiser was gone, Max's government had evaporated, and a republic had been declared. The Great War officially ended on November 11, mere hours after the demise of its central protagonist, Wilhelmine Germany.

WILSON AND THE ALLIES

Wilson considered the Central Powers the main but not the sole obstacle to his vision of the postwar world. The Allies, he felt, also practiced the old-school politics he wanted to transcend; their behavior too would have to change if things were to be truly different after the war. Four main points were in contention. First, the Allies wanted to treat the Central Powers harshly in defeat while Wilson wanted to bring a democratized Germany back into the community of nations on generous terms. Second, the Allies wanted to rely on their own strength and alliances for security, while Wilson wanted general disarmament supported by a collective security system institutionalized in the League of Nations. Third, Britain wanted to retain naval hegemony while Wilson wanted guaranteed freedom of the seas for all (and particularly the United States). Finally, the Allies wanted to pursue their own economic interests through exclusive arrangements, while Wilson wanted to create a multilateral liberal order based on free trade.

Wilson had kept these differences in mind when he joined the war, intending to deal with them at the close of hostilities. He spelled out his strategy in a letter to House during the summer of 1917:

> England and France *have not the same views with regard to peace that we have* by any means. When the war is over we can force them to our way of thinking, because by that time they will, among other things, be financially in our hands; but we cannot force them now. . . . [T]hese are very real difficulties and disclose some deep dangers. Our real peace terms—those on which we shall undoubtedly insist—are not now acceptable to either France or Italy (leaving Great Britain for the moment out of consideration).[38]

At the beginning of 1918 Wilson decided to state his own war aims explicitly, partly in response to the ideological challenge posed by the Bolsheviks in Russia and partly in an attempt to develop the contradictions within Germany. These famous fourteen items included, in addition to demands for the evacuation of occupied territories and other boundary issues, calls for a new and open diplomacy, freedom of the seas, freer trade, disarmament, and the creation of a League of Nations.[39] These themes were elaborated (and their details somewhat modified) in other Wilson speeches during the year.

No real effort was made, however, to coordinate this peace program with those of the Allies. As their military successes gained momentum and victory seemed increasingly certain, House raised this question with the president. "Do you not think," he wrote on September 3, "the time has come for you to consider whether it would not be wise to try to commit the Allies to some of the things for which we are fighting? As the Allies succeed, your influence will diminish. This is inevitable. . . . Therefore I believe that you should commit the Allies now to as much of your program as is possible."[40] This led to a speech by Wilson on September 27, "stat[ing] . . . this government's interpretation of its own duty with regard to peace." The speech called again for a League of Nations and demanded impartial justice for all in a consistent general peace settlement, no separate security or economic arrangements between nations outside the League framework, and public revelation of all treaties.[41]

Not surprisingly, the arrival of the first German peace note soon afterward focused attention on transatlantic divisions. The Germans appealed to Wilson deliberately and he just as deliberately tried to keep control of the subsequent negotiations. The British and French, meanwhile, watched anxiously from the sidelines; they called for more stringent armistice conditions than Wilson was discussing and suggested that Wilson finally send an American political representative to the Supreme War Council (the body that coordinated the Allies' strategy) so that disagreements among them could be settled.[42] As the Allies' desire for coordination matched the American desire to secure acceptance of the Fourteen Points, House was dispatched to Europe in mid-October as Wilson's representative.

By the time he arrived in Paris near the end of the month, the situation had progressed to the point where only the details of the armistice terms remained for discussion. Wilson had demanded guarantees of outright victory, the Germans had grudgingly accepted, and the correspondence had been forwarded to the Allies. Wilson persisted in wanting more generous terms than others, however, both to avoid driving Germany into revolution and to maintain German power as a balance against England and France in the postwar world. As he cabled House, "My deliberate judgment is that our whole weight should be thrown for an armistice which will prevent a renewal of hostilities by Germany but which will be as moderate and reasonable as possible within those limits, because it is certain that too much success or security on the part of the Allies will make a genuine peace settlement exceedingly difficult if not impossible. . . . Foresight is wiser than immediate advantage."[43]

The tokens of victory demanded by Allied military leaders in late October and the German domestic collapse in early November combined to produce a far greater disparity in strength between the European belligerents than Wilson desired. As German capitulation neared, however, the American president continued to insist that the Allies accept his peace program prior to the war's end. When House told his friend that their counterparts were dragging their feet, Wilson instructed him to force a showdown: "England cannot . . . dispense with our friendship in the future and the other Allies cannot without our assistance get their rights as against England. If it is the purpose of the Allied statesmen to nullify my influence, force the purpose boldly to the surface and let me speak of it to all the world. . . ."[44] Wilson told him to threaten the Allies with the prospect of a separate peace: "I . . . authorize you to say that I cannot consent to take part in the negotiation of a peace which does not include freedom of the seas because we are pledged to fight not only to do away with Prussian militarism but with militarism everywhere. Neither could I participate in a settlement which did not include league of nations because peace would be without any guarantee except universal armament which would be intolerable."[45]

After intense debates, the Allied leaders offered a compromise: they would accept Wilson's program subject to two tweaks. They refused to accept "certain interpretations" of the phrase "freedom of the seas" and they insisted on a provision stating that German reparations would cover "all damage done to the civilian population of the Allies," not merely the restoration of invaded territories. Wilson was upset with these conditions, particularly the former. On House's recommendation, nevertheless, he consented to this arrangement and sent his final note to Germany informing it that armistice terms were ready.

As one fight ended, however, Wilson girded himself for another. He decided to slow the flow of American help to the Allies to express his displeasure and started planning for future tension. "I wish no ships & nothing done till peace," Wilson told his cabinet on November 6. "I intend to carry as many weapons to the peace table as I can conceal on my person[.] I will be cold & firm. GB [is] selfish."[46]

EXPLAINING WILSON'S WAR AIMS

During the fall of 1918, the Wilson administration made three crucial decisions: to demand acceptance of the Fourteen Points by all the belligerents, to press Germany for democratic reforms, and to acquiesce in pressing Germany for armistice terms guaranteeing complete Allied military superiority. Interestingly, each decision was largely independent of the others, the product of different influences requiring separate consideration.[47]

The administration's overarching war aims, for example, encapsulated in the Fourteen Points, were a combination of routine items advancing American national interests and a more distinctive insistence on generous treatment of the vanquished powers and their integration into the postwar political and economic system. The former would have been pursued by most leaders in Wilson's position; the latter were driven more by Wilson's personal experiences and liberal political ideology.

From early on in the war, Wilson "hope[d] for a deadlock in Europe." A military stalemate would dispirit potential aggressors all around; "the chance of a just and equitable peace, and of the only possible peace that will be lasting," he noted in December 1914, "will be happiest if no nation gets the decision by arms; and the danger of an unjust peace, one that will be sure to invite further calamities, will be if some one nation or group of nations succeeds in enforcing its will upon the others."[48] This is easily interpretable as that classic American strategic goal of a balance of power in Europe. To the extent that Wilson held on to this goal even after entering the war—and it is clear that in key respects he did, believing his fight to be with the German regime and not the German nation—this aspect of his plan was reminiscent of Castlereagh's in 1815: Wilson wanted to make the United States part of a European concert, to check British and French hubris, and to make a revived Germany a key part of the postwar system.

Other elements of the desired American settlement are also consistent with routine realist predictions. "There was only one point on which an island nation could not yield," it has been written of Britain at the Congress of Vienna: "that of maritime rights."[49] This held true a century later as well. By the end of the First World War, the development of American industry and commerce, together with its status as a continental island, made Washington care about maritime rights because of material interests as much as legalism or moralism. In late 1916 Wilson wrote that "the absolute control of the seas by Great Britain" was a menace as great as "German militarism";[50] not surprisingly, the secretary to the British War Council told his prime minister that if the United States insisted on freedom of the seas, "the American peace would be more dangerous to the British Empire than the German War."[51] When the British balked at accepting this part of Wilson's vision in early November 1918, the president was furious, and told House to remind them that "if [they] cannot . . . accept the principle of the freedom of the seas, they can count upon the certainty of our using our present great equipment to build up the strongest navy our resources permit, as our people have long desired."[52] American insistence on freer trade, furthermore, is precisely what a realist would expect from a nation whose industry and technology had become the most advanced in the world.

But in his thinking about the postwar world, Wilson was clearly an idealist as well. Commentators usually view this in intellectual terms, as a matter of political ideology, but its true source might well lie in something more personal. At the start of a speech in 1909, Wilson noted that "it is all very well to talk of detachment of view, and of the effort to be national in spirit and in purpose, but a boy never gets over his boyhood, and never can change those subtle influences which have become a part of him, that were bred in him when he was a child. So I am obliged to say again and again that the only place in the country, the only place in the world, where nothing has to be explained to me is the South."

He went on to speak that day about Robert E. Lee, whom Wilson had met as a child and whose presence and cause had dominated the American South for half a century. "The Civil War," Wilson remarked, "is something which we cannot even yet uncover in memory without stirring embers which may spring into a blaze." In going to war to defend convictions and character, he argued, the South had done the right thing, and in the process "retained her best asset, her self-respect."[53]

The true imprint on a southerner of Wilson's generation, however, was not really the war itself—he was eight years old at its close—but its aftermath, Reconstruction. From the perspective of southern whites, that era consisted of vindictive havoc wreaked by northern conquerors. Writing at the turn of the century, when "Reconstruction [was] still revolutionary matter," then-professor Wilson noted how "that dark chapter of history" made "the name of Republican forever hateful in the South. . . . The negroes were exalted; the states were misgoverned and looted in their name; and a few men . . . went away with the gains." He argued that an important cause of these events was "the dangerous intoxication of an absolute triumph upon the side which won [the war]."[54]

Some months after his 1901 article on Reconstruction, Wilson closed his introduction to an encyclopedia of U.S. history thus: "A nation hitherto wholly devoted to domestic development now finds its first task roughly finished and turns about to look curiously into the tasks of the great world at large, seeking its special part and place of power. . . . A new age has come . . . but the past is the key to it; and the past of America lies at the centre of modern history."[55] As president a decade and a half later, Wilson would give those words life; the minister's son would do unto the beaten Germans as he wished others had done unto the beaten confederates.

But generous treatment of his defeated enemies was also part of a more comprehensive attempt to transcend international politics as ordinarily conceived. The first of the Fourteen Points, for example, famously called for "open covenants of peace, openly arrived at," directly challenging the theory and methods of the Old Diplomacy. This was no mere rhetorical flourish; to the astonishment and horror of the Allies, Wilson at the end of the war actually tried to put such concepts into practice. The fourth point called for general international disarmament, which again was not mere rhetoric but something Wilson considered crucial to his overall vision. The fifth point called for handling colonial claims with equal attention paid to the interests of the colonized as well as the colonizers. Various planks called for self-determination of peoples and adjustment of borders based on national lines. And capping it all off, of course, there was the League of Nations.

The British director of intelligence in the United States, Sir William Wiseman, understood what was going on and tried to explain it to his government in October 1918: "It would be misleading . . . to take any one of the Fourteen Points . . . and separate it from the rest of the speech. Each of the fourteen propositions put forward simultaneously . . . constitutes a part of a complete and consistent whole. In the President's mind, the whole future peace of the world is a single conception based on the League of Nations. If that fails, all is useless."[56]

The League was the centerpiece of Wilson's program, designed specifically to overcome what he saw as the inevitable troubles that arose when individual countries tried to solve their security problems alone. "If [the war] be only a struggle for a new balance of power," he asked in early 1917, "who will guarantee, who can guarantee, the stable equilibrium of the new arrangement? . . . There must be, not a balance of power, but a community of power; not organized rivalries, but an organized common peace."[57] The concert Wilson had in mind was not a great power condominium, but a universal collective security system; it would, as the fourteenth point put it, guarantee "political independence and territorial integrity to great and small states alike."

These ideas drew on a distinct liberal theory of international relations dating back to the early nineteenth century and beyond. According to this view, war was the product of nations' self-interested jockeying for power in an uncertain environment; if a general institutional framework could regulate international interactions and guarantee security to all, conflict could be eliminated. Arms races fueled destructive competition; popular will and commerce, on the other hand, were pacific, and if given free rein would produce a natural harmony of interest in the international sphere. Unlike those who stressed premeditated German aggression, Wilson saw the Great War as having arisen from the basic fact of competition under anarchy, and he was determined to attack this problem at its source. As he put it only six months before American entry into the war,

> Have you ever heard what started the present war? If you have, I wish you would publish it, because nobody else has. So far as I can gather, nothing in particular started it, but everything in general. There had been growing up in Europe a mutual suspicion, an interchange of conjectures about what this government and that government was going to do, an interlacing of alliances and understandings, a complex web of intrigue and spying, that presently was sure to entangle the whole of the family of mankind on that side of the water in its meshes. Now, revive that after this war is over, and, sooner or later, you will have just such another war. . . . We must have a society of nations.[58]

The creation of such a society was the core of Wilson's program because it addressed what he considered the fundamental cause not simply of this particular war, but of War in general. Without it, there was no hope for the world; once it started to work its beneficent effects, any residual problems could be settled within its framework.

Liberals in other countries held similar views; with the exception of the freedom of the seas plank, in fact, "the Fourteen Points . . . constituted the most comprehensive and striking presentation yet of a liberal program, almost exactly endorsing the aims of the British radicals."[59] In the United States, however, unique social conditions gave these traditions a special and widespread resonance, and favorable economic and geopolitical circumstances facilitated their adoption as a national program. Although a bit oversimplified, Gordon Levin's interpretation seems generally correct: "Unlike the European liberals and democratic-socialists, who operated in societies in which pre-liberal military and traditional values were still powerful, . . . Wilson was the leader of a nation-state in which pre-liberal values and classes did not exist." In these particular historical circumstances, the liberal foreign policy program served both American values and American interests. "For Wilson, there was no conflict between the needs of a burgeoning American political-economy to expand commercially and morally throughout the world and the European liberal-internationalist and moderate democratic-socialist program of a progressive, rationalized, and peaceful international-capitalist system."[60]

THE DEMOCRATIZATION OF GERMANY

In his notes to Germany, Wilson himself distinguished between his general peace program and his calls for democratization. Unlike the Fourteen Points, moreover, which were stated clearly before the war's endgame and accepted in toto by the Germans from the beginning of the negotiations, American demands for domestic reform in Germany were expressed vaguely and shifted over time in response to the changing situation. So even though the two issues are often linked, in fact they require separate treatment.

Wilson's own liberalism placed the greatest emphasis on problems stemming from the anarchic nature of the international system in general, as opposed to its constituent units. His solutions, accordingly, were also systemic: international institutions, freer trade, collective security. Another strand in liberal thought about war and peace, however, emphasized the importance of domestic sources of aggressive foreign policy behavior. According to this view, militaristic or atavistic elites caused wars; the way to eliminate aggression, consequently, was not to reform relations *between* nations, but to reform politics *within* them, and in particular to spread democracy.

Secretary of State Robert Lansing expressed this latter view well in a letter to House in the spring of 1918:

> No people on earth desire war, particularly an aggressive war. If the people can exercise their will, they will remain at peace. If a nation possesses democratic institutions, the popular will will be exercised. Consequently, if the principle of democracy prevails in a nation, it can be counted upon to preserve peace and oppose war. . . . [I]t comes down to this, that the acceptance of the principle of democracy by all the chief powers of the world and the maintenance of genuine democratic govern-

> ments would result in permanent peace. If this view is correct, then the effort should be to make democracy universal. With that accomplished I do not care a rap whether there is a treaty to preserve peace or not. I am willing to rely on the pacific spirit of democracies to accomplish the desirable relations between nations. . . . It seems to me that the proper course, [therefore,] . . . is to exert all our efforts toward the establishment of the democratic principle in every country of sufficient power to be a menace to world peace. . . .

When dealing with Germany, in other words, Lansing felt that acceptance of the Fourteen Points and the League was not enough: "We must crush Prussianism so completely that it can never rise again, and we must end Autocracy in every other nation as well. . . . Let us uproot the whole miserable [German] system and have done with it."[61]

Wilson was not unsympathetic to such views. He detested what he saw as the political philosophy underpinning the Kaiserreich's political system and, more important, he became convinced during the course of the war itself that the German leadership could not be trusted. So he agreed that German domestic reform and democratization should be a prerequisite for a settlement. When Allied fortunes looked grim in the spring of 1918, he discussed with Wiseman the possibility of "sign[ing] a peace with the Military Party in Germany," commenting that it was an "appalling prospect"—since the existing German regime could not be trusted and thus would have to be dealt with through traditional power politics. "The treaty itself with such people would be only a 'scrap of paper,' but they might be restrained from violating it by material rather than moral considerations."[62]

But if Wilson knew that he wanted regime change in Germany, he was less certain about what the successor regime should look like. Relying on advisers such as Walter Lippmann and William Bullitt, he followed German politics closely during the war and tailored his speeches to encourage the Social Democrats in the Reichstag. And to the dismay of Allied leaders, he called openly on the German people to rise up against their government. Nevertheless, these appeals were couched in vague terms. This was due partly to Wilson's fear that specific demands would backfire, creating a groundswell of support for hard-line militarists or triggering a full-scale revolution. (To critics advocating harsher political demands, he pointedly asked, "Had you rather have the Kaiser or the Bolsheviks?")[63] Yet Wilson also seems to have relied on what might be called a "Potter Stewart" conception of German democratization: he could not define it in the abstract, but he would know it when he saw it.

What the American president did not seem to grasp fully was that his real political mission in Germany was not democratization but parliamentarization. The Kaiserreich was not a democracy, but its political institutions did include the ingredients to build one.[64] The Reichstag in particular was a true national legislature, elected on the basis of direct, secret, universal male suffrage from the 1870s on; in the early twentieth century its effectiveness was limited almost as much by failures of political will and skill as by the Bismarckian constitution. So the challenge for Wilson or other outsiders was not to create democratic institutions from scratch, but rather to readjust the wiring on the German political circuit board so that the democratic parts of the existing institutional structure received power and the nondemocratic parts were cut out, rather than vice versa.

By 1917, four alternative futures for the Kaiserreich were conceivable: 1) maintenance of the status quo; 2) democratic reform within the existing constitutional framework; 3) formation of a new, republican polity; and 4) revolution along Soviet lines. Wilson wanted to avoid the first and the fourth, and preferred the third. During October 1918, however, he was confronted with the second, and did not know how to respond. Moreover, he had been so careless in discussing these issues with the Allies and the American public that whatever he might have come to decide himself, there was no guarantee that others would agree. As a result, his eventual demands of Germany stemmed more from the pressures of domestic politics than from his own previous ideological position.

The first German note in early October put Wilson on the spot, because it forced him to evaluate whether Prince Max's government passed muster politically. As House noted in his diary, "The President thought that if such an offer had been made by a reputable government, it would be impossible to decline it."[65] But quite apart from a general desire to press for full German defeat, most people in the United States did not believe that Max represented something dramatically new. Joseph Tumulty, one of Wilson's closest aides, put this view bluntly to the president on October 8: "It is the hand of Prussianism which offers this peace to America. . . . The other day you said 'we cannot accept the word of those who forced this war upon us.' If this were true then, how can we accept this offer now? Certainly nothing has happened since that speech that has changed the character of thos[e] in authority in Germany." Instead of "any attempt to deal with the present Prussian rulers of Germany," Tumulty advised Wilson to make "a reply along the lines of your last speech," pressing for a change in German leadership.[66]

Wilson's first, instinctual response to the note had not referred to German domestic politics at all; the president's political advisers, more in tune with their nation's political temper, thought it too soft. Wilson "seemed much disturbed when I expressed a decided disapproval of it," House noted; "I told him that I had thought of something quite different; that I did not believe the country would approve of what he had written." Further drafting and rewriting yielded the final version—including the query about whether Max spoke "merely for the constituted authorities of the Empire who have so far conducted the war"—which was sent only after it had been vetted by Tumulty.

The German reply to Wilson's note pointed out that Prince Max's government, unlike its predecessors, "has been formed by conferences and in agreement with the great majority of the Reichstag." This again put Wilson on the spot, because it represented a major step toward democratization *within the existing German political system.* At this point, the president received a detailed memorandum from the journalist David Lawrence analyzing "public opinion as it is reacting on the German note of yesterday," stressing that the American public would be outraged if Wilson did not press for removal of the Kaiser and suggesting that the president point out that the terms accepted included his earlier remarks on the abolition of autocracy in Germany. It is worth quoting at length to give a sense of the domestic political context within which Wilson was operating:

> Fortunately or unfortunately, America has been fed . . . hatred of the Kaiser and the Hohenzollerns by Liberty Loan posters, unchecked newspaper propaganda, and speeches galore. To a surprising extent the Kaiser has become the single issue. . . . The man on the street today doesn't believe Germany 'has been licked enough.' . . . [That] carries with it two implications—that the Kaiser and his family must be swept from power and that the men who broke their pledges with the United States shall never be given an opportunity to make any more pledges. . . . You asked, first, if Germany accepted not your program but your terms. Germany

> said 'Yes.' You asked, secondly, if Germany would withdraw from all invaded territory for purposes of an armistice. Germany said 'Yes.' But your basic question which was the base of the pyramid itself was number three. On its answer depended the validity of number one and number two.... Unfortunately, our people have not been acquainted with the nature of the recent reforms and the decree of September 30th or they would see in ... [the German] answer a very hopeful sign.... But we must face facts. Even if our people were fully acquainted with the tremendous strides that have been made toward reform, they would not be satisfied that the Thing as you so aptly christened the system of Prussianism had been totally eradicated.... [A]nything short of a positive definition of the issue as between the 'constituted authorities who have thus far conducted the war' and the elimination of those authorities before conditions one and two of your inquiry can be further considered, would be disastrous not merely to [your] prestige ... but disastrous to the application of moral force.... [W]ould it not be in order to make your answer to the German note of last night a single question, asking, in effect, if the German people read and if their answer means they have agreed to that portion of your speech of September 30th referring to the present government of Germany[?] ... Until the Hohenzollerns are gone ... the American people will not be ready to accept Germany as a partner in [the] League.[67]

And Tumulty wrote again, drawing Wilson's attention to a series of newspaper editorials and statements from prominent citizens demanding further German reforms.[68]

These were the pressures that led Wilson to include in his second note the paragraph reminding the Germans of his demand for "the destruction of every arbitrary power" and his comment that "the power which has hitherto controlled the German Nation is of the sort here described." Despite the seeming definitiveness of these words, however, Wilson actually left unclear just how much of the Kaiserreich's political structure he would permit the Germans to keep. His note was *not* a specific demand for the abolition of the monarchy, as can be seen by the caveat that Wilson would accept the "reduction ... [of the arbitrary power] to virtual impotency." The president would keep his own counsel as to "the definiteness and the satisfactory character of the guarantees which can be given in this fundamental matter."[69]

As noted above, the other clauses of this note precipitated a political crisis in Germany because of the demand for a guarantee of permanent Allied military superiority. During that crisis Prince Max's cabinet—representing the majority parties of the Reichstag—began to take control of the German state apparatus. In order to protect itself from future insubordination, moreover, as well as to meet Wilson's demands, the government tabled a long list of important reforms locking democratization into the constitution. Prince Max announced these changes in a dramatic speech to the Reichstag on October 22, and hearing the news, Bullitt—the State Department's real expert on German politics—decided that the new regime might now meet Wilson's conditions: "If these reforms shall indeed be passed by the Reichstag and the Bundesrat, the chief obstacle to a government by the representatives of the people will have been removed." Max's speech, however, was delivered two days *after* the German reply to Wilson, and was read in Washington as the next American response was being sent.[70]

Bullitt was also the exception among Wilson's advisers, both in his openness to changes in Germany and his focus on foreign policy considerations as opposed to domestic politics in the United States, where a midterm election was now only two weeks away. When discussing how to respond to the second German note, for example, Lansing had said bluntly that "we had to keep in mind the coming elections."[71] Wilson and House had demurred, but House was now on his way to Europe and others pressed Lansing's point home. Several advisers linked the reply to the third German note to the elections, stressing the American public's hatred of the German wartime leaders. As one "old hand at sounding public thought" put it, "never have I detected greater and more vigorous unanimity of opinion on any one subject."[72] A craving for more German reforms, said another, was "the almost universal temper of our people, and any answer which does not in substance, expression, and form speak the word which the people want to have spoken might lead to political disaster."[73]

Wilson himself was torn. "Public sentiment here wants blood or to put [the] Kaiser on St. Helena," the cabinet was told; the president felt this was "ridiculous." There was "such intolerant hatred of Germans," Wilson said, that "I may have to become their advocate for justice and against American Prussianism." On the other hand, he noted, "public opinion . . . was as much a fact as a mountain and must be considered." So Wilson decided to compromise: he would accept the German note and formally pass the correspondence on to the Allies, but he would also tack on to his acceptance a rhetorical flourish demanding further German democratization, going so far as to pay lip service to the public cry for "unconditional surrender." This course, he recognized, would not be entirely popular, but nor would it be politically suicidal: "What effect on politics? On election?" the cabinet asked about his proposed reply. Wilson "could not avoid thinking of that and [said] he might find popular opinion so much against he might have to go into [a] cyclone cellar for 48 hours. But after 48 hours, the people would quit being hysterical and become reasonable and prefer getting what they are fighting for now than to fight on to Berlin and keep up war."[74]

Despite what practically all Germans and Americans thought at the time and what most historians have written since, Wilson was not actually hell-bent on getting rid of the Kaiser. Klaus Schwabe's conclusion about these events seems valid:

> [T]he abdication of the Kaiser would certainly have been useful to Wilson and his party in the impending elections, but . . . it was not what Wilson was most intent upon achieving. His main goal was the rapid and most complete possible acceptance of his peace plan on the part of the Allies. The essential point in Wilson's third note is the President's favorable response to Germany's request for an armistice and for peace . . . but the approaching elections in the United States obliged Wilson to veil this attitude in a language which seemed "strong" and carried heavy ideological overtones.[75]

Over the next several days, Wilson kept silent about German politics, responding neither to further German messages of reform nor to speculations that the continued existence of the German monarchy was holding up the settlement. This was caused both by a desire to allow German reforms to evolve further and by the fact that the final negotiations that had to take place were within the victorious coalition, not between the two sets of belligerents.

Had there been any political will in Germany to maintain a reformed parliamentary monarchy, in short, the Americans might well have accepted it. That the Kaiser's descendants, and not simply Wilhelm himself, had no political future was due more to events within Germany than to pressure from without.

THE PUSH FOR MILITARY VICTORY

Beyond the general Wilsonian peace program and the pressure for democratic reform, the third aspect of American behavior that needs to be explained is the formulation of the specific armistice terms Germany was called upon to accept. These too shifted over the course of the October negotiations, and here again domestic political pressures help explain the evolution of the American position. In this case, however, Wilson overrode the most specific imperative of domestic politics, which was to demand unconditional surrender of Germany.

Wilson's basic idea for the end of the war was to use a curbed and reformed Germany as a counterweight to the Allies; the United States, led by Wilson and aided by public opinion abroad, would then oversee the evolution of a new world order institutionalized in the League of Nations. Crucial to this plan was reasonably generous treatment of the defeated Germany—both to forestall feelings of bitterness and revanchism that might poison postwar international relations, and to restrain the Old Diplomatic ambitions of Britain and France. When the first German note arrived on October 6, therefore, Wilson himself was most concerned about acceptance of his political program, evacuation of occupied territories, and an end to what he considered the immoral conduct of the war by German forces. Much to his dismay, he found that the American people wanted just the sort of harsh settlement he sought to avoid—and that rather than a negotiated truce they wanted complete submission.[76]

While Wilson was writing the polite first draft of his reply on October 7, for example, a Republican senator was declaring to his colleagues: "The only condition of an armistice ought to be an allied victory; unconditional surrender of our enemies. Anything else would be approaching in a degree the betrayal of the great cause for which we are fighting, and would be action along the line of what the Bolsheviki of Russia perpetrated in a larger degree." Every senator who took the floor during this debate agreed; one noted, "A wide pathway of fire and blood from the Rhine to Berlin should be the course our Army should take; and when our armies have reached Berlin, in the city of Berlin, the German government will be told what the peace terms will be." At the end of the day, a resolution was introduced to the effect that "there should be no cessation of hostilities and no armistice until the German government had disbanded its armies, had surrendered its arms and munitions, and had unreservedly agreed to the principles of compensation, reparation, and indemnity."[77]

The following day, not surprisingly, Wilson was sobered. "I found the President's viewpoint had changed during the night," House wrote in his diary. "He did not seem to realize before, the nearly unanimous sentiment in this country against anything but unconditional surrender. He did not realize how war mad our people have become." House's conclusion was impeccably Wilsonian: "This, I thought, had to be taken into consideration, but not, of course, to the extent of meeting it where it was wrong."[78] The tone of the first American note was therefore strengthened, and time bought by responding not with an answer but with more questions.

Wilson knew that the Allied nations also favored harsh terms. Alerted by an intercepted copy of the first German note, on October 6 their representatives had drafted a list of armistice conditions including evacuation from occupied territories, cessation of submarine warfare, and continuance of the naval blockade; two days later they added a variety of other conditions.[79] Soon, noting with dismay Wilson's inclusion of evacuation as his only material request of the Germans, they "drew the entire attention" of the president to the fact that "the conditions of an armistice cannot be fixed until after consultation with military experts."[80] Going some way to meet these fears, Wilson reassured an Allied representative that "it went without saying that the military commanders were alone competent to fix terms."[81]

The second German note accepted the initial U.S. conditions, but Wilson included major new conditions in his response: an end to unrestricted submarine and "scorched earth" tactics during the German retreat and "absolutely satisfactory safeguards and guarantees" of Allied military supremacy after the fighting ceased. These new demands were ultimately accepted, Wilson passed the correspondence on to the Allies, and final armistice terms were drawn up and then presented (and accepted) in November.

Some have argued that the reason for the new harshness in Wilson's position was his outrage at the sinking of the mail steamer *Leinster* in the English Channel on October 10. In fact, however, Wilson privately argued that the sinking had probably stemmed from a bureaucratic snafu rather than brazen German perfidy.[82] The real explanation is more banal: with the correlation of forces having turned so clearly against the Germans, there was no natural stopping point short of absolute military defeat. While the Germans could still put up resistance and delay an outright Allied victory for several months, everyone knew that their relative strength would only diminish further. Once the negotiations began, therefore, it was only a matter of time before the actual Allied military superiority expressed itself in the armistice terms. Wilson made a halfhearted attempt to prevent this, but had few cards to play.

What molded the armistice terms into their final, implacable form, interestingly, was simple bureaucratic politics. Wilson sought only to keep the Germans from renewing the battle; he "stated that armistice terms framed by Naval and Military Officers must be viewed in [the] spirit that undue humiliation would be inexcusable except insofar as such terms are necessary to prevent [the] enemy taking advantage of armistice to reform their forces and better their position." But even though he was "outstandingly fearful" that the Allied military bureaucracies would generate precisely such "humiliating" conditions, he did not interfere much in the actual armistice-drafting process.[83]

Wilson's liberal abhorrence of war led him to assume absolute control over the ends of American policy (to make sure they would not be polluted by traditional motives of self-interest). A corollary of this, however, was his view that the administration of its means was something best left entirely to professionals. The Allied military chiefs sought, when given the opportunity, to write total defeat into the armistice terms, and they succeeded. (The chief dissenting voice among them was Britain's Douglas Haig, but not out of any softheartedness: he just thought the Allied military situation was a bit less ideal than his colleagues did, and so did not want the terms so harsh that the Germans might refuse them.)

Ultimately the Germans were required to surrender vast amounts of military materiel; permit the occupation of a crucial stretch of their country for an indefinite period; surrender their submarines and most of their surface fleet; and agree to pay an amount of reparations to be named later. The Allied blockade of Germany, moreover, with all its attendant economic and human devastation, was to be kept in place.[84] At the last minute, U.S. general John Pershing called for unconditional surrender instead of an armistice; Wilson quickly suppressed such insubordination, but more telling was the comment of the senior Allied commander: "Marshall Foch is in complete accord with your idea," Pershing was told. "However, he says . . . [the Armistice] might not bear the name of unconditional surrender but virtually it would approximate to that."[85]

When Erzberger's delegation arrived at Compiègne to hear the terms of their country's capitulation, they were appalled. They had little choice but to sign, and eventually did so; but their post-signing statement "stress[ed] forcibly the point that the execution of this treaty can precipitate the German people into anarchy and famine. After the discussions that brought about the Armistice, we expected conditions which, while assuring full and complete military security to our adversary, might bring the end of suffering to the noncombatants, the women and children."[86] The president of the United States could have said the same thing.

WILSON IN RETROSPECT

During the endgame of the Great War, Woodrow Wilson sought to usher in a new era of international relations. He wanted to spare Germany the ravages that had befallen his beloved South after its total defeat a half century earlier, which he saw as a recipe for lasting bitterness. He wanted to rid Germany of what he considered its untrustworthy authoritarian leadership. And he wanted to bind his friends as well as his enemies to his vision of a peaceful future built on democracy, free trade, and the League of Nations. He failed, and in the process helped ensure that the very things he feared most—revanchism and future war—would come to pass.

Wilson's dream had its source in the liberal values that formed the heart of the United States' own political tradition. Yet the extrapolation of those values to the world at large was driven not only by idealism but also by American power. Precisely because American relative strength was so great, and because, unlike the other belligerents, its borders and domestic security were not directly at stake in the conflict, the United States could afford to fight for its ideals and not simply its material interests. France needed to regain its occupied territory, Wilson noted to a British colleague in early 1918; Belgium, its independence; Italy, its ethnic irredenta. But the United States and England, he continued, "the two most powerful countries on the Allied side, had no such [issues]. This, he thought, was a good thing, because it made us better umpires, more disinterested in our discussion of the peace terms."[87]

If the United States was strong enough to harbor such grand ambitions, it was not strong enough to impose them upon the surrounding world by fiat. Wilson's recognition of this American position, as first among several powers, conditioned his behavior during the endgame. While he wanted to defeat the German war machine and abolish what he considered the domestic sources of German Machtpolitik, he wanted to leave Germany some residual strength at the end of the war in order to restrain what he considered the traditional, self-interested ambitions of the Entente powers. The armistice, he reminded House, should not leave the Allies with "too much success or security"—both because that would tempt them to exact revenge and because it would diminish their reliance on the United States. With the help of a reformed Germany and a balance of power in Europe, Wilson believed, the United States, through the League, could break the competitive cycle of world politics and allow a natural harmony of interests to emerge.

The feasibility of Wilson's ultimate vision was always doubtful, but the odds against achieving it were increased dramatically by the president's naïvete and cluelessness. Even though he did not consider himself to be *of* the world of power politics, he should have recognized that he was *in* it, and thus at the mercy of its unforgiving logic. He trusted too much in the power of world public opinion to bend foreign leaders to his will, just as he trusted too much in his ability to lead American politics in the direction he wished.[88] Just as important, he failed to use the leverage he had over his co-belligerents to lock them into his program when they were most in his control.

The Allies, on the other hand, were quite aware of their dependence and fearful of what it might portend. As Wiseman noted succinctly to his superiors in August 1917, "Our diplomatic task is to get enormous quantities of supplies from the United States while we have no means of bringing pressure to bear upon them to this end."[89] During the negotiations at the end of the war, the American military representative on the Supreme War Council told his superiors that the British and French "think they have got the Germans on the run and that they now do not need as much help as a little while ago they were crying for." He passed on a comment he had heard: "a gentleman in high position here [said] that the United States was building a bridge for the allies to pass over; that the time for the United States to secure acquiescence in its wishes was while the bridge was building; that after the allies had crossed over the bridge they would have no further use for it or for its builders."[90]

Wilson's triangular diplomacy was frustrated not only by the Allies, but by his own nation as well. Having failed to articulate his vision of the peace with sufficient precision, and having alienated crucial elements of his domestic political coalition through wartime repression, the president found few in agreement with his intricate plan. Theodore Roosevelt's call to "dictate peace by the hammering guns" rather than "chat[ting] about peace to the accompaniment of the clicking of typewriters" was in tune with the national will in the fall of 1918; many agreed as well with his puzzlement over Wilson's conception of a distinct American role in the war.[91] So too was Wilson's program undercut by the bureaucratic imperatives of the military chiefs who drew up the actual terms of the armistice.

In the end, however, the internal collapse of Germany made all such considerations moot and provided the Allies with just the dominance that Wilson had feared. The implosion had not been foreseen, and the combination of a foe weak at present but strong in prospect led the Allies to exact a settlement different from the one the Germans felt they had been promised by Wilson's endgame negotiations. Together with the cover-up of Germany's true military position by Ludendorff and his cronies and their deliberate falsification of history later on, this shift would feed the poisonous passions that roiled the Weimar Republic.

EPILOGUE: FROM THE ARMISTICE TO THE TREATY OF VERSAILLES

On November 10, House cabled Wilson, "You have a right to assume that the two great features of the armistice are the defeat of German military imperialism and the acceptance by the Allied Powers of the kind of peace the world has longed for."[92] This was correct only in the most superficial sense; the defeated Germany was already slipping into chaos and the Allies had no intention of implementing a purely Wilsonian peace settlement. House had been closer to the mark a few days earlier, when he had written the president that "I doubt whether any other [of the] heads of the governments with whom we [have been] dealing realize quite how far they are now committed to the American peace programme."[93] Why this should be a source of glee for the U.S. leadership is hard to fathom and demonstrates just how much faith they placed on verbal commitments and the enforcement powers of benevolent public opinion.

At some level, Wilson understood that to bring his new world order into effect he needed the United States behind him, the Allies somewhat off balance, and a democratic Germany revived and reintegrated into Europe. If he had had a Bismarckian sense of the ways of power and the ruthlessness to use them, it is barely conceivable that he might have gotten a postwar settlement incorporating the bulk of his agenda. By November 1918, however, the cards were heavily stacked against him; when he played his hand poorly, the result was never in doubt.

The November 1918 elections at home had returned a Republican Senate, whose capacity to frustrate his designs Wilson realized far too late. The implosion of the Kaiserreich reduced Germany to the status of an international beggar, allowing the Allies to concentrate on extracting whatever they wanted over the short term. And since the Pre-Armistice Agreement that House had been so proud of contained no mechanism for enforcement, it could be ignored at will. Historians have spent many pages debating Wilson's "mistakes" in deciding to go to the peace conference himself and in stacking the U.S. delegation chiefly with his own men. The latter choice did represent a missed opportunity to mend fences at home, but the real problems for a Wilsonian settlement lay abroad. When Wilson toured Europe he was met by adoring crowds, but in the crunch those foreign populations either could not shape their governments' policies or, even worse, cared more about their nations' own material interests than anything else.

Despite all Wilson's talk of a League, French premier Georges Clemenceau declared at the end of the year that as far as he was concerned, "There is an old system which appears to be discredited today, but to which . . . I am still faithful. Here in this system of alliance . . . is the thought which will guide me at the conference."[94] While he would go on to stymie Wilson time and again during the peace conference, there is good reason to believe that any French leader would have been forced to do the same, if not worse. British prime minister David Lloyd George, meanwhile, pandered to his constituents' demands and supported stiff reparations from Germany to cover the costs of British war pensions, and there was little Wilson could do to stop him. And as for Italy, Prime Minister Vittoria Orlando and Foreign Minister Sidney Sonnino—driven by the same frenzied crowds that had turned out for the American prophet at the end of 1918—sought nothing more nor less than territorial gains at the expense of their neighbors.

These positions were hardening just as Wilson was getting his practical plans for his beloved League into focus, and the canniness of the other major players caught him in a trap. His European opponents at the conference could "wrest from him something of the practical substance of an issue in exchange for formal recognition of the finer principle involved; or, in certain circumstances, they could deflect his sermons with menacing references to the League."[95] A sense of how things went is caught in a private Lloyd George remark from late February 1919: "The old dog [Clemenceau] does not believe in all these new fangled schemes. He thinks the world will go on much as before, and you can't really alter things. Well, Wilson has gone back home with a bundle of assignats. I have returned home with a pocket full of sovereigns in the shape of the German colonies, Mesopotamia, etc. Everyone to his own taste."[96]

Some thought Wilson could have pressed his advantages more. Harold Nicolson was a young Wilsonian on the British side, and wondered why he did not: "We were all, at that date, dependent on America, not only for the sinews of war, but for the sinews of peace. Our food supplies, our finances, were entirely subservient to the dictates of Washington. The force of compulsion possessed by Woodrow Wilson in those early months of 1919 was overwhelming. It never occurred to us that, if need arose, he would hesitate to use it."[97] But Wilson, whether because it was not in his character or because he did not want to jeopardize the realization of his vision, harangued rather than threatened, and his opponents simply held their ground.

By mid-spring, Republicans were in open revolt at home. While Wilson was back in the United States trying to handle the situation, House—savvy enough to recognize the need for compromises, but also very friendly to Allied and particularly French interests—made some concessions that were difficult to undo. And then Wilson developed some medical problems that wore him down further. The chaotic peace conference finally drew to a close in early summer; its product was imposed on the representatives of Germany by fiat. Wilson could not get the treaty ratified by the U.S. Senate, and so when the League finally began its operations, Americans watched from the sidelines.

In later years, it became a truism in many circles that the harshness of the Versailles Treaty and American failure to join the League doomed the world to a cycle of instability, tyranny, and war. With generations of hindsight, however, the treaty seems more balanced now than it did then, a mixture of discordant elements that was neither Carthaginian nor Metternichian.[98] As for the League, its pure collective security aspect—the source of so much controversy at the time—would almost certainly have been ineffective even with formal American participation. Again with generations of hindsight, the true lost chances may have been the failure to devise a generous postwar financial settlement (through which American support might have reduced conflict between France and Germany) and the failure to weave the United States into a global institutional network (thus possibly slowing the rush to protectionist autarchy that hastened the world into depression a decade later). Given the expectations and realities prevailing at the end of the war, however, the history of the peace conference was preordained. The drama played itself out in public during 1919, but the script had been written long before, and the events of October–November 1918 are best understood as a dress rehearsal.[99]

Later American policymakers would draw several lessons from Wilson's experiences. What they really should have learned, however, was the importance of selecting realistic war aims, developing a practical strategy for achieving them, and paying close attention to the execution of that strategy during the final stages of the conflict.

3

WORLD WAR II—EUROPE

At the end of 1761, Frederick the Great was in trouble. What history would later call the Seven Years' War was winding down and Prussia's chances of victory were dwindling fast. Seventeen fifty-nine had seen major defeats at the hands of the Russians and Austrians and the trend continued over the next two years. By January 1762, Frederick was down to his last sixty thousand troops and his enemies were tightening the noose. "If Fortune continues to pursue me mercilessly," the king wrote to a friend from his winter quarters, "I will most certainly succumb; now it is only she who can pull me out of the situation I am in."[1]

Then came a miracle—the death of the Russian czarina Elizabeth and the succession of her Prussophile nephew, Peter. A century later, Frederick's Scottish biographer, Thomas Carlyle, painted the scene in dramatic colors:

> Hardly had he been five weeks at Breslau, in those gloomy circumstances, when . . . there arrive rumors, arrive news—news from Petersburg; such as this King never had before! "Among the thousand ill strokes of Fortune, does there at length come one pre-eminently good? The unspeakable Sovereign Woman, is she verily dead, then, and be-

> come peaceable to me forevermore?" We promised Friedrich a wonderful star-of-day; and this is it. . . . Peter, the Successor, he knows to be secretly his friend and admirer; if only, in the new Czarish capacity and its chaotic environments and conditions, Peter dare and can assert these feelings? What a hope to Friedrich, from this time onward! Russia may be counted as the bigger half of all he had to strive with; the bigger, or at least the far uglier, more ruinous and incendiary; and if this were at once taken away, think what a daybreak when the night was at the blackest![2]

Sure enough, on ascending to the throne the new czar immediately pulled Russian forces back from the outskirts of Berlin and signed a generous separate peace, allowing Frederick to escape and fight another day.

Eighty years after Carlyle wrote, a German leader was in trouble once again. In the spring of 1945, Adolf Hitler was in the sixth year of a terrible global war; he too was about to succumb to the armies of an opposing coalition that had already reached Berlin; he too needed a miracle. Hitler idolized Frederick, hanging a beloved portrait of his predecessor wherever he went and gazing at it for inspiration. As the Nazi leader huddled in his fortified bunker deep beneath the Reich Chancellery, Joseph Goebbels would read him passages from Carlyle's biography to cheer his spirits. "What an example to us and what comfort and consolation in these dark days!" the propaganda chief noted in his diary in early March. "One's heart lifts as one reads this account. There have been periods in Prussian-German history when the fate of the country and the people has been on an even sharper knife-edge than it is now. Then there were a few great men who saved the people and the country; it must be the same again now."[3]

On April 12, Fortune seemed to play her part, with word reaching Berlin that night that Franklin Roosevelt had died. Returning to the bunker after presiding over the last wartime concert of the Berlin Philharmonic—with a specially selected program of Beethoven's Violin Concerto, Bruckner's Fourth Symphony, and the final scene of Wagner's *Götterdämmerung*—Albert Speer was accosted by the Führer:

> Hitler caught sight of me and rushed toward me. . . . He held a newspaper clipping in his hand. "Here, read it! Here! You never wanted to believe it. Here it is!" His words came in a great rush. "Here we have

> the miracle I always predicted. Who was right? The war isn't lost. Read it! Roosevelt is dead!" He would not calm down. He thought this was proof of the infallible providence watching over him. . . . Now history was repeating itself, just as history had given a hopelessly beaten Frederick the Great victory at the last moment. The miracle of the House of Brandenburg! Once again the Tsarina had died, the historic turning point had come, Goebbels repeated again and again and again.[4]

The American president was not only one of the leaders of the opposing coalition, but also a personal enemy. "An unfortunate historical accident," Hitler had ranted to his secretary Martin Bormann in February, "fated it that my seizure of power should coincide with the moment at which the chosen one of world Jewry, Roosevelt, should have taken the helm in the White House. . . . Everything is ruined by the Jew, who has settled upon the United States as his most powerful bastion."[5] Now that his nemesis was gone, the tensions within the anti-Nazi alliance could finally erupt. Yes, Hitler acknowledged, the Russian and Anglo-American forces would likely continue their advances and meet up south of Berlin. But the Soviets would inevitably keep going, not content to stop where they had agreed at Yalta. Then the Americans would "be forced to push the Russians back by force of arms, and that . . . and *that* will be the point at which I'll be offered a high price for my participation in the final war—on one side or the other!"[6]

It soon became clear, however, that this time there would be no reprieve. On being sworn in as president, Harry Truman pledged to carry on Roosevelt's policies and the war continued as before. "Perhaps fate has again been cruel and made fools of us," Goebbels lamented. "Perhaps we have counted our chickens before they are hatched."[7] Russian and Anglo-American forces met up at Torgau on April 25, but the Grand Alliance would hold together for several months instead of several days.

Eventually even Hitler knew it was over and made his final arrangements, political and personal. During the evening of April 29, his pilot Hans Baur came to pay his respects, pleading to be allowed to fly his master away from the crypt. Hitler demurred, then made a last request. "I want to give you that picture hanging on the wall there," he said. "It's a portrait of Frederick the Great by Anton Graff. It cost 34,000 marks in 1934. Many of my pictures are much more valuable, but I'm very fond of that one and I don't want it to be lost."[8] A few hours later the leader of the Third Reich closed himself in his study with his new bride and shot himself through the mouth.

Viewed from one angle, the American effort in World War II was a fight *against* the Axis. The Roosevelt administration decided from the beginning to press for total victory over Germany and Japan and was able to carry out the decision. "All the rest," as Winston Churchill foresaw when Pearl Harbor brought the United States into the battle, "was merely the proper application of overwhelming force."[9] The European endgame of this struggle was shaped by the answers to three questions: whether to attempt a compromise settlement of the war with the Nazis; whether to attempt a compromise settlement with their internal opponents; and whether to continue cooperating with the Soviet Union during the war's final operations. The first two questions were answered in the negative with the decision to strive for unconditional surrender, the third was answered in the affirmative with the decision not to race for Berlin in 1944–45, and the final scenes in Hitler's bunker were the result.

Viewed from another angle, however, the American effort was a fight *for* a certain vision of international political and economic order. Even before the Japanese attacked, American leaders hoped for a postwar settlement that would provide their country and the world with lasting peace and prosperity—the former through a collective-security-system-cum-great-power-concert, the latter through global multilateral capitalism. "The United States did not enter the war in order to reshape the world," Warren Kimball has noted, "but once in the war, [a] conception of world reform was the assumption that guided Roosevelt's actions."[10] The European endgame of this second struggle centered on a fourth question, how to lay the groundwork for realizing the American postwar vision—to which the wartime answer was the creation of an institutional framework composed of the Bretton Woods system and the United Nations.

Nevertheless, although the negative and the positive struggles occurred simultaneously, American policymakers failed to link them as well as they might have. They never fully confronted the fact that the defeat of the Axis was a necessary condition for the emergence of their desired world order, but not a sufficient one. By contracting out the bulk of the fight against Nazi Germany to the Soviet Union, the Western Allies accepted a Faustian bargain that resulted in the occupation of

Central and Eastern Europe by an undemocratic, anticapitalist tyranny. The sheer magnitude of devastation stemming from Nazi domination and total war, moreover, led to political and economic chaos across the continent after the shooting stopped, while the costs of the fighting drained the strength of America's true allies. This situation was hardly conducive to the creation of America's postwar vision, and in fact provided fertile ground for its opposite—the emergence of radical, Soviet-controlled regimes in the industrial heart of Europe.

The European endgame of America's positive struggle, therefore, continued long after VE Day, concluding years later with the establishment of what has been termed "consensual American hegemony" in the West or "empire by invitation"—a system grounded in a second set of more practical institutions designed to organize, reconstruct, and defend a greatly expanded U.S. sphere of interest.[11] The Cold War, in other words, is best understood as a consequence of the Truman administration's decisions to pursue what remained of the positive goals America fought for during World War II in the face of Soviet decisions to do the same on their side.

Given the conflicting visions of order and security held by these two great powers and the conditions existing in Europe in 1945, such an enduring ideological and geopolitical clash seems inevitable; only one side's abdication of the field could have prevented it. Much of the disillusionment and hysteria accompanying the onset and early decades of the "long twilight struggle," on the other hand, was not inevitable, and stemmed from the wartime failure by the Western Allies to acknowledge the gap between their positive and negative efforts—to accept with open eyes the full consequences of partnering with one world-historical monster to destroy another. For this, as well as for the initial postwar fumbling and confusion, the leaders of the early 1940s were indeed responsible. George Kennan put it well:

> [Neither Churchill nor Roosevelt] could have done much more than they did to prevent the Russian conquest of half of Europe. That was a function and consequence of Western weakness in the pre-war period, and of America's own simultaneous involvement with Japan. But the things they said about Russia could have been different; and they could, by virtue of that difference, have stimulated fewer false hopes and accepted, for themselves and their countries, a smaller responsibility for the secondary tragedy they were unable to prevent.[12]

Throughout these years, American officials saw themselves as replaying the last war and correcting what they perceived as their predecessors' mistakes. Supported by a growing cushion of relative power, they generally did so successfully, bequeathing to posterity the framework of the world we have lived in ever since. It is thus ironic that their most significant failure lay in ignoring what should have been one of the central lessons of the previous conflict—the need to confront squarely and plan carefully for handling the differing war aims embraced by members of the winning coalition.

THE COURSE OF THE WAR IN EUROPE

During the interwar years, American plans for a future conflict focused on the Pacific and the use of the navy. By 1938, however, events in Europe caused a strategic reevaluation that culminated in a reversal of emphasis onto the threat posed by Nazi Germany and the importance of Britain as a first line of defense. By the end of 1940—after the fall of France, England's victory in the Battle of Britain, and Roosevelt's reelection—officials in Washington began practical planning for a combined Anglo-American effort aimed at the total defeat of the Axis. Although Roosevelt did not commit the country to war, he crafted policies to keep Britain supplied with crucial materiel while his military chiefs laid the groundwork for future combat.

Because Germany represented the strategic center of gravity of the Axis coalition and because German actions directly threatened British survival, policymakers decided to focus on the defeat of the Nazis first. Plans for the European theater were developed at Anglo-American military conferences in the spring of 1941. These envisioned an economic blockade, strategic bombing, the support of resistance movements, and the securing of bases on the European periphery, all preparatory to a final offensive on the continent in which Allied armored divisions would meet and destroy the German army on the ground. Shortly after these conferences, Hitler invaded the Soviet Union. When the danger of an immediate Soviet collapse passed, the Roosevelt administration incorporated the Soviet Union into its strategic framework, sending as much aid as possible to bolster Stalin's resistance.

Once the United States became an active belligerent after Pearl Harbor, the Western Allies debated whether to move toward the defeat of Germany directly, as the Americans wished (through an early cross-Channel invasion), or indirectly, as the British wished (through peripheral operations, bombing, and a blockade). Over fierce opposition from his military advisers and in the face of Soviet pressure to open a major "second front," Roosevelt sided with the British, committing the United States to a 1942 campaign in North Africa.

At the Casablanca conference in January 1943, Anglo-American planners decided that logistical considerations in the European theater favored further efforts in the Mediterranean and chose a July invasion of Sicily as the next major operation, which led in turn to an attack on the Italian mainland in September. But U.S. military leaders grew increasingly impatient with what they considered the diversion of resources from an early direct attack on Germany into "political" operations serving British imperial interests. And so, as the dominant contribution of troops and war production within the alliance shifted from Britain to the United States, control of Allied strategy followed, along with a stress on a cross-Channel attack.[13]

During a series of inter-Allied conferences from early summer to late fall 1943, the strategy for the remainder of the Anglo-American war in Europe was mapped out: some resources would be devoted to continuing operations in Italy and perhaps elsewhere in the Mediterranean, but the dominant campaign would be an invasion of the continent through landings at Normandy, scheduled for May–June 1944. Coordinated with Soviet offensives in Eastern Europe and increasingly devastating bombardment from the air, the thinking went, land operations following a successful invasion at Normandy would crush Nazi strength through Allied pressure on all sides.

While the United States was transforming its latent strength into actual capabilities and the Anglo-American forces were knocking Italy out of the war and gaining control of the seas and the skies, the Soviet Union was busy breaking the back of the Wehrmacht on the Eastern Front. In brutal combat from Stalingrad to Kursk in 1942–43, Soviet forces halted the German advance and began to push back. The Western Allies welcomed these successes, bought at horrendous cost, for the crucial role they played in weakening Germany. Their practical result, nonetheless, would be to leave Eastern Europe under Soviet control at the end of the war.

There were even grounds to worry that, precisely because of the high costs of war in the east, Stalin was exploring the possibilities of a separate peace during the brief period in 1943 when Soviet and German strength was evenly matched. Partly for this reason, in an attempt to assuage Stalin after yet another postponement of the promised second front, Roosevelt formalized the U.S. plan for total victory by announcing at Casablanca that he would pursue the war until the "unconditional surrender" of the Axis. Nothing ultimately came of the discreet Soviet contacts with the Germans, and by the spring of 1944 the end of the war in Europe was clearly in sight. The details of the dénouement would be determined only by the success of the cross-Channel invasion, the speed of subsequent Allied land operations from east and west, and the timing of the collapse of the Nazi regime.

THE ALLIES AND THE GERMAN OPPOSITION

Apart from Rudolf Hess's odd mission to Great Britain in 1941 and some feeble gestures from Heinrich Himmler and Hermann Goering in April 1945, nothing remotely resembling a peace offer came to the Western Allies from the Nazi hierarchy during World War II. This did not matter much, since no such offer would have been accepted anyway, given the determination of Britain and the United States to press for the overthrow of the Nazi regime. Both during the war and afterward, however, some in the West suggested trying to end the conflict sooner by offering encouragement and negotiations to Hitler's opponents within Germany. The Western Allies' decision to shun such contacts was therefore a conscious choice that shaped the war's endgame.

Broadly speaking, there were three kinds of German resistance to the Nazis: focused but impotent efforts from former political opponents now in exile; scattered gestures from individual members of the clergy, trade unions, and ordinary citizens inside Germany; and resistance by officials within the regime itself, from positions in the army and bureaucracy. Sadly, once Hitler's dictatorship had consolidated its rule, only the last had any chance of major impact.

From the late 1930s onward, a loose network of prominent German officials did indeed work to undermine the regime internally. These dissidents were split among themselves, however, over what kind of action to take against the government and even whether to take action at all. Because they could not get popular backing, they felt it necessary to enlist the aid of the senior leadership of the army, but almost all of the generals dragged their heels when asked to take part in anything resembling a coup d'état. Furthermore, until quite late in the war both the generals and the more conservative elements of the opposition held out for settlements so favorable to Germany that there was never a chance that the Western Allies would accept them.

Churchill grew disillusioned with Hitler's domestic opponents after various British contacts with them during the late 1930s led to few practical results. He set the wartime policy of the British government in January 1941, telling Foreign Secretary Anthony Eden that "our attitude towards all such enquiries should be absolute silence."[14]

American officials were less averse than the British to keeping abreast of developments inside Germany (notably through OSS officer Allen Dulles in Switzerland), but were equally hostile to any actual negotiations or compromise settlements. Once Roosevelt set out his demand for unconditional surrender in January 1943, a willingness to agree to it became the minimum American officials demanded before negotiations could begin. Since few members of the opposition would accept such terms, this effectively eliminated any possibilities for concerted action.

The Soviet Union, for its part, flirted during 1943 with various compromise settlements short of total victory, including accommodation with the Nazi leadership or a successor regime. Only after these courses revealed themselves to be unpromising and the Western Allies committed themselves to an invasion of the continent did Stalin halt all feelers regarding a separate peace.[15]

By June 1944, the remaining members of the opposition understood they would receive no promises of a favorable settlement before a coup actually took place, and with the war clearly lost and Germany's defeat in sight they decided to move ahead. They hinted at their plans to Dulles, who passed word on to Washington along with a recommendation for U.S. support and encouragement. The head of the OSS brought these reports directly to Roosevelt in the days before and after the July 20 attempt on Hitler's life, but to no avail. The president basically ignored the whole episode.[16]

WESTERN MILITARY OPERATIONS AFTER D-DAY

Allied success at Normandy was not inevitable. Hitler's restrictions on his generals' control over German reserves, major contributions from Ultra (top secret intelligence derived from broken German codes), a break in the weather—without these, the landings might have gone awry, with dramatic consequences for the rest of the war.[17] Once the Anglo-American forces had established a solid foothold on the continent, however, it was simply a matter of time before the Nazi regime succumbed to punishing blows from the east, west, south, and above. From mid-June 1944 onward, therefore, the endgame decisions for the United States in the negative struggle involved merely where and when to send its troops into the heart of Europe.

After taking and expanding the invasion beachheads, Anglo-American forces spent a month solidifying their positions and occupying the surrounding area. From late July through August they broke out and destroyed most German strength nearby. By the end of the summer, the Allied high command found its troops in excellent positions along the northeastern borders of Belgium and France, facing beaten German forces and relatively open ground, and a passionate debate erupted over what to do next.

Bernard Montgomery, the British commander of the Twenty-first Army Group on the left (northern) wing, proposed halting other Allied troops, strengthening the forces under his authority, and using those for a direct strike into Germany aimed ultimately at the capture of Berlin. Some American commanders such as George Patton wanted to try a similar move farther south, using their troops rather than Montgomery's. Dwight Eisenhower, from September 1 the Supreme Commander of the Allied forces in Europe, opted instead for a slower attack along a broader front. This more cautious approach reduced the risk of a major setback, but also the chance for a quick end to the war.

During the fall of 1944, logistical difficulties and stiffened German resistance led to a pause in operations on the Western Front, and in December the Germans launched a surprise counterattack in the Ardennes. What would come to be known as the "Battle of the Bulge" had little effect on the war's ultimate outcome but threw the Anglo-American forces back on their heels and reinforced American caution regarding remaining Nazi strength and determination.

By the time Western armies were on the move again in early 1945, Churchill had begun to worry seriously about Soviet domination of postwar Europe. In mid-spring, therefore, he suggested that Eisenhower direct Anglo-American forces to conquer as much of Germany as possible and attempt to take Berlin in particular. Eisenhower disagreed strongly on practical grounds and refused to change his plans for measured occupation of Germany west of the Elbe unless he was given direct orders from his political superiors to do so. Churchill tried to gain the approval of Roosevelt and then Truman for his Berlin strategy, but could not convince the American leaders or his own military chiefs to change their course. Similar efforts by Churchill to get the Western Allies to move on Vienna and Prague met a similar fate. The decisions regarding the placement of Anglo-American forces in Europe throughout the spring and summer of 1945, therefore, were made by the commanders in the field on the basis of immediate practical concerns; their political superiors chose to continue the wartime policy of cooperating fully with the Soviet Union in preparation for joint postwar control of Germany and its environs.

This cooperative policy was put to one final test prior to the war's conclusion. Just before Hitler committed suicide in his bunker, he passed control of the Nazi regime to Admiral Karl Doenitz, along with instructions to continue the fight to the bitter end. Doenitz realized that future resistance was hopeless but tried to surrender only to the Western Allies while holding the line against rapacious Soviet armies in the east. Adhering strictly to the policy of a universal, unconditional surrender, Eisenhower rejected all moves toward a separate peace or even a delay in the formal capitulation. Giving in to the inevitable, Doenitz agreed on May 7 to a general unconditional surrender, which took effect the following day.

THE U.S. POSTWAR PROGRAM AND THE FIRST WAVE OF INSTITUTIONAL PLANNING

The details and shadings of American plans for the postwar order evolved over time in response to circumstances, but the overarching vision was strikingly consistent. It had both economic and political aspects, with the two realms linked by a distinct liberal theory of international relations and international political economy, one that promised peace and prosperity for all with relatively few costs. The most passionate and articulate proponent of this theory was Cordell Hull. In his memoirs, he described "the philosophy I carried throughout my twelve years as Secretary of State":

> to me, unhampered trade dovetailed with peace; high tariffs, trade barriers, and unfair economic competition, with war. . . . I reasoned that if we could get a freer flow of trade—freer in the sense of fewer discrimina-

> tions and obstructions—so that one country would not be deadly jealous of another and the living standards of all countries might rise, thereby eliminating the economic dissatisfaction that breeds war, we might have a reasonable chance for lasting peace.[18]

Trade and growth were seen as near universal solutions for the world's problems. As one 1943 planning document put it, "A great expansion in the volume of international trade after the war will be essential to the attainment of full and effective employment in the United States and elsewhere, to the preservation of private enterprise, and to the success of an international security system to prevent future wars."[19] One pillar of the Roosevelt administration's new order, therefore, would be the construction of a multilateral economic system characterized by lower and nondiscriminatory barriers to trade.

A second pillar of the new order would be a global security system, established to deal with any remaining problems and recalcitrant members of the international community. This system would rest on a postwar concert of the great powers, institutionalized through the United Nations. Hull continued to believe even after the war that

> [t]he creation of the United Nations organization, embracing all the major peace-loving nations, was . . . a turning point in the political development of the world. . . . It would be impossible to exaggerate the importance to nations and peoples of maintaining at all times a spirit of peace and of cooperation to maintain peace—by force if necessary. This common world undertaking must contemplate the availability of armed forces at all times sufficient to prevent the use of any kind of military force or any kind of weapon capable of undermining, materially injuring, or destroying the world structure of peace based on world order under law.[20]

The crucial American decisionmaker, of course, was never Hull but rather his boss, who was somewhat tougher-minded in his assumptions—less concerned with trade and international law and more enthusiastic about the great-power-concert aspects of the new system than the orthodox collective-security aspects. But if Roosevelt could be Machiavellian in his means, it would be a mistake to exaggerate the Machiavellianism of his ends; there seems little doubt that at base he shared the same general vision as his secretary of state. Beneath his idealistic rhetoric was realist calculation, and beneath that was another, deeper layer of idealism.[21]

The positive U.S. program was prefigured well by the Atlantic Charter, issued by Roosevelt and Churchill in August 1941. This document may have been written largely to garner domestic support for a future war effort and certainly contained generalities and loopholes, but it nonetheless expressed the essentials of the Roosevelt administration's vision of a postwar world: no territorial aggrandizement; plebiscites for disputed territories; democratically elected governments; freer, nondiscriminatory trade; freedom of the seas; and forced disarmament for "nations which threaten, or may threaten, aggression," a step that would facilitate reduced military expenditures for the others.[22]

As far as the Roosevelt administration was concerned, four things were necessary to implement this program:

- First and most important, the Axis powers would have to be removed from the scene entirely, so as not to disrupt the postwar harmony of interests. This would be accomplished by pressing for total defeat and then reconstructing the vanquished along new lines.
- Second, the American people would have to be stopped from relapsing into isolationism after the war. This would be accomplished by locking the country into the United Nations and other international institutions before the fighting ended.
- Third, Britain would have to be educated into playing a constructive role in the new order. This would be accomplished by suggesting decolonization and by using wartime aid to pry open British imperial trade preferences.
- Fourth, the Soviet Union would have to cooperate with the grand design. This would be accomplished by allaying all its reasonable security concerns and coaxing it along the road to normalcy.

Creating a tabula rasa on which the new order could be inscribed was the task of the negative war, managed by Roosevelt and his military advisers largely without State Department involvement. Co-opting the Soviet Union was a governing principle of much of American policy during the war, ordered by and reliant on the president himself.[23] The remaining elements in the plan—devising the postwar international economic and security arrangements and pressing Britain to accede to American demands—were entrusted to American diplomats and Treasury Department representatives.

One set of institutions was designed to foster a stable and prosperous capitalist system in the postwar world. These included the International Bank for Reconstruction and Development (a.k.a. the World Bank), meant to provide aid for European reconstruction; the International Monetary Fund, meant to police and manage a new system of fixed exchange rates; and the International Trade Organization, meant to oversee a new international commercial order based on freer trade. The IBRD and IMF were created at Bretton Woods in July 1944, and Congress authorized American participation a year later. (Planning for the ITO began in 1943, although a charter was not drawn up until 1947 and ultimately was withdrawn from congressional consideration in 1950.) Late in the war it became clear that the second most important economy in the system, Britain's, needed major direct help—and that the U.S. Congress was serious about not using Lend-Lease aid to finance postwar reconstruction. So American officials added to the mix a substantial bilateral loan from the United States to Britain, signed in December 1945 and agreed to by Congress the following summer.

Planning for another set of institutions designed to handle postwar security issues, featuring the United Nations, began in early 1943 during British foreign secretary Anthony Eden's visit to the United States and was followed up at the Moscow and Tehran conferences later that year. Specific negotiations about the new organization's structure began during the meetings at Dumbarton Oaks from August to October 1944, continued at Yalta in February 1945, and were brought to fruition at the San Francisco Conference that April. Roosevelt originally conceived of a three-tiered pyramid involving a general body of nations at the base, a smaller executive committee above, and the "four policemen" (the United States, the Soviet Union, Britain, and China) at the apex. This evolved, over time, into a bicameral structure in which great-power influence could be exerted through permanent presence on the Security Council.

By 1945, then, the armature of what American officials thought would be a global postwar political and economic system was largely in place. Some major issues, chief among them Germany's future status, were left undecided because Roosevelt wanted it that way. The gaps in the framework, however, did not seem crucial. Although somewhat concerned about Soviet behavior in Eastern Europe and the transition from a wartime to a peacetime economy, Roosevelt died in April 1945 generally confident that his hopes would be realized: postwar cooperation among the great powers, working through the United Nations; a reasonably smooth revival of the European economies; and a transition to a new and lasting monetary and commercial regime.[24]

EXPLAINING UNCONDITIONAL SURRENDER

Two days after Pearl Harbor, Roosevelt told the nation that in the coming conflict, "the United States can accept no result save victory, final and complete. Not only must the shame of Japanese treachery be wiped out, but the sources of international brutality, wherever they exist, must be absolutely and finally broken."[25] By gratuitously declaring war on the United States, Hitler included his regime among those marked for destruction. Given the German leader's behavior over the years, the American refusal to deal with him once the war began was uncontroversial and overdetermined.

With the signing of the Declaration of the United Nations on January 1, 1942, the United States took on an additional commitment regarding the war's end: "not to make a separate armistice or peace with the enemies."[26] And within months, American planners settled on their preferred mode of war termination: the conflict should end with forced capitulations, giving the United States and its allies a free hand to treat the defeated Axis powers just as they pleased. Officials "rapidly reached the consensus that nothing short of unconditional surrender by the principal enemies, Germany and Japan, could be accepted, though negotiation might be possible in the case of Italy."[27] This recommendation was passed along to Roosevelt in May 1942, and he eventually discussed his intentions to adopt it with both Churchill and the American Joint Chiefs of Staff. Far from the spontaneous utterance he later claimed, therefore, Roosevelt's unconditional surrender proclamation at Casablanca in January 1943 was merely the public announcement of what was already a de facto policy. The notes in front of the president as he spoke spelled out a considered position:

> The President and the Prime Minister . . . are more than ever determined that peace can come to the world only by a total elimination of German and Japanese war power. This involves the simple formula of placing the objective of this war in terms of an unconditional surrender by Germany, Italy, and Japan. Unconditional surrender by them means a reasonable assurance of world peace, for generations . . . [It means] the destruction of a philosophy in Germany, Italy and Japan which is based on the conquest and subjugation of other peoples.[28]

The United States kept strictly to the letter of this policy with regard to Germany throughout the war.

By setting and keeping unconditional surrender as their chief war aim, American leaders placed strong constraints on their behavior in Europe during World War II. So why did they do it? The simplest explanation is that such a course was the easiest way to keep the anti-Axis alliance intact for the duration of the war. The United States and the Soviet Union, lacking ideological agreement or common positive interests, had to find some mechanism to keep each partner from defecting from the coalition should an opportunity present itself, and the unconditional surrender pledge served just that purpose.

The timing of the announcement shows that such logic was indeed part of Roosevelt's thinking. By early 1943, the Soviet Union had borne the brunt of the fighting in Europe and the Western Allies were about to renege yet again on their promise of a major invasion of the continent. Roosevelt's declaration was a means of "reassuring the Russians that, in spite of necessary delays over the opening of the second front, it was still the Western determination to press on unremittingly to victory, in fulfillment of Allied commitments, as soon as the physical forces could be assembled to do the job."[29] As a general statement of war aims, the slogan had major strengths: it served as a "lowest common denominator to which the Allies could subscribe. It was simple; it was a good rallying cry for rapid victory; and above all, it provided the best possible insurance against a separate peace."[30]

That said, if such a purely realist utilitarian logic was the only thing at work, one should find American planners at least considering the potential benefits of cooperation with the German opposition before rejecting it—estimating the relative threat a non-Nazi regime might pose in the postwar era, comparing it with the threat from a strengthened Soviet regime, and so forth. But such calculations simply did not occur.[31] Even those within the American government who advocated revising or clarifying the unconditional surrender policy were tentative. Allen Dulles and William Donovan of the Office of Strategic Services, for example, put the question to Roosevelt just before the July 20, 1944, coup attempt: "Those opposed to the Nazis . . . recognize that the next few weeks may be their last chance to show that they are willing to take some risks in making the first move to clean their own house. We must judge, on our side, whether the encouragement of any effort towards a revolution in Germany will, at this juncture, help to save thousands of lives of Allied soldiers fighting on the various fronts." Their concrete policy suggestion, however, was merely to issue a statement saying "that the fate of the individual German, after . . . [unconditional] surrender, and his future will be tolerable; that a reformed, demilitarized Germany has a necessary and vital place in the life of Europe."[32]

Unpersuaded, Roosevelt remained silent. Any public clarification of the policy would have required him to consider concrete plans for postwar Germany, something he was loath to do. Moreover, since at the time the thinking of the Allies ran toward a decidedly punitive peace, clarification might not have helped the situation. As Churchill noted privately in January 1944, "a frank statement of what is going to happen to Germany would not necessarily have a reassuring effect upon the German people, and . . . they might prefer the vaguer terrors of 'unconditional surrender,' mitigated by such statements as the President has made."[33]

So if alliance solidarity prevented the Roosevelt administration from actually making a deal with the German opposition, what kept the president from even considering it seriously was something else—namely, his belief that Hitler's domestic opponents were reactionary authoritarians who were equally unworthy potential partners for the United States. He had no intention, as he is reported to have said in response to a peace feeler in 1943, of dealing with "these East German Junkers."[34] Ideological distaste merged here with the lessons policymakers drew from history. As Kennan—who was friends with some in the opposition—wrote later, "I was shocked to realize, in talking to President Franklin Roosevelt . . . that he was one of the many people who could not easily distinguish World War II from World War I and still pictured the Prussian *Junkertum* as a mainstay of Hitler's power just as it had been, or had been reputed to be, the mainstay of the power of the Kaiser."[35]

As assistant secretary of the navy, Roosevelt had favored unconditional surrender and a harsh settlement at the end of World War I, noting in his diary in July 1918 that "the one lesson the German will learn is the lesson of defeat."[36] A generation later, he remained convinced that Wilson and the Allies should have forced the Germans to admit defeat more fully and eradicated German militarism—and he made plain both publicly and privately his intention to correct those mistakes this time around. As he told Churchill in early 1944, he was demanding unconditional surrender so that he could have a free hand in remaking German society after the war as he saw fit: "The United

Nations have no intention to enslave the German people. We wish them to have a normal chance to develop in peace, as useful and respectable members of the European family. But we most certainly emphasize the word 'respectable,' for we intend to rid them once and for all of Nazism and Prussian militarism and the fantastic and disastrous notion that they constitute the 'master race.' " Roosevelt used the same phrase on his return from Yalta; Allied policy, he told Congress, would destroy the military potential of the Third Reich so that "neither the Nazis nor Prussian militarism could again . . . threaten the peace . . . of the world."[37]

In fact, American officials in general worked from the premise, in the words of Assistant Secretary of State Breckinridge Long, that "we are fighting this war because we did not have unconditional surrender at the end of the last one."[38] Long's notes from the earliest meetings of the committees entrusted with postwar planning show just how directly lessons from 1918 informed U.S. policy a generation later: "The General and the Admiral are of mind that only an unconditional surrender will assure the future against German and Japanese aggressions. We had the Pershing memos of the last Armistice period—for study and discussion. I agree their objective is best. . . ."[39]

A strictly military logic of tactical cost-effectiveness, by contrast, had little impact on surrender policy, at least after late 1942. When Allied troops landed in North Africa, Eisenhower decided to smooth the way for his invasion by cutting a deal with the local Vichy representative, Admiral François Darlan. "Existing French sentiment in North Africa," he wrote to Roosevelt defending his move, "does not even remotely resemble prior calculations. . . . [N]o one who is not on the ground can have a clear appreciation of the complex currents of prejudice and feeling that influence the local situation." The alternative to dealing with Darlan was fighting, and for Eisenhower the priorities were clear. Roosevelt accepted this argument and the deal but made plain that it was only a temporary measure, writing back that "it is impossible to keep a collaborator of Hitler and one whom we believe to be a fascist in civil power any longer than is absolutely necessary."[40] And when similar instincts reemerged within the American military as officials considered the surrenders in Italy and Germany, requests for the authority to make further "Darlan"-style deals were overruled.

Domestic politics, finally, seems to have exerted a moderate constraint on overt deals with known fascists. Much of the American public, for example, was outraged by the Darlan deal, which appeared to taint the noble ideals of the Atlantic Charter. Of course, Roosevelt proved that he could buck such protests by sticking with the deal, responding to criticism with the argument that the arrangement was temporary and that it had saved American lives. Still, the experience left an unpleasant aftertaste and there seems little doubt that it reinforced his aversion to future compromises. Nevertheless, as late as the spring of 1944 the president's pollsters advised him that a survey found 38 percent of the American public favoring peace negotiations with German generals, giving the president something to work with had he ever considered changing his mind.[41]

COOPERATION WITH THE SOVIETS DURING OPERATIONS IN GERMANY

Once the decision had been made to conquer and occupy the Axis nations, the logic of American policy necessitated cooperation with the Soviet Union through the final military operations of the war. After D-Day, nevertheless, two separate attempts were made by the British to challenge this policy: Montgomery's pressure for a "narrow thrust" instead of a broad front and Churchill's agitation in favor of racing the Soviets to Berlin.[42]

When Montgomery argued at the end of the summer of 1944 for a single drive that would supposedly take Berlin and end the war quickly, Eisenhower opposed it for a variety of reasons. Logistical considerations weighed heavily against it; Ultra information promised better results on other stretches of the front; Montgomery's deliberate style was inconsistent with the bold execution the plan required for success; and bureaucratic and domestic politics made it problematic for American forces to stand idle while a British general with largely British troops hogged the limelight. As Stephen Ambrose wrote, "Under [Eisenhower's final] directives no army would take heavy casualties, no general would lose his reputation, credit for the victory could be shared by all, and there was no chance that the Germans would reverse the situation by surrounding and destroying an advanced force."[43] In retrospect, even most Montgomery fans admit that this particular plan was, in Michael Howard's words, "a gigantic gamble on the state of German morale, and there was little evidence in the behavior of the German armies either before or later to indicate that it might have come off."[44]

When the Western armies finally moved forward again in early 1945, Germany's defeat was imminent and national leaders were pondering the postwar settlement. The increasing truculence and harshness of Stalin's foreign policies led Churchill, along with a few other British and American officials, to favor a policy shift. He wanted to abandon Roosevelt's strategy of trying to win Stalin's friendship through unreciprocated concessions and switch to an attempt at inducing Soviet cooperation through coercive bargaining. The more territory and capitals the British and Americans conquered, Churchill felt, the stronger would be their postwar negotiating position. The problem was that this ran smack into what had passed for Allied occupation planning up to that point—and a dying Roosevelt and his neophyte successor were not about to shift course lightly.

Aside from his general desire to extirpate Nazism and militarism, Roosevelt had few settled ideas about what to do with Germany after the war.[45] Throughout the conflict, he did what he could to stifle discussions about postwar German policy within the American government and among the Allies because of his personal preference for improvisation over long-range planning and his desire to avoid binding commitments and domestic political controversy.

Because there was an obvious need for *some* mechanism to coordinate Allied plans for war termination and postwar planning, Roosevelt agreed in late 1943 to the establishment of the European Advisory Commission, an organization based in London facilitating regular meetings between representatives of Britain, the United States, and the Soviet Union. But few Americans, and certainly not the president, had any desire for the EAC to play an important role in hashing out a settlement: "We must emphasize," Roosevelt wrote to Hull in late 1944, "the fact that the European Advisory Commission is 'Advisory' and that you and I are not bound by this advice. This is something which is sometimes overlooked and if we do not remember that word 'advisory' they may go ahead and execute some of the advice, which, when the time comes, we may not like at all." As Kennan, who served for a time as political adviser to the EAC's American delegate, remembered bitterly, "So far as I could learn . . . attitude toward the commission was dominated primarily by a lively concern lest the new body should at some point and by some mischance actually do something, and particularly lest the American delegation, through overeagerness or inadvertence, contribute to so unfortunate an occurrence."[46]

Among the few things the EAC was permitted to handle were the details of occupation zones—the areas each victor would administer during what was supposed to be a temporary transition period between the end of hostilities and the ultimate postwar settlement. The British took the EAC more seriously than their allies, and at the beginning of 1944 they submitted a plan that would divide Germany into three roughly equal parts, assigning each to a different country based on the directions from which the respective armies would converge on Germany: the British from the northwest, the Americans from the south, the Soviets from the east.[47] Berlin, well within the Soviet zone, was to be an enclave jointly occupied by the victors. No one had any intention whatsoever that these lines would become lasting political boundaries.

The Soviets quickly accepted the British proposal, but the Americans did not. Roosevelt wanted the United States and Britain to trade zones, because he did not want the American zone to be landlocked or tied to France, potentially saddling him with extended postwar commitments or responsibilities.[48] Moreover, in 1944 the president flirted with Secretary of the Treasury Henry Morgenthau's plan to ravage and "pastoralize" postwar Germany, basically ignoring the EAC and its deliberations. By early 1945, nonetheless, Roosevelt's advisers finally persuaded him that the Morgenthau Plan was ill-considered and the zonal switch a logistical nightmare, so the United States finally agreed to the British proposal. At Yalta in February, the Big Three decided to include the French in the occupation as well, and so a zone for them was carved out from the British and American areas. At that point the Allies also agreed to make the Berlin occupation arrangements a microcosm of those for the rest of the country.

Given the vagaries of war, at different times from the beginning of 1944 onward it seemed that either the Soviets or the Western Allies would get to the heart of Germany first. In the spring of 1945, however, the former bogged down while the latter moved forward quickly, creating a glimmer of a chance that much of the country, including the capital, might be conquered by Eisenhower's troops. This was the moment when Churchill suggested, as he wrote Roosevelt in early April, that "we should join hands with the Russian armies as far to the east as possible and, if circumstances allow, enter Berlin."[49]

Despite what Churchill later claimed in his memoirs, this change was tactical rather than strategic; the British leader did not suggest a full-fledged policy of containment.[50] He had, rather, two less drastic things in mind: first, he wanted to use a retreat from the final Western positions to the agreed-upon occupation zones as a bargaining chip to garner Soviet concessions on other issues, and second, he wanted the Western Allies to capture Berlin so that they would carry a psychological edge into the postwar period. Churchill was hesitant, however, to express such politically incorrect sentiments to Americans determined on a more cooperative approach. So he kept quiet about the first idea, phrased the second poorly, and generally couched his pleas for new policies in terms of their alleged military benefits.

Eisenhower, for his part, viewed the matter in strictly military terms. His orders were to "enter the continent of Europe, and, in conjunction with the other United Nations, undertake operations aimed at the heart of Germany and the destruction of her armed forces."[51] He intended to do precisely that, then implement the agreed-upon occupation policy; consequently he saw no reason to incur huge losses simply to get to the rubble of Berlin first and then withdraw.[52] Eisenhower wanted to defeat the western German armies in detail, feared die-hard resistance by the Nazi hierarchy in what his intelligence staff told him was a proposed "Alpine redoubt" around Berchtesgaden, and worried about how to prevent clashes between American and Soviet armies rapidly converging from east and west. For these reasons, he decided to stop at the Elbe and not race ahead for the German capital.

Laying out his plans to Montgomery, he wrote, "You will note that in none of this do I mention Berlin. That place has become, so far as I am concerned, nothing but a geographical location, and I have never been interested in these. My purpose is to destroy the enemy's armed forces and his powers to resist." But Eisenhower was no MacArthur: he was fully prepared to accept and implement a change in orders should one be forthcoming, as he wrote to George Marshall on April 7:

> At any time that we could seize Berlin at little cost we should, of course, do so. But I regard it as militarily unsound at this stage of the proceedings to make Berlin a major objective, particularly in light of the fact that it is only thirty-five miles from the Russian lines. I am the first to admit that a war is waged in pursuance of political aims, and if the Combined Chiefs of Staff should decide that the Allied effort to take Berlin outweighs purely military considerations in the theater, I would cheerfully readjust my plans and my thinking so as to carry out such an operation.[53]

No new directives came down from above, and so Eisenhower continued on his course.[54]

Within a week of the transition from Roosevelt to Truman, Churchill tried to convince his new partner at least to stall on a withdrawal to the agreed-upon occupation zones. The gloomy warlord sketched out his reasoning in early May:

> I fear terrible things have happened during the Russian advance through Germany to the Elbe. The proposed withdrawal of the United States Army to the occupational lines which were arranged . . . would mean the tide of Russian domination sweeping forward 120 miles on a front of 300 or 400 miles. This would be an event which, if it occurred, would be one of the most melancholy in history. . . . It is just about time that these formidable issues were examined between the principal powers as a whole. We have several powerful bargaining counters on our side, the use of which might make for a peaceful agreement. First, the Allies ought not to retreat from their present positions to the occupational line until we are satisfied about Poland, and also about the temporary character of the Russian occupation of Germany, and the conditions to be established in the Russianised or Russian-controlled countries in the Danube valley. . . .[55]

This discussion was prescient except for one item: rather than being "just about time" that such issues were discussed, it was far too late. Not only did the Americans reject a radical course change; the Soviets made clear that the price for cooperation in the occupation in general and permission for the Western Allies to cross their lines to Berlin in particular was a retreat to the original zonal borders. (As the Soviet commander Marshal Zhukov would tell his American counterpart at the end of the month, "the quicker the move [back], the quicker the entry into Berlin.")[56] The Western Allies had not planned for such a contingency, and were over a barrel; Truman overruled Churchill and accepted the deal.[57] At the end of the summer of 1945, therefore, each member of the Grand Alliance rested precisely, except for the addition of the French, where the original British plan for the occupation of Germany had envisioned them.[58]

As with unconditional surrender, the explanation for the general pattern of cooperation by the Western Allies with the Soviet Union during the endgame in Germany is straightforward: no other course could guarantee the defeat of the Nazi regime. As Hitler himself recognized until the end, his only hope for survival after the Normandy landings lay in the development of dramatic new weapons or in a split between the opposing coalition members. An open break with the Soviets prior to the overthrow of the Nazis would clearly have harmed the material interests of the Western Allies, which is why even the most anti-Soviet of U.S. officials had few practical alternative courses to propose.[59]

Such hardheaded realism, however, cannot explain the complete absence of any contingency planning on the part of the Americans (and the British, too, for that matter) eventually to redirect politico-military efforts against the Soviets should a cooperative policy not work out. Perhaps the best example of this oversight is the planning for occupation and administration of Germany after the war. As late as Yalta, each of the Big Three favored partitioning Germany, with the only questions being where and into how many parts. Yet even as these plans were gradually shelved during the spring of 1945, no new ones officially emerged in the West to take their place.

EXPLAINING THE POSITIVE WAR

While the American armed forces were pursuing the total defeat of Nazi Germany, American politicians and diplomats were creating a framework for the postwar world. Economically, the United States would lead, in conjunction and competition with Britain and other Western European countries. Politically, the United States would continue to exercise a benign hegemony in the Western Hemisphere while Western Europe would be a British sphere of influence and Eastern Europe a Soviet one; in the Pacific, the United States would share responsibilities with China as European colonialism was phased out. Germany and Japan were to be purged and demilitarized; beyond that their fates were left undecided.[60]

In their public rhetoric, American officials eschewed realist rationales for such plans. Hull often pictured the new economic order as one in which all would prosper through a harmony of interests, and Roosevelt described the new security order as follows: "It ought to spell the end of the system of unilateral action, the exclusive alliances, the spheres of influence, the balances of power, and all the other expedients that have been tried for centuries—and have always failed. We propose to substitute for all these, a universal organization in which all peace-loving Nations will finally have a chance to join. . . . [T]he results of [the Yalta] Conference [will be] the beginnings of a permanent structure of peace. . . ."[61]

U.S. officials often used similar language in private as well, and many probably did see their own actions as fundamentally different from those of their Allies. Roosevelt, for example, was undoubtedly sincere when he berated Churchill for attributing cynical designs to everyone: "Winston, [altruism] is something which you just are not able to understand. You have 400 years of acquisitive instinct in your blood and you just don't understand how a country might not want to acquire land somewhere if they can get it."[62] And indeed, compared to the behavior of other powerful conquerors throughout history, U.S. motivations and conduct were remarkably benign.

Nevertheless, the happy consonance of American values and interests, and the great relative power that American officials enjoyed, make it difficult to characterize U.S. behavior unambiguously. As Charles Maier has written, it makes little sense to see American conduct as either purely idealistic or purely realistic, "because the same policies could serve both aspirations. Washington's neo-Cobdenite mission did aim at higher world levels of exchange and welfare. Simultaneously, it was intended to benefit American producers who could compete vigorously in any market where the 'open door' and the free convertibility of currencies into dollars facilitated equal access."[63]

"The United States," Bruce Kuniholm agrees, "with its vast resources and productive strength could afford to advocate principles which, if no less self-serving than those which guided the Soviet Union, nonetheless were more benevolent. . . ."[64] Hull may have considered American economic plans disinterested, but not all would have characterized the same policies the same way. "Since the early 1940s," D. C. Watt notes, "British students had been faced with examination questions on the statement: 'Free trade is the imperialism of the strong.' "[65]

Apart from the difficulty of disentangling the threads of power and principle in American designs, another problem in assessing the initial U.S. plans for the postwar order derives from those plans' confusion and impracticality, with the United Nations being a prime example. One could classify as idealist a collective security system that weighted all states equally and expected them to sacrifice blood and treasure for nonvital interests. One could classify as realist a great-power condominium that granted, de jure or de facto, each major state the right to control its strategic environs without interference. One is at a loss in classifying the United Nations as originally set up, however, because its American founders honestly seem to have expected it to provide a solution to the dilemmas of international anarchy at no cost to anyone's interests. What might happen should members of the Security Council disagree was not dwelt upon. The question of how such a global security system would relate to existing or potential regional systems was left unresolved. The contradictory purposes the organization was meant to serve, and the different understandings its members held of the role it would play in resolving international disputes, were never clarified.[66]

Such blurred vision was partly the result of the deep cleavages within the Roosevelt administration. The State Department was excluded from the conduct of the war but entrusted with the planning of the peace. The Treasury Department had its own ideas, and because of the personal relationship between Morgenthau and Roosevelt these went well beyond purely financial matters. And because the armed services played such an important role during the war, they had much to say about postwar planning, and their opinions differed greatly from those of their diplomatic colleagues.

Conflicting bureaucratic interests and perspectives sometimes led to governmental paralysis. For example, one of the crucial issues for the immediate postwar period was what to do about the German economy—but here, as even policymakers themselves noted, "divergences among government departments on basic issues . . . prevented the formulation of an agreed American position." The State Department wanted to assume control of the economy and revive production in order to make Germany a stable postwar ally. The Treasury and War departments disagreed, preferring to take on "limited liability" for German economic affairs. As one State Department memorandum put it,

> The War Department favors this limited definition of the Army's tasks because (1) they favor a simple, clear-cut military occupation, (2) they wish, by limiting the task, to minimize the need for consultation and negotiation among the commanders of the several zones of occupation, and (3) they wish to keep the job within the capabilities of the occupation forces. The Treasury supports the doctrine of limited liability because (1) they consider that extreme disruption in Germany is not in conflict with Allied interests, and (2) acceptance of any responsibility for the minimum functioning of the German economy would cause us to make compromises with respect to elimination of Nazis.[67]

Another memo captured the point more pithily: "The Treasury and War Departments advocate the same policy for different reasons: Treasury wants chaos; War wants decentralization and complete authority for its zone commander."[68] The final result was an inconsistent occupation policy straddling different visions—and so, unsurprisingly, in the end American officials ended up reacting to events on the ground more often than guiding them.

If this picture of government as anarchy among bureaucratic fiefdoms resembles that painted by bureaucratic politics theorists, however, it differs in one crucial respect: the chaos was neither inevitable nor unwanted. In fact, it was the direct product of, and served the peculiar purposes of, the ruler of the system. As Alexander George observed, Roosevelt "deliberately exacerbated the competitive and conflicting aspects of cabinet politics and bureaucratic politics. He sought to increase both structural and functional ambiguities within the executive branch in order to better preside over it."[69]

FDR once admitted, "I never let my right hand know what my left hand does. . . . I may have one policy for Europe and one diametrically opposite for North and South America. I may be entirely inconsistent, and furthermore I am perfectly willing to mislead and tell untruths. . . ."[70] In foreign as in domestic policy, he was addicted to improvisation, creating a system that concentrated decisionmaking power in his hands and gave him the utmost flexibility. He preferred to conduct all important wartime diplomacy through personal summitry or, if that could not be arranged, through loyal personal representatives such as Harry Hopkins. He downgraded the State Department's role because he did not trust more conservative elements there to implement his policies faithfully. And he chose a cipher (Edward Stettinius) as secretary of state in the final, crucial months of the war precisely to avoid having a powerful, independent foreign policy voice in the government.

When American officials in Moscow protested against giving the Soviet Union Lend-Lease aid without any quid pro quo—or even transparency about what the money was being used for—the president simply bypassed them by setting up a special agency to distribute the funds independent of the normal bureaucratic channels. When Eisenhower tried to get the president to relax the unconditional surrender policy in Italy and Germany, the president simply refused to do so, and the discussion ended there. Roosevelt had no intention of allowing anybody else to determine what U.S. postwar policy would be, and he wasn't going to decide himself until he absolutely had to. Thus, for example, Roosevelt actually embraced what others might regard as irresponsible neglect of planning for Germany's postwar fate. As he wrote Hull in late 1944, "I dislike making detailed plans for a country which we do not yet occupy. . . . Much . . . is dependent on what we and the Allies find when we get into Germany—and we are not there yet."[71]

Some have argued that "both before and during the war, what best explains Roosevelt's foreign policies was his inclination to mirror American public opinion."[72] Clare Booth Luce expressed this view succinctly. "Every great leader" during the war, she was once described as saying, "had his typical gesture—Hitler the upraised arm, Churchill the V sign. Roosevelt? She wet her index finger and held it up."[73] And it is true that domestic political concerns were often on the president's mind. Thus he implored General Marshall, regarding the invasion of North Africa, "Please make it before Election Day,"[74] and asked Stalin for token concessions at Yalta because "there are six or seven million Poles in the United States. . . . It would make it easier for me at home if the Soviet Government could give something to Poland."[75] Roosevelt also felt constrained by broader trends of public opinion. At Yalta, for example, he told the other Allied leaders that "he did not believe that American troops would stay in Europe much more than two years [after the war]. He went on to say that he felt that he could obtain support in Congress and throughout the country for any reasonable measures designed to safeguard the future peace, but he did not believe that this would extend to the maintenance of an appreciable American force in Europe."[76]

Regarding the larger questions of inter-Allied policy that arose at the end of the war, the British chief of staff, Hastings Ismay, felt that domestic politics were a major constraint:

> For over three years, public opinion in America and Britain had been led to believe that Russia was a brave and faithful ally who had done the lion's share of the fight, and endured untold suffering. If their Governments had now proclaimed that the Russians were untrustworthy and unprincipled tyrants, whose ambitions must be held in check, the effect on national unity in both countries would have been catastrophic. . . . One is forced to the conclusion that such a reversal of policy, which dictators could have taken in their stride, was absolutely impossible for the leaders of democratic countries even to contemplate.[77]

Many in the U.S. government felt the same way. On the eve of Yalta, for example, Kennan wrote to his fellow State Department Russia expert Charles Bohlen as follows:

> I am aware of the realities of this war, and of the fact that we are too weak to win it without Russian cooperation. . . . [But] I fail to see why we must associate ourselves with this political program, so hostile to the interests of the Atlantic community as a whole, so dangerous to everything which we need to see preserved in Europe. Why could we not make a decent and definitive compromise with it—divide Europe frankly into spheres of influence—keep ourselves out of the Russian sphere and keep the Russians out of ours?

Bohlen responded with an appeal to what he considered a higher realism, that of domestic politics and values: "The 'constructive' suggestions that you make are frankly naive to a degree. They may well be the optimum from an abstract point of view. But as practical suggestions they are utterly impossible. Foreign policy of that kind cannot be made in a democracy. Only totalitarian states can make and carry out such policies."[78]

Nevertheless, if domestic politics provided a general constraint upon U.S. decisionmaking, it was a manipulable one. Thus the Roosevelt administration set its sights on Germany rather than Japan as the initial and primary military target. Warren Kimball notes, "Had the President been a prisoner of public opinion, as he is so often depicted, he would have followed the instincts and emotions of Congress, the press, and the public, and turned westward, to respond to the Japanese attack."[79] Moreover, when American hostility toward the Soviet Union in the early 1940s inconvenienced the president's plans for the Grand Alliance, he launched a campaign to change it—and eventually created a new dynamic that supported cooperation with Moscow. And then, when such concerns threatened to interfere with actual policy—as with public pressure for a "second front" in 1942—Roosevelt used his authority to dampen debate.[80]

By the midpoint of the war, popular and congressional opinion would have prevented any move for a compromise peace with a Nazi regime even had the president for some reason decided to favor one. Popular attitudes regarding the Soviet Union were mixed, and might have been played upon in any of a variety of ways.[81] As for the war's positive program, meanwhile, the public and Congress were confused.

Isolationists had been discredited by Pearl Harbor and took chastened refuge in bipartisanship. Public disapproval was sufficient to constrain "secret treaties," and many obviously were concerned with deviations from the principles of the Atlantic Charter, but no clear direction was provided for postwar foreign policy. Far from being a response to popular demands, for example, the Roosevelt administration's postwar institutional framework had to be carefully marketed to pass Congress. Key congressional figures such as Senator Arthur Vandenberg sought to play a major role in foreign policy formation, but could be co-opted.[82] A survey of public opinion throughout this period concludes:

> It would have required courage and leadership, but there is strong reason to believe that Presidents Roosevelt and Truman and their secretaries of state could have told the American people throughout 1945 of America's and Russia's new power and of the new realities of the international order. . . . [I]t is quite likely that most Americans would have accepted their leaders' assessments of the postwar world order. In fact, that is precisely what the majority of the people had done when their governmental and other leading opinion makers favored pro-Russian attitudes during the war, and it is also what the people did when these leaders adopted a "get-tough-with-Russia" stance in 1946 and 1947.[83]

So what really drove key U.S. decisionmakers as they formulated the war's positive program? Their burning desire to avoid what all perceived as the dramatic failure of American policy in 1918–19.[84] Roosevelt expressed this pithily at the end of 1943:

> After the Armistice in 1918, we thought and hoped that the militaristic philosophy of Germany had been crushed; and being full of the milk of human kindness we spent the next twenty years disarming, while the Germans whined so pathetically that the other Nations permitted them—even helped them—to rearm. . . . The well-intentioned but ill-fated experiments of former years did not work. It is my hope that we will not try them again. No—that is putting it too weakly—it is my intention to do all that I humanly can as President and Commander in Chief to see to it that these tragic mistakes shall not be made again.[85]

These attitudes led directly to the policy of unconditional surrender, but explain a wealth of other behavior as well.[86]

There was striking agreement among U.S. policymakers during the 1940s about just what the lessons—in this case, the mistakes—of the past were. This consensus ran as follows: The Wilson administration had been soft on Germany and hard on Russia; it had permitted the other Allies to make secret agreements and hold acquisitive war aims; it had waited until after the war to establish an institutional framework for ordering the peace; it had failed to secure congressional approval of American participation in the League of Nations; the League itself had not taken sufficient account of power differentials between nations; and subsequently the United States had retreated into isolation while others had adopted nationalistic economic policies. These bankrupt policies had led, the consensus argued further, directly to World War II: the Allies' wartime alliance fractured; the League foundered, because it lacked the United States and because it was too idealistically conceived; trade barriers spurred economic depression; and eventually a tyrannical Germany, carelessly left intact, rose up again and was not checked in time.

It was this vision—or rather, this remembered nightmare—that lay behind the entire complex of U.S. planning for the postwar order. First, as Roosevelt put it bluntly, "It is of the utmost importance that every person in Germany should realize that this time Germany is a defeated nation."[87] Second, the Soviet Union would not be shunned and all attempts would be made to keep the victorious wartime alliance intact. Third, an institutional framework for such collaboration would be negotiated during the war itself, so that it could be in place to smooth postwar difficulties. Fourth, the institution would acknowledge the different roles in maintaining world order played by great powers and lesser states. Fifth, congressional approval would be won at all costs. Sixth, wartime commitments would be kept to a minimum so that the institution would not have to deal with the baggage of secret treaties. Seventh, the vanquished nations, once purged and democratized, would not be burdened with crushing reparations debts. And eighth, steps would be taken to ensure that the cornerstone of the postwar economic order would be multilateral free trade. Hitler, in short, was not the only one determined to ensure that "the year 1918 will . . . not repeat itself."[88]

LESSONS AND POWER

During the endgame of World War II, American policymakers wanted to repeat what they considered the tragedy of the Great War a second time, not as farce but as triumph. Their behavior was not driven by ideas alone, however—because the ideas themselves, not to mention the attempt to implement them, cannot be understood without reference to the extraordinary relative power position the United States enjoyed at the end of the latter conflict.

The lessons American policymakers in the 1940s drew from the botched endgame of World War I seemed obvious, and many were indeed quite sensible. But lots of different lessons could have been drawn from precisely the same experiences, and in fact were drawn by other observers at other times. What was notable about the reading of history that became conventional wisdom in the Roosevelt administration was that it favored more rather than less American action and involvement in the external world—something that was a direct, if only partly conscious, reflection of the material power at the administration's disposal.

The first wave of American "lessons learned" from the Great War, after all, blamed the Wilson administration for getting too involved in the troubles of the Old World and concluded that American interests should be protected through isolation rather than engagement. Only the second wave aspired to create a global order of peace and prosperity on American terms. And while American leaders saw Weimar Germany as having been whipsawed by the gap between a generous armistice based on the Fourteen Points and the punitive peace of Versailles, they might have concluded that the way to eliminate such a gap (and the "stab in the back" legend it enabled) was to remain committed to a generous settlement, a "Peace Without Victory," throughout the postwar period. Instead they chose to avoid charges of betrayal after World War II by refusing to make any promises to the Germans whatsoever—a course that required physically conquering Germany and remaking its political system from the ground up.

American leaders could contemplate the more expansive, and more expensive, options only because in 1945 the United States possessed the greatest relative material strength any nation has ever had or is ever likely to have. This peculiar situation was the result of the simultaneous flowering of the American economy and military-industrial establishment and the destruction of everybody else's. In the half decade after

1945, the United States was responsible for roughly one-half of the world's total product. "American blast furnaces produced 50 percent of the world's steel. Americans owned 70 percent of the world's merchant marine fleet and about 78 percent of the world's transport and commercial airplanes."[89] America harvested one-third of the grain and one-half of the cotton grown on the planet; it refined 60 percent of the world's oil, produced 90 percent of its natural gas, and mined more coal than anybody else. By late summer 1945, moreover, the nation was the sole possessor of the most powerful weapon ever known.

In late 1944, Roosevelt declared that "at the end of this war this country will have the greatest material power of any Nation in the world." Within months Truman would concur: "We tell ourselves that we have emerged from this war the most powerful nation in the world—the most powerful nation, perhaps, in all history. That is true."[90] In June 1945, Bernard Baruch told Truman not to worry too much about repeated crises because "it is on the productive capacity of America that all countries must rely for the comforts—even the necessities—that a modern world will demand. We have the mass production and the know-how. Without us the rest of the world cannot recuperate; it cannot rebuild, feed, house or clothe itself."[91] Economists in the Office of International Trade noted later in the decade that "the United States is now the greatest single economic force on earth, and the kind of foreign economic policy we follow now and in the next few years will inevitably determine in large measure the policies to be followed by the rest of the world."[92]

Other players in the international game understood this power disparity even better, as weaker partners often do. Smarting under criticism of his supposedly selfish and old-fashioned thinking, Churchill exclaimed bitterly in January 1945 that he wished his colleagues across the Atlantic would "give me a definition of 'power politics.' . . . Is having a Navy twice as strong as any other 'power politics'? Is having an overwhelming Air Force, with bases all over the world, 'power politics'? Is having all the gold in the world buried in a cavern 'power politics'? If not, what is 'power politics'? Is it giving all the bases in the West Indies which are necessary to American safety to the United States—is that 'power politics'?"[93] Sometimes these feelings of frustration and resentment at the ongoing hegemonic transition would come out in the open. Frustrated at one conference late in the war by Roosevelt's delay in initialing an aid agreement, the British leader burst out: "What do you want me to do? Get on my hind legs and beg like Fala?"[94]

Of course, the link between what a Marxist would call the material base and the ideational superstructure of American power was not immediate, smooth, or even fully acknowledged. The country's growing strength often operated, as structural factors generally do, at a subconscious level, implicitly skewing the risk assessments and cost-benefit calculations policymakers engaged in or leading them to be more ambitious than they might otherwise have been. Thanks to intellectual inertia, moreover, official Washington, however grand its wartime planning, ended up backing grudgingly into many of the less appetizing practical aspects of its new imperial role. In the early 1940s, for example, few in Washington envisioned a postwar foreign policy based on continual presence and intervention abroad—and most would have scoffed at and disapproved of those who did. But as the decade wore on, the combination of domestic strength and foreign weakness worked like a giant vacuum sucking American influence and commitments outward.

Perhaps the best representation of this process was the change in attitudes of the American military, neatly captured in the intellectual journey of George Marshall's chief long-range planner, General Stanley D. Embick. Embick began the war as a committed isolationist, favoring a purely continental defense policy and opposing major commitments abroad. By 1943, however, he had changed his mind about the Pacific and Far East, advocating long-term American involvement in those regions and the acquisition of bases there. Nevertheless, Embick still fought against any postwar involvement in European affairs, happily conceding to the Soviets all control over the eastern and southeastern parts of the continent and advocating whatever concessions were necessary to keep them happy. This was the reigning policy of the U.S. military throughout the war, even though the younger officers at a rival planning outfit were beginning to maintain that Embick's "premise that the U.S.S.R. must be appeased in order to keep peace is basically unsound."[95] But during the fall of 1945, with the contours of the new world clearly visible, Embick finally rejected his belief in continental self-sufficiency and moved to embrace the global role he had so long eschewed.

The story of what the United States did later with its new status as the dominant Western power—meeting the Soviet challenge and trying to salvage what remained of its original postwar vision—is the story of the Cold War.

FROM HOT TO COLD WAR

Contrary to American expectations, the end of World War II ushered in a period of confusion and instability rather than harmony—or rather, vastly greater confusion and instability than anybody had predicted. American officials, moreover, following the lead of their wartime president, had neglected practical short- and midterm planning for a broad range of postwar scenarios. So at the close of the fighting, those officials faced a new and daunting set of challenges: "Britain was weaker than they thought; European financial problems more intractable; German and Japanese economic woes more deep-seated; revolutionary nationalism more virulent; Soviet actions more ominous; and American demobilization more rapid."[96]

From 1945 to 1947, the Truman administration gradually realized just how mistaken previous American assumptions about the postwar world had been and just how inadequate were the international institutions that had been created to manage it. During the same period, moreover, they grew skeptical about Soviet willingness to help create a stable new order. As Melvyn Leffler has written, "At the end of the war, U.S. officials did not think that they were engaged in a zero-sum game of power politics with the Soviet Union. They wanted to cooperate with the Kremlin. But they harbored a distrust sufficiently profound to require terms of cooperation compatible with vital American interests."[97] By 1947, they decided that in order to salvage as much as possible of the American postwar vision, the institutional framework so recently and laboriously constructed would have to be set aside and a new one created based on more realistic, less universal assumptions. The period from 1945 to 1949 is best understood, therefore, as the second phase of the endgame of the positive war.

During 1945, the attention of the American public followed American soldiers, shifting from Europe to the Pacific and then back to the United States. Officials in the Truman administration, however, found themselves dealing with foreign dilemmas requiring more American attention and involvement rather than less—something for which both the new president and his advisers were largely unprepared. Truman's predecessor had played a double game with regard to the territories occupied by the Soviet Union. As Bruce Kuniholm writes: "Because Roosevelt could neither concede portions of Eastern Europe to Stalin, nor deny them to him . . . in effect [he did] both—the former through implicit understandings . . . [and] the latter through the promulgation of principles that were interpreted differently by the Soviets and by the American people."[98] The Truman administration faced the inevitable returns on such a dual policy, which had been complicated by the fact that Roosevelt had never fully acknowledged the tensions in his machinations to others—and perhaps not even to himself.

For foreign policy advice, Truman initially relied heavily on Secretary of State James F. Byrnes, who in turn looked to Bohlen. Bohlen resolved the contradictions in Roosevelt's policy by making clear what many in the State Department had been thinking: the United States would accept a Soviet sphere of influence, but only an "open" one. The Soviets would be permitted to control their satellites' foreign and security policies, but not dominate their domestic or economic realms. As he wrote in a memo for Byrnes in October 1945:

> While recognizing fully the legitimate interest of the Soviet Union in [Central and Eastern Europe] we should continue to oppose any extensions of this into illegitimate fields leading towards the establishment of a rigidly and exclusively Soviet-controlled bloc. The chief difficulty in the situation is that from all our indications the Soviet mind is incapable of making a distinction between legitimate and illegitimate influence; to distinguish between influence and domination, or between a friendly and a puppet government. . . . It should, therefore, be a constant endeavor on the one hand to demonstrate to the Soviet Government that they will receive American cooperation and help to the degree to which they are prepared to limit their influence to the legitimate sphere, and unmistakably on the other to demonstrate that such help and cooperation will not be forthcoming either diplomatically or materially in any attempt to translate a legitimate interest into domination and exclusion.[99]

The tensions between the victorious great powers' conflicting visions of the postwar order had now risen fully to the surface, and events during the fall of 1945 demonstrated that possession of the atomic bomb would not, in spite of the early hopes of some, guarantee U.S. diplomatic victories across the board.

At this point, while American officials were still pondering the import of Soviet moves in Eastern Europe, events in the Near East helped crystallize official American views regarding what the Soviets were doing, why they were doing it, and how the United States should respond. In early 1946, Soviet actions in Iran seemed to show Moscow's aggressive, destabilizing intentions. Kennan's "Long Telegram" from Moscow argued that since those intentions were driven by internal causes, American appeasement would not work. And the eventual Soviet retreat in Iran seemed to show that a confrontational policy could be effective.

By late 1946, moreover, the true dimensions of the postwar economic and political crisis in Western Europe had become clear. Reinterpreted in light of the new view of the Soviet Union, anarchy in the continent's industrial heartland now appeared as a strategic vacuum drawing in an opportunistic enemy. The harsh winter of 1946–47 pushed Europe even closer to chaos, galvanizing American officials (after prodding from their allies) into a dynamic response. In addition to dispatching a quick infusion of cash late in 1947, Truman administration officials launched a massive new aid program, the Marshall Plan, to fuel the reconstruction of Western European economies. When Britain sent word early in 1947 that it could no longer afford its commitments in Greece and Turkey, the U.S. administration responded with the Truman Doctrine, taking over the commitments as its own and making plain its intention of blocking further advances of Soviet influence, whether direct or indirect. Finally, developing an idea first proposed by British foreign secretary Ernest Bevin, by the end of the decade the Truman administration helped found the North Atlantic Treaty Organization, formally committing the United States to the defense of Europe from a Soviet attack.

With these bold and unprecedented steps, American officials salvaged a portion of their wartime vision, establishing a new set of commitments and institutions to supplement and partly supplant those they had embraced only a few years before.[100] Together, the Marshall Plan, the Truman Doctrine, and NATO provided a practical basis for a postwar order conducive to U.S. interests. Once established, in turn, this order would eventually be maintained with the help of some of the institutions of the "first wave" of endgame activity—the IMF, the World Bank, and the General Agreement on Tariffs and Trade (what remained of the wreckage of the ITO).

In contrast to the expectations of the early 1940s, the new system was limited to portions of a divided world. For the United States, moreover, it came with the burdens of continuing high defense expenditures, the actuality of limited wars, and the threat of a general conflagration, together with popular hysteria and global ideological conflict. But the presence of such threatening conditions facilitated a cohesion within the American sphere and domestic American support for an expanded global role that might not have been forthcoming otherwise. A return to the Roosevelt administration's dream—the gradual extension of the American sphere of peace, prosperity, and freedom to the world at large—would take another four decades and the final collapse of its problematic wartime ally.

In later years, the Roosevelt and Truman administrations would come in for much criticism over their supposed strategic mistakes in handling the end of the war. What stands out today, however, is how few of those criticisms, whether from the right or the left, actually hold up. Unconditional surrender was not a mindless policy that prolonged the fighting; it was a wise response to a total war fought by a fragile coalition. Eastern Europe was not given away at Yalta; it was seized by the Red Army, at a price the Western Allies would never have dreamed of paying. Eisenhower was not wrong in rejecting a race to Berlin; he was prudent and sensible. Truman did not start the Cold War through clumsiness or belligerence; he and his colleagues grudgingly recognized its imminence and on balance responded appropriately. Run the events of the 1940s through innumerable computer simulations, with different strategic choices made by American leaders at key moments, and the vast majority of outcomes would be far less attractive than the results actually achieved.

If the standard criticisms can be readily dismissed, however, a less common one cannot be. The Roosevelt administration was indeed guilty of negligence in not preparing backup plans for adverse contingencies abroad or at home. Trying to keep the Grand Alliance going throughout the war and after made sense, as did bending over backward to alleviate Soviet concerns about security. But there was no reason why such efforts could not have been supplemented by practical planning for what to do if the alliance broke down anyway.

In his most recent analysis of the origins of the Cold War, John Lewis Gaddis wondered why anybody was surprised or alarmed by the postwar falling-out, since knowledgeable people should have "expected exactly what took place. Certainly a theorist of international relations would have."[101] This is unfair. Several of the most serious and practical-minded international relations theorists in the country actually addressed precisely this subject in early 1945 and came to a less definitive conclusion. "Even though history may abound with instances in which the 'allies of today' proved to be 'the enemies of tomorrow,' " they noted in a report for the Pentagon, "it would be criminal folly to jettison our wartime alliance in the moment of victory in the mistaken belief that war with the Soviet Union is 'inevitable.' . . . While the United States can afford to make no concessions which leave its security or vital interests at the mercy of the Soviet Union, there is almost no other concession which it can afford not to make to assure Soviet collaboration in the maintenance of security." [102] Given what the Cold War ultimately cost, it is not at all surprising or inappropriate that American leaders hoped and planned for the wartime alliance's continuation. The real wonder is that they did nothing else.

The most astonishing example of such complacency comes from the debate over occupation zones in Germany. In 1944 and 1945, Roosevelt and the American military were obsessed with specifying in advance, down to the last comma, arrangements for moving troops and supplies between the American zone and the coast—that is, through the British zone. But until practically the day of the German surrender, barely a thought was given to the question of how to supply or even reach the Western sectors of Berlin—located deep within the Soviet zone—should the Soviets not prove cooperative.[103] Military officials saw no need to hammer out access rights in advance, assuming arrangements could be worked out easily later on. "I must admit that we did not then fully realize," the responsible officer would sheepishly write afterward, "that the requirement of unanimous consent would enable a Soviet veto in the Allied Control Council to block all of our future efforts." [104]

Some might claim that developing backup plans for the breakdown of the alliance would itself have raised Soviet suspicions, running the risk of creating a self-fulfilling prophecy. Sure: prenuptial agreements are hardly conducive to romance. But geopolitical marriages of convenience are not love matches, and the interests at stake were too important to be left to chance. So the practical argument against contingency planning does not wash.

It is more likely that what was going on was a psychological blocking mechanism. World War II was the worst conflict in human history, having followed the next worst by only one generation. British officials were so traumatized by their experiences in the Great War that many of them found it difficult to consider actually engaging the German army ever again. Their American counterparts, fully engaged only the second time around, must at some deep level have felt the same about a follow-on geopolitical conflict with the Soviet Union. Assuming that the only choice was between great power harmony or a third unbearable world war, they committed themselves wholeheartedly to the former, never realizing that a middle ground was possible—even though that was actually what eventually emerged.

Similarly, Roosevelt and those around him must have found it difficult to face the prospect that he was mortal. The president had dominated American politics so completely for so long, steering the country so skillfully through crises of all kinds, that life without him must have been hard for many to imagine. Throughout 1944 and early 1945, accordingly, even as Roosevelt's physical condition deteriorated visibly and rapidly, nobody made any preparations for his passing. When Truman was suddenly catapulted into the most powerful office in the land at one of the most critical moments in world history, he was at a near-complete loss because he had never been taken into his predecessor's confidence on any of the myriad crucial questions of the day. "He never did talk to me confidentially about the war, or about foreign affairs, or what he had in mind for the peace after the war," the new president confided to his daughter.[105] Truman's critics at the time and later scorned his ordinariness and supposed lack of fitness for the job. But it was his ostensibly greater predecessor who really deserved the censure, for irresponsibly ignoring any planning for a succession.

On May 8, 1945, writing to his mother and sister, the thirty-third president described his first few weeks in the new job: "Things have moved at a terrific rate here since April 12. Never a day has gone by that some momentous decision didn't have to be made. So far luck has been with me. I hope it keeps up. It can't stay with me forever however and I hope when the mistake comes it won't be too great to remedy."[106]

A modest, decent, hardworking man, Truman worried that he was not up to his new responsibilities, and he had a lot of company. In fact, the country, and the world, got lucky. For it was in large part thanks to the new president's common virtues and good sense—and his administration's ability to improvise successfully—that over the next few years the Western Allies' wartime gains were consolidated and extended as much as they actually were.

4

WORLD WAR II—PACIFIC

In the early hours of Wednesday, August 15, 1945, General Korechika Anami poured himself a tumbler of sake, downed it, then poured another. "I'm thinking of committing suicide," he said. "If you keep drinking like that, won't you flub up?" asked his brother-in-law, Lieutenant Colonel Masehiko Takeshita. "I have a fifth-degree rank in kendo," Anami replied, "so I won't fail. When you drink sake, you bleed more profusely. That way you're certain of dying. Anyway, should something go wrong, I want you to assist me."[1]

Four months earlier, Anami had been appointed war minister of Imperial Japan, a position with veto power over all national policy. He had known the war was going badly, but remained confident his forces could mount a last-ditch effort to disrupt the coming American invasion of the Japanese home islands. That might buy enough time and space to arrange a compromise peace—and if it didn't, well, then at least the army would go down fighting. As his colleague General Yoshijiro Umezu, the army chief of staff, noted, "The word 'surrender' is not in the Japanese military lexicon. In our military education, if you lose your weapons, you fight with your bare hands. When your hands will no longer help, you fight with your feet. When you can no longer use your hands and feet, you bite with your teeth. Finally, when you can no longer fight, you bite off your tongue and commit suicide. That's what I teach."[2]

Throughout the summer Anami had held his ground, even as the noose drew tighter around his country's neck and its people were incinerated by endless waves of American bombers. In the space of four days the previous week, however, the Americans had dropped two atomic bombs on Japan and the Soviets had launched a surprise attack on Japanese positions in Manchuria. Even after these blows, the six members of the cabinet's inner circle had remained split over how to respond. Three "moderates" favored surrendering according to the terms of the Potsdam Declaration, with one additional condition—that the Japanese monarchy be preserved. Anami, Umezu, and a third colleague insisted on three further conditions. But in an unprecedented move, the emperor himself had intervened in the decisionmaking process, declaring his preference for the moderate position. Anami and the other two hard-liners had bowed to his will, and notification was duly sent to Washington on August 10.

The Americans, taken aback, had replied with a note parrying the request for clarification on the emperor's postwar status—leading to another three-three deadlock in the Japanese cabinet, one that had been broken by another imperial intervention in favor of the moderates that very morning. In the afternoon, as the emperor and his advisers began to prepare a radio message announcing the surrender, Anami had broken the news to his staff:

> Three hours ago the emperor commanded that Japan accept the enemy terms. The army will obey the emperor's command. He offered to come here and speak to you himself. I replied that that would not be necessary. The army, I said, will, like the rest of the country, obey the emperor's command. . . . No officer in the army will presume to know, better than the emperor and the government of the country, what is best for the country. . . . The future of Japan is no longer in doubt, but neither will it be an easy future. You officers must realize that death cannot absolve you of your duty. Your duty is to stay alive and to do your best to help your country along the path to recovery—even if it means chewing grass and eating earth and sleeping in the fields![3]

Takeshita found his brother-in-law at home just after midnight. Despite Anami's orders, some fanatical junior officers had refused to accept capitulation and were about to launch a coup to prevent it. Anami had known about their plot for days, even flirted with leading it, but at the crucial moment had backed away, unwilling to disobey a direct request from his lord and master. Takeshita had been sent by the plotters to make one last plea for Anami's participation; when he continued to refuse, the two of them just talked and drank instead.

Around 2 A.M., shots rang out from the palace nearby, but Anami remained calm. He predicted that without his own participation and that of other senior military commanders the coup attempt would fail, and he was right: although the plotters penetrated the palace and killed some guards, they never managed to capture the emperor or destroy the two hidden recordings of his surrender message, set for broadcast at noon.

About 4 A.M., Anami put on a loose white shirt that the emperor had given him as a present years before and drew his short sword from its lacquered sheath. A maid came in to say that a police official had arrived with a report, and Takeshita went out to handle it. When he returned, he found his relative kneeling, covered in blood with his stomach sliced open. Then Anami plunged a dagger into his neck and slumped forward. Noticing that he was still alive, Takeshita administered a coup de grâce. The leader of Japan's army left behind two cryptic notes. One said: "Believing firmly that our sacred land shall never perish, I—with my death—humbly apologize to the Emperor for the great crime." The other said: "Having received great favors from His Majesty, the Emperor, I have nothing to say to posterity in the hour of my death."

Eight hours later, gathered around radios across Asia, the Japanese people and armed forces heard their ruler's voice for the first time. "Despite the best that has been done by everyone," they were told, "the war situation has developed not necessarily to Japan's advantage." As a result, the throne had "resolved to pave the way for a grand peace for all the generations to come by enduring the unendurable and suffering what is insufferable." Within three weeks, the war in the Pacific was over.

Because of the limited connection between the European and Pacific theaters during World War II, it is useful to think of the United States fighting two related, simultaneous wars in those years rather than making one global effort. Both struggles drew on the same national resources and stocks of materiel, yet different services predominated, different passions motivated American soldiers and civilians, and different attitudes toward U.S. policy and interests often prevailed.

The Japanese attack on Pearl Harbor was the catalyst for American operations in both theaters, but soon afterward the Roosevelt administration reaffirmed its intention to focus on defeating Nazi Germany first and more or less kept to this position during the years after. By the start of 1945, American strategists thought fighting in the Pacific might well continue for a year after it had stopped in Europe and planned accordingly. As it happened, however, punishing blows from land, sea, and air caused the endgame there to begin in earnest just as the guns fell silent on the other side of the globe, and the emperor's broadcast of surrender followed the fall of Germany by a scant hundred days.

U.S. behavior during the European endgame turned on four central questions: whether to attempt a compromise settlement of the war with the Nazis; whether to attempt a compromise settlement with their internal opponents; whether to continue cooperating with the Soviet Union during the war's final operations; and how to lay the groundwork for America's preferred postwar order. As described in the previous chapter, the first two questions were answered in the negative with the decision to strive for unconditional surrender, the third was answered in the affirmative with the decision not to race for Berlin in 1944–45, and the fourth was answered with a network of international institutions—the Bretton Woods regime and the United Nations—designed to promote multilateral capitalism and global security.

Four comparable questions drove events during the Pacific endgame, but the second and fourth can be dealt with summarily. Japanese opposition figures were as scarce as reasonable Nazis, so the possibility of dealing with them was never an issue. And postwar planning applied broadly to both theaters. When American policy shifted in the late 1940s, moreover, the impetus for change came from events in Europe and the Near East rather than Asia—and the American approach to occupied Japan switched gears just like the approach to occupied Germany, away from domestic reform and toward the new goal of integrating the former enemy into a capitalist, anti-Soviet, U.S.-led alliance system.[4]

The key questions for U.S. behavior during the Pacific endgame, therefore, were the first and third: whether the United States should bargain with a still-powerful Imperial Japanese regime and whether it should continue cooperating with the Soviet Union during the war's final stages. But the denouement in the Pacific was complicated by three new factors: an attempt by Japanese leaders to try to negotiate an end to the war short of total defeat, increasingly obvious U.S. and Soviet divisions, and the availability of the atomic bomb.[5]

All this led to heated debates in Washington during the summer of 1945 about how the Pacific war could and should be brought to a close. For guidance, the Americans looked, as in Europe, primarily to the lessons of the past and national ideology rather than to calculations of Realpolitik. In addition, American public opinion, inflamed by Pearl Harbor and racism, played a somewhat larger role in the Pacific theater, reinforcing pressure for a hard-line policy toward Japan. Once again, however, a crucial yet often neglected factor driving American decisions—underwriting policymakers' uncompromising course and ambitious postwar vision—was the strongest relative power position the world has ever seen. In the end, a long war's worth of devastation, decisionmaking, and drama was packed into one final tumultuous week, with the clear cessation of hostilities that resulted being a much chancier thing than many realize even today.

THE COURSE OF THE PACIFIC WAR

In December 1941, Japanese forces launched surprise attacks on Western possessions and strongholds throughout Southeast Asia and the Pacific, including the U.S. Navy's main fleet docked at Pearl Harbor, in Hawaii.[6] These thrusts gained the Japanese control of a vast area in a short time, but were eventually halted short of Japan's overall military objectives. During the first half of 1942, the Allied forces remaining in the Pacific tried to block Japanese progress toward India and Australia while their countries mobilized new legions at home. In June, the U.S. Navy inflicted a major defeat on its Japanese counterpart at Midway, and during the second half of the year the Allies—for all practical purposes, now only the United States—began to push the Japanese back.

Washington decided to press for total victory even as Tokyo remained defiant, so the challenge for American officials became how to bring U.S. material advantages to bear and methodically destroy Japan's capacity to make war. The basic plan was set early on: two major thrusts would converge on the Japanese home islands, one by the army in the South Pacific under General Douglas MacArthur and the other by the navy in the Central Pacific under Admiral Chester W. Nimitz.

At the same time, U.S.-aided Chinese forces would fight on the Asian mainland while strategic bombers operating from China and Pacific island airstrips would destroy Japanese industry and morale.

Japan's wartime political system was a hybrid of monarchy, militarism, and cabinet government. The Meiji Constitution of 1889 enshrined a semi-divine emperor at the apex of the national polity but made the position largely symbolic, with the monarch floating above most actual decisionmaking.[7] The Diet, Japan's bicameral legislature, was largely impotent. Important political choices were made by unanimous vote of senior members of the cabinet, including the war and navy ministers and the army and navy chiefs of staff (all four of whom were appointed by the services themselves). If the cabinet could not reach a consensus, it would disband and a new one would be formed, with the premier selected by a council of political elders and ratified by the emperor. By the 1930s, civilian cabinet members were cowed into submission by freelance political violence from right-wing nationalists and policy was dominated by leaders of the armed forces—who were themselves wary of crossing increasingly radical junior officers under the spell of a quasi-fascist imperial ideology.[8]

General Hideki Tojo had become premier in the fall of 1941 and led the nation during the first years of the war. His government collapsed after the United States conquered the crucial island stronghold of Saipan in July 1944. Tojo was succeeded by General Kuniaki Koiso, but during the latter's nine-month tenure the war continued as before, with U.S. forces slowly pushing the Japanese back on all fronts. By the fall of 1944, U.S. bombers could reach the Japanese home islands and began subjecting the country's military installations, industrial infrastructure, and central cities to increasingly withering attacks. In early 1945, Koiso and the Foreign Ministry tentatively and secretly explored some avenues of negotiation with the Allies through China and Sweden, but these were neither pressed nor reciprocated. That March, the United States inaugurated a new phase of the air campaign with an incendiary raid on Tokyo that killed more than eighty thousand people and destroyed a quarter of the capital. When U.S. troops successfully landed on the island of Okinawa in April, Koiso's cabinet collapsed. He was succeeded by retired admiral Kantaro Suzuki and the war continued.

Seeing no evidence of changes in Japanese attitudes, U.S. leaders pressed all their various operations forward simultaneously. The logic of the island-hopping campaigns implied an eventual final hop to invade the Japanese home islands if necessary, but some thought the naval blockade and air campaign, separately or together, might force a Japanese capitulation short of an invasion. Each branch of the American military tended to value its own efforts most highly and believe that they held the key to concluding the war successfully. The few senior leaders who knew about the secret Manhattan Project, meanwhile, hoped that atomic weapons—expected to be ready by the summer of 1945—might also play a role. Nevertheless, the stiffness of Japanese resistance made everybody uncomfortable and led them to search for additional help wherever they could find it, such as the possible entry of Soviet forces into the fight.

In January 1945, the Joint Chiefs of Staff outlined Washington's official plans for the war's final stages, a logroll that combined elements of each service's approach:

> [F]orce the unconditional surrender of Japan by:
>
> 1. Lowering Japanese ability and will to resist by establishing sea and air blockades, conducting intensive air bombardment, and destroying Japanese air and naval strength.
> 2. Invading and seizing objectives in the industrial heart of Japan.[9]

The invasion of Kyushu, the southernmost home island, was scheduled for November. Planners expected resistance to be furious, comparable to that on islands such as Iwo Jima or Okinawa, where Japanese troops fought practically to the last man (and woman and child, since most of the islands' civilian populations perished as well). American casualties during an invasion were expected to number from tens to hundreds of thousands, depending on how long the campaign lasted.[10]

At the Yalta Conference in February 1945, the Allies decided that the Soviet Union would enter the Pacific war within months of the defeat of Germany, and in April, the Soviets notified the Japanese of their intention not to renew the Neutrality Pact between the two countries the following year. Responding to this and the worsening war situation, in May the Japanese cabinet's "Big Six"—the premier, foreign minister, war and navy ministers, and army and navy chiefs of staff, now formalized as the Supreme Council for the Direction of the War—decided to open talks with Moscow, pursuing three graduated objectives: "first, to keep the U.S.S.R. out of the war, a necessity which was felt strongly by all; second, to induce her to adopt a friendly policy toward Japan; and third, to seek her mediation in the war."[11]

On June 8, the Japanese government officially adopted a document titled "The Fundamental Policy to Be Followed Henceforth in the Conduct of the War," which envisioned a furious total defense of Japan. Less than two weeks later, however, it decided to step up appeals for Soviet help in negotiating a settlement. U.S. cryptanalysts had broken Japanese diplomatic codes years earlier and so were able to read the increasingly urgent messages about these negotiations that passed during the summer between Tokyo and Moscow. In mid-July, for example, the Americans read the following instructions from the foreign minister to the Japanese ambassador:

> . . . if only the United States and Great Britain would recognize Japan's honor and existence we would terminate the war and would like to save mankind from the ravages of war, but if the enemy insists on unconditional surrender to the very end, then our country and His Majesty would unanimously resolve to fight a war of resistance to the bitter end. . . . [Invite the Soviet Union to mediate an end to the fighting, but this] does not include unconditional surrender; please understand this point in particular.[12]

A few days later U.S. officials could read the foreign minister's further orders: "We cannot accept unconditional surrender . . . in any situation. Although it is apparent there will be more casualties on both sides in case the war is prolonged, we will stand united as one nation against the enemy if the enemy forcibly demands our unconditional surrender. It is, however, our intention to achieve, with Soviet assistance, a peace which is not of unconditional nature. . . ."[13]

And a few days later still:

> . . . it is impossible to accept unconditional surrender under any circumstances, but we should like to communicate to the other party through appropriate channels that we have no objection to a peace based on the Atlantic Charter. The difficult point is the attitude of the enemy, who continues to insist on the formality of unconditional surrender. Should the United States and Great Britain remain insistent on formality, there is no solution to this situation other than for us to hold out until com-

> plete collapse because of this point alone. . . . [I]t is necessary to have them understand that we are trying to end hostilities by asking for very reasonable terms in order to secure and maintain our nation's existence and honor.[14]

THE PACIFIC ENDGAME

By the summer of 1945, all belligerents in the Pacific understood that the tide had turned irreversibly against Japan. The question was no longer who would win, but how the war would end, when, and on what terms. The Japanese cable traffic indicated that something was going on behind the scenes in Tokyo, but it was not clear exactly what. Brigadier General John Weckerling, the deputy assistant chief of staff of G-2, army intelligence, summarized for Army Chief of Staff George Marshall the situation as of July 13:

> [T]here are a number of interesting deductions suggested by [the cable traffic up to that point]:
>
> 1. That the Emperor has personally intervened and brought his will to bear in favor of peace in spite of military opposition;
> 2. That conservative groups close to the Throne, including some high ranking Army and Navy men, have triumphed over militaristic elements who favor prolonged desperate resistance;
> 3. That the Japanese government clique is making a well coordinated, united effort to stave off defeat believing (a) that Russian intervention can be bought by the proper price, and (b) that an attractive Japanese peace offer will appeal to war weariness in the United States.
>
> Of these, (1) is remote, (2) a possibility, and (3) quite probably the motivating force behind the Japanese moves. Mr. Grew agrees with these conclusions.[15]

The intercepts confirmed the feelings of some American officials that the war could be ended quickly by letting the Japanese know that "unconditional surrender" would not necessarily mean the destruction of the imperial institution. The most vocal advocate of this view was the prewar ambassador to Japan, Joseph Grew, who badgered Truman about it while serving as acting secretary of state in the spring of 1945. "The greatest obstacle to unconditional surrender by the Japanese," he told the president in May, "is their belief that this would entail the destruction or permanent removal of the Emperor and the institution of the Throne. If some indication can now be given the Japanese that they themselves, when once thoroughly defeated and rendered impotent to wage war in the future, will be permitted to determine their own future political structure, they will be afforded a method of saving face without which surrender will be highly unlikely."[16]

What was at issue was essentially the conditions surrounding "unconditional" surrender. The Allies—at least the Americans and British—did not intend to annex the Axis powers or destroy their peoples, and had said so in various proclamations. Grew and others favored a statement that Japan might retain its distinctive *kokutai* ("national polity"), symbolized by the emperor, as one more unilateral statement of generous treatment of the defeated enemy.

On July 27, Allied leaders publicly issued the Potsdam Declaration, calling once again for Japan's unconditional surrender but specifying several examples of the moderate treatment Japan could expect afterward. The document did not include an explicit comment on the emperor, but noted that eventually the Allies would permit a government "established in accordance with the freely expressed will of the Japanese people." The declaration closed with a threat of "prompt and utter destruction," but did not mention two new factors: impending Soviet entry into the war and already-scheduled atomic strikes.[17] With the cabinet divided over how to respond, Premier Suzuki used the phrase *mokusatsu*—he would ignore the declaration, "treat it with silent contempt." This infelicitous refusal to engage the Allied statement, picked up and amplified by newspapers on both sides, was taken as a rejection by the Americans, and at this point Truman gave the final go-ahead for dropping the bomb.[18]

On August 6, the city of Hiroshima was destroyed. On August 8, the Soviets announced they were entering the war against Japan, slicing through weakened positions in Manchuria and removing any last hopes of mediation. And on August 9, a second atomic bomb was dropped, on Nagasaki, casting a further pall over the deadlocked meetings of the Japanese leadership. Premier Suzuki, Foreign Minister Shigenori Togo, and Navy Minister Mitsumasa Yonai favored accepting the declaration so long as they could receive assurances that the emperor would be protected, while Anami and the two service chiefs of staff wanted to continue fighting unless three additional conditions were accepted (self-disarmament of the Japanese armed forces, no Allied occupation of Japan, and no war crimes trials). On the night of August 9, in a move orchestrated by court officials and moderates in the cabinet, the question was presented to the emperor, and for practically the first time in modern Japanese history he strongly advocated a particular course of action, personally asking the cabinet to stop the war. Shocked but reverent, the hard-liners bowed to the imperial will, and the Japanese government sent a note to the Americans (through the Swiss government) accepting the Potsdam Declaration "with the understanding that the said declaration does not comprise any demand which prejudices the prerogatives of His Majesty as a Sovereign Ruler."

This created a quandary for the Americans because it challenged the notion of unconditional surrender and reopened the internal debate they had been having over whether to preserve the emperor's status. Truman instructed Secretary of State James F. Byrnes to come up with a reply; others, including Grew, gave their unsolicited advice. In the end, the U.S. response, transmitted back through the Swiss on August 11, fudged the issue, saying, "From the moment of surrender the authority of the Emperor and the Japanese Government to rule the state shall be subject to the Supreme Commander of the Allied Powers who will take such steps as he deems proper to effectuate the surrender terms."

This, in turn, created a quandary for the Japanese, producing the same three-three split among the Big Six as before—with the moderates arguing that preservation of the imperial institution could be read into the American note while the hard-liners demanded an explicit guarantee. Ultimately the dispute was resolved the same way as before, with a direct intervention by the emperor on August 14 imploring the hard-liners to submit, leading to the frantic final hours before surrender recounted above.

REALISM AND THE EMPEROR DEBATE

Realists think states will approach war termination, like other national security issues, with a goal of maximizing their material power. According to such a logic, as a nation nears victory it should weigh the material gains and costs of continuing to fight against those of settling. A prominent early student of the Pacific endgame, in fact, interpreted it just this way. Thus, according to Paul Kecskemeti, while by late 1944 the trend of the Pacific war was indeed clear to both sides, the Japanese believed their power to inflict casualties during an American invasion of the home islands gave them a bargaining tool. The Americans were loath to admit this, but implicitly recognized it by adding to their continued attacks an eventual compromise on the emperor: "The Japanese surrender illustrates the use of a defeated power's residual strength, combined with an insular position and an extreme will to resist, for the purpose of obtaining political concessions in return for surrender."[19] Such an interpretation is problematic, however, because in the end there was no such compromise.

At the war's start, Japanese leaders did indeed expect it to end with a negotiated peace. But they thought the impetus for such a settlement would come from the demoralized Allies and were taken aback by their opponent's determined response.[20] During the conflict's middle years, they resisted acknowledging the political implications of military setbacks and did not seriously explore possibilities other than increasing their military efforts. Postwar interrogations revealed that key navy personnel "consider[ed] either Midway or Guadalcanal as *the* turning point. . . . The loss of Saipan, which is also mentioned from time to time, is generally considered to be several steps beyond the turning-point stage. Those who continued to hope, after Midway, for a favorable change in fortune knew, after Saipan, that their hopes had lost all meaning." Army men were more optimistic, but even the pessimists did not press for negotiations: "As the physical bases for predicting victory gradually disappeared, many of Japan's leaders . . . began re-emphasizing the importance of *Nippon seishin:* the mind, the soul, the spirit of Japan. Their plea was simply this: 'Japan may be weak in resources, but she is strong in *spirit*. This will lead the nation to victory!' "[21]

Japanese military leaders felt that they could inflict substantial damage on U.S. forces, and they were correct. The United States Strategic Bombing Survey, commenting on the enemy's resort to kamikaze tactics during the war's final years, notes: "This was a measure of desperation, but the results obtained were considerable and, had they been much greater, might have caused us to withdraw or modify our strategic plans."[22] But whatever power resources Japan possessed, it never tried to translate them into a political settlement. Hard-liners were able to force a prosecution of the war without negotiations while simply waiting for some kind of military success—in the early years, a "decisive" one; in the later years, a tactical one. As Lieutenant General Seizo Arisue, the head of the Japanese army's intelligence operations, put it,

> We thought that although it was extremely difficult we had at least enough strength to continue fighting. At the time the Army was not damaged at all. At least *it could fight in Japan proper*. We thought that way. We did not think we could drive out the Americans and recover Maruta or Okinawa. *In one way Japan had the power to continue and in another way Japan had not.* Generally speaking, we who were engaged in the war had the feeling that provided we had any strength left we wanted to do something.[23]

Those few in the Japanese military who did advocate compromise were helpless. In the summer of 1943, for example, Rear Admiral Sokichi Takagi, ordered by navy leaders to study the "lessons of the war," took the liberty of assessing the overall situation. The devastating report he finished in February 1944 argued that Japan could not win and had to seek a compromise peace, which would have to include at a minimum withdrawal from China, Manchuria, and Sakhalin. Deciding his superiors would not accept these conclusions, Takagi kept his report closely guarded. Soon afterward, a farsighted colonel on the army general staff put together a report on "Measures for the Termination of the Greater East Asia War," recommending that Japan should try to end the war when Germany surrendered and suggesting specific compromises; for his troubles, he was reassigned to the expeditionary forces in China.

Some Japanese political elders and court officials eventually came to favor exploring the possibility of a negotiated settlement. In February 1945, for example, the former premier Prince Fumimaro Konoye presented a memorial to the throne (an official message to the emperor) that reviewed the status of the war and concluded that Japan had to end it or face an internal Communist revolution afterward.[24] The government as a whole, however, did not systematically attempt to exit the conflict or probe the possibilities of a negotiated settlement until the late spring of 1945, well after the war had become unwinnable and the home islands were being devastated through incendiary attacks. Even then it clung to the hope that the Soviet Union might help—rejecting the reports of Japanese diplomats there who scorned the idea—and did not deal with the Americans directly until after the atomic bombs had been dropped.[25]

If Japanese leaders did not act like realists, what about their American counterparts? Did they focus primarily on questions of relative material power during the war's endgame? By the summer of 1945, Japan posed little immediate threat to the United States; the question for U.S. policymakers was how to terminate a war that had already been won. Senior national leaders discussed five policy alternatives: an invasion of the home islands (favored by the army); a blockade of the home islands with continued air bombardments (favored by the navy and airpower advocates); the use of atomic bombs; Soviet entry into the war; and a statement clarifying Japan's future status that might lead to an early surrender. The first two were combined in official military plans, into which the third fit easily when nuclear weapons became available. Military leaders agitated for the fourth alternative, Soviet entry, until practically the end of the war, when they decided that their own operations had sufficiently reduced the threat Japanese forces in Manchuria posed. Grew favored the fifth option and thought that including a promise about the emperor might induce a capitulation. Secretary of War Henry L. Stimson agreed, but thought more along the lines of an ultimatum whose threats might compel a surrender.

The original impetus for such a statement had come from Winston Churchill. At a meeting of the Combined Chiefs of Staff during the Yalta Conference, the British leader

> expressed the opinion that it would be of great value . . . [to issue] a four-power ultimatum calling upon Japan to surrender unconditionally, or else be subjected to the overwhelming weight of all the forces of the four powers. Japan might ask in these circumstances what mitigation of the full rigour of unconditional surrender would be extended to her if she accepted the ultimatum. . . . [He felt] there was no doubt that some mitigation would be worth while if it led to the saving of a year or a year and a half of a war in which so much blood and treasure would be poured out.[26]

This approach appealed to those in the U.S. military who had always found a strict adherence to unconditional surrender impractical. During the spring and summer of 1945, therefore, army planners called gently but persistently for a public clarification of what American demands actually were. As a report from senior military planners noted in April, it was not clear whether a truly unconditional surrender could "be brought about by any means." But

> [w]hat can be accomplished is decisive military defeat and the results equivalent to unconditional surrender, similar to the present situation in Germany. In no case to date in this war have organized Japanese units surrendered. The concept of "unconditional surrender" is foreign to the Japanese nature. Therefore, "unconditional surrender" should be defined in terms understandable to the Japanese, who must be convinced that destruction or national suicide is not implied. This could be done by an announcement on a governmental level of a "declaration of intentions" which would tell the Japanese what their future holds. Once convinced of the inevitability of defeat, it is possible that a government could be formed in Japan that would sign and could enforce a surrender instrument. Unless a definition of unconditional surrender can be given which is acceptable to the Japanese, there is no alternative to annihilation and no prospect that the threat of absolute defeat will bring about capitulation.[27]

The army also came to believe that the emperor might be useful in implementing the terms of a Japanese surrender and easing the costs of a postwar occupation, which led it to question the idea of committing the United States to abolishing the imperial institution. Thus at the end of June a report could note: "The present stand of the War Department is that Japanese surrender is just possible and attractive enough to the U.S. to justify us in making any concession which might be attractive to the Japanese, so long as our realistic aims for peace in the Pacific are not adversely affected."[28] At one crucial meeting, Admiral William D. Leahy, the president's senior military adviser, "said that he could not agree with those who said to him that unless we obtain the unconditional surrender of the Japanese that we will have lost the war. He feared no menace from Japan in the foreseeable future, even if we were unsuccessful in forcing unconditional surrender. What he did fear was that our insistence on unconditional surrender would result only in making the Japanese desperate and thereby increase our casualty lists. He did not think that was necessary."[29] This is exactly the sort of calculated bargaining that realist theory predicts for war termination. The only problem is that the chief concession under discussion—a guarantee of the emperor's postwar status—was not made. When the Allies released the Potsdam Declaration in late July, no statement regarding the imperial institution was included.

This silence is all the more striking because both the British and the Soviets favored conceding the point. Never enthralled with repeated public statements of the unconditional surrender policy because they might increase the resistance of defeated enemies, neither Stalin nor Churchill could understand the American position. From Moscow in May, Harry Hopkins cabled Truman that Stalin

> made it quite clear that the Soviet Union wants to go through with unconditional surrender and all that is implied with it. . . . However, he feels that if we stick to unconditional surrender the Japs will not give up and we will have to destroy them as we did in Germany. . . . Should the Allies depart from the announced policy of unconditional surrender and be prepared to accept a modified surrender, Stalin visualizes imposing our will through our occupying forces and thereby gaining the same results. . . . In other words, it seemed to us that he proposes under this heading to agree to milder peace terms but once we get into Japan to give them the works.[30]

(This seems to have been Stalin's standard operating procedure. Yugoslavia's Tito told the following story about a June 1944 conversation with the Soviet leader: "Stalin began to assure me of the need to reinstate King Peter [of Yugoslavia after the war]. The blood rushed to my head that he could advise us to do such a thing. I composed myself and told him it was impossible. . . . Stalin was silent, and then said briefly: 'You need not restore him forever. Take him back temporarily, and then you can slip a knife into his back at a suitable moment.' ")[31]

Churchill was less cynical, and describes his July conversations with Truman in his memoirs:

> I dwelt upon the tremendous cost in American and to a smaller extent in British life if we enforced "unconditional surrender" upon the Japanese. It was for him to consider whether this might not be expressed in some other way, so that we got all the essentials for future peace and security and yet left them some show of saving their military honour and some assurance of their national existence, after they had complied with all safeguards necessary for the conqueror. The President replied

> bluntly that he did not think the Japanese had any military honour after Pearl Harbor. I contented myself with saying that at any rate they had something for which they were ready to face certain death in very large numbers, and this might not be so important to us as it was to them.[32]

We now know that, given the depth of the division within the Japanese cabinet, explicitly guaranteeing the emperor's future status would not by itself have ended the war sooner. Prime Minister Suzuki's comment to an aide about the Potsdam Declaration shows just how far even the moderates were from hopelessness and total capitulation: "For the enemy to say something like that means circumstances have arisen that force them also to end the war. That is why they are talking about unconditional surrender. Precisely at a time like this, if we hold firm, then they will yield before we do. Just because they broadcast their declaration, it is not necessary to stop fighting. You advisers may ask me to reconsider, but I don't think there is any need to stop [the war.]"[33] And even after two atomic bombs and the Soviet invasion of Manchuria, several key decisionmakers were holding out for additional surrender terms so generous they resembled more an armistice than a capitulation. But separate from the question of whether such a guarantee would have achieved its goal is the question of why it was never really offered—something standard realism has a very hard time explaining.

EXPLAINING THE EMPEROR DECISION

Why did American decisionmakers not try to induce a Japanese surrender by offering a guarantee of the emperor's future status? Because they didn't want to—and felt strong enough to get away with not doing it.

The immediate causes of the emperor decision lay in ideology, perceived lessons of history, and domestic politics. Truman and his advisers felt that the imperial institution was a major cause of Japanese aggression. They were eager to curb its powers if not eliminate it entirely, and were reluctant to tie their hands in advance regarding possible postwar reforms. These inclinations were shored up by the strong anti-Japanese feelings of the American people, many of whom would have criticized compromises with the villains of Pearl Harbor.

Just as crucial to the story, however, was American leaders' ability to give these attitudes free rein. In contrast to both Britain and the Soviet

Union, by the summer of 1945 the United States was flush with victory, aware of its extraordinary relative power, and the proud possessor of the most devastating weapons in world history. Whatever strict Realpolitik might dictate, American leaders could afford not to dicker with an enemy they hated and felt needed transformation—and they did not.

The ultimate decision about whether to include a guarantee about the emperor in the Potsdam Declaration lay, of course, with President Truman. But he delegated it to his secretary of state, Byrnes. Also new to his position and unsure what to do, Byrnes called his predecessor Cordell Hull for *his* opinion. Hull advised Byrnes against a guarantee because "the statement seemed too much like appeasement of Japan. . . . I said that the Emperor and the ruling class must be stripped of all extraordinary privileges and placed on a level before the law with everybody else."[34] Byrnes took this advice and opposed a guarantee; Truman followed Byrnes.

Domestic political concerns facilitated the decision. The emperor was extraordinarily unpopular in the United States, and the Pacific war in general was marked by a higher level of public passion than its European counterpart. As the historian John Dower has noted,

> In the United States and Great Britain, the Japanese were more hated than the Germans before as well as after Pearl Harbor. On this, there was no dispute among contemporary observers. They were perceived as a race apart, even a species apart—and an overpoweringly monolithic one at that. There was no Japanese counterpart to the "good German" in the popular consciousness of the Western Allies. . . . Not until May 1945, when the Nazi death camps were exposed, did public horror and indignation against the Germans reach, at least in the United States, a pitch comparable to the feelings directed against the Japanese. And by that time, the Germans had already surrendered.[35]

In response to a December 1944 poll asking "what do you think we should do with Japan as a country after the war?" 13 percent of Americans wanted to "kill all Japanese" and 33 percent wanted to destroy Japan as a political entity. The poll's comparable question on Germany did not even include the first option.[36]

A June 1945 Gallup poll on postwar treatment of the emperor, meanwhile, showed that 33 percent favored execution, 17 percent favored a war crimes trial, 11 percent favored imprisonment, and 9 percent favored exile. Only 4 percent wanted to spare him on grounds that he was merely a figurehead and only 3 percent wanted to use him to run Japan after the war.[37] The public also seemed ready to bear the burdens of a no-concession policy. Another June 1945 poll asked: "Japan may offer to surrender and call her soldiers home provided we agree not to send an army of occupation to her home islands. Do you think we should accept such a peace offer if we get the chance, or fight on until we have completely beaten her on the Japanese homeland?" Eighty-four percent favored fighting on; only 9 percent said they would accept.[38] When the Japanese made their initial offer on August 10 to accept the Potsdam Declaration on condition that the emperor's status be guaranteed, public opinion in the United States strongly opposed any such deal. A Gallup poll found an almost two-to-one margin against the concept; the *Washington Post* judged sentiment in Congress closer to three-to-one against.[39]

At the same time, however, the American public was growing tired of the war. In fact, one of the central reasons army strategists disliked navy plans for a peripheral strategy in the Pacific was that it would not deliver immediate results: "the prospect of a prolonged siege would only aggravate the skittishness of the American people."[40] With this in mind Marshall and his planners supported, despite the apparent contradiction, both a relaxation of the unconditional surrender policy *and* a direct invasion of the Japanese home islands. The nature of the domestic political constraints on officials has been well summed up by Leon Sigal: "In this political climate, anyone who tried to change America's war aims unilaterally had to undo an oft-stated policy that had overwhelming domestic political support, leaving himself open to attack from right and left. . . . But a slogan was not much of a policy. The closer the United States drew to victory, the less guidance unconditional surrender gave to officials who were planning for war's end."[41]

Those policymakers most sensitive to public opinion—either for bureaucratic reasons (such as Archibald MacLeish, as assistant secretary of state for public and cultural affairs, and Dean Acheson, as assistant secretary for congressional affairs) or political ambition (such as Secretary of State Byrnes)—were indeed the strongest opponents of any compromise, but it is not clear that domestic politics was the sole factor driving their positions. Acheson "argued that [the emperor] should be removed because he was a weak leader who had yielded to the military demand for war and who could not be relied upon."[42] The liberal

MacLeish actually wanted to do away with the emperor primarily for ideological reasons, but raised the specter of a domestic political backlash instrumentally to support his case—understanding that the way any concessions were portrayed would affect how the public would react.[43]

Still, it is clear that domestic opposition to such a compromise was indeed on many minds. A State Department briefing paper for the Potsdam Conference concluded: "There are indications that the Chinese may favor the abolition of the institution of the Emperor and public opinion in the United States increasingly seems to prefer this solution."[44] Hull had Grew pass along to Byrnes at Potsdam a letter cautioning him against "a proposed declaration by the Allies now that the Emperor and his monarchy will be preserved in event of allied victory. . . . I am stating this rather broadly but as the general public will doubtless construe it. The proponents believe that this step might shorten the war and save allied lives. . . . The other side is that no person knows how the proposal would work out. The militarists would try hard to interfere. Also should it fail the Japs would be encouraged while terrible political repercussions would follow in the U.S."[45] Truman himself responded to Leahy's explication of the logic of concessions with the comment "that it was with that thought in mind that he had left the door open for Congress to take appropriate action with reference to unconditional surrender. However, he did not feel that he could take any action at this time to change public opinion on the matter."[46]

If domestic politics pushed American leaders, however, it pushed them in a direction they already wanted to go. As discussed in the last chapter, Americans saw World War II as a clash between good and evil and viewed their task as the punishment of aggressors. In the previous war, the Allies had preceded the harsh terms of Versailles by a mere armistice, a seeming duplicity that gave credence to the "stab-in-the-back" theory and hence Nazi revanchism. As the former German ambassador to the United States put it, because of Woodrow Wilson's promises, "The Peace of Versailles . . . became the breach of an undertaking, when it would otherwise have merely been the consequence of our military defeat."[47] American leaders drew from this experience the twin lessons that drastic internal reform of Germany would be necessary in order to curb its aggressive tendencies and that the full measure of this bitter medicine should be publicly accepted beforehand by the vanquished.

"With regard to Japan," as Ernest May wrote, "the previous war provided no comparable guideline, for Japan had then been an ally. Planning for the defeat of Japan therefore borrowed from planning for Germany."[48] The lessons were simply transferred from one theater to another. Roosevelt captured this logic succinctly in 1944: "Practically all Germans deny the fact they surrendered in the last war, but this time they are going to know it. And so are the Japs."[49] The interwar Germany analogy was an integral part of the backdrop of debate over postwar Japanese reform. As one Asian expert stressed in January 1945, "Japan must not be permitted to follow the same course as Germany did after World War I, and the continuance in power of groups among Japan's civilian bosses—big business monopolists, bureaucrats, politicians or nobility—could fatally compromise the nation's transformation into a law-abiding state and risk a renewal of Japanese aggression at their first opportunity."[50]

Roosevelt told Congress in the fall of 1943, "there is one thing I want to make perfectly clear: When Hitler and the Nazis go out, the Prussian military clique must go with them. The war-breeding gangs of militarists must be rooted out of Germany—and out of Japan—if we are to have any real assurance of future peace."[51] He drilled the point home again after Yalta: "the unconditional surrender of Japan is as essential as the defeat of Germany. I say that advisedly, with the thought in mind that that is especially true if our plans for world peace are to succeed. For Japanese militarism must be wiped out as thoroughly as German militarism."[52]

In the summer of 1945, many still agreed with MacLeish, Acheson, and Hull that, in the words of a MacLeish memo:

> What has made Japan dangerous in the past and will make her dangerous in the future if we permit it, is, in large part, the Japanese cult of emperor worship which gives the ruling groups in Japan—the *Gambatsu*—the current coalition of militarists, industrialists, large land owners and office holders—their control over the Japanese people. . . . [T]he institution of the throne is an anachronistic feudal institution, perfectly adapted to the manipulation and use of anachronistic, feudal-minded groups within the country. To leave that institution intact is to run the grave risk that it will be used in the future as it has been used in the past.[53]

If there was even a chance that abolishing the throne would be the course ultimately decided upon, American leaders were not going to foreclose their options. The Potsdam Declaration, they decided, would not become another Fourteen Points. And the conclusion of the leading American student of the occupation would seem to vindicate their judgment:

> Shortly after the occupation began, Assistant Secretary of State Dean Acheson formulated [the American] vision in blunt terms. The goal of the occupation, he stated, was to ensure that "the present economic and social system in Japan which makes for a will to war will be changed so that the will to war will not continue." . . . Such an audacious undertaking by victors in war had no legal or historical precedent. With a minimum of rumination about the legality or propriety of such an undertaking, the Americans set about doing what no other occupation force had done before: remaking the political, social, cultural, and economic fabric of a defeated nation, and in the process changing the very way of thinking of its populace. . . . The radicalism of these policies shocked the elites who held power when the war ended. Had men of influence from the emperor on down been left to their own devices, they would never have dreamed of initiating anything remotely approximating such drastic reforms; and had the government actually been conceded a "conditional" surrender in the closing stages of the war, it might have been in a position to cut American reformers off at the knees.[54]

REALISM, THE RUSSIANS, AND THE BOMB

Some have argued that realist considerations lay behind another feature of the Pacific endgame, the decision to drop the bomb. The revisionist historian Gar Alperovitz, for example, has suggested that "Hiroshima and Nagasaki [were] bombed primarily to impress the world with the need to accept America's plan for a stable and lasting peace—that is, primarily, America's plan for Europe."[55] The Truman administration, in this view, made a conscious decision in the late spring and summer of 1945 to check Soviet power. Knowing that the war with Japan was practically over, and therefore that dropping the bomb was not necessary to win, American leaders dropped it anyway to cow the Soviets and end the fighting before they could reap any gains.

By the summer of 1945, many U.S. officials had indeed begun to question the Roosevelt administration's policy of cooperating with the Soviet Union, so there is some evidence for this interpretation. And the news of the successful Alamogordo nuclear test, received during the Potsdam Conference, was certainly bracing. Stimson recorded in his diary a conversation he had with Churchill soon afterward:

> He told me that he had noticed at the meeting of the Three yesterday that Truman was evidently much fortified by something that had happened and that he stood up to the Russians in a most emphatic and decisive manner, telling them as to certain demands that they absolutely could not have and that the United States was entirely against them. He said "Now I know what happened to Truman yesterday. I couldn't understand it. When he got to the meeting after having read this report [about the test] he was a changed man. He told the Russians just where they got on and off and generally bossed the whole meeting."[56]

After hearing about Alamogordo and discussing Japanese peace feelers with Stalin, Truman noted in *his* diary: "Believe Japs will fold up before Russia comes in. I am sure they will when Manhattan appears over their homeland."[57] Churchill wrote to Eden a few days later, "It is quite clear that the United States do not at the present time desire Russian participation in the war against Japan."[58] And Secretary of the Navy James Forrestal noted in *his* diary on July 28 that "Byrnes said he was most anxious to get the Japanese affair over with before the Russians got in, with particular reference to Dairen and Port Arthur. Once in there, he felt, it would not be easy to get them out."[59]

Nevertheless, few experts now subscribe to the revisionist interpretation, since the weight of contemporaneous evidence shows that despite their increasing misgivings, U.S. officials remained committed to a policy of cooperation with the Soviets until after the war was over, considered beating Japan the main task at hand, and approached the bomb in that context.

Senior military leaders had long been among the most vociferous advocates of U.S.-Soviet cooperation. At a crucial meeting in April 1945, for example—sometimes seen as the beginning of the Cold War because of Truman's sharp words to Soviet foreign minister Molotov directly afterward—Marshall opposed any change in Roosevelt's policy. He said that he "hoped for Soviet participation in the war against Japan at a time when it would be useful to us. The Russians had it within their power to delay their entry into the Far Eastern war until we had done all the dirty work. . . . He was inclined to agree with Mr. Stimson that possibility of a break with Russia was very serious."[60] Although held with increasingly less passion, this basic attitude persisted as the summer wore on. As the historian Michael Sherry has written,

> To the last moment [the U.S. high command] still considered invasion a possibility, did not foresee fully the impact of the atomic weapon, and did not appreciate the significance the Japanese had attached to the now-severed negotiations with the Soviet Union. . . . Service leaders undoubtedly surmised that their use of the atomic bomb would alarm Soviet leaders and might carry at least the collateral benefit of stiffening American policy toward the U.S.S.R. Yet . . . they had not yet decided how threatening [Soviet] ambitions were, or whether Japan or Germany might not still pose the greater danger.[61]

Since Japan was still the enemy throughout that summer, "Far from regarding Russian entry into the war as an alternative to other methods of forcing surrender, the military hoped to assemble all possible means to convince Japanese leaders to submit."[62] As late as July 24, the U.S. and British chiefs of staff ratified in writing their desire to "Encourage Russian entry into the war against Japan. Provide such aid to her war-making capacity as may be necessary and practicable in connection therewith."[63]

So if the bomb was not dropped to intimidate Russia, then why was it used? Because a total war was on and bureaucratic and cognitive inertia made any other course almost unthinkable. Its use was simply a continuation of existing policy, which was to deploy all force available. "At no time, from 1941 to 1945," Stimson would write later, "did I ever hear it suggested by the President, or by any other responsible member of the government, that atomic energy should not be used in the war."[64] When the new weapons became available, "There were no moral, military, diplomatic, or bureaucratic considerations that carried enough weight to deter dropping the bomb and gaining its projected military and diplomatic benefits."[65] The fact that it came on line just when Japan was trying to surrender and inter-Allied relations were fraying was a historical accident; it would have been used directly no matter when it had arrived.

Unsurprisingly, the strongest advocates of the bomb's use were the leaders of the Manhattan Project and the politicians who had devoted $2 billion to it. As the project's director, General Leslie Groves, said, "From the day that I was assigned to the Project there was never any doubt in my mind [that] my mission . . . was to get this thing done and used as fast as possible, and every effort was bent toward that assignment, you might say." Groves used strong bureaucratic and political arguments in internal debates:

> I said they could not fail to use this bomb because if they didn't use it they would immediately cast a lot of reflection on Mr. Roosevelt and on the basis of that why did you spend all that money and all this effort and then when you got it, why didn't you use it? Also it would have come out sooner or later in a Congressional hearing if nowhere else just when we could have dropped the bomb if we didn't use it. And then knowing American politics, you know as well as I do that there would have been elections fought on the basis that every mother whose son was killed after such and such a date—the blood was on the head of the President.[66]

The other military services were indifferent, largely because they did not think the bomb's use would be necessary or decisive to ending the war and because a revolutionary change in weaponry would render their own contributions less important in the future. (Chief of Naval Operations Ernest King, for example, noted almost ruefully in his memoirs that "had we been willing to wait, the effective naval blockade would have starved the Japanese into submission.")[67]

Two bombs were dropped without a real pause not because there was a conscious, separate decision to hit Japan twice, but because two were available and the operation was "planned initially to deliver them as soon as they were available, one after another, until the order was given to stop. Thus an order was not needed to drop a second bomb, only an order if a second bomb was *not* to be dropped."[68] This fit in nicely with the wishes and interests of the Manhattan Project's leaders. They had developed two separate kinds of nuclear weapon, a gun type ("Little Boy") and an implosion type ("Fat Man"). "Nothing short of dropping two bombs on Japanese cities would silence doubts at home about the necessity of building both types."[69]

The targeting decisions were driven in part by strategic considerations and in part by parochial concerns of the project's leaders, both of which argued in favor of a dramatic bolt from the blue that would show off just how devastating the new weapons really were. This meant picking cities relatively undamaged by previous conventional bombing and with the proper size and topography to determine the bombs' uncertain blast effects. Stimson's sentimental decision to spare Kyoto because of its cultural and imperial heritage had to be forced through the bureaucracy several times, because those in charge of the bomb considered it the perfect target: "[Kyoto] was large enough in area," Groves argued, "for us to gain complete knowledge of the effects of the atomic bomb. Hiroshima was not nearly so satisfactory in this respect."[70]

In fact, in this case, bureaucratic politics explains not only many of the details of the bombing decision, but also much of the war's course in general. The two-pronged American strategy in the Pacific—the central strategic decision in the theater for most of the war—was devised not because a unified "America" thought this was the best way to achieve its political or military goals, but as a compromise to mollify army and navy leaders who each thought their service alone could win the war and should be given the chance to do so. If anything, Japanese service rivalries were worse. Moreover, to a large extent it *is* possible to predict where participants stood on war termination issues from where they sat. The armies on both sides—which would bear the brunt of fighting but also take center stage in the event—argued in favor of permitting an invasion of the Japanese home islands. The American navy opposed such an invasion, not least because it would inevitably play a secondary role. Senior figures in the Japanese navy were substantially more moderate than their army counterparts, not least because by 1945 they had no effective service left and hence would not be involved in any further prosecution of the war. And the U.S. Army Air Forces, which gained substantial autonomy during the war, argued vociferously for strategic bombing—the only practice that could justify their independent bureaucratic status.

Still, there are crucial exceptions as well. According to bureaucratic politics theory, Byrnes, as secretary of state, should have advocated the views of the professional diplomats in his department and become Grew's patron; instead it was Stimson, the secretary of war, who did so. Hull, outside the government, had no bureaucratic affiliation; to the extent that he retained one, it too should have placed him with Grew. Moreover, the ultimate decisions on both sides were made by leaders with substantial freedom of choice. The Japanese emperor broke historical precedent by personally intervening in the policy process at the end of the war; Truman could and did listen to any advisers he chose, and agreed or disagreed with their recommendations as he pleased.

Bureaucratic politics sees Truman as forced into a position where he had no choice but to use the bomb, since that was the only real option presented to him by the processes going on at lower levels. In the words of General Groves, by July 1945 the president was "like a little boy on a toboggan. He never had the opportunity to say 'we *will* drop the bomb. All he could do was say 'no.' "[71] But this glosses over the fact that he believed as strongly as anyone that the Japanese had to be punished through complete defeat. Explaining his reasoning in a letter written a few days after the attack on Nagasaki, Truman wrote: "Nobody is more disturbed over the use of the Atomic bombs than I am but I was greatly disturbed over the unwarranted attack by the Japanese on Pearl Harbor. The only language they seem to understand is the one that we have been using to bombard them. When you have to deal with a beast you have to treat him as a beast. It is most regrettable but nevertheless true."[72]

HISTORY AND HISTORIOGRAPHY

Unlike the final acts of most wars, which languish in relative historical obscurity, the Pacific endgame of World War II has received a vast amount of attention. The main historiographical debates have generated more heat than light, however, because most work has been hobbled by an excessive focus on the American side of the conflict, an anachronistic obsession with the bombing of Hiroshima and Nagasaki, and a simplistic, apolitical conception of what war termination involves.

The debate about whether dropping the bomb was "necessary" to head off an invasion of the home islands, for example, makes sense only in retrospect, when so many people felt so bad about the bomb's use and focused on it in isolation from the rest of the conflict. Viewed in prospect, by people knowledgeable about and charged with responsibility for the war effort in general, the question was not about necessity but about expected utility—might it help convince the Japanese to surrender?—and the answer was clearly yes.

Given what other miseries were being inflicted and suffered, the bomb did not stand out as much from the background of events then as it does now, and not nearly enough to make it a dramatic exception to the rule of fighting the war with whatever tools were at hand.[73] Postwar guilt over the infliction of mass noncombatant deaths attached itself to the atomic bombings rather than the incendiary bombings less because of any significant moral difference between them than because the latter occurred routinely during the war while the former coincided dramatically with its end.[74] At the time, the bomb and other strategies were understood as complementary and not mutually exclusive—as can be seen from the post-Nagasaki discussions over tactical use, when the American military leadership considered integrating the next available atomic bombs into the invasion planning.[75]

Similarly, the debate on whether the bomb was dropped to intimidate the Soviets reads later attitudes back into wartime decisionmaking, not to mention reversing the sign on American and Soviet moral and strategic calculations. American behavior during the Pacific war was shocking and the human results of its strategies sickening. But Japanese and Russian behavior was worse, both at the micro and the macro level, toward every category of population—occupied peoples, prisoners of war, even their own combatants and citizens. *Every month* in 1945 until the war's end, Japanese forces caused the deaths of 100,000–250,000 noncombatants across Asia.[76] The possibility that the atomic bombs might induce a Japanese surrender prior to Russian entry into the war was indeed an added attraction for the American leadership in general, and an important consideration for some officials, but it was only the Russians who were truly "racing the enemy" to get into the war, and for utterly cold-blooded reasons. Stalin ordered the Soviet invasion of Manchuria speeded up to be sure his forces were in a position to reap the spoils of peace and he kept them fighting for weeks longer in order to seize more territory. Hearing news of Japan's capitulation, Truman immediately ordered his forces to suspend offensive operations; Soviet forces not only continued their advances but stepped up the pace.[77] And the human cost of these little-studied final Soviet operations dwarfed those of the atomic bombs: following their entry into the war, Stalin's forces captured about 2.7 million Japanese nationals, of whom 350,000–375,000 ended up dead or permanently missing. Six hundred and forty thousand Japanese prisoners of war seized by the Soviets in August 1945 were sent to slave labor camps in the U.S.S.R.[78]

Regarding the much-debated question of whether it was the atomic bombings or Russian entry that triggered Japan's surrender, there is really no way of knowing for sure, since they happened nearly simultaneously and the relevant counterfactual analysis depends heavily on subjective assumptions about the psychology of a few key individuals under great stress. It is possible that either might have produced a comparable result by itself, and even if neither occurred, there were other factors that might well have intervened to head off an invasion. Like a patient with multiple organ failure, Imperial Japan was dying from several causes simultaneously; which one actually finished the job was largely a matter of chance.[79]

As for the emperor decision, finally, English-language commentators have spent far too much time probing the American side of this issue and far too little probing the Japanese side. As discussed in the last chapter, unconditional surrender was both a logical mechanism for binding the Grand Alliance together through the end of hostilities and a permit for a free hand in politically reengineering the defeated Axis powers afterward. Although the Truman administration was not prepared to abandon the concept with regard to Japan, it was indeed prepared to modify it, so the emperor question on the American side boiled down to what sort and what scale of modifications should be made. For all that analysts have pilloried American officials for not addressing the question as calmly and carefully as they might have, however, the other side of the debate was even more important and even less calmly and carefully handled, and remains much less appreciated even several decades later.

What the Americans thought of as a question of the emperor, the Japanese thought of as a question of their *kokutai*, generally translated into English as "national polity." Just what this term meant in practice, however, was never really clear—or rather, was contested, with different Japanese political factions favoring different interpretations and all trying to clothe themselves in the concept's legitimacy.[80] In its final decade, Imperial Japan could be legitimately viewed from any of several vantage points: as a homogeneous society bound together by ethnicity, history, and geography; as a religious or ideological community bound together by particular beliefs; and as a political regime with a particular set of institutions and procedures. The concept of *kokutai* jumbled all of these together into one emotionally resonant whole, symbolized in the person of the semi-divine emperor, representing his people and regime and claiming direct descent over thousands of years from the sun goddess Amaterasu Omikami.[81] At issue in the summer of 1945 was not simply how the Pacific war could be ended, but how much this concept could and should be deconstructed and what would happen if it were.

On the American side, this meant pondering how deep the roots of Japan's aggression lay and hence what had to be done to eliminate them. No American leaders truly favored a genetic explanation, and so all were prepared to guarantee the Japanese people's continued existence as a community in situ. They were divided, however, as to whether it was the community's beliefs or institutions that were the key problem, and decided to play it safe by keeping the option open of reforming both. This was the meaning of both the Potsdam Declaration's terms and the subsequent Byrnes note: no "enslavement as a race or destruction as a nation"; continued Japanese possession of the home islands; and a temporary occupation in order to guarantee an end to militarism and authoritarian rule and the establishment of a liberal democratic regime, with details to be filled in later according to the "freely expressed will of the Japanese people."

On the Japanese side, deconstruction meant determining whether *kokutai* was at root about people, ideas, or institutions. Despite what they occasionally claimed, no Japanese leaders seemed to care much about people qua people or follow a utilitarian calculus; all were ready to sacrifice countless lives of ordinary Japanese to protect their ideological, religious, or political visions.[82] The hard-liners in the cabinet, and the fanatics in the military ranks below them, defined *kokutai* as essentially a mystical conception of autonomous Japanese statehood, with sovereign authority contained in and represented by the emperor. From this perspective, both occupation and democracy were inconsistent with it, and so the only options in 1945 were a true compromise settlement or a full-scale fight to the death. That is why the cabinet hard-liners argued for continuing to fight even after the atomic bombs and the Soviet entry, and why their zealous junior colleagues launched a coup attempt to save the emperor from his own decision to surrender. The moderates in the cabinet, meanwhile, were prepared to gamble that the Americans would retain the basic outlines of the imperial institution, and decided that—given growing domestic dissent—this was the best chance left of preserving a version of *kokutai* they could live with.[83] If the hard-liners' position was essentially "better dead than American," in other words, the moderates' position was essentially "better American than dead or red."

Emperor Hirohito himself came to agree with the moderates, influenced in part by increasing worries over the fate of the imperial regalia—the three sacred relics, a mirror, curved jewel, and sword, whose possession legitimized his dynasty and symbolized its divine origin. As he put it some months later, one of the main motives behind his intervention to break the cabinet deadlock was that "if the enemy landed near Ise Bay, both Ise and Atsuta Shrines would immediately come under his control. There would be no time to transfer the sacred treasures of the imperial family and no hope of protecting them. Under these circumstances, protection of the *kokutai* would be difficult."[84]

The debate over what *kokutai* really involved came to a head during the final exchanges between the belligerents, since the hard-liners' position remained outside the Americans' "negotiating space," the moderates' position edged into that space during the last few days of the war, and the Japanese government had no established mechanism for breaking a deadlock. What the atomic bombs and Soviet entry really did was give the emperor and his advisers an excuse to intervene in support of the moderates' position (of Potsdam plus a single condition regarding the emperor). But the *expression* of that condition in the Japanese note of August 10 (crafted by the conservative baron Kiichiro Hiranuma) was deeply problematic, since it was couched not in moderate terms but in the extreme *kokutai* rhetoric of the hard-liners, thus almost defeating its purpose. Luckily for all involved, the Byrnes note of August 11 handled the issue delicately enough to set the stage for a second imperial intervention on August 14 that would allow the war to end relatively cleanly.

The historian Herbert Bix puts it well: "Knowing they were objectively defeated, yet indifferent to the suffering that the war was imposing on their own people, let alone the peoples of Asia, the Pacific, and the West whose lives they had disrupted, the emperor and his war leaders searched for a way to lose without losing—a way to assuage domestic criticism after surrender and allow their power structure to survive." This is why navy minister Yonai could say to a colleague on August 12, "I think the term is perhaps inappropriate, but the atomic bombs and the Soviet entry into the war are, in a sense, gifts from the gods. This way we don't have to say that we quit the war because of domestic circumstances."[85]

STAYING THE COURSE

The Japanese decision to sue for a negotiated peace during the summer of 1945 threatened to throw a wrench into the U.S. government's plans for total war and absolute victory. Roosevelt had given orders to suppress all information about the German opposition precisely because he wanted the American public to view the struggle as an uncomplicated contest that did not require difficult, unpleasant trade-offs.[86] The Japanese peace moves, together with the rising tensions in the Grand Alliance, forced the Truman administration to consider, at least for a moment, whether to change its course with regard to the end of the Pacific war.

Because there was so much intellectual, bureaucratic, and political inertia behind existing policies, however, changing directions would have been unpleasant and difficult. Three factors made it unnecessary: public attitudes toward Japan, the emergence of the bomb as a usable weapon, and the recognition of American power. Speaking to the nation about the Potsdam Conference on August 9, Truman explained what lay behind the atomic attacks:

> Having found the bomb we have used it. We have used it against those who attacked us without warning at Pearl Harbor, against those who have starved and beaten and executed American prisoners of war, against those who have abandoned all pretense of obeying international laws of warfare. We have used it in order to shorten the agony of war, in order to save the lives of thousands and thousands of young Americans.[87]

The president thus managed to link together, perhaps unconsciously, three separate yet complementary rationales. Bureaucratic politics would indeed have dictated that whenever the bomb happened to be "found," it would be used. But any qualms that might have attached themselves to such an engine of mass destruction were overcome, for leader and public alike, by the fact that its target was considered such a devious and even bestial "other." Finally, the substitution of technology for troops had practically come to define the American way of war, and the bomb fit snugly into existing strategic doctrine and self-interest.

Even if the bomb had never been invented, however, American policy in the summer of 1945 would have been essentially the same—because the nation was strong enough to shun distasteful compromises with what were regarded as the forces of darkness. A few paragraphs later in his speech, Truman continued: "We tell ourselves that we have emerged from this war the most powerful nation in the world—the most powerful nation, perhaps, in all history. And that is true. . . ." The material foundations of American strength were there, Truman argued, but the ideals they supported were even more important. "Let us use that force and all our resources and all our skills," he concluded, "in the great cause of a just and lasting peace!" His predecessor had struck a similar note with greater eloquence the year before: "The power which this Nation has attained—the political, the economic, the military, and above all the moral power—has brought to us the responsibility, and with it the opportunity, for leadership in the community of nations. It is our own best interest, and in the name of peace and humanity, this Nation cannot, must not, and will not shirk that responsibility."[88]

5

THE KOREAN WAR

Like most people, Dwight Eisenhower enjoyed a good night's sleep—and as president of the United States, he needed his rest more than others. So White House aides knew not to disturb him once he had gone to bed. In the early hours of June 18, 1953, however, they woke him up to deal with a breaking national security crisis—the first and only such nocturnal intervention during his eight years in office.

The crisis had been triggered by Syngman Rhee, the president of the Republic of Korea. Rhee was a classic example of what foreign policy wonks call a "friendly tyrant"—a brutal local strongman seen as generally serving America's geopolitical interests. As the saying goes, Rhee was an SOB, but he was *our* SOB, and so American leaders tolerated his many shortcomings. By the spring of 1953, however, the objectives of the United States and its South Korean ally had diverged significantly. Official Washington had reluctantly come to recognize that the Korean War was a stalemate and that the least bad option was to end it by accepting a modified version of the status quo ante. But Rhee, a passionate Korean nationalist appalled by the division of his country, refused to give up his dream of total victory and unification of the peninsula under his control—even though he had no realistic prospect of achieving that on his own. So when the outlines of a compromise settlement finally started to fall into place during early summer, he decided to disrupt it—to kick over the board of a game he felt he was about to lose.[1]

The way Rhee tried to do this was by opening the doors of U.N.-run POW camps on his territory and letting the prisoners inside scatter to freedom. This might seem like an odd way to create a crisis, but in context it made perfect sense. Prisoner issues had been the chief sticking point in the armistice negotiations for almost a year and a half, with an incredibly intricate arrangement for handling them only recently agreed on after endless negotiations among several parties. With a signing ceremony days away, what Rhee did was basically remove and pocket a key piece of the puzzle. This forced the Eisenhower team, as the *New York Times* put it, to scramble "to save a Korean truce that some responsible men regarded as all but lost through South Korea's angry defiance of the United Nations. The position was described authoritatively as the gravest since June 25, 1950—the day the Communists invaded the Republic of Korea."[2]

Administration officials were furious with Rhee for his actions and his charges that "counsels of appeasers have prevailed" in Washington. General Mark Clark, the commander of U.N. forces in Korea, publicly told the South Korean president, "I must inform you with all the sincerity which I possess that I am profoundly shocked by this unilateral abrogation of your personal commitment." In private, Clark was even more scathing, writing a friend a couple of weeks later, "Rhee is as unscrupulous a dictator as has ever lived. . . . Through duplicity and underhanded methods, [he] blocked the armistice which was about to be consummated. . . . During the time that he has blocked an armistice, we have had approximately 25,000 battle casualties."[3]

Some American conservatives took a different view. Wisconsin Republican senator Joseph McCarthy, for example, said that "freedom-loving people throughout the world should applaud [Rhee's] action." And California Republican William F. Knowland—the acting majority leader of the Senate—said, "I don't think [Rhee] has done anything that warrants anyone to say we can't trust him," adding that if he were Rhee, "he would not settle the Korean war 'without a united Korea.' "[4]

"When and how the desperate impasse, with its high potential of human misery and expanding war, will ultimately be resolved is beyond the prophetic powers of anyone," intoned the prominent pundit Arthur

Krock. "The mood generally" in Washington, reported the *Times*, "is one of complete anxiety and complete frustration. Nobody really has any answer and at bottom nearly everybody just wants to leave it to Eisenhower."[5]

The president, for his part, didn't know what to do, either. Two days after his middle-of-the-night awakening, the man who had managed D-Day was moved to comment, "I can't recall when there was ever a forty-eight hours when I felt more in need of help from someone more intelligent than I am."[6] As he and his advisers waited to see how the Chinese would react to Rhee's gambit, they frantically debated their own options, considering whether to put into effect a detailed plan for a coup against their truculent partner (something the Truman administration had longingly considered a year earlier) or even walk away from Korea entirely.[7]

Luckily for everybody, the Chinese reaction was critical but distinctly muted, and after some additional maneuvering—both between and within the opposing coalitions—the war did in fact end a few weeks later. But it was a close call, and understanding why holds the key to understanding both the final years of the conflict and the practical impact of America's unprecedented power in the middle of the twentieth century.

Overshadowed by the sheer magnitude of its predecessor, World War II, and the domestic trauma of its successor, Vietnam, the Korean War has been almost as unpopular with historians as it was with contemporaries. When it is remembered, moreover, people generally focus on the dramatic events of the war's first year: the North Korean invasion; the defense of the Pusan Perimeter; Inchon; the Chinese entry; the Truman-MacArthur controversy. Almost half of all U.N. casualties occurred after the start of peace negotiations in July 1951, but the final two years represent the forgotten part of the forgotten war. In particular, few have asked what would seem to be an obvious question: why did the belligerents wait so long, and fight so hard, before accepting in July 1953 a settlement that was practically identical to their positions two years earlier?

None of the major conceptual approaches to the war are much help in solving this puzzle. Left-wing interpretations, put forward by iconoclasts such as I. F. Stone at the time and revisionist historians later on, see the struggle as an American attempt at imperial expansion.[8] They usually account for the two-year delay in ending the war by viewing it as a cynical cover for domestic rearmament: "The war had to be prolonged," one scholar has written, "to buy time to implement NSC 68 [the national security strategy for the early Cold War], to so institutionalize it that domestic political vagaries could not undo it."[9] The problem with this argument is that overwhelming evidence exists that U.S. officials actually *did* want to end the war, and viewed themselves as trying to do so (albeit while pursuing some other goals as well). The Truman administration's inability to exit the conflict, moreover, was a major factor in the Democratic defeat in the 1952 presidential election. It would be an extraordinary example of partisan self-abnegation for such a loss to have been stoically endured simply to lock in a particular view of defense policy.

Right-wing interpretations, put forward at the time by MacArthur and many Republicans, saw the conflict as a belated American response to Communist expansion that was ultimately betrayed by Truman's acceptance of limits on the war effort.[10] This school, however, has no explanation for why the administration continued to pour men and materiel into a conflict it was determined to limit when a status quo ante deal was on offer as early as the summer of 1951.

Centrist interpretations, finally, advanced by the Truman and Eisenhower administrations at the time and the vast majority of historians since, flip the right-wing interpretation on its head and view the acceptance of limited war as an act of sober realism. The problem here is that the American position on the issue that delayed a settlement the longest—whether Communist prisoners of war should be repatriated against their wishes—had nothing to do with realism and, at least on the surface, everything to do with the most altruistic ideals imaginable.

So what did drive U.S. policy during the final phase of the war? What was America really fighting for, and why was it considered worth the sacrifice of tens of thousands of American casualties, the political fortunes of an incumbent administration, and ultimately the risk of global nuclear war? The answers lie in a subtle interplay of humanitarianism, incompetence, and stubbornness that unfolded against the backdrop of America's extraordinary mid-century hegemony.[11]

THE COURSE OF THE KOREAN WAR

When North Korean troops surged across the 38th Parallel in late June 1950, the senior figures of the Truman administration interpreted the attack as a major salvo in the increasingly tense Cold War. They quickly decided to meet the challenge, and within a week had committed the United States to the defense of South Korea and arranged for U.N. sponsorship of the effort.

During the summer of 1950 the North Koreans pushed their way down the peninsula, eventually pinning the U.N. forces into a small area around the southeastern port of Pusan. Despite military setbacks, President Truman and Secretary of State Dean Acheson resisted efforts by Britain and India to try to end the fighting, refusing to make political concessions to the Communist camp as part of a settlement.

In September, MacArthur's successful amphibious landing at the port of Inchon behind enemy lines reversed the trend of the war, and soon U.N. troops were pushing the North Koreans backward. At this point the ambiguity of the U.S./U.N. war aims became clear. The objective had originally been framed, back in June, as being "to repel the armed attack and to restore international peace and security in the area." But in early October, flush with victory and sensing an opportunity to unify the peninsula on South Korean terms, the Americans and British pushed through a new U.N. resolution calling for "all appropriate steps . . . to ensure conditions of stability throughout Korea." U.S. leaders gave MacArthur the freedom to pursue operations well into North Korean territory, which he promptly exploited to the limit and beyond.

As the U.N. armies moved ever northward in November, the war once again switched directions, as Chinese troops came to the aid of the North Koreans and forced the U.N. soldiers to beat a hasty retreat back south. With the full dimensions of the new war clear, Britain and India again pressed the United States to begin negotiations for a cease-fire, based on a deal that would include the admission of China to the United Nations and the abandonment of Taiwan. But the Truman administration refused to adopt such a course, deciding instead to hold its future plans in abeyance until it knew for certain whether its forces could retain any foothold at all in Korea.

A new ground commander, General Matthew Ridgway, did indeed manage to revive the U.N. side's fortunes, leading to yet another reversal of the trend of battle. By early 1951 Ridgway's troops were slowly grinding their way back up the peninsula, and both sets of belligerents began to realize that moving beyond a stalemate would be extraordinarily costly. American leaders decided, therefore, to move toward a negotiated end to the war on a rough basis of the status quo ante.

MacArthur disagreed with this policy choice, and deliberately set out to sabotage U.N. peace feelers; in response, Truman and the Joint Chiefs removed him from overall command in April, replacing him with Ridgway. Over the next two months U.N. forces in Korea thwarted a massive Chinese offensive, while Truman administration officials at home used the hearings convened to investigate MacArthur's dismissal as a vehicle for explaining their view of the stalemate to Congress, the nation, and the world at large. On June 23, Soviet U.N. ambassador Jacob Malik suggested in a radio address that both sides agree to an armistice at the 38th Parallel. On July 10, after some diplomatic pirouettes, direct cease-fire negotiations between the belligerents began in the Korean town of Kaesong, near Chinese lines.

To contemporary observers, agreement seemed only a matter of time. The first Americans coming to the negotiations were told to pack dress uniforms, for a signing ceremony; the first Chinese took only summer clothing. "The Joint Chiefs thought the talks would last about three weeks, but being military men they also had to be realistic. It might take as long as six weeks to get an armistice."[12] Their guess was off by a hundred weeks.

THE ENDGAME UNDER TRUMAN

Soon after the armistice negotiations began, it became clear that the two sides still had some major disagreements. The U.N. side envisioned orderly proceedings moving from agreement on an agenda, to negotiations over a cease-fire line, to negotiations over the terms of the truce. The Communists, on the other hand, envisioned quick acceptance of a cease-fire along the 38th Parallel, followed by the withdrawal of all "foreign" forces (that is, non-Korean and non-Chinese) from the peninsula. But they soon agreed to let the agenda's reference to an eventual cease-fire line remain vague and put off "political" questions until later, and so by the end of July the two sides had agreed that the remainder of the negotiations would take place over four consecutive stages: the establishment of a demarcation line between the armies, arrangements for a cease-fire, arrangements relating to prisoners of war, and recommendations (on "political" issues) to the governments of the countries involved.

The debate over the demarcation line was simple but heated. The U.N. team wanted to base it on the line of contact between the two forces, which would allow the U.N. Command to retain the solid defensive positions just north of the 38th Parallel it had seized during the early summer. The Communists, on the other hand, wanted to reinstate the exact prewar border. Delegates on both sides were intransigent, and those on the Communist side were abusive as well; the talks got nowhere. On August 10, for example, the two sides met and, after perfunctory opening remarks, sat in absolute silence for two hours and eleven minutes. (For such a serious venue, things could get incredibly childish. During the silence, the North Korean delegates, trying to get a rise out of their South Korean counterparts, passed a note among themselves that read, in large Korean characters visible to everybody, "The Imperialist errand boys are lower than dogs in a morgue.") Finally, on August 24, using as a rationale the latest in a series of trumped-up "incidents" around the negotiating area, the Chinese broke off the formal negotiations.[13]

With the suspension of the talks, combat heated up once more as the armies struggled for position on the ridges in the middle of the peninsula. In order to avoid future "incidents," Ridgway demanded that any resumption of negotiations take place on truly neutral ground; during October the Communists agreed, and on October 25 the talks began again in a new location, the town of Panmunjom. Within days, the Communists abandoned their insistence on the 38th Parallel, basically accepting the U.N. position that the eventual demarcation line should follow the line of contact. Ridgway wanted to hold out for slightly better positions, but the senior leadership of the Truman administration overruled him, and the demarcation issue was largely settled.

At the start of December the U.N. delegation suggested speeding up the talks by having subdelegations discuss cease-fire arrangements and prisoners of war concurrently; the final point, "political" recommendations, was added to the mix a bit later. The cease-fire talks boiled down to debates over what restrictions would be placed on the two sides' freedom of action in the period after the armistice and which countries would serve on the commission policing the accords. After intense haggling, a rough trade-off on these issues was reached during the following spring, and acknowledged in May. The recommendations question, meanwhile, was dealt with quickly, with a vaguely worded statement agreed to in mid-February after less than three weeks of negotiation. On February 8, 1952, therefore, Acheson could write Truman a memo that began: "It now appears likely that the prisoners of war issue will shortly become the sole remaining fundamental issue in the Korean armistice negotiations."[14] That topic did indeed take center stage in the following weeks, and remained there until the armistice was signed almost a year and a half later.

The prisoner issue was not what one might think, however. Western publics were outraged at the brutal treatment of U.N. captives in the "death camps on the Yalu" and by the "brain-washing" and occasional collaboration by American prisoners that occurred there, later immortalized in popular culture through novels and films such as *The Manchurian Candidate*. And the treatment of pro-Communist prisoners in U.N. hands also created headlines at the time, especially when they rioted on cue as part of Soviet and Chinese propaganda campaigns. But what Acheson had in mind was the disposition of *anti*-Communist prisoners in U.N. hands.

Simply put, the ideological passions raised in the Chinese and Korean civil wars dominated life in the U.N. prisoner-of-war camps, making them important battlefields in the larger regional and global conflict. With external help and encouragement on both sides, supporters of Chiang Kai-shek and Syngman Rhee fought with their Communist counterparts for the allegiance of, and control over, the rank-and-file prisoners in the camps. By the time the armistice talks reached item four of the agenda during the winter of 1951–52, it had become clear to American decisionmakers that while the Communist side would insist on the repatriation of all the prisoners, some prisoners would violently resist the journey north.[15]

The notion that the U.N. side should use captured prisoners as propaganda weapons had been part of American strategy in Korea from Inchon onward. A National Security Council directive approved by Truman on September 11, 1950, for example, stated in part:

> In order to effect the reorientation of the North Korean people, to cause defection of enemy troops in the field, and to train North Korean personnel to participate in activities looking to unification of the country, the following steps would be appropriate:

a. Establish the principle that the treatment of POW's, after their transfer to places of internment, shall be directed toward their exploitation, training, and use for psychological warfare purposes, and for the tasks specified above.
b. Set up immediately [facilities for the] . . . interrogation, indoctrination, and training . . . of those POW's now in our hands in Korea.[16]

Early efforts along these lines collapsed with the Chinese intervention two months later, but in the spring of 1951 the United Nations started a new program to handle the "orientation" of what had become a steadily growing prisoner population. As the operational chief of the enterprise put it,

> We mean to provide an ideologic[al] orientation towards an orderly, responsible, progressive, peaceloving, and democratic society. We wish to promote a comprehension of, faith in, and adoption of the concepts, institutions, and practices of democracy. Specifically we would like to see these people develop a conviction that they and their people would be better off socially, politically, and economically under a democratic rather than totalitarian regime. We would also like to see develop a support of an independent, democratic, unified Korean nation.[17]

There was a qualitative difference in the means used by the two sides to capture the "hearts and minds" of prisoners during the war. In the Chinese and North Korean camps, food rations were manipulated and force used as part of attempts to "reeducate" the dazed soldiers, in an Asian variant of methods developed in the Soviet gulag. In the U.N. camps, by contrast, prisoners were given some health care, food, and clothing.[18] But the two sides' attempts at indoctrination did have some things in common. In the Chinese and North Korean camps, the captives were given harangues such as "The Soviet Union Heads the World Peace Camp" and "Churchill, Tool of the Truman-MacArthur-Dulles Fascist Clique." In the U.N. camps, prisoners were shown *Miracle on 34th Street* and *Life Begins for Andy Hardy*, and instructed on topics such as "The People of the U.S. Work for World Peace" and "Our Friends, the Policemen and Firemen."[19]

Since many of the Communist prisoners had been impressed into the Chinese and North Korean armies against their will, Truman administration officials debated—as a matter of both propaganda and morality—whether it was appropriate to send them back home at the end of the war if they did not want to go. On January 2, 1952, the U.N. negotiating team at Panmunjom formally suggested that the disposal of the prisoners respect the "freedom of choice on the part of the individual, thus insuring that there will be no forced repat[riation] against the will of the individual."[20] The Communists adamantly rejected this proposal, insisting instead on an all-for-all exchange of the prisoners held by each side. This was the problem that Acheson described in his memo to Truman on February 8.

The crucial decision was taken at a cabinet meeting in the White House on February 27, in response to a telegram from Ridgway begging for negotiating instructions. "The President expressed his decision," the State Department notetaker recorded, "that the final U.S. position should be that the U.S. would not agree to the forcible repatriation of POWs and that State and Defense should draft appropriate instructions to General Ridgway for the President's approval."[21]

During the following weeks, U.S. policymakers searched for ways to implement the decision without disrupting the talks. Chinese negotiators hinted that they might accept a compromise solution involving a U.N. "screening" of the prisoners and subsequent quiet removal from the lists of those who would violently resist repatriation—a concession that came after the U.N. negotiating team had guessed that such a procedure would permit the return of 116,000 of 132,000 prisoners. In early April, therefore, the U.N. screened the prisoners to determine precisely how many would forcibly resist repatriation.

The results shocked practically everybody: only 70,000 of the 132,000 agreed to return, including only 5,000 of the 21,000 Chinese prisoners.[22] When the U.N. team presented these figures at Panmunjom on April 19, the Communists were visibly shaken and immediately called for a one-hour recess. When they returned, with barely controlled emotion they read carefully from a written statement: ". . . this figure by no means can be a basis for further discussion. If your side is willing to negotiate for a solution of the POW matter on a fair & reasonable basis, we request your side to reconsider fundamentally this estimated figure. *I repeat, this figure absolutely by no means can be a basis for further discussion.*"[23]

Understanding that the screening results made an armistice agreement practically impossible anytime soon, yet being unwilling to back off of its position, the Truman administration instructed the U.N. negotiators to present the Communists with a "package proposal" that bundled the prisoner question with two other disputed issues.[24] The Communists responded by splitting the bundle and accepting a deal on the other two, leaving prisoner repatriation as the sole remaining important issue in contention, and the talks broke down on May 7. The deadlock persisted with only minor changes until Truman left office eight months later.

THE ENDGAME UNDER EISENHOWER

In December 1953, talking to British and French leaders at a top-secret conference in Bermuda, Secretary of State John Foster Dulles went over some recent history. "The principal reason we were able to obtain the armistice" in Korea, he explained, "was because we were prepared for a much more intensive scale of warfare. It should not be improper to say at such a restricted gathering that we had already sent the means to the theater for delivering atomic weapons. That became known to the Chinese Communists through their good intelligence sources and in fact we were not unwilling that they should find out."

A dozen years later, when Lyndon Johnson was grappling with how to achieve U.S. objectives in Vietnam and asked Dwight Eisenhower to brief him on the Korean endgame, the former president said the same thing. He had passed word through various channels "telling the Chinese that they must agree to an armistice quickly, since he had decided to remove the restrictions of area and weapons if the war continued." That had done the trick, he said, and a comparably tough-minded attitude should work in Vietnam, too.[25]

Whatever the Eisenhower team may have told itself and others, however, the real story of their Korean experience was rather different. Despite what he implied during the 1952 presidential campaign, Eisenhower took office without a new Korea policy. He still faced the same three unappetizing options that had bedeviled his predecessor: escalate the fighting and risk a global conflict, stay the course in a frustrating and costly limited war, or back off American demands regarding prisoner repatriation.

From the start, Eisenhower ruled out the third option. Two weeks after the election he met with Truman and Acheson and was persuaded to publicly endorse their repatriation policy. As he said a few months later, he felt there were "certain principles inherent in the UNC [U.N.

Command] position which are basic and not subject to change. No prisoners will be repatriated by force. No prisoners will be coerced or intimidated in any way. And there must be a definite limit to the period of their captivity. The procedures in handling the prisoners must reflect these principles." As a result, during the first months of his term he chose the second option—continuing to fight "Truman's war"—while threatening the first, escalation.[26]

By May 1953, Eisenhower had indeed gone so far as to endorse a fundamental change in American policy if the war could not be ended soon, up to and possibly including the use of atomic weapons against China. But in the end he never had to decide whether to make good on the veiled threats his administration offered with increasing frequency and intensity, because the Chinese decided to concede on the prisoner issue themselves, thus paving the way for an agreement.

It now seems clear that the most important factor in breaking the logjam was Stalin's death on March 5, 1953. Although Stalin had never wanted a war with the United States over Korea—he had originally authorized the North Korean invasion in 1950 only because he was confident the United States would not intervene—by late 1951 he was comfortable allowing a contained conflict to continue. As Kathryn Weathersby puts it,

> After the initial opportunity for a negotiated settlement collapsed in August 1951, Stalin considered it in the Soviet interest for the war to continue, as long as there was no danger that U.S./UN troops would advance into North Korea again. After the war was reduced to a stalemate, it benefited the Soviet Union in several ways. It tied down American forces, rendering the United States less able to engage in military action in Europe; it drained American economic resources; and it caused political difficulties for the Truman administration. It also provided the Soviet Union with a superb opportunity to gather intelligence on U.S. military technology and organization. And the war in Korea created great hostility between the Chinese and Americans and thus tied the People's Republic more firmly to Moscow.[27]

So Stalin stiffened the spine of (and helped support) the Chinese, who in turn kept the North Koreans in line. Once he died, however, his successors in the Kremlin embraced a more conciliatory approach to the armistice negotiations as part of a more general international "peace offensive":

> Stalin's death . . . resulted in a radical change in the Soviet approach to the Korean War and hence in the position of the Chinese and North Koreans as well, as they were dependent on Soviet support and therefore subordinate to Moscow's directions. Despite the great uncertainty and anxiety within which the new collective leadership operated, it nonetheless moved immediately to bring an end to the war in Korea. On March 19 the Council of Ministers adopted a lengthy resolution on the war, with attached letters to Mao Zedong and Kim Il Sung . . . outlin[ing] statements that should be made . . . [by all three Communist governments] indicating their willingness to resolve the outstanding issues in order to reach an armistice agreement.[28]

Before the end of the month, in response to a fairly routine request from the U.N. Command, the Communists agreed to a mutual return of sick and wounded prisoners, adding that they wanted the exchange "to lead to the smooth settlement of the entire question of prisoners of war, thereby achieving an armistice in Korea for which the people of the world are longing."[29] Two days later, Chinese premier Chou En-lai proposed that prisoners unwilling to be repatriated could be transferred to a neutral state. On April 20 the exchange of sick and wounded prisoners began, and a week later formal negotiations between the two sides kicked into gear at Panmunjom.

Among the first statements by the Communist team at the talks was a new proposal on the POW issue, suggesting that prisoners opposed to repatriation be handed over to a neutral third party after the armistice. The belligerent governments would then have six months to try to convince these prisoners to return, and the fate of the final holdouts would be settled by the political conference that was already scheduled to follow the armistice. (Few expected such a conference to settle anything, and yet few expected the war to be renewed as a result of this failure. Referring questions to the post-armistice political conference, then, basically meant accepting the strong possibility that the existing state of affairs would persist.) Although the U.N. team rejected the plan, negotiations began within its general framework, and by the end of April the issues under contention had been narrowed down to who would serve as the neutral power; where they would hold the nonrepatriates; how long the period of attempted convincing would be; and what would happen to the ultimate holdouts.

On May 7, the Communists presented a new plan that incorporated major concessions. A week later, the U.N. team responded aggressively, grabbing what disputed ground was left between the two sides and even reopening issues that had already been settled; in the words of the U.S. Army's official history, "the UNC had taken a leaf from the Communist book, accepted the concessions, and then pressed for more."[30] The Communist negotiators were furious, and the talks seemed once again on the verge of breaking down.

Realizing that it had overreached but unwilling to tolerate the frustrating dickering much longer, the Eisenhower administration decided to combine a minor retreat with a declaration that this was absolutely the final U.N. position. This was when it resolved to expand the war if no progress were made, underscoring its determination with four separate actions: a meeting with Indian prime minister Jawaharlal Nehru at which Secretary of State Dulles delivered an ultimatum;[31] instructions to the U.N. negotiating team to present a "final" position; a letter to the senior Communist commanders reinforcing these instructions; and a signal to the Soviet leadership by the U.S. ambassador in Moscow, Charles Bohlen.[32] As Rosemary Foot has written, by late May "the threat had been made, the opponents in the conflict had supposedly been apprised of the position, and the United States was potentially one week away from a new and much more dangerous phase of the Korean conflict."[33] On June 4, however, the Communists shifted somewhat and accepted the bulk of the U.N. "final offer," and on June 8 the senior negotiators for each side initialed an agreement on the prisoner issue.

It was then that Rhee decided to take matters into his own hands, as described above, trying to derail the approaching truce by ordering his troops to let the anti-Communist North Korean prisoners loose. After a nail-biting two weeks, the administration relaxed a bit when the Chinese signaled that they would, in effect, overlook this infraction but wanted reassurances that there would be no more in the future.[34] Specifically, they wanted guarantees that Rhee would not unilaterally violate the armistice once it was signed. During the succeeding month, therefore, the United States threatened and cajoled Rhee into accepting the situation, and he ultimately agreed to honor the armistice even though he would not sign it. After a final, intense series of Communist military offensives (launched in retaliation for the prisoner release) were beaten back, an armistice ending hostilities was signed by the military commanders of both sides on July 27, 1953. In terms of actual combat, at least, the Korean War was finally over.

EXPLAINING THE ENDGAME

The Truman administration's initial decision to begin armistice negotiations was a pragmatic concession to the realities of power. As far as Acheson and others were concerned, the Korean War was absorbing human and political capital far out of proportion to its strategic importance. The opportunistic attempt to unify the peninsula by force after Inchon had led to Chinese intervention and disaster; once the front was stabilized by Ridgway and the chance for a roughly status quo ante peace seemed possible, the administration was determined to seize it. National leaders felt that a decision to escalate rather than accept a draw in such a secondary theater of the Cold War might well bring on, as Omar Bradley put it during the MacArthur hearings, "the wrong war, at the wrong place, at the wrong time and with the wrong enemy."[35]

In June 1951, then, the Truman administration was trying to liquidate its involvement in Korea without further embarrassment. In response to a senator's question about the U.N. Command's objectives, Acheson said: "Our aim is to stop the attack, end the aggression on that [South Korean] Government, restore peace, providing against the renewal of the aggression. Those are the military purposes for which, as I understand it, the U.N. troops are fighting."[36]

During the ensuing months, the U.N. side fought hard on the battlefield and at the negotiating table for just such material considerations: a demarcation line that would allow them to retain strong defensive positions; restrictions on the post-armistice buildup of Communist forces; rules that would allow them to resupply and rotate their own troops over the long haul ahead. They focused on these matters because they sincerely feared a future replay of the North Korean invasion. As Acheson confided to a British colleague, the Truman administration had few illusions about the talks bringing a true peace:

> . . . my own attitude toward the possibility of success in the negotiations is one, more of caution than of optimism. I agree with you that the signs

> point to a desire on the part of the Russians to end the fighting, but I think that they wish to end it on terms and in a way which will not interfere with the achievement of their purposes. . . . [B]oth [the Russians and the Chinese] wish to achieve Communist control of the peninsula. . . . [T]he prospects of [achieving a general political settlement in Korea] are not good. I think it probable that we should regard an armistice as something with which we must live for a considerable time and that therefore it must be adapted to this end.[37]

There were important internal disagreements about strategy and policy on the U.N. side during these first months of the talks (between officials at State and Defense, between the U.N. Command and the Joint Chiefs, and even within each organization), but they were disagreements within a traditionally realist framework: about whether more force should be exerted to move the negotiations forward, how important such-and-such a position was for a solid defensive line, which restrictions on the other side were required for post-armistice security, and the like. The disagreements were resolved, moreover, before they hamstrung the negotiations. Whatever the merits of the negotiators' style or positions, the Truman administration's efforts in the second half of 1951 were clearly governed by a desire to end U.S. involvement in the war on terms that would allow for the protection of a non-Communist South Korea. If other objectives came into conflict with this goal, they were jettisoned.

By late February 1952, most of the items on the negotiating agenda had been settled, and it was at this point that the prisoner repatriation issue stalemated the talks for the rest of the war. On the surface, this seems a straightforward example of idealism in action—which is how it was perceived by Truman himself and how it was spun by Acheson and others. But the true explanation is more complicated, for two reasons: first, because the realities of life in the U.N. prison camps undermined the morality of the United Nations' negotiating position; and second, because U.S. leaders never dreamed, when they took their initial stance on forcible repatriation, that it would carry such an expensive price tag. It was only afterward that they realized what a wrench they had thrown into the works.

What this means is that there are really three parts to the endgame story: the initial acceptance of a stalemate, the decision to insist on nonforcible repatriation, and the refusal to abandon that insistence come what may. The first was extremely controversial at the time, but in retrospect seems a pretty obvious choice given the alternatives. However substantively important its impact, pragmatism is common and not particularly interesting. The second was mildly controversial at the time, at least within the ranks of the U.S. government, and calls for some discussion because of its deviation from standard practice before and after. Its roots turn out to lie in the personal characteristics of individual decisionmakers and the political circumstances of the day. The third was hardly controversial at the time—a fact that itself seems extraordinary now, given the incredible costs incurred for such a historically exceptional objective. What was unremarkable to contemporaries, in other words, is precisely what seems most puzzling in retrospect.

WHY FUSS OVER THE PRISONERS?

When Brigadier General Robert A. McClure, the army chief of psychological warfare, first proposed during the summer of 1951 that the U.N. side essentially grant asylum to those enemy prisoners who wanted it, he viewed his plan as a way of avoiding the human catastrophe that had occurred when Soviet prisoners had been forcibly returned by the Allies to the U.S.S.R. at the end of World War II. That process led to numerous suicides by prisoners and mass imprisonment, if not executions, for most of the returnees. It was traumatic for many of the Americans who authorized and executed it, and McClure didn't want to go through the experience again. He also noted that the prospect of asylum might induce defections by Communist soldiers in future wars.[38]

The Joint Chiefs of Staff saw problems with McClure's specific proposal and quickly discarded it. But they too were uncomfortable with the concept of forcible repatriation, and so they decided to float the idea with others in the Truman administration. As they wrote to George Marshall, now secretary of defense, in early August, "The Joint Chiefs of Staff, from the military point of view, have no objection to the adoption of the proposed policy ['not to repatriate prisoners of war to Communist-controlled territory without their full consent']. . . . On balance, they are inclined to favor it because of its extreme importance to the effectiveness of psychological warfare."[39]

Marshall forwarded the memo to Acheson, who did not like the idea. Noting that the JCS also wanted to make the safety and return of U.N. prisoners in Communist hands top priority, Acheson pointed out that the two goals would be in conflict. As he wrote back to Marshall: "the Department of State is seriously concerned over the possibility that the proposed policy might jeopardize the prompt return of all United Nations and Republic of Korea prisoners of war." He added:

> While the possible psychological warfare advantages of the proposed policy are recognized, it is difficult to see how such a policy could be carried out without conflict with the provisions of the 1949 Geneva Prisoner of War Convention . . . [which] requires, among other things, the prompt return of all prisoners of war upon the cessation of active hostilities. . . . United States interests in this and future conflicts dictate, in my opinion, strict observance of the provisions of the Geneva Convention.[40]

(One of the ironies of the prisoner repatriation issue is how almost everybody took different positions on it at different times. When the Geneva Convention had been debated only two years earlier, the issue of the day had been German POWs retained against their will as slave labor by the Soviet Union, and the Americans had pushed strongly *for* repatriation, while the Communists had adamantly opposed it. The German POW issue, in fact, was still a bone of contention even as the Korean prisoner issue was playing itself out, leading the German specialists at the State Department to file the bureaucratic equivalent of an amicus brief supporting an all-for-all exchange in Korea.)[41]

The kinds of arguments that Acheson raised persuaded the Joint Chiefs to change their mind, not least because Ridgway was adamant that releasing any prisoners prematurely would be a mistake and that forcible repatriation should be adopted if it was the only stumbling block to peace. As he put it bluntly to his superiors in October:

> From a humanitarian point of view, we sympathize with the various proposals re non-return to Communist control of Chinese nationals [and] NK PW who do not desire repatriation. . . . We believe however, no action should be taken now or during the negotiations which may jeopardize our basic objective to gain the release of UN and ROK PW nor should the UNC delegation press the Communists to include in the armistice agreement any exceptions or spec[ial] provisions which jeopardize the achievement of our basic objective. . . .

> [A]n all-for-all exchange should be auth[orized] if this appears nec[essary] to secure release of the max[imum] n[umbe]r of UN and ROK PW, or is nec[essary] to prevent breakdown in truce negotiations. In add[ition], it may be nec[essary], in an all-for-all exchange, to release to the Communists the fol[lowing] classes of pers[ons]:
>
> a. Suspected war criminals and witnesses to war crimes.
> b. Intel[ligence] prospects.
> c. Indiv[iduals] who have voluntarily aided UNC.
> d. Indiv[iduals] not desiring to return to Communist control.[42]

Ridgway's stance was exactly the same as that taken by Eisenhower and Roosevelt a few years earlier; it had been their concern for the fate of U.S. personnel in foreign hands that had led to forced repatriation at the end of World War II. Whatever they may have said later to ward off criticism or ease their guilty consciences, U.S. leaders in 1945 understood just what the consequences of their policies would be on the unfortunate souls being returned. In fact, as the leading historian of the episode put it, "Eisenhower and Marshall agreed to Moscow's insistence upon forced repatriation *because* they had no illusions about Russian ruthlessness and *because* they feared for the safe return of GIs stranded in Eastern Europe."[43] Such hard-edged utilitarian calculations may seem callous, but war is said to be hell for a reason, and the postwar fate of returned enemy prisoners has never been a high priority for any military commander.

But even as the Joint Chiefs were reversing their position, so was Acheson—not least because he discovered that Truman felt strongly about the issue. Presented with a memo on the prisoner issue only days after Ridgway's cable, the president commented that "he [did] not wish to send back those prisoners who surrendered and have cooperated with us because he believes they will be immediately done away with."[44] The deputy assistant secretary of state for Far Eastern affairs, U. Alexis Johnson, wrote on a copy of the notes from this meeting, "We should consider how to educate the Pres. a little on PW problem."[45] The secretary of state, however, apparently decided to join the president rather than "educate" him, because in the ensuing months he repeatedly framed the issue in terms calculated to reinforce Truman's anguish over forced repatriation. In his crucial memorandum of February 8, 1952, for example, Acheson wrote:

> Any agreement in the Korean armistice which would require United States troops to use force to turn over to the Communists prisoners who believe they would face death if returned, would be repugnant to our most fundamental moral and humanitarian principles on the importance of the individual, and would seriously jeopardize the psychological warfare position of the United States in its opposition to Communist tyranny. . . . It is therefore recommended that you approve the maintenance of the present United States position, namely that we will not accept Communist proposals which would require the use of force to repatriate to the Communists prisoners of war held by the United Nations Command who are strongly opposed to such repatriation and whose lives would probably be seriously endangered thereby. . . .

Acheson had been opposed to the repatriation of displaced persons to the Soviet Union and had helped stir the misgivings of the newly anointed President Truman on this issue in the fall of 1945. (He had nonetheless condoned the forced repatriation, to certain imprisonment and death, of Soviet prisoners who had collaborated with the Germans).[46] Seven years later, in the next war, the two men decided together to reverse what they had always considered a morally bankrupt policy.

There is every reason to believe that Truman was sincere. His diary entries throughout 1952 mirror his public statements and bear the unmistakable mark of the man's character.[47] When the talks broke down after the U.S. "package proposal" in May, Truman issued a public statement: "To agree to forced repatriation would be unthinkable. It would . . . result in misery and bloodshed to the eternal dishonor of the United States and the United Nations. We will not buy an armistice by turning over human beings for slaughter or slavery."[48] In private, provoked by fervid and utterly fraudulent Communist propaganda, he was even more emotional, setting out what he really wanted to say:

> What has happened to the 1,000,000 German prisoners the Soviet holds or have they also been murdered as the Poles were murdered at Katyn? How many South Korean and Allied prisoners have you shot without cause? . . . If you signed an agreement it wouldn't be worth the paper it is written on. You've broken every agreement you made at Tehran, Yalta, and Potsdam. You have no morals, no honor. . . . These lies of

> yours at this conference have gone far enough. You either accept our fair and just proposal or you will be completely destroyed.

Only a total cynic could believe that Truman was not completely honest when he longingly instructed his negotiators, in the same diary entry, "Read Confucius on morals to them. Read Buddha's code to them. Read the Declaration of Independence to them. Read the French declaration, Liberty & Fraternity. Read the Bill of Rights to them. Read the 5th, 6th, & 7th Chapters of St. Matthew to them. Read St. John's prophecy on Anti Christ and have your own interpreter do it."[49]

Idealists in lower positions, nonetheless, sometimes felt obliged to cloak their feelings in strategic garb. It is clear from several sources, for example, that Charles Bohlen—who had been Roosevelt's translator at Yalta—was racked with guilt over the forced repatriations after World War II and was determined to prevent their recurrence.[50] In discussions with skeptics, however, he would put forward "tougher" rationales. During one meeting the chief of naval operations, Admiral William M. Fechteler, groused

> that a number of fellows in Tokyo and Korea felt that if Washington would only give up its altruistic concern for a lot of worthless Chinese there wouldn't be any problem about POW's. Mr. Bohlen took issue . . . and stated that there was nothing altruistic about our position. We had attached great importance to the POW issue. . . . If . . . we should now cave in on it it would be convincing to the Communists that in a pinch we will cave in on anything, even if it is of great importance. . . . It would be interpreted as a real sign of Western weakness.[51]

The motives of Acheson—a man who exercised a powerful influence on Truman and who might have been able to sway him had he wished—were particularly complicated, as can be seen from the fact that he changed his position during the fall of 1951 and the fact that when he later learned that his rhetoric differed from reality, he did not change his mind back but rather lied to cover up his mistakes. When Acheson first came down hard in favor of voluntary repatriation, he expected that the prisoner issue might yield a moral and propaganda victory on the cheap. When Churchill and Eden asked him at the beginning of 1952, for example, what the prospects were for peace, Acheson "said that I thought there would be an armistice, and, if I had to make a guess, I would guess that it would come about toward the end of January."[52] This guess was based on the knowledge that the prisoner issue was the only remaining difficulty and on Acheson's confidence, as he would write as late as mid-March, that "most of the Communist prisoners" would be "quite ready to be repatriated."[53] Even in early April, at the start of the prisoner screenings to find out how many would resist repatriation, he still guessed that there would be a settlement within a month.[54] Unfortunately, as he put it delicately in his memoirs, "Circumstances unforeseen and embarrassing intruded."[55]

THE PRISON CAMPS IN PRACTICE

The results of the prisoner screening surprised almost everybody and derailed the armistice negotiations. The spin put on this at the time and later by the State Department was that the results simply reflected popular dissatisfaction with Communist tyranny, which had turned out to be even greater than anyone suspected. Trying to explain the diplomatic disaster to skeptical Australian allies—who "found it difficult to believe that approximately 70,000 prisoners of war including civilian internees will have their lives jeopardized if they are returned"—U.S. officials protested: "We ourselves were astounded at the large proportion who said they would resist being returned. [Assistant Secretary of State John D.] Hickerson stated that the figure has deeper significance than we realized of conditions in China."[56] In fact, however, the screening results said less about Communist China than they did about incompetence and bureaucratic politics in the United States.

Organizational theory suggests that bureaucracies follow established routines and interests; have substantial autonomy from their nominal bosses, particularly in the implementation of policy; and often produce chaos as a result. This is precisely what happened with the prisoner-of-war camps in Korea, left to founder without any proper supervision as a result of top officials' carelessness and incompetence. (Think Abu Ghraib in Iraq two generations later and you get the picture.)

Concerned about possible reprisals against its own soldiers in Communist hands, the U.S. Army had taken charge of the U.N. Command's prisoners in Korea soon after Inchon, "to ensure that all contingents observed the Geneva convention, particularly the ROKS who had 'a tendency to mistreat or kill POWs at the slightest provocation.' "[57] The central bureaucratic mission of an army, however, is combat. No task could be further removed from this mission than taking care of enemy prisoners, and so guard duty is perpetually neglected by military organizations and despised by ambitious, motivated soldiers. Korea was no exception to this rule; as a medical orderly who served in the U.N. camps remembered, "Anybody who couldn't make it on the line was sent down to do duty [in the Chinese prisoner-of-war compounds] on Koje-do. We ended up with the scum of the Army—the drunks, the drug addicts, the nutters, the deadbeats."[58] (Ridgway himself would later write: "The personnel we could spare to take charge of the camps was not of a quality to insure the alertness needed.")[59]

Huge numbers of prisoners were jammed into small compounds, living at four times the legal density of U.S. federal prisons, in conditions their captors "considered appropriate to Asian peasants. . . . Western treatment of the Koreans and the Chinese was dictated by a deeply rooted conviction that these were not people like themselves, but near-animals."[60] The few U.S. personnel in the vicinity paid scant attention to their charges. "Guards slept on duty and deserted their posts to visit prostitutes in the adjoining refugee camps. Morale amongst officers was low and there was a high turnover of camp commanders. In the 8th Army, Koje was regarded as 'the end of the line.' "[61]

Not surprisingly, the combination of such lax oversight with the ideological passions of the Korean and Chinese civil wars led to disaster—for while the U.S. Army may not have cared about the fate of the prisoners, Rhee, Chiang, Mao Tse-tung, and Kim Il Sung certainly did. Rhee, for example, set up a special section of his war ministry in order to whip up support for his regime among the Korean prisoners, and the Chinese Nationalists on Taiwan used the cover of various U.N. programs to promote anticommunism among the Chinese prisoners. The Korean and Chinese Communists, meanwhile, used the prisoners for propaganda purposes from the start, infiltrating cadres with detailed orders and staging "incidents" whenever appropriate. Some U.S. personnel sympathized with and aided the anti-Communist forces, but the real contribution of the U.S. Army to the bedlam was malign neglect.

Just as the Truman administration was making a definitive decision against forcible repatriation, therefore, the prison camps were becoming battlegrounds as contested as the ridges in central Korea. Ridgway was at least consistent: he cared little about the situation in the camps but did not want to make a big issue out of the fate of the prisoners. He warned, moreover, that once raised, the issue would be hard to back away from. Acheson and his aide U. Alexis Johnson, on the other hand, pressed to enshrine nonrepatriation as U.S. policy but did not bother to learn the true costs in advance. They assumed they could have their cake and eat it, too, never really worrying that their proposed course of action might destroy the prospects for an early armistice.

Various guesses as to how many potential nonrepatriates a screening would reveal were bandied about within the administration during early 1952, some of which were within the range the Chinese had indicated they might be willing to accept. Johnson, having taken a cursory tour of the U.N. POW camps in February, assured doubters back home that the number of returnees after a screening would be within the comfort zone—even when he should have known better thanks to accurate reporting from the U.S. ambassador to South Korea, John H. Muccio.[62] In January, for example, a member of the State Department's Policy Planning Staff had warned: "The prison camps for Chinese, on the basis of firsthand reports from Departmental officers, are in effect run by the inmates themselves. The exercise of authority . . . is direct, violent, and brutal . . . , in effect, a reign of terror."

In March, Muccio passed on to Johnson reports that fleshed out the story:

> Chinese prisoners of war are controlled by a thin veneer of PW trustees not freely elected by the prisoners whom they control, but appointed by US Army camp authorities on the basis of ostensible anti-Communism. . . . These trustees exercise discriminatory control over food, clothing, fuel and access to medical treatment for the mass of Chinese prisoners. With encouragement from Formosan Chinese . . . the trustees have for several months conducted a drive to collect petitions for transfer to Formosa. This propaganda drive is now reaching a climax with use of brutal force to obtain signatures. The trustees maintain control over the Chinese compounds by means of force and coercion. Beatings, torture and threats of punishment are frequently utilized to intimidate the majority of Chinese POWs. . . . This situation . . . [represents] an attempt at forced, coerced removal to Formosa in direct contradiction of the UNC stand at Panmunjom on voluntary repatriation of internees.[63]

What was Johnson's reaction to this news? "Thanks very much for your letter . . . on the problem of Chinese POWs. . . . All I can do now is to keep my fingers crossed and hope for the best."[64]

Further details about the conditions in the camps emerged from another report sent by Muccio to Acheson on May 12. It noted that the "outstanding feature [of the screening] was [the] extent pro-nationalist POW's . . . dominated proceedings through violent systematic terrorism and physical punishment of those choosing 'against going Taiwan' (as the issue was militantly advertised by pro-Nationalists) throughout both orientation and screening phases. Severe beatings, torture, some killings."[65]

Muccio continued to pass on such information in hopes that the problems could be corrected before a rescreening took place. In cables over the summer he reiterated the basic point that there had been "physical terror including organized murders, beatings, threats, before and even during [the] polling process."[66] And others within the State Department confirmed his findings. A lengthy July report from the Department's Office of Intelligence Research, for example, noted: "During the months preceding the screening, KMT POW trusties, with Chinese Nationalist and American encouragement and aid, had built up a police-state type of rule over the main Chinese POW compounds, which provided the foundation and means for powerfully influencing the screening against repatriation. . . ." The report detailed the "enforced tattooing of the POWs" with anti-Communist slogans and the "violent and terroristic coercion of the POWs by the KMT trusties during the screening," along with the "lack of UN foresight in anticipating and preparing to cope with such factors." It estimated that if these problems at the camps were thoroughly eliminated, "anywhere from 4,000 to 10,000 of the present 14,000 Chinese 'anti-repatriation' POWs might be expected to go over to the Communists."[67]

The U.N. negotiators knew about the problems, too, although they kept them quiet. Admiral C. Turner Joy, for example, the head of the U.N. delegation at the talks, noted in his diary immediately after the April screening:

> It seems that the compounds with pro nationalist leaders were completely dominated by those leaders, to such an extent that the results of the screening were by no means indicative of the POWs' real choice. [Lieuten-

> ants] Wu & May [his Chinese interpreters] believed that the removal of the leaders, coupled with a period of indoctrination of the POWs, would bring the percentage in those pro nationalist dominated compounds of those wishing to return to the enemy up from 15 to 85%.... [They] told of a mock screening which had taken place in compound 92 prior to the regular screening. The leaders had asked those who wished to return to step forward. Those doing so were either beaten black & blue or killed. Wu & May also said their experience watching Chinese POWs at the polls convinced them that the majority of the POWs were too terrified to frankly express their real choice. All they could say in answer to the questions was "Taiwan" repeated over & over again.[68]

But rather than reconsider an allegedly humanitarian policy in light of such facts, the senior leadership of the State Department decided to stonewall—to cover up the problems with the screening and redouble the United Nations' public rhetoric on the repatriation issue. One reason was not to give any credence to Communist propaganda, which made the situation in the prison camps seem even worse than it actually was. *Pravda*, for example, "featured a cartoon titled 'American benevolence' portraying a bleeding, half-naked Korean war prisoner lashed to a post. In front of him stood a two-star American general armed with a gore-splashed revolver, a monstrous hypodermic needle, bloody handcuffs, and a thick whip. The general held up the prisoner's bloody hand and said, 'Look, he doesn't want to be repatriated.' "[69]

The Soviet press repeatedly concocted absurd lies out of whole cloth, even comparing the POW compounds to Nazi death camps:

> Koje Island! Again the gloomy shadow of Maidanek has come upon the world, again the stench of corpses... again the groans of the tormented.... We have learned that "civilized" Americans can be yet more inhuman, yet more infamous than the bloody Hitlerites. Dachau was a death camp, Maidanek was a death factory. Koje is a whole island of death.... The American hangmen are torturing, tormenting, and killing unarmed people here. They are trying out their poisons on them. They have surpassed the Hitlerites; they have turned POWS into guinea pigs and are testing on them the strength of their germ "soldiers"—microbes.[70]

Pro-Communist prisoners, moreover—who were actually treated less badly than anti-Communist prisoners, since guards were too scared to enter their compounds at all—were instructed to riot and to kidnap the U.S. general in command of the camps, both of which actions brought the situation in the U.N. prisons worldwide prominence.

All of this exacerbated a split between the United States and its allies, whose private attitudes were captured succinctly by the Australian prime minister, Sir Robert Menzies: "If the allied choice lay simply between a continuation of the war and acceptance of forcible repatriation . . . [I] would have no hesitation in choosing the latter." (Ironically, even the new American commander of the POW camps felt the same, and he unilaterally—without telling his superiors—instigated a policy of "discouraging" any further anti-repatriation stands. "I did not want to risk any extension of the war," he would later write, "just so a few more prisoners could claim to be anti-communists.")[71]

In hopes of defusing the crisis, a meeting was held at the State Department on May 20, 1952, to discuss "Steps to be Taken and Questions to be Considered Arising Out of POW and Related Issues." The minutes noted that "neither we nor the Pentagon have full details as to current conditions or as to disclosures that may be made of an embarrassing nature in the future" regarding the prisoners, but nevertheless outlined a public relations campaign to defend the conduct of the U.N. Command. The minutes also discreetly referred, however, to

> [f]acts about which there is some doubt as to the desirability of full public disclosure at this time. (Paul Nitze described these as the "firecrackers under the table.")
>
> a. Chinese Nationalist influence prior to the screening of the Chinese POW's.
>
> b. Prisoner-to-prisoner brutality preceeding and during the course of the screening.[72]

The cover-up worked as intended: there is no evidence that Truman ever learned about the reality behind his cherished policy, and mainstream historians did not begin to treat the prisoner issue at any length or with any skepticism until the relevant documents became available to scholars three decades later.[73] And after May 1952, the U.S. position on the prisoner issue remained basically the same for the rest of the war. Repeating the incantations long enough, even the Joint Chiefs came to support the administration's stance because of a general unwillingness to concede anything to the Communists and a longing to compel a settlement rather than accept a stalemate.

WHAT DID THE AMERICAN PUBLIC WANT?

In July 1952, the Communists announced that "if the UNC would forcibly repatriate all the Chinese POWs, an armistice could be arranged."[74] This offer was repeated often afterward, leading to a major puzzle: why did two successive administrations in Washington choose not to take the actions within their grasp to bring the war to a close?

One possible answer is the influence of domestic politics and public opinion. Ridgway had warned in 1951, for example, that the concept of "giving asylum to POWs is so appealing to humanitarian sentiment, that once it is announced and publicized, the demand by our people to stand or fall on this proposal may preclude ultimate abandonment of this position."[75] But as it turned out, that was not what happened under Truman and only part of the story for Eisenhower.

It is true that right-wing Republicans in Congress were strong supporters of the nonrepatriation policy. As the Truman administration was deciding on its position in February 1952, for example, it "learned that a considerable group of Senators had expressed concurrence with a proposed Senate resolution initiated by Senator [William] Jenner calling for an inflexible U.S. position on voluntary repatriation."[76] Since this period was also a particularly low point in the Truman presidency more generally—the president's Gallup approval rating bottomed out at 22 percent that month and at the end of March he announced that he would not seek reelection—it is plausible that Truman was mulling ways to improve his hard-line, anti-Communist credentials in order to satisfy critics. A strong stand on prisoner repatriation would clearly help the president's image in the short term, while a decision to send screaming, crying, suicidal men into waiting Communist arms would be a public relations disaster.

Nevertheless, as Acheson wrote in his February 8 memo to Truman, "while domestic and international public opinion can be expected strongly to support the desirability of no forcible repatriation, if and when there is a belief that maintenance of this principle requires a continuation and probable spread of hostilities in Korea, support for it . . . will be much less." In a meeting the following month, the army's vice chief of staff put the question well: "Is there not real doubt concerning the attitude which the U.S. public will take on this matter? No one knows which position they will most strongly support. Will they advocate leaving our boys in communist hands or will they want to insist on the principle of no involuntary repatriation?"[77]

Before the Truman administration committed itself to voluntary repatriation as a principle, the American public cared little about Communist prisoners in U.N. hands and a lot about American prisoners in Communist hands,[78] and such feelings did not change dramatically throughout the war. Although no important American politicians questioned the new policy and all major newspapers supported it, public opinion was confused, fluid, and manipulable. Had the administration wanted to, it could have generated support for the opposite of its policy as well—something leaders understood from reports they were getting out of the State Department's Office of Public Opinion Studies. These are worth quoting at some length, to give a full picture of the domestic context of the repatriation issue and what the Truman administration knew about it:

March 3, 1952

On the prisoners-of-war issue, commentators have been . . . concerned and . . . divided. . . . From the time this issue first came into the news, some radio commentators and editors have stressed that it is more important to secure the release of American prisoners than to prevent the return of anti-Communists held by the UN. But the dominant view in public comment has been that the leading free world countries must not repeat their earlier mistakes of turning over anti-Communists to almost certain death—either execution or suicide. . . . During the last week or so, there has been considerable non-committal discussion of the "terrible dilemma" which confronts the UN negotiators on this question. This position may represent some movement away from the stand taken in earlier comment in support of the UN position.[79]

August 13, 1952

Americans agree on wanting to get the Korean War over with. . . . Americans are puzzled about how to put an effective end to the fighting. Some—about ¼th—would pull our troops out. More—perhaps

40%—would push ahead, militarily. . . . Specifically the UN position on repatriation of POWs has been reaffirmed by press and public. A July opinion survey shows an increase from 50% to 58% in the number upholding the UN stand. The few leading newspapers which earlier spoke of a "compromise" on the POW issue have not repeated that suggestion, although a few radio commentators are now talking of "compromise." A number of papers have reiterated their firm backing of the UN position. Of course, the general public continues to hold that the UN should give in *if it becomes necessary* in order to secure the return of Americans in Communist hands.[80]

September 15, 1952

In the present stage of the truce talks there is virtually no sentiment in favor of making "concessions" in order to reach an agreement. . . . Hardly any [commentators] believe we can or should retreat on the POW issue. . . . But when the general public is faced with the emotionally persuasive argument of returning all POWs for the sake of getting U.S. prisoners back, it favors giving up on this issue. A July 1952 survey found:

31% in favor of returning all POWs now
40% in favor of returning all POWs if necessary to get our men back

——

71%

20% would "never" return anti-communist POWs
 9% no opinion[81]

At most, in other words, public opinion permitted the administration's prisoner stand; it certainly did not require it.

Moreover, far from being a slave to domestic opinion, the Truman administration actively tried to master it, and used the prisoner issue for its own purposes. The leading study of the subject puts it nicely:

Having decided to hang tough on voluntary repatriation, the White House and State Department faced the problem of selling this policy to the public. Convinced that there was little popular support for their po-

> sition, officials decided they would have to stimulate it. Recognizing that the public would prefer a swift end to the war and the immediate return of American prisoners, they concluded that potential opposition would have to be neutralized.
>
> One way to drum up public support would be to use voluntary repatriation to turn the war into a moral crusade for human rights. Ever since the administration had backed away from the clear goal of unifying Korea, UN aims, as [the State Department's Office of Public Affairs] privately conceded, had become "more and more beclouded and misunderstood." Now, however, the administration had a chance to turn the war into something more than just killing the enemy.[82]

Truman's underlings saw their chance and took it, and fanned the flames of ideological conflict as a result.

Eisenhower's situation was slightly different. He understood that the American electorate had given him a mandate to do something new in Korea, as well as some freedom to decide what that would be. Although he never seriously considered dropping the insistence on voluntary repatriation, he did decide that the war had to be ended relatively quickly, both for domestic political reasons and because he was outraged by the continuing high defense expenditures it required. When the Communist stand on repatriation finally began to weaken during the spring of 1953, for example, Secretary of State John Foster Dulles wanted to take advantage of the shift and grab a substantial portion of North Korea. In the words of an NSC notetaker,

> In view of the changed situation and the possible desire of the Communists for an armistice, it seemed to Secretary Dulles questionable whether we should feel bound now by the other provisions in the armistice to which we had agreed earlier. . . . Secretary Dulles stated his belief that it was now quite possible to secure a much more satisfactory settlement in Korea than a mere armistice at the 38th parallel. . . . [H]e personally would like to be able to say to the Communists that unless we could divide Korea at the waist rather than at the 38th parallel, we would call off the armistice.[83]

But Eisenhower dealt with the suggestion shortly, demonstrating his view of domestic constraints in the process: "The President stated his belief that it would be impossible to call off the armistice now and to go to war again in Korea. The American people would never stand for such a move."

A month later, when the prospect of an armistice began to seem real, an adviser raised the question of whether "a truce [would] cause a public outcry, since negotiations that had been extended for two years 'of savage fighting' [would have brought] so little at the peace table and on the battlefield. Eisenhower flashed his famous temper: 'If the people raise Hell,' he said, ask them if they are prepared to 'volunteer for front-line action in a continued Korean War.' "[84] Given his strong feelings on the need to end the war for political and economic reasons, and yet his apparent unwillingness to compromise on the repatriation issue (in sharp contrast to his actions at the end of World War II), just what Eisenhower would have done had the Communists not given in when they did is a fascinating, if unanswerable, question.

POWER AND THE PRISONERS

So why *did* American leaders ride the prisoner issue so far and so long? Ultimately, because they could. American decisionmaking during the Korean endgame cannot be understood apart from America's extraordinary relative international power at the time. In 1950, the United States had three times the total gross national product of the second-largest power in the world and five times that of the third, and by the war's endgame two years later, it had translated a significant amount of that economic strength into military capacity.[85] Like the eight-hundred pound gorilla in the old joke, it could sit wherever it wanted. In this case, that meant choosing to focus on the personal destinies of former enemy soldiers. Rarely in human history has a great power war been fought over such an issue—but then, rarely has a state had such relative strength, and hence the luxury of being able to relegate its narrowly material security needs to a secondary position.

Once the Truman administration managed to recover its military position after the Chinese intervention, it moved to extricate itself from the war. Few senior administration figures wanted to risk a major global confrontation over such a geostrategic triviality as the fate of North Korea; they had tried to snatch it in the first place only because they were confident the operation would be cheap and easy. Ridgway's success in stabilizing the line, it was felt, had earned the United Nations at least a draw; accepting it was seen by U.S. officials as the triumph, at least the second time around, of discretion over valor.

Yet because they consciously chose this outcome rather than having it forced on them, Truman and his advisers were prepared to hold off signing an agreement until they got one that offered a bit more than simply the status quo ante. One commentator has put it succinctly: "The major obstacle to the swift negotiation of an armistice was the American position that the U.S. had the moral right and responsibility to demand terms that, although essentially restoring the status quo of a divided Korea, would tip the balance sufficiently in South Korea's favor so as to guarantee its future security."[86] During the fall of 1951, these issues were largely hammered out—both at the talks and on the battlefield—and by the end of the year an armistice seemed imminent.

Then, unexpectedly, the prisoner repatriation issue moved to the front burner. American military leaders felt that the result of granting asylum, as the United Nations' chief negotiator passionately argued, would be "that the Commies would retaliate by not returning all of our POWs that they hold. In short we would sacrifice our men for a bunch of Chinese & NKs who were formerly our enemies and who had shot at us."[87] They felt that the results of any screening of the prisoners would become written in stone, and that a screening was therefore "impractical, undesirable, unnecessary, and dangerous to [the] UNC position."[88]

Truman and Acheson, however, were uncomfortable with replaying the end of World War II: "The memory of Yalta, of hundreds of thousands of doomed, desperate Russians being herded by the Western Allies back into the bloody maw of Stalin in 1945, hung heavy" over their heads.[89] Still smarting over having to accept a stalemate at all, they decided that there was no reason they had to witness such scenes this time around, and understood that the issue would be marvelous propaganda as well. So the president simply ended the internal administration debates and decided national policy by fiat. If Acheson had given more thought to the affair, he might have realized the gamble he was taking and tried to lead the president in a different direction. But he did not, and soon the issue exploded with worldwide repercussions.

There were legitimate and noble moral concerns regarding the forced repatriation of the prisoners of war in Korea. Even those Communist prisoners who returned voluntarily did indeed face terrible treatment—since after the war their very existence was seen by their countries' leaders as an embarrassment, a possible source of ideological contamination, and a demonstration of insufficient ideological commitment (*true* Communists, after all, would never have let themselves be taken alive in the first place).[90] Still, simple humanitarianism is not by itself a good explanation of American behavior, even though it has been offered as such by many commentators, both at the time and since.

Why not? First, because the moral issue was never as black-and-white as the Americans presented it. The number of would-be nonrepatriates was boosted dramatically by the harsh control of the camps enforced by Rhee's and Chiang's minions, and the authoritarian regimes in South Korea and Taiwan (under which the nonrepatriate prisoners ultimately found themselves) were lesser evils rather than shining outposts of truth, justice, and the American way.[91] And second, because at the very same time the prisoner drama was playing itself out, American forces were quite casually sacrificing the lives of several times as many Korean combatants and civilians on both sides—even deliberately flooding large sections of North Korea.[92] If humanitarianism or idealism had truly been the dominant factor consistently driving American foreign policy in this period, things would have looked quite different on a number of fronts.

Moreover, about 45 percent of the United Nations' own casualties during the war occurred after negotiations began; more than 124,000 of them, including 9,000 American dead, came during the period when prisoner repatriation was the sole contested issue. It is difficult to calculate the monetary costs of the stance, but it clearly was at least several billion 1952 dollars (which would amount to tens of billions today). Given the notorious unwillingness of nations to bear heavy burdens for nonmaterial interests, if in fact the Korean prisoner case did represent simple humanitarianism in action, it has to be regarded as a glaring anomaly in world history rather than an obvious consequence of American purity.

The same can be said for the latest conventional wisdom, among postrevisionist scholars, that the U.S. stance on the repatriation issue was driven by a desire to gain a propaganda victory. Such concerns were indeed present in the minds of key decisionmakers, but their willingness to bear such high costs for nonmaterial objectives in what all agreed was a secondary theater of the Cold War is less an explanation than a puzzle in its own right, given how bizarre it is by historical standards.

No, what really shaped American behavior during the Korean endgame was the abundance of relative power that provided a general context for U.S. actions, enabling American leaders to avoid repeating what they saw as the mistakes of the previous war while also indulging their annoyance at not winning a clear victory. At one point during the negotiations, Admiral Joy told his opposite number, "Apparently you cannot comprehend that strong and proud and free nations can make costly sacrifices for principles because they are strong; can be dignified in the face of abuse and deceit because they are proud, and can speak honestly because they are free and do not fear the truth."[93] The last two assertions, regarding the dignity and honesty of the U.N. stand, were valid in a relative sense only. The first, however—regarding American power and the extent to which it yielded a historically remarkable freedom of action—was indisputably correct.

Ironically, it was the Chinese who understood this better than the Americans. They themselves didn't care about the prisoners as people, but rather as symbols. What mattered to them was the forward march of communism, not the life prospects of a few thousand conscripts, and letting some of those publicly repudiate the one true faith while embracing the hated enemy would send a terrible signal about the course of history.[94] What also mattered was status, and an all-for-all prisoner exchange would formally ratify the equal standing of the two sides. When the Americans revealed their unusual prisoner stance at Panmunjom, the Chinese saw it as dirty pool, an "unreasonable and unfair" attempt at bullying and humiliation. Having earned a tie on the battlefield, the Chinese felt, they were not going to accept less than a tie at the negotiating table—which is just what the smug, self-important Americans were trying to impose. "This negotiation is not one between winners and losers," the head of the Communist negotiating team privately told his staff in November 1951:

> Reasonably speaking, the talk is between two sides which have fought to a draw on the battlefield. Even so, the other side has refused to accept such a fact. America is the number one power in the world. It will hardly get down from its high horse. On the other hand, we are the people who have just achieved our own liberation. No power in the world can possibly overwhelm us. Here is the fact that the enemy wants to overpower you, but you do not want to accept his suppression. . . . [H]e plays all the games at the talks . . . the other side does not intend to reach an agreement with us easily and quickly.[95]

Debatable as this may be as an analysis of the previous few months (during which both sides had played similar games), it is not at all unreasonable as a characterization of what was soon to come.

After the U.S. adoption of the nonforcible repatriation policy turned the conflict into a low-grade war of nerves and attrition, relative power factors actually shaped the behavior of all the belligerents. The North Koreans were the weakest of the bunch, and they sought to bail out during 1952—but were overruled by the Chinese. The Chinese, in turn, tried to bail next—but were overruled by the Russians. Then the Russians, after Stalin's death, decided to cut their losses, and it was this that eventually led to the negotiating breakthroughs in the spring of 1953. By releasing the prisoners in June, Rhee played his weak hand boldy, managing to extract a hard security guarantee from Washington that he probably would not otherwise have gotten. The Americans, finally, strongest of all, used their power to endure longer than the rest and force their enemies to allow tens of thousands of prisoners to switch sides in the Cold War. Whether that was a wise and deliberate use of such power was a question almost never discussed.

6

THE VIETNAM WAR

Henry Kissinger and his aide Winston Lord could hardly believe what they had just heard. "We've done it!" they said to each other, shaking hands as they walked in a park during a break in the negotiations, discussing the deal the North Vietnamese had just proposed. Alexander Haig said he thought they had saved the honor of the soldiers who had fought and died in the war. John Negroponte was skeptical about what Saigon would think, but he was always a grumbler, wasn't he? "I have participated in many dramatic events," Kissinger would write later, "but the moment that moved me most deeply has to be that cool autumn Sunday afternoon, while the shadows were falling over the serene French landscape and that large quiet room, hung with abstract paintings, was illuminated only at the green baize table across which the two delegations were facing other. At last, we thought, there would be an end to the bloodletting in Indochina and the turmoil in America."[1]

Four days later, on October 12, 1972, the national security adviser was back in Washington briefing the president on the breakthrough. White House Chief of Staff H. R. Haldeman recorded the scene in his diary:

> K[issinger] opened by saying, Well, you've got three for three, Mr. P[resident] (*meaning China, the Soviet Union, and now a Vietnam settlement*). . . . The P was a little incredulous at first and sort of queried Henry a bit. Henry started to outline the agreement from his secret red folder. Made the point overall that we got a much better deal by far than we had expected. The net effect is that it leaves Thieu in office. We get a stand-in-place cease-fire on October 30 or 31. They have to agree to work together to set up a Council on National Concord and Reconciliation, but any action by this council has to be by unanimous vote, so it can't effectively hurt Thieu any. The cease-fire would be followed by a complete withdrawal of [U.S.] troops within 60 days and a return of the [U.S.] POW's in 60 days. We'd have everything done by the end of the year. . . . The real basic problem boils down to the question of whether Thieu can be sold on it. . . . Overall, it boils down to a super-historic night if it all holds together, and Henry is now convinced it will. He thinks that he's really got the deal. So we'll see.[2]

Both the pessimists and the optimists were right—the deal would indeed be tough to sell to Thieu, but in the end it would be the Nixon administration's ticket home.

Kissinger knew that he had gotten the best agreement possible. But he also knew that it stacked the odds against the long-term survival of the Saigon regime. (His own deputy had opposed the deal only a week before, "because he thought we were screwing Thieu.")[3] To bypass South Vietnamese objections, therefore, Kissinger had decided to keep the last stages of the negotiations secret and force Saigon to accept a fait accompli. But the stratagem backfired when Thieu balked.[4]

Like his South Korean counterpart Syngman Rhee two decades earlier, Nguyen Van Thieu had agreed to let negotiations in his country's stalemated civil war move forward, but only because he had never dreamed the talks would actually get anywhere. Now, as details of the breakthrough leaked and the South Vietnamese leader was briefed on the situation, he was shocked to realize that his American patrons were finally ready to leave. He pleaded in tears for the Americans to hold out for better conditions. When informed of the problem, Nixon refused to force Thieu into signing, and Kissinger had to tell the North Vietnamese that the deal they had just negotiated was being postponed. The North Vietnamese, in turn, now suspected they had been duped into making concessions for nothing, and retaliated on October 26 by publicly revealing the draft agreement—and the American promise to sign it.

This was the point at which Kissinger, desperate to keep the settlement from slipping out of reach, took to the airwaves himself and plaintively assured the world that "peace is at hand."[5] Three months later—after an American election, further bitter and exhausting negotiations, secret promises to Thieu, and the most intense bombing of the war—it was, on roughly the terms agreed to in mid-October.

Twenty-six months after that, South Vietnam ceased to exist.

Successful belligerents face difficult choices at the ends of wars; unsuccessful belligerents confront far worse. The losing side in Vietnam, as in other wars, had to perform political triage—decide which of its goals were still worth fighting for and how they could be achieved against lengthening odds. For the United States, unlike its South Vietnamese ally, defeat did not directly threaten the nation's physical security or sovereignty. But American leaders still found it so excruciating to bring the war to a close that the endgame took as long, and cost as many U.S. casualties, as the entire preceding American intervention.[6]

In the 1960s, U.S. leaders believed that the fall of South Vietnam to communism would have terrible consequences at home and abroad, so they decided to do what was necessary to prevent such an outcome. At first, this meant providing U.S. aid and advisers. Then it meant facilitating the overthrow of South Vietnamese president Ngo Dinh Diem. Then it meant bombing North Vietnam and sending U.S. ground troops to fight Communist forces directly.

Throughout the Kennedy and Johnson administrations, policymakers in Washington refused to address the toughest question of all—whether to accept the true costs of victory or defeat. Wishing on a star, they hoped that if the United States gradually increased the scale of its effort, the Communists could be persuaded to cease and desist.[7] Once the patience of the American public wore thin, such an approach was no longer feasible. By 1968, the war was causing such domestic turmoil and costing so much blood and treasure that it could no longer be justified by the old goal of preventing a Communist takeover in the South. This aim was still important, but finding a way out now became at least as crucial, and at this point the war's endgame began.

Lyndon Johnson never accepted defeat in Vietnam; even as he capped the war's escalation during his final year in office, he never let go of his basic conviction that the Saigon regime could and should be preserved and the war should continue. The limits he set on American forces and the unilateral bombing halt he declared, however, became political facts that restricted the choices available to his successor. Presiding over the endgame from 1969 onward, Johnson's heirs inherited a fundamental imperative to finish the war along with little political capital for new ventures.

Richard Nixon had thought about "Asia after Vietnam" even before taking office, and set his sights on larger issues of superpower relations.[8] Neither he nor Kissinger ever contemplated simply abandoning the war, but they understood that it had to be ended, and relatively soon. Their first strategy sought to achieve old goals through a new mixture of force, fraud, and bluff. They hoped the strategy's four components—cowing the North Vietnamese with blows and threats, inducing the Soviets and Chinese to help, supporting the South Vietnamese with aid and training, and pacifying the American public with token troop withdrawals—would yield an agreement formalizing simultaneous American and North Vietnamese military disengagement. But the strategy failed, and the war dragged on.

By the fall of 1969, the Nixon administration was back where it had begun on Vietnam, except that U.S. troop withdrawals had already started. For its second try, the administration adopted a strategy of extrication, gradually diminishing its own military involvement while maintaining its commitment to the existing Saigon regime. Eventually, the twists and turns of policy and negotiations yielded an agreement permitting the United States to walk out, get its prisoners back, and not formally betray an ally. That same agreement, nevertheless, paved the way for the fall of South Vietnam two years later.

The Nixon administration's first strategy stemmed directly from the lessons policymakers had drawn from the endgame of the Korean War: negotiations with Communists could be successful if you continued military operations and threatened radical escalation. When that didn't work, the domestic political imperative to exit provided the context for the administration's second strategy. But public opinion was confused and contradictory, giving the administration some maneuvering room. Ultimately, it followed what appeared to be a politically palatable middle course, reducing the U.S. role in ground combat while fending off a South Vietnamese collapse.

The goal Washington retained the longest and fought for most tenaciously was distancing itself from the end of Thieu's regime. Deposing Thieu themselves, Nixon and Kissinger felt, would debase the currency of U.S. commitments across the globe—something the administration was increasingly worried about because of broader adverse geopolitical trends. "[Nixon] came into office," Kissinger remarked at the former president's funeral, "when the forces of history were moving America from a position of dominance to one of leadership."[9] Yet as Kissinger went on to note, dominance reflects objective strengths, while leadership reflects others' subjective perceptions. Relative decline thus made policymakers even more obsessed than usual with the credibility of American commitments—because they feared that their carefully planned global strategic withdrawal could turn into a rout.

For a while, at least, the second Nixon strategy worked as intended: the Paris Accords did not achieve a true peace but did permit American extrication from the war. Whether the 1973 status quo in Indochina could have been maintained indefinitely had Watergate not crippled the administration is a fascinating question, one with a less clear answer than partisans on all sides usually admit.

In the endlessly divided literature on Vietnam, critics portray Nixon and Kissinger as lying monsters who prolonged a brutal and unwinnable war, while supporters see them as noble statesmen who snatched victory from the jaws of defeat until stabbed in the back by their domestic opponents. Each perspective picks up something real, but tells only part of the story. William Safire—a Jewish, libertarian Nixon loyalist who found out late in the game that his longtime boss was an anti-Semite who had tapped his phone—captured the paradoxical truth: "As a person, Richard Nixon is an amalgam of Woodrow Wilson, Nicolo Machiavelli, Teddy Roosevelt, and Shakespeare's Cassius, an idealistic conniver evoking the strenuous life while he thinks too much. . . . Nixon is both great and mean, bold and vacillating, with large blind spots in a remarkable farsightedness."[10] Much the same could be said about Kissinger.

Together, these two complicated figures seized control of American foreign policy and ran it as their personal preserve, scheming and deceiving and cutting corners all the way. The great irony, however, is that for all the neuroses and procedural irregularities of the Nixon administration, the basic foreign policy course it pursued was sane and moderate, a reasonable attempt to chart a path out of the wilderness. And it almost worked—until blowback from the administration's own flaws brought everything down in flames.

THE ROOTS OF AMERICAN INVOLVEMENT

At the height of the Cold War in the early 1950s, senior U.S. officials believed that Indochina was crucial to their policy of global containment, largely because of the ripple effects that might follow its fall to communism. Despite their disapproval of European colonialism, therefore, they increasingly underwrote the costs of the French war against the Vietminh, the local Communist-led revolutionaries. Although the Eisenhower administration chose not to stave off French defeat in 1954, neither did it question the basic premises behind previous U.S. policy. So when Ngo Dinh Diem began establishing control over South Vietnam in the mid 1950s, the United States supported him with arms, aid, and advice. "The loss of South Viet-Nam," the president reaffirmed in 1959, "would set in motion a crumbling process that could, as it progressed, have grave consequences for us and for freedom."[11]

John F. Kennedy agreed. As a senator, he had declared that South Vietnam represented "the cornerstone of the Free World in Southeast Asia, the keystone to the arch, the finger in the dike. Burma, Thailand, India, Japan, the Philippines and obviously Laos and Cambodia are among those whose security would be threatened if the Red Tide of Communism overflowed into Vietnam."[12] As president, Kennedy was eager to demonstrate his toughness and confident that an aggressive strategy of counterinsurgency could deal with what Soviet leader Nikita Khrushchev called "wars of national liberation." Since North Vietnam had decided in 1959 to resume its military struggle to unify the country under Communist rule, Kennedy's decision to stand by the Diem regime resulted in increasing U.S. involvement.

During 1961, the situation in South Vietnam deteriorated and a special commission recommended sending increased U.S. aid, additional advisers, and a contingent of combat troops to signal U.S. resolve. Kennedy accepted the basic rationale of the commission's plan along with many of the less extreme recommendations. But Diem's troubles continued. Unwilling to embrace the reforms suggested by his American advisers and unable to marshal the skill, strength, or popularity necessary for victory, he retreated into ever-greater seclusion and repression.

Finally, in 1963, the Kennedy administration tried to coerce Diem into reforms and when that didn't work it sanctioned a coup by a group of South Vietnamese generals.

Kennedy was assassinated a few weeks after Diem and bequeathed to his successor Lyndon Johnson chaos in South Vietnam, a strong U.S. commitment, and a coterie of advisers who advocated staying the course. The situation gradually worsened over the next year and a half, with occasional American retaliatory attacks on the North doing little to arrest the slide. In early 1965, U.S. planners decided to try more sustained aerial punishment. "Dropping bombs," then-undersecretary of state George Ball would acidly remark, "was a pain-killing exercise that saved my colleagues from having to face the hard decision to withdraw."[13]

The new raids achieved little; if anything, they actually stiffened the enemy's resolve. The bases from which the bombers were launched, however, now represented targets for the Communists to attack, and so the administration agreed to General William C. Westmoreland's request for U.S. combat troops to protect them. Thus did the first few thousand Marines come ashore in March 1965 at Da Nang. Within weeks, 20,000 more were authorized, together with a change in mission permitting them to take the offensive. A few weeks later still, the number of troops authorized rose to 90,000, and by the end of 1965 the total had reached 180,000. These measures were adopted from a mix of despair and confidence: despair that without them the South would fall to communism, and confidence that with them such an outcome could be averted. What almost all could agree on was that southern defeat was imminent. Faced with a stark choice between withdrawal and escalation, Johnson and his advisers opted for the latter, even as they also decided to put strict limitations on the overall U.S. effort.[14]

1965–1968: JOHNSON'S WAR

The Johnson administration's plan for fighting and ending the war was captured well in a June 1965 cable from General Maxwell Taylor, then ambassador in Saigon:

> [O]ur strategy must be based upon a patient and steady increase of pressure following an escalating pattern while making maximum effort to turn the tide here in the South. This does not mean that we must "win" in the South to bring about a change in DRV [North Vietnamese] at-

> titudes, but rather the DRV must perceive that the tide has turned or is likely soon to turn. Hopefully at this point the DRV will seek to find some way out, and if and when it does, there could be a "bandwagon" effect that would so lower VC [Viet Cong] morale and so raise that of South Vietnam as to permit bringing major hostilities to a reasonably early conclusion.[15]

The strategy had three offensive components: limited bombing in the North (and enemy-held areas in the South); defeating Communist forces in pitched battles in the South's hinterlands; and "nation-building" in the South's core. Together, these would supposedly convince the North to call off the war, permitting the United States to go home. Two other, more forceful alternatives—all-out bombing in the North and attacking Communist sanctuaries in Laos and Cambodia—were rejected in order to avoid provoking Chinese intervention and to facilitate bargaining between the two sides.[16]

Unfortunately, this approach to the war had three crucial flaws, summed up in Taylor's retrospective comment, "We didn't know our ally. . . . We knew even less about the enemy. And the last, most inexcusable of our mistakes was not knowing our own people."[17] The South Vietnamese government simply did not have much popular legitimacy or independent strength.[18] The Vietnamese revolutionaries, on the other hand, were adept at creating strong political institutions and mobilizing popular support.[19] They also proved to be superb and tenacious fighters. Finally, the American public proved unwilling to support a costly and inconclusive conflict so removed from its shores. The first two problems kept anything resembling a U.S. victory far out of reach; the third set a timer on how long the attempt itself could be made.

During 1966 and 1967, the Johnson administration bombed and fought with few results except increased destruction.[20] Although the most perceptive observers had always understood that the war would be a long, drawn-out struggle, the president and his advisers felt compelled for domestic political reasons to give the impression of progress, if not imminent success. When the communist Tet Offensive erupted in February 1968, therefore, it had a psychological impact in the United States out of all proportion to—in fact, in contradiction to—its impact on the military balance within Vietnam. Key sectors of the American establishment became disillusioned with the war effort, and its leading figures advised Johnson to move toward disengagement.[21]

Taken aback, Johnson decided that escalating any further would be extremely unpopular and not necessarily productive, but he also ruled out withdrawal. Instead he hunkered down. He renounced his reelection attempt, capped troop deployments, restricted bombing in the North, and pleaded with the enemy for negotiations (an offer that was soon accepted). As George Herring has put it, with such adjustments, "Johnson hoped to salvage his policy at least to the end of his term, and he felt certain that history would vindicate him for standing firm under intense criticism. Johnson's [March 31, 1968] speech did not represent a change of policy, therefore, but a shift of tactics to salvage a policy that had come under bitter attack."[22]

The year following the war's supposed "turning point" witnessed the most intense sustained fighting of the entire conflict, as each side tried to break the stalemate and seize the initiative. During the fall of 1968, in an attempt to move the negotiations forward and to boost Hubert Humphrey's campaign, the president announced a halt in American strategic bombing. This last move of the Johnson administration in Vietnam produced little more than its predecessors: Humphrey still lost, and the negotiations still dragged on without progress.[23]

THE FIRST NIXON STRATEGY

Coming to office in January 1969, Richard Nixon understood that part of his mandate was to end the war somehow. Separate from domestic pressures, moreover, he and his chief foreign policy lieutenant, Kissinger, wanted to concentrate on superpower relations and a general reorientation of American diplomacy.[24] Still, they had no intention of "losing" the war outright or of abandoning South Vietnam under pressure from the enemy. Ruling out both a massive escalation and an immediate withdrawal, therefore, they devised what might be termed the first Nixon strategy. Its objective was familiar: negotiated North Vietnamese acquiescence in a settlement leaving the Saigon regime intact and secure (at least from external threats). As Kissinger put in a *Foreign Affairs* article published just as the administration was taking office, "The limits of the American commitment can be expressed in two propositions: first, the United States cannot accept a military defeat, or a change in the political structure of South Viet Nam brought about by external military force; second, once North Vietnamese forces and pressures are removed, the United States has no obligation to maintain a government in Saigon by force."[25] What was new were the means to be used: removal of certain limits on American operations in Indochina, together with threats of further escalation; pressure on Moscow to restrain its proxy, together with incentives for doing so; and attempts to transfer the capacity and responsibility for fighting to the South Vietnamese themselves.

The chief reason for the North Vietnamese to cooperate, Nixon and Kissinger thought, would be the punishment inflicted by powerful blows and the fear of even greater punishment in the future. The concept was similar to the Johnson administration's "slow squeeze" strategy, except that the tempo of the bombings and the number of targets would be increased. This time, it was felt, the North Vietnamese would understand that the Americans were serious, and feel threatened enough to buy American withdrawal with concessions at the negotiations. Accordingly, in March 1969 the president approved a JCS plan to bomb heretofore-unscathed Communist base areas in Laos and Cambodia (ordering as well that the attacks be kept secret from the press and American public).

Cooperation was also supposed to emerge as a result of Soviet (and, to a lesser extent, Chinese) urgings. Since great power relations played a central role in Nixon's and Kissinger's worldview, it was only a short step to link them to Vietnam diplomacy. As Kissinger put it in his memoirs, "we made progress in settling the Vietnam war something of a condition for advance in areas of interest to the Soviets, such as the Middle East, trade, or arms limitation."[26] The North Vietnamese, by this logic, would be forced by Soviet pressure and reduced aid to accept the American offers then on the table and agree to continue their struggle by political rather than military means.

Finally, the new administration sought to bolster the southern war effort and reduce American casualties. Shifting the burden of the war to the South, it was felt, would spur the North Vietnamese to negotiate by presenting them with new facts on the ground; reducing the American combat role, on the other hand, would quiet domestic dissent and thus buy time for a sustainable long-term American involvement. The Johnson administration had begun similar policies in its last years, but the Nixon administration gave what it called "Vietnamization" far more attention, and started some limited American withdrawals in June.

Nixon and Kissinger truly believed that their new approach would lead to a satisfactory settlement within months. Haldeman recounts how Nixon wanted to combine a "threat of excessive force" with "generous offers of financial aid to the North Vietnamese":

> [W]ith this combination of a strong warning plus unprecedented generosity, he was certain he could force the North Vietnamese—at long last—into legitimate peace negotiations. The threat was the key, and Nixon coined a phrase for his theory. . . . He said, "I call it the Madman Theory, Bob. I want the North Vietnamese to believe I've reached the point where I might do anything to stop the war. We'll just slip the word to them that, 'for God's sake, you know Nixon is obsessed about Communism. We can't restrain him when he's angry—and he has his hand on the nuclear button'—and Ho Chi Minh himself will be in Paris in two days begging for peace."[27]

Kissinger too thought the change in administration would produce results. As one member of the NSC staff put it, "Our biggest problem at first was to convince Henry that the North Vietnamese were not going to change what they had been insisting on for the better part of a decade simply because Henry was talking with them."[28]

Still, the first Nixon strategy failed. The Soviets either could not or would not pressure the North Vietnamese strongly enough to make them accept a settlement, and the Communists neither collapsed nor blinked under the new attacks. There were no breakthroughs at either the formal peace talks in Paris or the secret meetings between Kissinger and the North Vietnamese that began in August. Far from buying time for diplomacy, moreover, the removal of a few American troops whetted rather than satisfied the public's desire for further withdrawals (and gave Hanoi incentive to wait Washington out). So the war just kept going and going, and American frustration continued to mount.

THE SECOND NIXON STRATEGY

Halfway into its first year, the Nixon administration was back to where it had started on Vietnam, except that unilateral troop withdrawals had already begun. Haldeman noted in his diary over the summer: "K is discouraged, because his plans for ending [the] war aren't working fast enough and [Secretary of State William] Rogers and [Secretary of Defense Melvin] Laird are constantly pushing for faster and faster withdrawal. K feels this means a 'cop out' by next summer, and that, if we follow that line, we should 'cop out' now. He wants to push for some escalation, enough to get us a reasonable bargain for a settlement within six months."[29]

The national security adviser instructed his staff to prepare plans for a "savage, punishing blow" against the enemy: "I can't believe," he told them, "that a fourth-rate power like North Vietnam doesn't have a breaking point."[30] In the hope that actually implementing such a plan would not be necessary, Nixon and Kissinger gave an ultimatum to the Soviets and the North Vietnamese to make concessions or else. When the ultimatum was ignored, however, they decided not to make good on their threats.

Rejecting escalation, the administration nevertheless refused to accept major concessions, and so found itself at a loss. At this point, a division emerged between Nixon and Kissinger, one that would persist until the end of the war. The president seized on the opinion offered to him by British counterinsurgency expert Sir Robert Thompson that Vietnamization might really work—that is, might produce, over the long run, a viable non-Communist South Vietnam capable of defending itself even without American troops.[31] Kissinger was more skeptical about Vietnamization and more concerned that continued unilateral withdrawals would undercut his ability to achieve results at the negotiating table.[32] He was also more willing than Nixon to pressure Thieu, and less concerned to secure a settlement that would guarantee long-term South Vietnamese independence. Whatever their differences, however, both Nixon and Kissinger agreed that during the period of American withdrawal they could neither abandon Thieu outright nor permit the South to be overrun.

Ultimately, they settled on what might be termed the second Nixon strategy, the goal of which was American extrication no later than the end of 1972. This approach consisted of gradual U.S. withdrawal and formal protection of the Thieu regime, with a concerted effort to enshrine these elements in a negotiated settlement. It began with Nixon's dramatic call on November 3, 1969, for the nation's "silent majority" to rally round his Vietnam policies and grant enough time for them to work. The strategy of extrication then guided all the major U.S. actions from late 1969 through 1973—steady troop drawdowns, Vietnamization and pacification, attacks on Communist sanctuaries in Cambodia and Laos, and concessions at the bargaining table together with intransigence on one issue alone.

In the spring of 1969, there were almost 550,000 American troops in Vietnam. By the spring of 1970, there were just over 400,000; by the end of 1970, 280,000; by the end of 1971, just over 150,000; by late spring 1972, fewer than 70,000. These troops had entered the fighting in the mid-1960s in order to stave off imminent defeat and had succeeded in this primary aim, defending the South ever since. Because the Communists had not stopped fighting, the only way for the troop withdrawals not to lead directly to an enemy victory was to have them replaced with something else. A vital part of the replacement package was aid and training for the South Vietnamese army (ARVN). Still, most observers understood that this alone could not create a true bulwark in the time allotted. So the Nixon administration supplemented aid to ARVN with other measures to keep the Communists off balance and entice them into a negotiated agreement.

One set of actions sought to make progress in the war against the guerrillas. The strength of the Viet Cong had been crippled during the Tet Offensive, and it appeared that a powerful effort by the South Vietnamese government could dispose of them once and for all. In order to press this advantage, the Nixon administration placed even greater emphasis than before on measures to "pacify" the South. The Phoenix program targeted the remaining VC infrastructure in southern villages; the Chieu Hoi program tried to attract Communist defectors; and the Americans finally pushed Thieu to institute wide-ranging land reforms.

Another set of actions constituted, in effect, a proactive defense. The Communist leadership clearly intended to continue launching offensives until the Saigon regime was brought to its knees. Rather than wait passively for these attacks to emerge, Nixon and Kissinger sought to disrupt them by striking at the base areas from which they would be launched. A coup by a pro-American faction in Cambodia during the spring of 1970 provided an opportunity (and a perceived need) for just such a disruption, and so the administration decided to move. The resulting U.S.-ARVN assault on Communist sanctuaries in Cambodia threw a wrench into Communist plans and reduced South Vietnamese vulnerability. But it also provoked even greater protests in America than had been expected, particularly after four students were killed during antiwar demonstrations at Kent State University, in Ohio. The following year a similar operation, launched against part of the Ho Chi Minh Trail in Laos (this time by South Vietnamese ground forces with U.S. air support), achieved little.

The Nixon administration's military actions from late 1969 onward can be summed up as follows: U.S. troop withdrawals undermined the long-term security of the Thieu regime, but other U.S. measures made sure that regime was protected over the short term. The same pattern was displayed in the administration's behavior at the negotiating table. Kissinger met repeatedly in secret with the North Vietnamese in an attempt to formalize the American extrication in a written agreement, but to little avail. Step by step, he offered a series of minor concessions. "Within nine months of entering office," he would ruefully recall, "the Republican Nixon Administration had exceeded the dove platform of the Democratic Party [which had been rejected by the 1968 Democratic National Convention]."[33]

In September 1970, Nixon and Kissinger went so far as to agree that the North's troops could remain after a settlement in the parts of the South they controlled. Such a cease-fire-in-place would allow the Communist forces to renew their offensives with ease once the Americans had left; any agreement based on it would make an eventual Communist victory likely.[34] The North Vietnamese were unmoved, however, and persisted in demanding the one concession American leaders refused to make—direct betrayal of Thieu in the short term. "Hanoi," Kissinger would write,

> continued to insist that the United States establish a new government [in the South] under conditions in which the non-Communist side would be made impotent by the withdrawal of the American forces and demoralized by the removal of its leadership. . . . It was not just a matter of our pulling out and letting the chips fall where they may, nor of pulling out abruptly without any quid pro quo whatever. Our unilateral exit was not enough; we had to engineer a political turnover before we left, or else the war could not end, we would have no assurance of a safe withdrawal of our remaining forces, and we would not regain our prisoners. Our dilemma was that Hanoi maintained this position until October 1972.[35]

Although the administration was prepared to offer a lot for American prisoners and extrication—even conditions leading in all probability to eventual Communist success—it was not prepared to formally abandon its client Thieu.

THE ROAD TO THE PARIS AGREEMENT

Thanks to an intricate sequence of events in a changed international context, the second Nixon strategy eventually resulted in the 1973 Paris Accords. The process began in the spring of 1972, when the North Vietnamese—eager to take advantage of the near-complete withdrawal of U.S. troops—launched a massive attack on the South. This Easter Offensive made significant advances at first, but was eventually halted by a combination of ARVN resistance, American tactical air support, and American strategic bombing. (U.S. bombers struck for the first time at Hanoi itself and mined the harbor of its port, Haiphong.) By this point, moreover, the Nixon administration had established good relations with the Communist superpowers through détente and the opening to China, and so the North's key patrons now sought to dampen rather than fan the flames of the war. By late summer 1972, the North Vietnamese, facing few opportunities for further military success and calculating that Nixon might be more motivated to cut a deal before reelection than after it, appeared willing to continue their struggle on the political front alone for a while. The Nixon administration, for its part, wanted to take credit for ending the war during its first term—and if still unwilling to dump Thieu, was nonetheless prepared to make further concessions affecting the long-term viability of his regime.

Under these conditions, the negotiations began to move forward. The United States agreed to accept the formation of a tripartite electoral commission—made up of the Thieu government, southern neutralists, and the Viet Cong—which would be formally responsible for resolving the political issues remaining after a cease-fire-in-place. The North Vietnamese agreed to permit the continuation of the Thieu regime—as long as the legitimacy of the southern Communists' political entity, the PRG, was acknowledged as well. By mid-October, as noted above, Kissinger and his counterpart Le Duc Tho had worked out a draft agreement calling for the removal of the remaining U.S. troops and the return of the U.S. prisoners of war within sixty days after a cease-fire. The political future of the South would then be handled by the tripartite National Council of Reconciliation and Concord, which would administer elections and police the agreement. Both men agreed to be responsible for the compliance of their respective sides in the conflict and they set a signing date for the end of the month.

Thieu refused to cooperate, however. "President Nguyen Van Thieu said tonight that all the peace proposals discussed by Henry A. Kissinger and the North Vietnamese in Paris so far were unacceptable," reported the front page of the *New York Times* on October 25. A cease-fire would be acceptable, Thieu declared, "only if it was Indochina-wide, guaranteed and involved the withdrawal from the South of all North Vietnamese troops."[36] That sort of complete withdrawal would indeed have been a fine way to guarantee the future security of the Saigon regime, but by this point in the war it was also pie in the sky, as Thieu well knew (or should have known).[37] So the negotiations stalled.

As the American election came and went, the deadlock remained. In return for his acquiescence, Thieu demanded a variety of changes to the agreement, both minor and major. Kissinger agreed to present Thieu's demands to the North Vietnamese, but signaled to them that he actually sought only minor concessions. Yet the Communist negotiators were in no mood to grant favors and refused to make any changes at all, even revoking some of their earlier compromises.

Tantalized and frustrated by the prospect of a settlement just out of reach, Nixon and his advisers decided on a final pair of moves to end the war. First, to corral Thieu, they ordered a massive quick infusion of aid to the South and secretly promised to "respond with full force" to any Communist violations of the accords, while at the same time threatening to abandon him if he didn't fall into line. "I have asked General Haig to obtain your answer to this absolutely final offer on my part for us to work together in seeking a settlement along the lines I have approved or to go our separate ways," Nixon wrote to Thieu in mid-December. "You must decide now whether you desire to continue our alliance or whether you want me to seek a settlement with the enemy which serves U.S. interests alone."[38]

Second, to get the North Vietnamese back to the table, they ordered devastating air strikes. This "Christmas Bombing" succeeded in the limited goals of extracting a few minor concessions, compelling a North Vietnamese signature, and showing everybody that Nixon could buck public outrage. It also helped cover up American insistence that the South sign an agreement similar to the one negotiated in October. (As Kissinger's aide Negroponte would quip, "We bombed the North Vietnamese into accepting our concession."[39])

Pulling along a reluctant ally and enemy, the United States signed the Paris Accords on January 27, 1973, formally extricating itself from the Vietnam War. The Nixon administration's policies had enabled the United States to get its troops out and its prisoners back without directly betraying its client. The conditions of the agreement, however, made that client's ultimate survival unlikely.

THE DYNAMIC DUO

It is ironic that bureaucratic politics theory burst onto the intellectual scene during the Nixon administration, because of all the periods in American history, it probably has least applicability to this one—for reasons that highlight both a key problem with the theory and important aspects of the Nixon administration's foreign policy. The main points of the bureaucratic politics approach, after all, are that decision-making power is dispersed inside the government, players follow their parochial bureaucratic interests, and as a result national policy ends up being a mess or a compromise. It was precisely because Nixon and Kissinger were fully aware that this was how government often worked, however, that they took extraordinary pains to make sure it didn't happen on their watch, deliberately centralizing power in the hands of the president and his closest advisers. The result was a secretive, byzantine policymaking process that worked largely as intended—until the system's dysfunctions eventually brought the whole administration crashing down.

Nixon and Kissinger both distrusted the national security bureaucracy, for different reasons. The president was convinced that it was the preserve of a liberal eastern establishment that loathed him personally, disagreed with his politics, and wanted to subvert his chosen policies. As he put it to his cabinet in 1971, "Down in the government are a bunch of sons of bitches . . . [who] are out to get us. . . . We've checked and found that 96 percent of the bureaucracy are against us; they're bastards who are here to screw us."[40]

Kissinger, on the other hand, considered the bureaucracy to be a sump of mediocrity, one that would suck any original or creative initiative into its nether regions and spew forth only sludge. Well before holding important office, he wrote about bureaucracies' rigidity and sluggishness, their "bias against novel conceptions which are difficult to adapt to an administrative mold."[41] An oft-repeated Kissinger comment was that when the bureaucracy was asked to provide a range of alternative approaches to a problem, "There are always three choices:

war, surrender, and present policy."[42] Leaders who wanted striking results, he thought, had no choice but to fight the system: "Faced with an administrative machine which is both elaborate and fragmented, the executive is forced . . . in the direction of extra-bureaucratic means of decision."[43]

The very first task the president and his national security adviser tackled during the postelection transition, accordingly, was minimizing the role of the bureaucracy and maximizing the foreign policy power of the White House. Kissinger was ordered to come up with a plan and he enlisted his aide Morton Halperin to help. In place of a system in which policies bubbled up from below, they created a system in which the White House framed questions from above and asked for raw information.[44] Combined with the personal characteristics of the two chief decisionmakers—their taste for secrecy, manipulation, and absolute control—this system largely achieved its procedural goals. One staff member described how it worked:

> There was a major effort to collect all the options, all the information, all the different points of view. I mean, the White House sought these, drew them in, and listened to them. Then the President went off and made his decision, usually in collaboration with his security adviser. . . . [T]he centralized presidential decision-making under Nixon and Kissinger was probably the most coherent policy-making we are ever going to get, whether you like the content or not.[45]

Much has been made over the years of the constant infighting that took place within the Nixon administration, the sordid gambits with which the highest officials of the nation vied for access and advantage, displaying a ruthlessness, pettiness, and paranoia worthy of the Borgias. Practically everybody, for example, was spying on everyone else. Nixon's White House taping system was known only to the innermost circle; the private phones of many White House staffers were secretly tapped; official records of military operations were falsified to keep them hidden; Kissinger even created a subterranean communications network designed solely to bypass his State and Defense department rivals.

Perhaps the best indication of the depths to which matters sank was the capture, in late 1971, of a mole on the NSC staff. This agent would take notes on sensitive conversations, forage in Kissinger's briefcase, even go through each day's "burn bags" in search of discarded documents—and then transmit all this information to his handlers. One might think that such an event would be big news, especially since the mole revealed, under interrogation, who his handlers were. But one would look in vain for coverage of this security breach in the newspapers of the day, since the agent in question turned out to be working not for the Russians, nor even for the French, but rather for the U.S. Joint Chiefs of Staff![46]

Yet far from being a sign that bureaucratic politics was important in setting administration policy, all this frenzy indicates just the reverse. Kissinger's endless machinations to keep the secretaries of state and defense in the dark and shut them out of the decisionmaking process were successful: eternal vigilance was the price of his liberty. Other bureaucratic players faced the opposite problem. *Their* endless machinations were aimed at getting *into* the process, chipping away somehow at the man "who became for all intents and purposes the de facto chairman of the Joint Chiefs of Staff, who managed to poach on the territory of the Secretary of Defense, and who in essence usurped the responsibilities of the Secretary of State."[47]

I LIKE IKE

Even though Nixon and Kissinger had watched the Johnson administration self-destruct over Vietnam, they took charge of the war effort themselves without trepidation. In the months after the inauguration, they confidently and repeatedly predicted, in public and in private, that the war would end soon and with a favorable settlement to boot. Addressing his cabinet in March 1969, for example, Nixon "stated flatly that [the] war will be over next year."[48] "Give us six months," Kissinger told a group of concerned Quakers in May, "and if we haven't ended the war by then, you can come back and tear down the White House fence."[49] This optimism stemmed from the knowledge that they did indeed have what they considered a new approach to the war.

Domestic politics does not help much in explaining the first Nixon strategy. Nixon and Kissinger felt a general imperative from the American political scene to end the war quickly, but such pressures had little to do with the substance of the administration's new course. Perhaps its most crucial element, after all, was the bombing of Communist sanctuaries in Cambodia and Laos, attacks the administration knew would be extraordinarily controversial. Instead of forgoing them, however, they simply kept them hidden from the American public. Nor was bureaucratic politics important, as noted above. Domestic values also explain little here. By the most generous conceivable reckoning the secret bombings were an amoral operation, undertaken for strictly pragmatic reasons, and in lying to Congress and the public about what it was doing the administration betrayed the American Creed rather than embodying it. And as for realism, while the initial Nixon strategy is consistent with it (because it used the classic tools of Realpolitik statecraft to pursue goals related to American national interests), that doesn't say much, because a wide range of other policies would have been as well.

What really explains the first Nixon strategy is the lessons of the past. A decade and a half before assuming the presidency, Richard Nixon had watched from a ringside seat as another Republican president extricated the United States from a frustrating and bloody civil war in Asia. The lesson Nixon took from that experience was that credible threats of massive escalation could force the enemy to give in. When he found himself in a similar position in 1969, therefore, he tried to follow in what he believed to be his mentor's footsteps. "Nixon not only *wanted* to end the Vietnam War, he was absolutely convinced he *would* end it in his first year," Haldeman noted.

> He saw a parallel in the action President Eisenhower had taken to end another war. When Eisenhower arrived in the White House, the Korean War was stalemated. Eisenhower ended the impasse in a hurry. He secretly got word to the Chinese that he would drop nuclear bombs on North Korea unless a truce was signed immediately. In a few weeks, the Chinese called for a truce and the Korean War ended. . . . Nixon didn't have [Eisenhower's military] background, but he believed his hard-line anti-Communist rhetoric of twenty years would serve to convince the North Vietnamese equally as well that he really meant to do what he said. He expected to utilize the same principle of a threat of excessive force.[50]

Speaking to some delegates at the 1968 Republican National Convention, Nixon spelled out the analogy himself: "How do you bring a war to a conclusion? I'll tell you how Korea was ended. We got in there and had this messy war on our hands. Eisenhower let the word go out . . . to the Chinese and North [Koreans] that we would not tolerate this continual ground war of attrition. And within a matter of months, they negotiated. Well, as far as negotiation is concerned [in Vietnam] that should be our position."[51]

Kissinger was also thinking of the Korean endgame, but he had learned a slightly different lesson. He focused less on Eisenhower's 1953 nuclear threats than on the Truman administration's June 1951 decision to curtail operations on the eve of negotiations. More than a decade before becoming national security adviser, he had written: "Our decision to stop military operations, except those of a purely defensive nature, at the very beginning of the [Korean] armistice negotiations reflected our conviction that the process of negotiation operated on its own inherent logic independently of the military pressures brought to bear. But by stopping military operations we removed the only Chinese incentive for a settlement; we produced the frustration of two years of inconclusive negotiations."[52] Rather than being eager like Nixon to repeat successful policies, therefore, Kissinger was concerned to avoid making the same mistake twice. This time, he felt, a settlement would come quickly, because Hanoi could not "risk a negotiation as prolonged as that of Panmunjom a decade and a half ago."[53]

The implications of both men's interpretations of American policy toward the end of the previous conflict were clear: bold offensive maneuvers and threats of future punishment were necessary to make progress in the negotiations with the North Vietnamese. The Korean example told them no major changes in U.S. war aims were necessary and that public opinion could be ignored in the short term—because if the escalation threats were credible, enemy concessions and a settlement would emerge in short order.

The only problem was that the two wars differed in such a crucial respect that the analogy was worthless. The outcome achieved by Eisenhower in Korea had been a permanent cease-fire, one that was stable primarily because it was possible to draw a clear and defensible demarcation line between the northern and southern halves of the country. The non-Communist regime in Seoul had been strong enough to suppress its domestic insurgency and "pacify" its own territory, and with the help of a continuing U.S. military presence was able to deter renewed attacks from the North after the armistice was signed. Indochina's peculiarly inhospitable geography, however, made such an outcome impossible in Vietnam: instead of a short line cutting directly across a peninsula, the relevant contested borders of South Vietnam were long, remote, and indefensible. Kissinger recognized the problem clearly:

> If there existed a front line with unchallenged control behind it, as in Korea, the solution would be traditional and relatively simple: the two sides could stop shooting at each other and the ceasefire line could follow the front line. But there are no front lines in Viet Nam; control is not territorial, it depends on who has forces in a given area and on the time of day. If a ceasefire permits the Government to move without challenge, day or night, it will amount to a Saigon victory. If Saigon is prevented from entering certain areas, it means in effect partition which, as in Laos, tends toward permanency. Unlike Laos, however, the pattern would be a crazy quilt, with enclaves of conflicting loyalties all over the country.[54]

In other words, the conditions did not exist in Vietnam for a durable geopolitical stalemate corresponding to the war's temporary military stalemate. The Vietnamese Communists, masters of the Ho Chi Minh Trail, understood this better than anyone. So during Nixon's first year in office they called his bluff—and in this case the savvy poker player, knowing he didn't have the cards, sheepishly backed down.

THE IMPERATIVE FOR RESOLUTION

It was only in the fall of 1969 that Nixon and Kissinger came face-to-face with the true dilemma of the U.S. endgame. Given the unbridgeable gulf between Hanoi and Saigon, the North's greater cohesion, and its determination to unify the country under Communist rule, U.S. policymakers had only two variables to manipulate: their own military involvement and their support for the southern regime. These could have been combined in four different ways:

1. Washington could have continued its support for the Thieu regime while increasing its own military involvement, pursuing a strategy of escalation.
2. It could have continued supporting Thieu while keeping its own military involvement constant, pursuing a strategy of persistence.
3. It could have maintained support for Thieu and reduced military involvement, pursuing a strategy of extrication.
4. It could have decreased both its support for Thieu and its own military involvement, pursuing a strategy of concession.

The first option would have involved actually carrying out the measures the first Nixon strategy had mostly threatened—all-out strategic bombing; invasion of the North; even, hypothetically, the use of nuclear weapons. The second option would have involved staying the course, continuing to bear the costs of the war indefinitely in order to prevent a Communist takeover. The fourth option would have involved acquiescing in the removal of the Thieu regime (and eventually, therefore, in a Communist or Communist-aligned South). The third option—the one Nixon and Kissinger chose—involved trying to end direct U.S. involvement in the ground war while leaving the ultimate political future of the South up for grabs.

The reason Nixon and Kissinger passed over options one and two, escalation and persistence, is simple: domestic politics. The broad outline of the American public's attitudes toward the war is easily sketched. Apathy before 1965 was followed by a surge of support for direct American involvement, which then ebbed consistently as the Johnson administration's policies produced few results. Most distressing, apparently, was the combination of continued casualties and the war's inconclusiveness. By November 1967, only 4 percent of those polled supported the current course, while fully 55 percent favored escalation. Thirty-four percent favored extrication ("start negotiations, decrease fighting"), while 10 percent favored complete withdrawal.[55] Over the next year and a half, the withdrawal option gained ground among the public while the escalation option lost it, but in March 1969 polls showed that "go all out, escalate" was still the single most popular alternative, garnering a plurality of 32 percent.[56] The Nixon administration's initial strategy of bombing and threats was controversial enough to be kept secret, but it was hardly beyond the mainstream of national opinion at the time.

In the second half of 1969, however, two new elements began to constrict the administration's choices. First, public support for escalation continued to drop; by December, the option "send more troops to Vietnam and step up the fighting" was being selected by only 11 percent of respondents.[57] Second, the troop withdrawals proved to be quite popular. Asked in October whether they approved of Nixon's removal of a further 35,000 soldiers, 71 percent of one poll's respondents said yes while only 15 percent said no. Another poll found 31 percent favoring continued withdrawals at the present rate, while 45 percent favored withdrawing even faster.[58] Rather than creating the basis for a sustainable long-term American commitment, in other words, the reductions had created new demands for swifter extrication.

This was not what the president and national security adviser had expected. At the start of the Vietnamization process in June, Kissinger wrote in his memoirs, Nixon had been "jubilant."

> He considered the announcement [of the first troop withdrawal] a political triumph. He thought it would buy him the time necessary for developing our strategy. His advisers, including me, shared his view. We were wrong on both counts. We had crossed a fateful dividing line. The withdrawal increased the demoralization of those families whose sons remained at risk. And it brought no respite from the critics, the majority of whom believed that since their pressure had produced the initial decision to withdraw, more pressure could speed up the process, and who did not care—nay, some would have rejoiced—if accelerated withdrawals produced a collapse.[59]

Yet if Kissinger was discomfited, the true architect of the withdrawals—Laird—was not. Perhaps the most astute and wily politician in the entire administration, the secretary of defense was playing his own game and serving as the internal proxy for trends in American public opinion at large. "I never was a great supporter of the Vietnam War," he would say later. "I was a great supporter of getting the hell out of there." He wanted to start drawdowns precisely in order to create a self-fulfilling prophecy: "His political instincts told him that if he could just get that first contingent of troops out, it would be impossible for Kissinger or Nixon or the commanders to stop the momentum."[60]

The American public knew what it did not want—further war. It was still sharply divided, however, over whether to accept the true political consequences of defeat. Throughout the conflict, in fact, there had been a "persistent ambivalence between competing goals—peace and an honorable conclusion. It was never completely clear what the people wanted most and few political candidates had the courage to suggest that America would have to choose between one or the other."[61] The endgame forced that question onto the agenda, and the answer was murky enough to give policymakers some freedom of action when selecting among the two strategies still available.

When asked in October 1969 whether they favored continued withdrawal "even if [the] South Vietnam government collapses," 47 percent of respondents said yes while 38 percent said no. By April 1970, 56 percent said yes to the same question while 27 percent said no. Despite all the protests, the invasion of Cambodia had little impact on these broad opinion trends; in July, the answers were 58 percent and 24 percent respectively.[62] These figures suggest that despite a general desire to end the war quickly, a significant portion of the population preferred extrication to concession, thus introducing some noise into the signals policymakers received.

More importantly, the hawkish portion of the public formed a key part of the Nixon administration's political base, which gave its opinions added importance and made the administration leery of adopting any concession strategy. In 1971, for example, Kissinger purported to explain why the administration could not withdraw abruptly: "If we had done in our first year what our loudest critics called on us to do, the 13% that voted for Wallace [in 1968] would have grown to 35 or 40%. The first thing the President set out to do was to neutralize that faction."[63] Sometimes, when describing the domestic backlash that might follow defeat, Kissinger went so far as to raise the specter of Weimar Germany.[64]

Whether or not the president and his advisers truly believed that defeat would risk the stability of the republic, Nixon never let electoral considerations get far out of sight. At one point in 1970, for example, Nixon was considering a complete withdrawal (largely for its public relations value). Haldeman noted in his diary that Kissinger was opposed: "He thinks that any pullout next year [1971] would be a serious mistake because the adverse reaction to it could set in well before the '72 elections. He favors, instead, a continued winding down and then a pullout right at the fall of '72 so that if any bad results follow they will be too late to affect the election:"[65] Ironically, that Nixon and Kissinger could both argue from domestic politics in this instance and yet still favor different strategies shows how nebulous the political constraints really were—at least, that is, with regard to a choice between the last two options.

The Nixon administration's actions, in the end, offer a good example of what savvy politicians can do to shape their political environment rather than merely respond to it. When he decided to forgo escalation in the fall of 1969, Nixon simply refused to accept a strategy of rapid withdrawal and concession. In his November 3 speech, he dismissed the vocal antiwar movement, appealing instead for support to what his instincts told him was a "great silent majority." The speech worked, serving to quiet criticism temporarily and mobilize his constituencies behind a strategy of extrication. Several months later, he once again simply refused to follow public opinion over the short term and ordered attacks on the sanctuaries in Cambodia. During 1972, he ordered measures such as the bombing of Hanoi, the mining of Haiphong harbor, and ultimately the Christmas Bombings, understanding in each case that the actions would provoke political firestorms yet being willing to weather them for the sake of his policy goals. Nixon was able to survive these unpopular actions, in turn, only because he agreed to give the general public what it wanted most: a steady reduction in American casualties and general involvement in the war.

THE CASE FOR CREDIBILITY

If escalation and persistence were ruled out by domestic politics, what led Nixon and Kissinger to try for extrication rather than some sort of managed concession? Their own take on realism combined with their sense of American decline.

Nixon and Kissinger both styled themselves realists when it came to foreign policy, and at least in retrospect, both questioned the Johnson administration's folly in committing the United States to a war of such difficulty and magnitude when so few material interests were at stake. Their predecessors, Kissinger said bluntly in early 1969, had been guilty of a "failure . . . to analyze adequately the geopolitical importance of Viet Nam."[66] Since by this point the war was harming the American economy, causing diplomatic embarrassments abroad, and diverting time and attention away from more significant issues, realism would rule out persistence. It would also rule out escalation, simply because the risks were disproportionate to the material gains it might bring.[67]

Like domestic politics, moreover, realism can also explain why the administration did not opt for complete capitulation—because of the damage such a humiliation would do to America's global standing. Kissinger was only expressing a realist truism when he wrote that precipitate withdrawal would cause diplomatic damage and that extrication should thus come "as an act of policy, not as a collapse, in a manner reflecting a national decision and not a rout."[68]

The most interesting question is why Washington chose a strategy of extrication over some form of managed concession. Striving for extrication prolonged the war at a high price in U.S. power, wealth, will, and domestic harmony in return for upholding the credibility of the nation's alliance commitments. Managed concession would have lanced the boil of U.S. involvement more quickly, but at a greater cost in terms of humiliation and loss of confidence, at home and abroad. The judgment of such trade-offs is inherently subjective, and realists working from similar premises could come down on different sides. In fact, they *did* come down on different sides.

Hans Morgenthau—the leading realist theorist of the era—favored managed concession. "If you believe," he wrote in 1968,

> that our military intervention in 1965 was a blunder and that, once the blunder had been committed, the issue before us was not how to continue the war but how to liquidate it as quickly and advantageously as possible, then you have no real problem in liquidating it now. You will simply see to it that a genuinely civilian government is established in Saigon, which inevitably will make it its first order of business to come to an understanding with the Viet Cong. That government would use the presence of our troops as a bargaining counter in the negotiations, after the completion of which it would thank us for our assistance and bid us farewell. The terms of the settlement would be none of our business, and we could not be blamed for them.[69]

George Kennan—the preeminent realist diplomat of the era—felt the same way. As early as 1966, he testified before the Senate Foreign Relations Committee as follows:

> If it were not for the considerations of prestige that arise precisely out of our present involvement, even a situation in which South Vietnam was controlled exclusively by the Viet Cong, while regrettable, and no doubt morally unwarranted, would not, in my opinion, present dangers great enough to justify our direct military intervention. . . . [A] great deal depends on how these things are done. If we get out in a gradual way, if there is some sort of political compromise which can help to explain our departure, that is one thing. But if we simply turned tail and fled the scene, obviously we would do great damage. . . . [E]ventually there must be some sort of a political compromise between the various factions involved in South Vietnam.[70]

Henry Kissinger, on the other hand—a realist theorist turned statesman—started from a similar worldview yet ended up at a strategy of extrication instead:

> [T]he commitment of 500,000 Americans has settled the issue of the importance of Viet Nam. For what is involved now is confidence in American promises. However fashionable it is to ridicule the terms "credibility" or "prestige," they are not empty phrases; other nations can gear their actions to ours only if they can count on our steadiness. . . . Those whose safety or national goals depend on American commitments could only be dismayed [by the collapse of the American effort in Vietnam]. In many parts of the world—the Middle East, Europe, Latin America, even Japan—stability depends on confidence in American promises. Unilateral withdrawal, or a settlement which unintentionally amounts to the same thing, could therefore lead to the erosion of restraints and to an even more dangerous international situation. . . . However we got into Viet Nam . . . ending the war honorably is essential for the peace of the world. Any other solution may unloose forces that would complicate prospects of international order.[71]

VIETNAM AND RELATIVE DECLINE

For Nixon and Kissinger, the choice of extrication over managed concession was not a matter of arbitrary personal or intellectual preference, or even a matter of honor (at least as ordinarily defined). It flowed directly from their sense of broader trends in geopolitics and the international balance of power.

One afternoon during the fall of 1972, Kissinger ruminated on the foreign policy challenges facing a falling hegemon: "How do you withdraw?" he asked. "How do you get out of a situation where every single crisis around the globe gets dumped on us?"[72] The need to bring America's commitments into line with its reduced capabilities reinforced the domestic imperative of withdrawal from Indochina; the dangers inherent in retrenchment, on the other hand, made protecting the credibility of American promises seem more important than ever.

In the years since the end of the country's last war, the U.S. economic position relative to others had shrunk. Hegemony came with burdens as well as privileges; Europe and Japan had grown by leaps and bounds; the Johnson administration had weakened the U.S. economy by spending lavish sums on both guns and butter while letting the bills accumulate. U.S. relative military strength had also deteriorated, and the Soviet Union was approaching nuclear parity. The Nixon administration decided that the nation could simply no longer afford the full costs of global leadership, that the nation's foreign and military policy had to become more selective.

"The driving force of the Nixon Strategy," one commentator noted, was "the compulsion to retrench, to alleviate America's material and political burden in supporting its commitments and other interests."[73] The administration closed the gold window in order to preserve its remaining freedom of action; adopted "sufficiency" rather than "superiority" as a guide in nuclear policy; and devised the Nixon Doctrine to reduce the emphasis placed on U.S. forces abroad. The end result of such contractions would be that Nixon's and his successor's tenure would witness "the most substantial reductions in American military capabilities relative to those of the Soviet Union in the entire postwar period."[74]

Still, the United States had not declined so far that it had to forswear all its aspirations. What Nixon and Kissinger truly sought was to keep the essence of the American position intact while paying less for it. The central problem for them regarding Vietnam was thus how to extricate the United States from the war without looking too bad. As a contemporary realist put it, "If a modest and orderly retreat of American power is to be undertaken without sacrifice of, or jeopardy to, the larger structure of interests on which America's world position continues to rest, it is essential that it not be done, and not *appear* to be done, as a response to defeat in Vietnam."[75]

This would not be easy, as the Johnson administration's Cassandra, George Ball, had argued in vain during the summer of 1965:

> Let us suppose that we commit 500,000 men to South Viet-Nam and blow to bits the economy of North Viet-Nam. . . . If after a protracted struggle we conclude that we cannot achieve the necessary solution . . . , we will still have to face the problem of getting out—which by then will have become highly complex. To admit defeat—or even to accept a qualified success—would, at this point, be far more costly in prestige and world support than a withdrawal carefully executed at a time when our commitment was still limited. We would have wasted lives and resources in a futile effort. . . . Furthermore, the elements working against US free-

dom of action would generate pressures and momentum of their own, depriving US policy of its lingering ability to extricate itself.[76]

Johnson's successors found themselves stuck in just this position. The local southern insurgency may have been largely defeated during the Tet Offensive and its aftermath, but the insurgency's northern patrons were ready and able to continue the war in other, more conventional ways. Precipitate withdrawal would lead directly to Communist victory, which was something the Nixon administration refused to accept. "We could not simply walk away from an enterprise involving two administrations, five allied countries, and thirty-one thousand dead as if we were switching a television channel," Kissinger would write.[77]

When its first strategy achieved little, therefore, the administration chose to disengage unilaterally while continuing to protect the Thieu regime. Such a gradual withdrawal might spell eventual doom for a non-Communist South Vietnam, but if the U.S. could credibly say that it had not betrayed an ally, the international ramifications and humiliation of such an outcome would be diminished—and that seems to have been senior policymakers' chief concern. As Kissinger notes, "Above all, the Nixon Administration was convinced that unilateral withdrawal would turn into a geopolitical disaster. . . . A 180-degree reversal of a major American commitment . . . would have produced profound disillusionment among America's allies, particularly among those most dependent on American support, regardless of whether they agreed with the details of America's Vietnam policy."[78] In the end, the Nixon administration pursued an Indochinese settlement in which the Asian belligerents would pause and accept the political status quo long enough for the United States to leave. It got precisely that.

EPILOGUE: FROM THE PARIS ACCORDS TO THE FALL OF SAIGON

The Paris Accords were acknowledged in Vietnam with a resignation that the true struggle continued, and with a sense on all sides that the North held major advantages unless the United States continued to back the South to the hilt.

After January 1973, as before, both Vietnamese belligerents saw the conflict as a zero-sum game for control of the South and kept up military pressure on each other. Small-scale fighting never stopped, and it seemed clear that major combat would soon resume as well. Perhaps 150,000 northern troops remained in parts of the South, and the Ho Chi Minh Trail running through Laos and Cambodia was upgraded to a modern highway in order to pre-position men and supplies for a future invasion. The Nixon administration had flooded South Vietnam with military assistance in the final months before the accords were signed, creating formidable strength on paper. But this might actually have hurt Saigon by saddling it with a war machine whose maintenance was far beyond its means.

Once its troops and prisoners were home, the American public tried to blot the war out of its memory, and largely succeeded. A dominant consensus formed that the United States should not reengage directly, and in fact should reduce its indirect involvement still further.[79] Reflecting this opinion, in June 1973 Congress ordered that all U.S. military operations in Indochina cease by the end of the summer, and in November passed the War Powers Act restricting the president's ability to send troops into battle without congressional authorization. Congress also cut the aid the United States gave to South Vietnam, from about $2.3 billion in 1973 to about $1 billion in 1974 and still less after that. In addition to the psychological blow involved, this made it difficult for Saigon to use the expensive high-tech war machine it had been given.[80] The 1973 oil crisis had the same effect, helping to cripple what remained of the South Vietnamese economy. By 1974 the country was racked with runaway inflation, massive unemployment, and low morale; an ARVN soldier's pay covered only about one-third of an average family's living requirements.[81]

In October 1974, the northern leadership met to consider plans for future operations. They agreed, in the words of one participant, that "the Saigon troops were growing weaker militarily, politically, and economically every day," while "[we] had increased our forces and our stockpiles of materiel, and had completed the system of strategic and tactical roads."

> One question was posed and discussed heatedly at this conference: Did the Americans have the ability to send troops back into the South when our large attacks led to the danger of the Saigon army's collapse? Everyone saw clearly . . . [that since the Paris Accords] the Americans had grown more confused and were in greater difficulty than before. . . . The Watergate affair had agitated the whole country and brought about

> the resignation of . . . Nixon. The United States was in a recession, inflation was increasing, unemployment had become serious, and the fuel crisis was continuing. . . . [North Vietnamese leader] Le Duan put the important conclusion into a resolution: "Now that the United States has pulled out of the South, it will be hard for them to jump back in."[82]

An attack on a province northeast of Saigon at the end of 1974 went smoothly and provoked no real American response, confirming the North's judgment of the correlation of forces. The conferees thus approved a two-year campaign designed to yield total victory.

The initial offensives of this campaign were launched in early 1975, and met stunning success, thanks partly to some strategic blunders by Thieu. Realizing that the ultimate prize was almost in its grasp, the North decided to accelerate its schedule of operations and conquer the South in one sweep. Kissinger, now Gerald Ford's secretary of state, recommended a final desperate burst of U.S. help, but the new president ultimately acquiesced to public and congressional objections. On April 23, Ford told a cheering crowd of students that national pride could not "be achieved by refighting a war that is finished as far as America is concerned."[83] Thieu outlasted Nixon by eight months; on May Day 1975, Communist soldiers hoisted their flag above the erstwhile capital of South Vietnam, now Ho Chi Minh City.

Was this outcome inevitable, a predetermined coda to the Paris Accords and the American withdrawal? Nixon and Kissinger always denied it. To allay Thieu's fears about the settlement he was being asked to sign, in November 1972 Nixon had given the South Vietnamese leader a private guarantee: "Far more important than what we say in the agreement . . . is what we do in the event the enemy renews its aggression. You have my absolute assurance that if Hanoi fails to abide by the terms of this agreement it is my intention to take swift and severe retaliatory action." With Thieu still hesitant, Nixon privately reiterated his commitment the following January: "you have my assurance of continued assistance in the post-settlement period and that we will respond with full force should the settlement be violated by North Vietnam."[84]

Nixon and Kissinger later argued that they intended to carry these promises out, and fully expected they would be able to. But then out of the blue, Kissinger would write, "Soon after the agreement was signed, Watergate undermined Nixon's authority and the dam holding back Congressional antiwar resolutions burst."[85] Congress denied

Nixon and his successor "the means to enforce the Paris Agreement at a time when the North Vietnamese were openly violating it . . . [and] began cutting back on military aid for South Vietnam. . . . The war and the peace . . . won at such cost . . . were lost within a matter of months once Congress refused to fulfill our obligations."[86]

Parts of this interpretation are valid: Watergate did drain the administration's attention and authority, Congress did restrict U.S. operations and cut aid to the South, and these moves did pave the way for the eventual northern victory. What Nixon and Kissinger leave out, however, is that such events were quite predictable and that the settlement they negotiated had left the South vulnerable to future attacks. To the American public, the most important fact about the accords was that American troops and prisoners came home; it was precisely because a guarantee of renewed U.S. military intervention in support of Saigon would have been political poison that Nixon had to make his promises to Thieu in secret. Even without Watergate, in other words, it would have been difficult for the Nixon administration to counter northern actions; with it, there was never a chance to try.

"I believed then, and I believe now," Kissinger wrote recently,

> that the agreement could have worked. It reflected the existing equilibrium of forces on the ground. We had no illusions about Hanoi's long-term goals. . . . Nor did we go through the agony of four years of war and searing negotiations simply to achieve a "decent interval" for our withdrawal. We were determined to do our utmost to enable Saigon to grow in security and prosperity so that it could prevail in any political struggle. We were convinced that Saigon was left strong enough to handle the enemy forces that remained in its country; that we would resist other violations of the agreement; that we would be able to distill from the Moscow-Beijing-Washington triangle and the possibility of economic reconstruction for Indochina additional incentives for restraint. We sought not an interval before collapse, but peace with honor.[87]

The problem for Kissinger is that there are numerous contemporaneous examples of him saying something else. The briefing book for Kissinger's trip to China in July 1971, for example, contained the following passage: "On behalf of President Nixon I want to assure the prime minister [Chou En-lai] solemnly that the United States is prepared to make a settlement that will truly leave the political evolution of South

Vietnam to the Vietnamese alone. We are ready to withdraw all of our forces by a fixed date and let objective realities shape the political future. . . . *We want a decent interval. You have our assurance.*"[88]

In his actual meeting with Chou, Kissinger expanded on the script:

> I would like to tell the prime minister, on behalf of President Nixon, as solemnly as I can, that first of all, we are prepared to withdraw completely from Indochina. . . . Secondly, we will permit the political solution of South Vietnam to evolve and to leave it to the Vietnamese alone. We recognize that a solution must reflect the will of the South Vietnamese people and allow them to determine their future without interference. We will not reenter Vietnam and will abide by the political process. But . . . the military settlement must be separated in time from the political issues. It is that which is holding up a solution. . . . If the government is as unpopular as you seem to think, then the quicker our forces are withdrawn the quicker it will be overthrown. And if it is overthrown after we withdraw, we will not intervene.[89]

Nine months later, meeting with Soviet Foreign Minister Andrei Gromyko in Moscow, he made a similar point: "If North Vietnam were wise—I'm being candid—it would make an agreement with us now and not haggle about every detail, because one year after the agreement there would be a new condition, actually. . . . [W]e will not leave in such a way that a Communist victory is guaranteed. However, we are prepared to leave so that a Communist victory is not excluded. . . ."[90]

And a month after that, meeting again with Chou, he spelled it out once more:

> I believe that if a sufficient interval is placed between our withdrawal and what happens afterward that the issue can almost certainly be confined to an Indochina affair. It is important that there is a reasonable interval between the agreement on the cease-fire and a reasonable opportunity for political negotiation. . . . The outcome of my logic is that we are putting a time interval between the military outcome and the political outcome. No one can imagine that history will cease on the Indochina peninsula with a cease-fire.[91]

Chou, in turn, relayed these points to the North Vietnamese. Just after the Christmas Bombings, he put it bluntly to Le Duc Tho: "Nixon has many international and domestic issues to deal with. It seems that the United States is still willing to get out from Vietnam and Indochina. You should persist in principles while demonstrating flexibility during the negotiations. The most important [thing] is to let the Americans leave. The situation will change in six months or one year."[92]

Fine, some might say—but what if the administration was just playing the Chinese and Soviets, giving them false assurances in order to facilitate a settlement, but intending all along to stand by Saigon come what may? Such deviousness would be nothing unusual for Nixon and Kissinger, but it can't explain why they would use even more direct language when alone in the Oval Office talking to each other (and to history, through the tapes spinning away automatically in the dark). On August 3, 1972, for example—a couple of months before the big negotiating breakthrough—they went right to the heart of the issue:

> NIXON: Let's be perfectly cold-blooded about it. . . . I look at the tide of history out there, South Vietnam probably is never gonna survive anyway. I'm just being perfectly candid. . . . [C]an we have a viable foreign policy if a year from now or two years from now, North Vietnam gobbles up South Vietnam? That's the real question.
>
> KISSINGER: If a year or two years from now North Vietnam gobbles up South Vietnam, we can have a viable foreign policy if it looks as if it's the result of South Vietnamese incompetence. If we now sell out in such a way that, say in a three-to-four-month period, we have pushed President Thieu over the brink—we ourselves—I think there is going to be—even the Chinese won't like that. I mean, they'll pay verbal—verbally, they'll like it—
>
> NIXON: But it'll worry them.
>
> KISSINGER: But it will worry everybody. And domestically in the long run it won't help us all that much because our opponents will say we should've done it three years ago.
>
> NIXON: I know.
>
> KISSINGER: So we've got to find some formula that holds the thing together a year or two, after which—after a year, Mr. President, Vietnam will be a backwater. If we settle it, say, this October, by January '74 no one will give a damn.[93]

And yet, and yet . . . if Nixon and Kissinger distorted the truth, so have their fiercest critics. The White House may have steeled itself to the possibility of accepting a South Vietnamese collapse after a "decent interval," but it certainly did not prefer or embrace that outcome, nor assume that it was preordained. Nixon and Kissinger hoped that it could somehow be avoided and intended to do what they could to keep it at bay.[94] Even the North Vietnamese themselves expected the war to continue for several more years: the plans for the final offensive had contingencies lasting into 1977.[95] Had events in Washington played out differently—with Watergate not crippling the administration and with Congress less hell-bent on slamming the door behind the departing U.S. ground troops—Nixon might have been able to send enough aid and bombs to keep the Thieu regime in power.[96]

Nixon and Kissinger were certainly guilty of many sins, but when it came to Vietnam the worst of them was having been in the wrong place at the wrong time—inheriting an impossible situation from grossly irresponsible predecessors. The simple fact of the matter was that throughout the third quarter of the century, for various reasons, the local balance of power in Vietnam favored what its proponents called "the Revolution." The United States could not alter that reality—which meant that the North was destined to win the war eventually unless physically prevented from doing so. The Kennedy and Johnson administrations chose to keep defeat at bay for several years, but only at the price of digging the United States ever deeper into a hole. Forced to clean up the mess Kennedy and Johnson left behind, Nixon managed to extricate the United States from the fighting and leave Saigon a chance of survival—no more and no less.

Attacks on the Nixon administration's policies from the right have focused on the supposed sellout of Saigon, but these seem facile. It is hard to see how any administration coming to power in 1968 could have pushed harder against the basic trend of American public opinion, kept the war going longer, fought it better, or got an agreement fundamentally more favorable to Saigon than the one that emerged.

Serious attacks from the left, meanwhile, have focused on the supposed needless prolongation of the war for little result. As Senator John Kerry put it to Kissinger in 1992, "what you wound up with in 1973 was extraordinarily close to the program tabled in 1969."[97] This argument comes in both a dishonest and an honest form. The dishonest one is to say, in effect, that 1973 could have been achieved in 1969. That is simply not true, since a key element of the 1973 settlement—Thieu's short-term and possibly long-term survival—was not available earlier.

The honest form is to say that 1973 implied 1975, and that 1975 could (and should) have been had in 1969. This puts the real issue squarely on the table, and whether one accepts the argument depends on how important one thinks it was (for whatever reasons) for Washington to give South Vietnam a shot at lasting past American withdrawal.

Americans have been so preoccupied with their own internal score-settling over the Nixon administration's Vietnam policies that few have looked at the question from the opposite side. If the deal the North got in 1973 was so favorable and so similar to what it could have had in 1969, it is worth asking, why did the *Communists* not grab something like it several years earlier? Writing just before night descended on the South, Sir Robert Thompson, Nixon's favorite counterinsurgency expert, offered a straightforward answer: because in earlier years Hanoi did not have sufficient forces in place in the South to give it a leg up in the ongoing Vietnamese struggle that all realized would follow the departure of U.S. ground troops. Then he twisted the knife: "There was a deeper, but very simple reason why Hanoi could not accept a settlement on [the 1973] or similar terms much earlier. Hanoi had to continue fighting until American will had been so eroded that the terms of the settlement would not be enforced against the North, and continued American support for the South, after a settlement, would at least be doubtful. That condition was definitely not present in 1966 and was still uncertain in 1970."[98]

By 1973, however, most Americans just wanted the whole subject to go away—and few really cared if the South went with it.

7

THE GULF WAR

Thursday, February 28

At about 6 A.M. the Apaches flew toward the crossroads in the Iraqi desert, looking for the enemy. The war was almost over, and a few hours earlier the 1st Infantry Division had actually been given orders to stop attacking. But then new orders came to start up again and head for this obscure spot in the middle of nowhere, just north of the Kuwaiti border. Who knows what's going on, thought the commanders in the field. Some enemy units were still fighting and others were trying to escape intact. Maybe the coalition's high command in Riyadh was concerned that the crossroads might be a route out. So the attack helicopters went to check, scouting for their colleagues on the ground. They saw a handful of vehicles driving north, but no major movement. They sent back their observations and flew on.[1]

An hour and a half later, a report of friendly fire came in. Coalition commanders were obsessed with the unexpectedly high number of such accidents and were doing everything they could to avoid more. So the ground operation to take the crossroads was put on hold, just to be safe. When the report turned out to be mistaken, orders were sent to start moving forward again. Then, at 8 A.M., orders were given to stop for good, and the war was over.

Friday, March 1

In the wee hours of the morning, Lieutenant General Fred Franks—the commander of the 1st Infantry Division's parent formation, the VII Corps—was woken by calls from his boss, Lieutenant General John Yeosock, the commander of the Third Army. Yeosock told him to prepare a site for cease-fire talks and asked about the crossroads. Surprised, Franks replied that in the chaos of the war's final hours, the crossroads hadn't actually been taken. Yeosock paused. That was going to be a problem, he said, because they had been ordered to seize it, had reported it seized, and the commander in chief of the coalition forces, General Norman Schwarzkopf, had already told Washington that the small airstrip near the crossroads was where the cease-fire talks should be held. As recriminations flew up and down the chain of command, Franks told his groggy subordinates their new mission: take the airstrip, the crossroads, and the nearby town without causing any trouble.

Starting out at first light, units from the 1st Infantry reached the airstrip quickly but found somebody else already there—an armored brigade of Iraq's elite Republican Guard. A puzzled Iraqi colonel came over to ask what the Americans were doing in Iraq, whether they were lost. Told that his forces had to move, he replied coolly that he had no orders to do so. But after some tense back and forth, the Iraqi unit backed down and started withdrawing toward Basra, Iraq's second-largest city, thirty miles north.

Nearby a similar drama was unfolding, as different units from the 1st Infantry also ran into the enemy—in this case, an infantry company from Tikrit, Saddam Hussein's hometown. These forces also refused to move, and made it clear they would fight back if pushed. To Schwarzkopf's increasing fury, the stalemate continued as the day wore on. (At 1:30 P.M., the Third Army's operations officer noted in his log: "CINC has repeatedly threatened to relieve Franks, Yeosock, et al.") Orders to force the issue came down from General Colin Powell himself, the chairman of the Joint Chiefs of Staff. By the time it passed to Colonel Tony Moreno, the senior American officer on the spot, the instruction was blunt: Tell the opposing Iraqi commander "that if he doesn't leave by 1600 you're going to kill him. You're going to kill all his forces and attack right through him." Moreno arranged his troops as menacingly as possible and delivered the message. Deciding that discretion was the better part of valor, these Iraqis too agreed to withdraw, and by early evening the entire area was securely occupied.

Sunday, March 3

Another group of Apaches flew toward the crossroads in the desert, this time accompanying three larger Black Hawks carrying Schwarzkopf and his retinue to the cease-fire meeting. They landed at the unprepossessing airstrip, a slab of asphalt on which coalition forces had hastily set up some meeting tents ringed by dozens of American armored vehicles, guns pointing inward. A delegation of Iraqi generals came to the meeting overland, having been transferred into American Humvees a few miles away. The event was orchestrated to convey the magnitude of the coalition's overwhelming victory, but at the same time had some overtones of chivalry. "I don't want them embarrassed, I don't want them humiliated," Schwarzkopf was overheard saying to an aide about the Iraqis, and when the visitors objected to being searched for weapons, he allowed himself to be patted down first as an example.

At a table inside the tent, the American commander was joined by his Saudi colleague, General Khaled bin Sultan, as triumphant but exhausted coalition commanders sat watching nearby. The two-hour meeting dealt mostly with technical details about the separation of forces and handling of prisoners, and the Iraqis generally agreed to the terms proposed—particularly when they realized, apparently for the first time, just how devastating their defeat had actually been. At one point, they asked for a partial exception to the ban on air travel inside Iraq so that helicopters could be flown. Considering how difficult ground travel around the country had become, and feeling grateful for the Iraqis' agreeable attitude at the meeting, Schwarzkopf said yes. Afterward, he and Khaled walked the Iraqis to their vehicles and shook hands goodbye. Then he spoke to a crowd of reporters: "I would say very candidly that the Iraqis came to discuss and to cooperate with a positive attitude, [and] that we are well on our way to a lasting peace."

Sunday, March 3–Thursday, March 7

The cease-fire meeting had originally been scheduled for Saturday, but was pushed back a day because the Iraqis had trouble getting to the venue. "I don't think they were worried too much about their safety," explained a coalition military spokesman, "just the chaos and upheaval that's going on." In fact, it came out later, the Iraqi delegation was fired on by insurgents en route to the meeting place and had to flank each of its staff cars with Republican Guard tanks in order to get there intact.

The unrest had started on Friday, as disaffected Iraqi soldiers retreating from Kuwait joined oppressed local Shiites in revolt. Two weeks earlier, President George H. W. Bush had called for the Iraqi army and people to overthrow Saddam. In their own ways, for their own reasons, many of Saddam's subjects were now trying to accomplish just that. While Schwarzkopf met with the Iraqi generals, the rebels were moving to seize control of not only Basra but also Najaf, Nasariya, and other cities across the south, executing regime loyalists as they went.

Saddam's forces, however, soon fought back strongly, deploying regrouped Republican Guard units that had escaped destruction during the war as well as the helicopter gunships whose use Schwarzkopf had permitted. On Tuesday, loyalist and rebel tanks were shooting it out face-to-face in Basra. By Wednesday, the rebels were being routed and refugees started streaming south toward the American forces still holding the area around the crossroads. On Thursday, bedraggled survivors told reporters there about mass public executions of hundreds of people by Saddam's revitalized troops: "Their hands were tied, then they tied them to tanks and shot them," one said. "The bodies are still there, bound by the wrists." "We want the allied forces to be here," he continued. "If they pull out, the government will come back and punish the protesters."

But it was not to be. As Secretary of Defense Dick Cheney said on Wednesday, the Bush administration would be pleased "if Iraq had a new government," but there were worse outcomes than Saddam's continued rule—such as the breakup of the country—and so the Americans had decided to sit out the turmoil on the sidelines. "I think it would be very difficult for us to hold the coalition together for any particular course of action dealing with internal Iraqi politics," Cheney commented, "and I don't think, at this point, our writ extends to trying to move inside Iraq." So while they put out the oil well fires Saddam had lit in Kuwait, the Americans just watched as Iraq itself burned.

The Iraqi town by the crossroads was called Safwan. Otherwise unknown to history, within the span of a single week in late winter 1991 the area witnessed a lot of it. The dispute over possession of the airstrip was embarrassing, but it had little strategic significance. Nor, ultimately, did the cease-fire meeting itself (since any of the arrangements decided upon there, including the one related to the helicopters, could have been adjusted later on). But the confusion surrounding the final stages of the fighting and the coalition's postwar role in the region was both important and revealing—a display in microcosm of Washington's ambivalence about what it was fighting for and how it could be achieved.

That such a carefully planned and lopsided victory could have had such an untidy and unsatisfying end has puzzled observers ever since. Yet such an outcome was probably in the cards all along. Six days after Iraq's invasion of Kuwait in August 1990, Bush gave a speech setting out his response. Announcing the dispatch of American troops to Saudi Arabia, he described the "four simple principles" guiding U.S. policy during the crisis: "First, we seek the immediate, unconditional, and complete withdrawal of all Iraqi forces from Kuwait. Second, Kuwait's legitimate government must be restored. . . . Third, my administration . . . is committed to the security and stability of the Gulf. And fourth, I am determined to protect the lives of American citizens abroad."[2] The second and fourth principles played little role in later events, but the first and third were crucial. The crisp clarity of "immediate, unconditional, and complete withdrawal" from Kuwait established the central U.S. demand on Iraq from which the president would never back down. But the vagueness of just what it meant to provide for "the security and stability of the Gulf" would bedevil not only Bush, but his successors for decades to come.

This tension between precision and ambiguity—between what might be called the Kuwait problem and the Iraq problem—can be followed like a bright thread all the way through the crisis.[3] Because of it, the ending of the Gulf War was always destined to be problematic, less a clean break than a shift from one difficult situation to another. By failing to plan carefully for managing the transition from war to peace, however, the Bush administration allowed events to spin even further out of control than they had to, and in the process tarnished its own impressive handling of the crisis.

In retrospect, the Gulf War is best understood as an early episode in a new chapter of U.S. global hegemony, one devoted to securing and stabilizing the greater Middle East. In 1980, President Jimmy Carter had declared, "An attempt by any outside force to gain control of the Persian Gulf region will be regarded as an assault on the vital interests of the United States of America, and such an assault will be repelled by any means necessary, including military force." Carter's national security adviser, Zbigniew Brzezinski, saw the new commitment as a logical extension of previous ones. "Until the 1970s," he wrote in his memoirs,

> U.S. foreign policy was anchored on the principle of interdependence with Western Europe, and then later with the Far East. The Middle East was viewed as a semi-neutral zone sealed off from Soviet power by a protective belt composed of Turkey, Iran, and Pakistan, with a neutral Afghanistan providing a buffer. . . . However, the collapse of Iran and the Soviet move into Afghanistan . . . created an urgent security problem for the region as a whole, prompting by 1980 formal U.S. recognition of the security interdependence of three, instead of two, zones of central strategic importance to the United States: Western Europe, the Far East, and the Middle East.[4]

When they issued their marker, Carter and Brzezinski had the Soviets in mind. President Ronald Reagan's administration followed a similar logic in using various measures to counter a different attempt at regional hegemony, this time from Iran. By the Bush years, the U.S. commitment to preventing a hostile power's domination of the Gulf had become policy orthodoxy. But with the Soviet Union expiring and Iran checked, it lay dormant—a check waiting to be cashed. Then Saddam's invasion of Kuwait did for the Carter Doctrine what Kim II Sung's invasion of South Korea had done for the Truman Doctrine and NSC-68: it led Washington to back up its words with deeds, militarized containment, and ushered in an open-ended and multigenerational American regional presence.

During the crisis, Bush administration officials grasped some of this larger context, which is why they were able to react so swiftly and surely when Saddam made his unexpected move. The choices they made from early August on were generally smart and sensible—far more so, in the aggregate, than those suggested by critics on both left and right. But Bush and his advisers had so much trouble getting themselves, their allies, and the American public to accept the need for the war itself that they had little stomach for thinking about the true scale of the burdens Washington would be called upon to shoulder afterward. Hoping to strike hard and fast and get home quickly, the president and his advisers defined their military objectives narrowly, never forcing themselves to decide in advance just how important it was for Saddam himself to exit the scene. This proved adequate to deal with the Kuwait problem, but it left the Iraq one up in the air—as the administration belatedly recognized in the weeks after the coalition's guns went silent. Just when Bush thought he was out, therefore, Iraq pulled him back in—but grudgingly and hesitantly, having already lost his best opportunity to shape the postwar situation to his liking.

Bush "promised the American people that Desert Storm would not become a Persian Gulf Vietnam," Powell would write later, "and he kept his promise."[5] True. But in his determination to avoid getting trapped in one sort of quagmire, he ended up with another—and in a bitter irony of history, he eventually saw the Vietnam nightmare visit his son, who would decide to take the United States into another war a decade later in a bungled attempt to solve the Iraq problem once and for all.

CRISIS AND RESPONSE

During the early hours of Thursday, August 2, 1990, Iraqi troops began pouring across the border into Kuwait. Tactical surprise combined with the great disparity in strength between the two sides made the invasion a walkover, and by Thursday evening the Iraqis had taken complete control of the country.[6]

The Iraqi move came as a shock to almost everybody. Saddam was generally regarded as a brute, but a pragmatic one.[7] Emerging from the Iran-Iraq War with little to show for it but massive debts, he had ratcheted up pressure on Kuwait, Saudi Arabia, and the other rich monarchies in the region, demanding that they forgive his war debts, raise oil prices, and otherwise help Iraq out of its plight. As the spring and summer of 1990 wore on, Saddam acted more and more truculently, going so far as to mass powerful forces near the Kuwaiti border in July. But people thought he was engaging in coercive diplomacy, a classic shakedown effort designed to extract concessions from his neighbors. Eventually, it was expected, his targets would give in and pay him off, and he would accept. At most, he would attempt a minor land grab, seizing some disputed offshore islands or the Kuwaiti portion of a shared oil field.

In Washington, the Bush administration was watching the situation with one eye. The United States had tilted toward Iraq in its war with Iran and then tried to entice Baghdad into better relations afterward. Saddam was seen as a ruler one could deal with. Sure, he invaded other countries, gassed thousands of his own citizens, and ran a totalitarian police state. But this was the Middle East, and one could not be picky. He kept the oil flowing, balanced Iran, bought American arms and grain, and was not a religious fanatic. Compared to other Sunni strongmen throughout the region, he did not seem exceptional. "We had no illusions about the character of this man at all," National Security Adviser Brent Scowcroft would say later, "but we did not see him necessarily as having serious unrequited aggressive aims."[8]

As Saddam's provocations intensified, American policymakers could tell their attempts at engagement were not working. Still, given what was going on elsewhere in the world—the end of the Cold War, the collapse of communism, the aftermath of the Tiananmen Square massacre, the first Palestinian intifada, etc.—crafting a new Iraq policy was hardly at the top of the administration's foreign policy to-do list. So in July, the State Department cabled a boilerplate position on the crisis to American diplomats in the region: "Disputes should be settled by peaceful means, not intimidation and threats of use of force. . . . The United States takes no position on the substance of bilateral issues concerning Iraq and Kuwait. . . . We remain committed to ensure the free flow of oil from the Gulf and to support the sovereignty and integrity of the Gulf states."[9] On July 25, U.S. ambassador April Glaspie was summoned to a snap meeting with Saddam, during which she expressed these positions. She came out of the session thinking that the crisis was likely to subside rather than escalate, reported her take to Washington, and did not change her plans to go on vacation a few days later.[10]

Glaspie's view was not an outlier; it tallied with what Bush and his senior advisers were hearing from everybody else, both in the region and outside it. So when Saddam's troops actually crossed the border and then swallowed up all of Kuwait, the near-universal reaction was shock—quickly followed by worry about what would come next.

Because of the time difference, news of the invasion reached Washington on Wednesday evening, and officials there immediately sprung into action. Helped by the brazenness of the attack, within hours they had mobilized a broad international coalition to counter it. At 4:30 A.M. Thursday, Scowcroft woke Bush to sign executive orders freezing Iraqi and Kuwaiti assets, denying Saddam one of the chief fruits of victory.[11] At 6 A.M., the U.N. Security Council voted 14–0 to pass a resolution condemning the invasion and demanding "that Iraq withdraw immediately and unconditionally all its forces."[12]

To coordinate this response, Scowcroft had chaired a midnight meeting attended by the "deputies," the seconds-in-command of the administration's major national security organizations. In the morning, the administration's "principals," the heads of those organizations, gathered with Bush to assess the situation, but their meeting was rambling and unfocused. Afterward, the president flew to Aspen, Colorado, where he was scheduled to deliver a talk on post–Cold War defense policy. During the flight, Bush conferred with other heads of state; in Colorado, he discussed the crisis with British prime minister Margaret Thatcher; and late that night, he flew back to Washington.

The principals met again with Bush first thing Friday morning.[13] Scowcroft and his staff had been upset with the previous meeting's drift and lack of urgency. Discussing matters on the plane to Aspen, the national security adviser realized that the president agreed, and "was prepared to use force to evict Saddam from Kuwait if it became necessary." So the two of them decided to start off the next meeting by getting right to the point. Bush himself set the stage:

> [Saudi Arabia's] King Fahd, [Jordan's] King Hussein, [Egyptian president Hosni] Mubarak, and [Yemeni president Ali Abdullah] Saleh and I talked at length. They expressed great concern. . . . [But] their reaction was hand-wringing. . . . Diplomatic efforts are underway to get Saddam to back off. He is ruthless and powerful. Others' efforts might not succeed to get his troops out, and Kuwait's ruler back in. We need to weigh the implications of taking this on directly. The status quo is intolerable.

Then, after a CIA update on the situation, Scowcroft laid down a marker:

> I appreciate the [intelligence] community's opinion and remarks. I detected a note in the end that we may have to acquiesce to an accommo-

> dation of the situation. My personal judgment is that the stakes in this for the United States are such that to accommodate Iraq should not be a policy option. There is too much at stake. . . . It seems while the alternatives are not attractive, we have to look at the possibility that we can't tolerate him succeeding.

Deputy Secretary of State Lawrence Eagleburger and Cheney weighed in on along the same lines, and after some talk of diplomatic and economic sanctions, the discussion turned to military issues. Powell described the options available to the administration even as he tried to steer talk in a different direction:

> Looking at force packages for a contingency, there are two: the first, to deter further Iraqi action with Saudi Arabia, would require U.S. forces on the ground. This is the most prudent option. . . . Saddam looks south and sees a U.S. presence. . . . The second would be to deploy U.S. forces against Iraqi forces in Kuwait to defend Saudi Arabia, or possibly go against Iraq. Looking at this option, this is harder than Panama and Libya. This would be the NFL, not a scrimmage. It would mean a major confrontation. Most U.S. forces would have to be committed to sustain, not for just one or two days. He is a professional and a megalomaniac. But the ratio is weighted in his favor. They also are experienced from eight years of war.

The meeting ended without major decisions, but the thinking of the major players—and the division among them—was already clear.[14]

Everybody now recognized that the key to the crisis was Saudi Arabia, both as the next possible target and the necessary staging area for any action to reverse the invasion. So after the meeting, Scowcroft discussed the situation with Prince Bandar bin Sultan, the Saudi ambassador. Bandar agreed that his country was threatened, and he and everybody else knew that Riyadh was far too weak militarily to defend itself against Iraq. And yet he was still not wild about the idea of accepting American forces for protection. When pressed on this apparent contradiction, he confessed that American military promises didn't always mean much. Just over a decade earlier, during the Iranian revolution, the United States had sent over a squadron of F-15s to signal its commitment to the defense of Saudi Arabia—but to avoid any controversy, while the planes were en route the Carter administration had announced they were unarmed, humiliating everybody involved. Then, in Lebanon a few years later, the United States had pulled its troops out after the bombing of the Marine barracks. Why, Bandar asked, should the Saudis take the Americans seriously this time?

Scowcroft's reply was, essentially, "because this time we mean it." He sent Bandar over to the Pentagon to get briefed by Cheney and Powell about just what sort of force the administration was prepared to send over—at that point, an initial deployment of about one hundred thousand troops. Impressed, Bandar agreed that it made sense for a high-level American delegation to consult with his uncle, King Fahd, and get formal approval for such a mission.

The next day, Saturday, August 4, senior administration officials met at Camp David to get a fuller briefing on military options. Schwarzkopf had flown up from Central Command headquarters in Tampa, Florida, a couple of days earlier and had attended the meeting on Thursday. Now he was told to present plans for action.

The gruff, burly general had had the forethought to start planning for an Iraq-related contingency months earlier, and as the invasion was playing out, his staff was actually conducting a war game based on a similar scenario.[15] Racing to update and transform the game plans into plausible military options, he and his air force commander, Chuck Horner, showed the fruits of their labors to the president and his senior advisers. They sketched out a deployment guaranteed to defend Saudi Arabia successfully, which they said would take three months to complete. Then Schwarzkopf hazarded a guess at the requirements necessary to go on offense and "kick the Iraqis out of Kuwait"—a force more than twice as large, needing perhaps eight to ten months to deploy.[16]

Nobody knew what Saddam was going to do next, but if he wanted to he could swallow up Saudi Arabia's major oil fields almost as easily as he had Kuwait, so preventing that was the first order of business. After a series of calls between American and Saudi officials Saturday afternoon, it was agreed that a high-level delegation led by Cheney would fly over for consultations on how to manage a vast U.S. military deployment to the region—something unprecedented and domestically problematic for both sides, but particularly the Saudis.[17]

Coming back to the White House for another meeting Sunday afternoon, Bush was met on the helipad by Richard Haass, the senior Middle East specialist on the NSC staff. Scanning updates about recent developments in the crisis—including continued waffling by several Arab countries as to what should be done—the president, annoyed, told reporters on the record what he had already been thinking for days: "This will not stand, this aggression against Kuwait."[18]

On Monday morning, Cheney reported from Riyadh that the Saudis had formally requested American help, and the deployment began that afternoon. That same day, the Security Council voted 13-0 to maintain comprehensive economic sanctions against Iraq until it withdrew. It was on Wednesday, with American planes already touching down in Saudi Arabia, that Bush took to the airwaves to tell the world about the multifaceted American policy that Saddam's actions had set in motion.

DESERT SHIELD

Within a week of the Iraqi invasion, the script for future events had already been written: the United States would lead a broad international coalition to push Saddam back, using all the policy tools at its disposal. As if following Chekhov's famous dictum, the gun appearing in the first act would ultimately be fired in the last one. To policymakers working in real time, however, things did not appear this clear. Holding the diplomatic coalition together, making the economic sanctions bite, preparing and using military force—none of these was as certain or as easy as it appeared in hindsight.

The first problem emerged soon, over the question of sanctions enforcement. The Security Council had banned most economic transactions with Iraq on August 6 but left open the issue of how the ban would be enforced. The matter was brought to a head two weeks later when a pair of tankers loaded with Iraqi oil brushed off warning shots from American warships in the Gulf and continued heading toward the Yemeni port of Aden. One camp of Western policymakers, led by Scowcroft and Thatcher, argued for military action to stop the tankers directly, relying for authority on Article 51 of the U.N. Charter (which affirms members' "inherent right of individual or collective self-defence"). Another camp, led by Secretary of State James Baker, argued against such a move because it would displease Moscow.

Soviet participation in the anti-Saddam coalition was always a delicate issue. Historically, the Soviet Union had been one of Iraq's major patrons, and strong constituencies inside the Soviet diplomatic and national security bureaucracies were aghast at the idea of siding with the

United States against their former client. With the collapse of the Soviet empire in Eastern Europe and the general discrediting of communism, moreover, sensitivities in Moscow were raw. The Bush administration had been deeply engaged in managing these sensitivities and seeing to it that the Cold War ended as smoothly as possible, and some of its senior officials approached the Iraq crisis through this prism.[19]

When the invasion took place, Baker happened to be traveling in Siberia with his Soviet counterpart, Eduard Shevardnadze, and the two had quickly collaborated on a joint statement of condemnation. The Soviets also voted in favor of all the early anti-Saddam resolutions in the Security Council. But Baker knew that Shevardnadze's liberal views were unrepresentative of the foreign ministry in general, and that Soviet president Mikhail Gorbachev, himself a reformer, was getting plenty of counsel opposing cooperation with American moves. So when the tanker issue emerged, Baker was keen to avoid responding in a way Gorbachev could not endorse.

With Baker concerned not to lose Soviet backing and the hard-liners concerned not to send signals of weakness and irresolution, the issue went to Bush for resolution, and he decided to compromise. Baker was authorized to tell the Soviets they had three days to try to fix the problem, after which the United States and Britain would act on their own. The gambit worked: after Saddam refused to budge, Gorbachev agreed to join the Americans, and the Soviet Union voted in favor of a new resolution specifically authorizing military enforcement of sanctions in the future.[20]

A few weeks later, as American forces continued to flow into the region, fears of an Iraqi attack on Saudi Arabia subsided and the Bush administration's attention increasingly turned north. Bush and his advisers had hoped that concerted diplomatic and economic pressure would convince Saddam to pull back, but the Iraqi leader did the reverse, digging in more deeply. On August 8, he formally absorbed Kuwait into Iraq (although the move was not recognized by others), and over succeeding weeks he mounted a brutal campaign to eradicate that country's separate identity and loot its resources. As summer turned to fall, therefore, the question for Washington was what to do next.

Powell and other moderates, reluctant to start down a path toward war, argued for giving sanctions plenty of time to work. Scowcroft and other hard-liners, concerned that coalition unity was a wasting asset, argued for escalating the pressure on Iraq. This time Bush, mindful of the destruction being wreaked on Kuwait, sided with Scowcroft.[21]

In mid-August, Powell had told Bush that there could be three possible phases of the deployment of U.S. forces to the Gulf, corresponding to three possible missions. By early September, enough troops and materiel would have arrived to have a good chance of deterring an attack on Saudi Arabia, and by early December, enough would have arrived to defend against such an attack successfully. Going on the offensive, however—launching a war against Iraq—would require even more forces, Powell noted, which would need to start flowing into the deployment pipeline during October.

In late September, Powell grew concerned that momentum was steadily—and unnecessarily—building toward that third mission, so he raised the issue with Bush directly, but got nowhere. Toward the end of the month, Schwarzkopf was ordered to send a team to Washington to brief senior officials on his plans for an offensive attack, using the forces agreed on for the first two phases of the deployment. The air war component of the plan was received favorably, but the ground component was not. It called for a straightforward attack through massed Iraqi defenses, and was mocked as being unimaginative and likely to yield high casualties. Coming to his commander's defense, Powell argued that it was the best that could be done with the forces then available—and that airpower alone couldn't do the job. The real choice, in other words, was either to stay on the defensive and let sanctions work or send more forces. How many more, he was asked? Twice as many as were already planned, he replied—another full army corps, brought down from Europe. Although some at the White House rolled their eyes, by the end of October the president made his call: give Powell and Schwarzkopf what they were asking for and tell them to come up with an offensive plan everybody liked.

Having decided to push Saddam out of Kuwait if necessary, the administration now turned toward lining up support for this course both abroad and at home. American officials saw the international arena as more important and more permissive than the domestic one, so they directed their attention there first. As with the decision over sanctions enforcement, Baker wanted to go back to the Security Council for a new resolution, while Cheney, Scowcroft, and others saw no need for it (and hence no reason to risk the embarrassment of trying and failing).

Once again, Bush sided with Baker, and by the end of November, the administration got what it wanted: Resolution 678, authorizing the use of "all necessary means" to eject Iraq from Kuwait if a complete withdrawal had not occurred by January 15, 1991.

Support on the home front was more difficult to achieve, as Congress was in the hands of Bush's political opponents and the public at large was not sold on the need for war. Once again taking Baker's counsel, Bush sought to convince Americans that he saw war as a last resort by offering Saddam a meeting prior to any ultimate decision. The session was ultimately held between Baker and Iraqi foreign minister Tariq Aziz in Geneva on January 9; its failure to produce a settlement, together with the authorization of the Security Council, allowed Bush to peel off just enough Democrats in the Senate to win congressional authorization of the war on January 12.

DESERT STORM

Had Saddam withdrawn completely and unconditionally from Kuwait anytime between August 2 and January 15, there would have been no war. Policymakers in Washington and elsewhere would have been happy to pocket the Iraqi pullback as a successful example of coercive diplomacy and avoid the costs and risks of a full-scale military confrontation.[22] As Saddam refused to budge, however, the Bush administration proceeded with its plans to force him out, launching air strikes against Iraqi positions soon after the U.N.'s deadline had passed.

From the beginning of military planning during the first week in August, commanders had respected the differences among the military services while trying to coordinate their efforts to achieve a common purpose. In the same way that the Bush administration wove together the diplomatic, economic, and military strands of its policies, so it would weave together attacks from the air, ground, and water. The debate over what airpower could be expected to achieve, in fact, resembled nothing so much as the debate over what sanctions could be expected to achieve. Advocates saw each as a potential silver bullet that could work wonders, if only used properly and for an appropriate length of time. Detractors saw each as foreplay, activities whose chief purpose was to prepare the ground for other, more decisive measures. In both cases, senior policymakers decided to split the difference between the two perspectives, settling on a phased approach that gave each tool a chance to work alone but continued up a ladder of escalation if it did not.

The initial air war plan had been developed during the first week of the crisis by a visionary officer named John Warden, who believed that modern technology had finally given airpower the ability to live up to the hopes of its earliest and most enthusiastic advocates. Warden argued that the proper objective of an air campaign was to compel the enemy's surrender by striking directly at his "centers of gravity"—the props of his power. Rather than attack Iraqi forces in Kuwait, accordingly, Warden wanted first to go after the regime's leadership and communications, its military-industrial capacity, its transportation networks, and its society—in that order of priority. For Warden and those who thought like him, taking the fight directly to Baghdad appeared a swifter and more efficient way of securing withdrawal from Kuwait than destroying the occupying army there.

Briefed on Warden's plan on August 20, Horner found some things in it that he liked, but thought it was incomplete. He sent Warden himself packing, kept some of his staffers, and used the plan as a first draft to be edited and expanded in subsequent months. After devoting particular attention to achieving air superiority quickly, the final plan struck at all kinds of targets simultaneously and repeatedly.

In practice, the air campaign went both better and worse than its planners expected. On the one hand, the technical and logistical feats involved in massing and delivering so much firepower so precisely were nothing short of extraordinary, and were accomplished with far fewer losses than anybody had dared predict. On the other hand, while it exacted a fearsome toll on Iraqi forces and infrastructure, the air war neither disabled the Iraqi regime nor produced a withdrawal from Kuwait. It also failed to anticipate the difficulty of suppressing a key Iraqi countermeasure, the launching of Scud missiles at Israel in an attempt to "heighten the contradictions" within the coalition. (When senior policymakers in Washington recognized this danger, they moved swiftly to counter it, ordering Schwarzkopf to dramatically increase Scud-hunting efforts and using skillful, aggressive diplomacy to keep the Israelis on the sidelines.)[23]

After a month of air strikes, Bush and his advisers found themselves in the same position that they had been in the previous October with sanctions, as some voices pushed for continuing the air war alone and others pushed to launch a ground attack. Now as then, moreover, a

Soviet peace initiative threatened to allow Saddam a face-saving escape from his cul-de-sac. Driven once again by a desire to achieve his prime objective before the coalition fell apart, the president declared that he would start the ground war if Saddam did not begin a complete and unconditional withdrawal by February 24. Like the note that Baker had handed to Aziz in Geneva a month and a half earlier, this ultimatum was a modern version of the Potsdam Declaration: "Back down or we will soon hit you very, very hard." And when Saddam, like the Japanese, did not comply in time, the boom was lowered as promised.[24]

Using the extra forces they had been granted, Schwarzkopf and his planners had eventually come up with a bold and imaginative plan for the ground campaign. As the Iraqis focused on apparent preparations for a major thrust up the center of their defenses and an amphibious landing near Kuwait City, the coalition was actually readying two different blows, a jab up the coast in the east and a massive left hook that would swing around Kuwait in the west, hitting Iraqi forces in the flank and back.[25] The deception worked beautifully, as did both of the actual blows. In fact, the jab worked too beautifully, and instead of "fixing" the Iraqi forces in place so that they could be struck from the side, it shot right through enemy positions and led to an Iraqi retreat north. By the time the elements of the left hook started to smash into their assigned targets, therefore, many Iraqi units were already on the run.

Receiving reports of the increasingly one-sided victory, the principals met with the president at the White House on February 27. With Iraqi forces defeated and Kuwait liberated, Powell argued, the coalition's objectives had been achieved, and further attacks on a prostrate enemy would tarnish the military's reputation and lead to a backlash. He suggested ending the war the next day. Bush raised the possibility of ending it that night. No one disagreed, and so the order went out to stop fighting at midnight—8 A.M. the following morning in the Gulf.

RESTORING KUWAIT

The core American demand during the crisis was that Iraq withdraw from Kuwait—quickly, completely, and unconditionally. Washington's decision to pursue this goal relentlessly drove events from start to finish. Why did it care so much?

Led by a man whose communication skills were so poor he once read out the stage directions on the cue card in front of him, the Bush administration offered many different rationales for its actions during the crisis, giving rise to some confusion. In truth, however, to any realist, the administration's thinking was straightforward, even obvious. As Cheney put it at the critical meeting on August 3, "[Saddam] has clearly done what he has to do to dominate OPEC, the Gulf, and the Arab world. He is 40 kilometers from Saudi Arabia, and its oil production is only a couple of hundred kilometers away. If he doesn't take it physically, with his new wealth he will still have an impact and will be able to acquire new weapons, including nuclear weapons. The problem will get worse, not better."

Bush's critics sometimes cracked that if Kuwait had produced bananas rather than oil, the United States would not have rushed to its defense. That was undoubtedly true, but it hardly invalidated the administration's concerns, which reflected a decade-old declared U.S. policy. Policymakers understood that the global capitalist economic system the United States had nurtured and presided over for half a century floated on a sea of cheap oil, and that if that sea were drained, the global economy would collapse. At the time, Iraq possessed over a tenth of the world's proven oil reserves. Kuwait possessed another tenth, and Saudi Arabia almost two more tenths. Saudi Arabia was not only the world's largest oil producer and held the world's largest reserves, but also had a majority of the world's excess production capacity, which it used to stabilize and control oil prices. As Bush and his advisers were deciding what to do that first week in August, in other words, Saddam already controlled one-fifth and was poised to control two-fifths of the world's oil. Even if he stopped at the Kuwaiti border, Saudi Arabia would be essentially "Finlandized," becoming an Iraqi protectorate in all but name. Allowing Saddam's move to stand unchecked would have given him a chokehold on the entire world.

Not only was Saddam's possession of such power inherently problematic, but so was the manner in which he had acquired it—both in its implications for future Iraqi behavior and in the example it would set for others. At the same August 3 meeting, Eagleburger had sketched the oil issue's broader regional and even global context:

> This is the first test of the post [cold] war system. As the bipolar context is relaxed, it permits this, giving people more flexibility because they are not worried about the involvement of the superpowers. . . . Saddam Hussein now has greater flexibility. . . . [I]f he succeeds, others may try

> the same thing. It would be a bad lesson. On the oil issue, he would dominate OPEC over time. As to his intentions, Saudi Arabia looks like the next target. Over time, he would control OPEC and oil prices. If he succeeds, then he would target Israel.

To the president and many of his senior advisers, the situation seemed clear: in order to protect a variety of critical U.S. national interests, Saddam's actions had to be countered and he had to emerge from the crisis with no clear benefit from having caused it. The wonder is not that the United States chose to use its power to reverse the Iraqi invasion, but that the decision to do so was at all controversial.

SECURING THE GULF

Getting Iraq out of Kuwait may have been the primary American war aim, but it was not the only one. Reversing the invasion was difficult, costly, and risky—not the sort of thing anyone wanted to have to do on a regular basis. So in addition to forcing Iraq to disgorge Kuwait, the Bush administration sought ways to ensure the smaller country would not be swallowed again down the road.

In theory, there were three possible routes to this goal: changing Iraq's desires, so that it would not *want* to attack again; changing Iraq's behavior, so that it would not *choose* to; and changing Iraq's capabilities, so that it would not *be able* to. Infused with a realist approach to foreign policy, the Bush team thought the first was impossible and the second unreliable, so they concentrated on the third.

The administration's thinking on these issues was captured well in a December cable sent to Baker by Charles Freeman, the U.S. ambassador to Saudi Arabia. "Possible objectives to be pursued in military action against Iraqi forces," Freeman noted, "may be divided into two categories:"

> A. Those stated by both the United Nations Security Council and Arab League which have been explicitly endorsed by all governments contributing forces to the coalition; and
>
> B. Those broadly agreed within the U.S. Government and implicitly (but not explicitly) endorsed by most (but not all) governments contributing forces to the coalition.

The first category included removing Iraqi forces from Kuwaiti territory, restoring Kuwaiti sovereignty, and reinstalling the pre-occupation government of Kuwait. (By this point, Iraq had already released its Western hostages.) The second category went further:

1. Eliminate or substantially reduce Iraqi weapons of mass destruction, including their delivery systems and Iraq's capacity to make more of them.
2. Establish stability and security in the Upper Gulf based on:

   A. Destruction of Iraq's capacity to make offensive war but not its capacity to defend itself;
   B. A restored balance of power between Iran, Syria, and a rehabilitated Iraq;
   C. Strengthened U.S. economic, political, and military cooperation with Saudi Arabia and other members of the GCC [Gulf Cooperation Council];
   D. Arrangements to prevent the future concentration of Iraqi forces on the Iraq-Kuwait border.

These latter objectives, Freeman continued, "which focus on reducing Iraq rather than on liberating Kuwait—lie . . . at the heart of our fundamental long-term interest in restored security and stability in the Gulf . . . [and] must be at the center of our war planning vis-à-vis Iraq."[26]

Other administration officials thought along similar lines, which is why the document officially authorizing the war—National Security Directive 54, issued on January 15—set out the conflict's military objectives as follows:

a. Defend Saudi Arabia and other GCC states against attack;
b. Preclude Iraqi launch of ballistic missiles against neighboring states and friendly forces;
c. Destroy Iraq's chemical, biological, and nuclear capabilities;
d. Destroy Iraq's command, control, and communications capabilities;
e. Eliminate the Republican Guards as an effective fighting force; and
f. Conduct operations designed to drive Iraq's forces from Kuwait, break the will of Iraqi forces, discourage Iraqi use of chemical, bi-

> ological, or nuclear weapons, encourage defection of Iraqi forces, and weaken Iraqi popular support for the current government.[27]

The Bush administration did not seek just to beat up Iraqi forces; it wanted to do so in a way that would send an unmistakable and humiliating message. The idea was to supplement the reduction of Iraqi capabilities with a crushing psychological burden of defeat. Aggression had to be punished and had to be seen to be punished, so that nobody could be left in any doubt about what had just happened.

These goals, it should be stressed, had little to do with internal Iraqi politics. Where followers of liberal theories of international relations might have located the root cause of the problem in the nature of the Iraqi regime or leader, and thus focused remedies on changing that regime or leader, Bush administration officials focused instead on manipulating the material incentives that would apply to any future Iraqi government. As a paper on "Post Crisis Gulf Security Structures" prepared for the deputies committee put it, "Regardless of Saddam Hussein's motivations, the Iraqi invasion of Kuwait was possible because of a collapse of the regional balance of power. . . . Therefore, a key [postwar U.S.] security objective is to help reestablish a balance so that future aggression directed against the GCC states by either Iraq or Iran will be deterred."[28] If Iraq's offensive capabilities were reduced and its attempt to grab Kuwait were shown to be a costly failure, the administration reasoned, then whoever was in power in Baghdad would think long and hard before causing trouble again.

It would be satisfying if Saddam himself left the picture, officials felt, but that was not a necessary precondition for the maintenance of regional order over the longer term—which would ultimately be guaranteed by realist measures such as balanced power, opposing coalitions, and the like. As Baker put it publicly on February 24, in response to a question about the administration's approach to the postwar era:

> The restoration of peace and stability in the gulf would be a heck of a lot easier if [Saddam] and his, and that leadership were not in power in Iraq. [But] [w]e don't know yet . . . exactly how the war is going to terminate. If they remain in power, there will be some things that we will want to continue to insist upon, as we've said before, such as an international arms embargo, perhaps, against the rebuilding of this very dispro-

> portionate military power and against trying to recreate the weapons of mass destruction that we have succeeded in degrading and destroying.[29]

Variations of this formula were common. Administration officials said they "would not shed any tears" if Saddam fell, "would not be upset" if he did, even "hoped" he would be deposed. But as Baker put it, they were "careful not to embrace it as a war aim or political aim."[30]

This linguistic delicacy related partly to the administration's interpretation of its legal obligations, which permitted strikes at military targets but prohibited the assassination of foreign leaders. As Baker described it later,

> We were very careful to observe the executive order which prevents action leading to the assassination of foreign leaders. On the other hand, I think the legal experts had told the military that it would be perfectly legal and within our laws and regulations, in the context of war, to kill anyone involved in the command and control establishment of Iraq. And since he was the commander in chief of the Iraq armed forces, if he were killed in combat that would not violate the executive order.[31]

Saddam thus became He-Who-Must-Not-Be-Named. The war plan targeted him, but everybody was loath to admit that publicly. When Warden's team first articulated the air campaign's objectives, for example, under "Leadership" they scribbled, "Saddam." Two days later, they changed that to "isolate and incapacitate Hussein's regime."[32]

The reasons for the administration's ambiguous talking points regarding Saddam went deeper, however, reflecting a real ambivalence about how much his fate actually mattered and an aversion to doing what might be necessary to affect it. The United States, it must be remembered, had dealt directly with Saddam until quite recently, and was allied with a variety of other unsavory regimes in the region—including the repressive traditional monarchy in Kuwait on behalf of which it was going to war. The only thing that had changed back in August was the administration's sense of Saddam's pliability. He had revealed himself to be not the pragmatist previously believed, but a risk-acceptant megalomaniac with ambitions beyond his station. Saddam's ouster would be desirable, accordingly—not least because it would send a strong signal to other potential troublemakers—but a number of officials did not see it as a big deal, figuring that even if he stayed in power he would have learned his lesson and be more docile in the future, and figuring that any likely replacement would be cut from similar cloth. As a National Intelligence Estimate put it,

> Saddam Husayn is a product of Iraqi political culture, not an aberration. In the short term, at least, it is likely that any successor to Saddam will share his perspective on the internal and external threats to Iraqi integrity and will have grown up in a culture in which suspicion—of both one's known enemies and apparent friends—is routine and perhaps even required and in which violence is an accepted political tool. Changing the nature of Iraqi politics is a long-term process not likely to be achieved by the fall of Saddam Husayn.[33]

Accepting that Saddam's fate did matter, moreover, had unsettling implications. The administration pondered the question of making Saddam's ouster a war aim, but the more it did so, the leerier it got. As Scowcroft put it,

> The problem was, apart from targeting him personally (itself extremely difficult with air strikes, and assassination was not an option), we did not know how this might be achieved. We could not make it a formal goal of the coalition, since it was well beyond the bounds of the UN resolutions guiding us. It might also split the coalition. If the United States made it an objective unilaterally, and declared it as such, we would be in a difficult bind politically and operationally. We would be committing ourselves—alone—to removing one regime and installing another, and, if the Iraqis themselves did not take matters into their own hands, we would be facing an indefinite occupation of a hostile state and some dubious "nation-building." Realistically, if Saddam fell, it would not be a democracy emerging but another, perhaps less problematic, strongman.

The administration's reasoning, in short, went as follows: it would be embarrassing and discomfiting to state a goal and then not achieve it; Saddam's ouster might be difficult and costly to achieve; therefore, we should not state it as a goal (even though it is something we actually would like to see accomplished). The administration thus decided that hope could indeed be a plan: "The best solution was to do as much damage as we could to his military, and wait for the Ba'ath regime to collapse. We would concentrate on liberating Kuwait and leaving the region as soon as possible—fulfilling our UN objectives and our promises to our Arab allies, and, we hoped, destroying Saddam's power base." [34]

NO MORE VIETNAMS

Bush administration policymakers had a number of contemporaneous reasons for not wanting to go to Baghdad. Reinforcing those, however—particularly for the uniformed military—was a specter from the past. As the Third Army's official history of the conflict puts it, "From the president downward through the chain of command, the ghost of the Vietnam War hovered over every proceeding. . . . Commanders were intent on avoiding what they regarded as the mistakes of the past. . . . This war would be everything the Vietnam War had not been." [35]

For the senior officers in the Gulf crisis, Vietnam had been the defining experience of their professional lives. They had watched their friends and charges die and their beloved institutions break down into a dysfunctional mess, all for the nation's first military defeat—and had then devoted their careers to overcoming the past and reestablishing American military competence and honor. Every action they took during the crisis was driven by those goals and seen in that light.

Powell, who served two tours in the earlier war, notes that throughout the early principals meetings, "Vietnam [was] running through my mind very much." [36] Fred Franks, the Third Army commander, had lost a leg there and says that Vietnam was "constantly in my mind. . . . [W]e all felt that we're going to do it right this time." [37] Warden, the creator of the concept for the air campaign, had flown in 266 combat missions in Indochina and named his plan Instant Thunder to emphasize that it was the opposite of Vietnam's Rolling Thunder. Walt Boomer, the Marine commander, said that "Vietnam was always lurking in the background for all of us that had served there. In my case, I served two tours. All of my commanders had been in Vietnam, at least two times. And I think what we were committed to more than anything else, was that we weren't going to make the same stupid mistakes that we made in Vietnam. And we weren't going to do some of the dumb things that we had been forced to do, as younger officers, we weren't going to tolerate it, and we didn't." [38]

For the military, the mistakes and lessons of Vietnam were obvious.

That conflict was seen as having been entered into casually and then fought slowly and halfheartedly for broad, vague political objectives. Avoiding a repeat meant doing the opposite at each decision point: keeping out of trouble unless absolutely necessary and then, if ordered to do so, fighting quickly with massive force for narrow and militarily achievable goals. In the context of the Gulf, this translated into skepticism about making the invasion of Kuwait a casus belli, reluctance to move from sanctions to war, insistence on overwhelming force to execute the mission given, and determination to limit the war's objectives and return home quickly.

In many if not most respects, the military's Vietnam obsession had beneficial consequences during Desert Shield and Desert Storm, resulting in an extremely high level of tactical and operational proficiency and professionalism. But at the strategic level, it produced an allergy to long-term, open-ended military commitments that was neither relevant nor helpful. For reasons having nothing to do with the realities of the Persian Gulf, the last thing anybody in the military wanted was to get trapped in some desert quagmire or dip their toes into Iraqi politics. As far as American commanders were concerned, what happened after the fighting stopped was somebody else's problem; they were going to Disney World.

The Vietnam obsession had a bureaucratic corollary to it as well: a desire to avoid the supposed sin of political micromanagement. As if to displace responsibility for all the unpleasantness of Southeast Asia onto somebody else's shoulders, American military leaders elevated one aspect of the earlier conflict, Lyndon Johnson's picking of bombing targets, above all else—if not a stab in the back, then at least a hand tied behind the back, the memory of which galled even decades later. Bush himself, for what it was worth, shared this opinion: "I did not want to repeat the problems of the Vietnam War," he wrote later, "where the political leadership meddled with military operations. I would avoid micromanaging the military."[39]

In sharp contrast, therefore, to, say, the Nixon administration, in which the president and national security adviser ran everything out of the White House, the situation in the Bush administration approximated what Samuel Huntington called "objective civilian control"—civilian leaders picked national goals and then left military professionals largely alone to decide how they should be achieved.[40] In theory, this created a division of labor that accorded each community precedence in its area of specialized expertise. In practice, however, it meant that postwar planning was stovepiped (handled in narrow bureaucratic channels) and politico-military affairs were less well coordinated than they might have been, with consequences that became apparent only as the war was drawing to a close.

FROM WAR TO . . . SOMETHING

Had Bush administration officials thought about it closely, they might have recognized that the simplicity of their Kuwait-related goals was matched by the complexity of their Iraq-related goals. Trying to create a stable postwar regional balance of power, they wanted to bring Iraq's capabilities down enough to prevent Kuwait and Saudi Arabia from being threatened, but not so much that Iran would gain a free hand. And trying to create a quiescent Iraq domestically, they wanted to hit the existing regime hard enough that it would learn a lasting lesson (and ideally oust its humiliated leader), but not so hard that the regime would collapse or the country break apart. Even if policymakers were correct that these middle-ground outcomes were the least bad ones available—*especially* if they were correct about that—they should have been worried, given how difficult such results would be to achieve. Closing out the Gulf War successfully was going to be like hitting a tough approach shot to a tiny green surrounded by bunkers and hazards on all sides.

There simply was no ideal level of Iraqi strength, for example, that could create a stable postwar regional balance of power without major and open-ended American involvement—something Powell pointed out later on: "Iraq, a nation of twenty million people, can always pose a threat to its tiny neighbor, Kuwait, with only 1.5 million people. With or without Saddam and with or without the Republican Guard, Kuwait's security depends on arrangements with its friends in the region and the United States. That is the strategic reality."[41]

And it was bizarre to think that Saddam's fate was not a big deal, as Bush himself repeatedly noted in his diary. On February 15, during a brief moment when he thought Saddam had agreed to withdraw, he put the issue clearly: "Now the question is, what comes next? But my emotion is not one of elation. We've got some unfinished business. How do we solve it? How do we now guarantee the future peace? I don't see how it will work with Saddam in power, and I am very, very wary."[42]

On February 20, he repeated his concern: "I don't quite see how Iraq with Saddam Hussein at the helm will be able to live peacefully in this family of nations. . . . [T]he dilemma is, 'What is victory—what is a complete victory?' Our goal is not the elimination of Saddam Hussein, and yet in many ways it's the only answer in order to get a new start for Iraq in the family of nations."[43] In an unguarded moment, Powell confessed the truth: "I think the interest of the region would be best served with Saddam Hussein out of power, and I think the interest of the region would be best served if Iraq remains a single country. How that comes about, I don't know."[44]

The administration managed to ward off such discomforting thoughts, however, by convincing itself that the Iraq problem would somehow be worked out on its own, thanks to the actions of an as-yet-unknown Iraqi military officer who would dispatch Saddam once the war's outcome was clear. This magical Iraqi would act as a deus ex machina, miraculously appearing onstage at the end of the play to resolve everybody's problems. As the president wrote in his diary on January 31:

> I just keep thinking the Iraqi people ought to take care of [Saddam] with the Iraqi military. Seeing their troops [and] equipment getting destroyed—they've got to do something about it. I wish like hell that we could. . . . This is a war and if he gets hit with a bomb in his headquarters, too bad. But it seems to me that the more suffering the people of Iraq go through, the more likely it is that somebody will stand up and do that which should have been done a long time ago—take the guy out of there—either kick him out of the country or do something where he is no longer running things.[45]

The president was hardly alone in thinking that a military defeat in Kuwait would lead to Saddam's fall in Iraq; this view was shared by most senior officials in the United States and other coalition countries, not to mention the intelligence community. Cheney went so far as to bet *New York Times* reporter Michael Gordon dinner "that Saddam Hussein would be gone in six months."[46] A CIA joke from the era ran, "I can't tell you the last name of Saddam's successor, but I can tell you his first name." "What is it?" "General."

With the ground war approaching, accordingly, American political and military leaders worried far more about the actual combat than what would follow it. They told themselves they had done appropriate due diligence, identified the mistakes of the past, and thought through how to avoid them. Schwarzkopf had a war termination specialist on his staff. Powell distributed copies of the leading book on the subject to his colleagues. State had coordinated its thoughts with its British counterpart. Haass had written and rewritten a memo on war termination for Bush and Scowcroft.[47] Still, when American tanks raced forward and Iraqi forces folded quickly, things flew apart.

Part of the problem was the inevitable fog of war, with different pictures of the battlefield emerging between headquarters and the front. Part of it was cockiness, with American officials assuming that their victory was so great that it would necessarily yield all the results they desired. And part of it was simple carelessness, with the principals making crucial calls on the fly, not properly staffing their decisions or considering all the consequences. The result of all this together was that at its end, the U.S. war effort split open at its politico-military seam—and like a James Bond villain who sets a death trap for the hero and then walks off before it snaps shut, the administration let its resourceful enemy get away.

The ground campaign began on February 24. By early February 26, Saddam had ordered the withdrawal of most of his forces, with the remainder fighting on in a covering action. On the evening of February 27, Schwarzkopf briefed the world on his triumph. "Our intention was purely to eject the Iraqis out of Kuwait and to destroy the military power that had come in there," he said, and that had been achieved. "To date, we have destroyed over twenty-nine—destroyed or rendered inoperable. . . . I don't like to say destroyed because that gives you the visions of absolutely killing everyone, and that's not what we're doing. But we have rendered completely ineffective over twenty-nine Iraqi divisions and the gates are closed. There is no way out. . . . [W]e've almost completely destroyed the offensive capability of the Iraqi forces within the Kuwaiti theater of operation." Asked about whether he was concerned about being allowed to complete his mission, Schwarzkopf replied: "I think I've made it very clear to everybody that I'd just as soon the war had never started and I'd just as soon never have lost a single life out there. . . . We've accomplished our mission and when the decision-makers come to the decision that there should be a cease-fire, nobody will be happier than me."[48] Before the briefing, he and Powell had talked and decided that the time for a cease-fire was rapidly approaching. "Do you realize if we stop tomorrow night," Schwarzkopf had said, "the ground campaign will have lasted five days? How does that sound to you: the 'Five-Day War'?" Powell chuckled and replied that he would pass the quip along.[49]

Just after Schwarzkopf's briefing had ended, the principals met with Bush in the White House. Powell led off with a summary of the military situation, wrapping it up by saying, "Mr. President, it's going much better than we expected. The Iraqi army is broken. All they're trying to do now is get out. . . . We don't want to be seen as killing for the sake of killing. . . . We're within the window of success. I've talked to General Schwarzkopf. I expect by sometime tomorrow the job will be done, and I'll probably be bringing you a recommendation to stop the fighting."

Bush responded, "If that's the case, why not end it today? . . . We're starting to pick up some undesirable public and political baggage with all those scenes of carnage. You say we've accomplished the mission. Why not end it?" Powell said that he wanted to consult Schwarzkopf, and they called him in Riyadh. Schwarzkopf raised no objection. White House Chief of Staff John Sununu pointed out that if they ended it at midnight, the ground campaign would have lasted precisely one hundred hours. That seemed an even better hook than the Israeli-topping Five-Day War, and clinched the deal. Soon Bush and his advisers were fanning out to brief coalition members and Congress, and at 9 P.M. that evening the president took to the airwaves to announce his decision:

> Kuwait is liberated. Iraq's army is defeated. Our military objectives are met. . . . After consulting with Secretary of Defense Cheney, the Chairman of the Joint Chiefs of Staff, General Powell, and our coalition partners, I am pleased to announce that at midnight tonight eastern standard time, exactly 100 hours since ground operations commenced and six weeks since the start of Desert Storm, all United States and coalition forces will suspend offensive combat operations.[50]

When Bush spoke, victory seemed to have come quickly, easily, and completely. Over the following days, however, the third of those attributes started to unravel, aided in part by the impromptu nature of the decision to halt operations. It turned out, for example, that Schwarzkopf had never consulted his commanders in the field before agreeing with Bush's decision to stop the war, nor verified the exact situation of his own forces and those of the enemy. Due to entirely predictable confusion and miscommunication, coalition forces proved to be not quite where he thought they were, and the enemy less fully destroyed or trapped than he had believed.[51]

Several of the administration's deputies, meanwhile, were surprised to find out on the afternoon of February 27 that their principals had decided to end the war just then. Unlike their military counterparts, many of the civilian policymakers were concerned less with pulling out quickly than with setting up postwar arrangements to stabilize the region. They had expected the war to continue another day, until the Iraqi forces had been fully surrounded and defeated in detail, and they were not particularly worried about a possible backlash from press accounts of the war's final stages. Still, nobody challenged the call—because the president, the principals, and the military leadership were content with it and because everybody assumed the magnitude of the victory was great enough to deliver the results they all wanted.[52]

Later on, when the discrepancy between the situation on the ground and Schwarzkopf's perceptions of it became clear, there was controversy about whether the "gate" had truly been closed and whether American military objectives had been met. This discussion has been mostly beside the point, however, as the real issue was not tactical or even operational, but strategic—what the war's military objectives really were, or should have been, and how they related to its political ones.

Interestingly, Powell's and Schwarzkopf's memoirs contain different accounts of the crucial war-ending phone call. After describing the president's suggestion to stop, Powell has Schwarzkopf agree by saying, "Our objective was to drive 'em out, and we've done it." Schwarzkopf quotes the same sentence this way: "Our objective was the destruction of the enemy forces, and for all intents and purposes we've accomplished that objective."

Since Powell had a limited conception of the mission from the very beginning of the crisis, and didn't want to fight even over Kuwait, let alone Iraq, it is hardly surprising that he defined the objective narrowly at this point—but it is somewhat surprising that other principals with a more hawkish bent did not counter his impulses.

Schwarzkopf, in turn, not only failed to check whether his own stated goals had indeed been fully achieved, but also failed to define and operationalize those goals precisely. In discussions during the war, "destroying" the Iraqi forces sometimes meant "beating them up badly," sometimes it meant "reducing them by 50%," and much of the time it seems to have meant "rendering them combat ineffective over some unspecified timeframe." This last usage made sense when talking about the current war: an Iraqi unit thus "destroyed" could no longer resist the coalition. But it made less sense when thinking about postwar regional security, because that same unit might still be able to reconstitute itself and play a role in some other conflict—which is precisely what happened in March, as some "destroyed" Republican Guard units managed to pull themselves together and go on to crush the Shiite and Kurdish uprisings.[53]

The administration's more general failure, however, lay in not linking its military operations directly to political objectives inside Iraq and not planning for a variety of postwar scenarios. Everybody simply assumed that a major military defeat would result in a military coup against Saddam, leaving a nasty but defanged and more pragmatic Iraqi regime securely in place. The postwar popular uprisings in the south and north thus took the administration by surprise.[54] Policymakers were loath to sit back and watch as their supposedly defeated and humiliated enemy regained his footing and proceeded to engage in mass murder with impunity—but they were even more loath to get trapped in a desert Vietnam. So they froze and did nothing as events on the ground played themselves out.

In the hours after he ordered the fighting stopped, Bush jotted down some dark thoughts in his diary, taking consolation from his assumption that somehow the situation would improve:

> Still no feeling of euphoria. I think I know why it is. After my speech last night, Baghdad radio started broadcasting that we've been forced to capitulate. I see on the television that public opinion in Jordan and in the streets of Baghdad is that they have won. It is such a canard, so little, but it's what concerns me. It hasn't been a clean end—there is no battleship Missouri surrender. This is what's missing to make this akin to WWII, to separate Kuwait from Korea and Vietnam. . . . The headlines are great—"We Win." The television accurately reflects the humiliation of Saddam Hussein and it drives the point home to the American people. But internationally, it's not there yet, at least in the Arab world that has been lined up with Saddam. He's got to go, and I hope those two airplanes that reported to the Baghdad airport [with bunker-busting

> payloads for one last attempt to kill the Iraqi leader] carry him away. Obviously when the troops straggle home with no armor, beaten up, 50,000 casualties and maybe more dead, the people of Iraq will know.[55]

Over the next several days, administration officials exhaled, began to pick up the pieces of their lives, and set in motion complex diplomatic efforts such as a Security Council resolution formalizing the end of the war and negotiations that would evolve into the Madrid peace conference. The meeting at Safwan was not given a huge amount of thought in Washington: it was considered a prosaic discussion of technical military issues, something that could and should largely be delegated to commanders on the ground. There was some debate in the White House about whether to demand that Saddam come to Safwan in person, but it was decided that the risks of such a demand outweighed the potential benefits. The choice was not seen as incredibly significant, because Saddam's fate was considered already sealed.[56]

Then the Shiite uprising erupted suddenly, only to be put down almost as quickly.[57] The Kurdish uprising took off a few days after the Shiite one and continued going strong into late March. News reports of Saddam's latest cruelties opened the Bush administration up to criticism in the press, but there was little appetite anywhere in Washington for additional intervention. As a "senior official" told the *Washington Post*, Bush believed that

> Saddam will quash the rebellions and, after the dust settles, the Baath [party] military establishment and other elites will blame him for not only the death and destruction from the war, but the death and destruction from putting down the rebellion. They will emerge then and install a new leadership and will make the case it is time for new leaders and a new beginning. And having gone through what they have gone through with the Iran-Iraq war, the Gulf war, and the civil war, the lessons will have been learned.[58]

The Bush team just wanted to hurry past the unpleasantness. "This is not a crusade," another official noted. "It is a somewhat painful acceptance of a certain reality. You manage it in as low-key a way as possible and hope you get through it."[59]

By the beginning of April, however, as Saddam retook the north, nearly two million Kurds fled into the mountains without food, water, or shelter. Unlike the Shiites, who were seen as proxies of the hated Iranians and thus relatively expendable, the Kurds were seen as innocent victims. Moreover, the Kurdish refugees were spilling into and destabilizing Turkey, a crucial NATO ally with a Kurdish problem of its own. The Kurdish crisis, finally, was playing out slowly, on a very large scale, with significant press attention, shaming the Bush team and allowing self-righteous policymakers in Europe to grab the spotlight. So the administration grudgingly began to reverse its course, agreeing to drop some care packages to the refugees from the air. Baker toured the Kurdish areas on April 7 and came away shaken by what he had seen. He was able to bring the principals around to favor some form of humanitarian intervention, and the result was Operation Provide Comfort, the establishment of a "safe haven" in northern Iraq for the displaced Kurds until they could be persuaded to return home.[60]

In May, finally recognizing that Saddam wasn't going to be toppled by anybody else, the administration changed its tune and made his ouster an official goal of U.S. policy. Unilaterally reinterpreting the massive Security Council cease-fire resolution passed just a month earlier, Deputy National Security Adviser Robert Gates announced the change of course on May 7, declaring that as far as the United States was concerned, "All possible sanctions will be maintained until [Saddam] is gone. Any easing of sanctions will be considered only when there is a new government."[61] Three weeks later, the president gave the CIA formal instructions to "create the conditions for the removal of Saddam Hussein from power"—two months after the best opportunity to do so had passed into history.[62]

HALFWAY GONE

Domestic politics explain little about U.S. behavior during the Gulf crisis. The key decisions regarding U.S. policy were made by a handful of people within a few days of the Iraqi invasion, with almost no involvement from Congress or the public at large. Those decisions were not particularly controversial at the White House, since they upheld a U.S. commitment to Persian Gulf security that had been proclaimed a decade earlier and were approved by key American allies abroad. But since most Americans knew little about the history of the country's involvement in the region and cared little about geopolitics, the administration simply went about its business without asking for permission.

Even six months later, congressional authorization of the war was considered a bonus rather than a prerequisite for action.[63]

Domestic values also explain little about American strategy. Whatever rhetorical points individual officials might have made in public or even felt strongly themselves, as a whole the administration's behavior was strikingly unsentimental and nonideological throughout. As Scowcroft would note drily, "The core of our argument rested on long-held security and economic interests: preserving the balance of power in the Gulf, opposing unprovoked international aggression, and ensuring that no hostile regional power could hold hostage much of the world's oil supply. President Bush, appalled by the evidence of Iraqi atrocities, added the Hitler, Holocaust, and morality arguments."[64] The world order that Washington fought for was not new, but several centuries old; the principles that guided the administration's grand strategy—stability, sovereignty, nonintervention in domestic affairs, a balance of power—represented Westphalian conservatism, not the revolutionary idealism of the American Creed.[65]

Organizational politics do not explain the general policy direction the Bush administration followed, but do help explain how that policy was executed. Far more than is usually recognized, the pace of events was set by the standard operating procedures of the U.S. military, which started its deployment five days after Saddam's troops crossed into Kuwait. In late summer and early fall, forces for the defense of Saudi Arabia flowed into the region, followed seamlessly in late fall and early winter by forces for going on the attack—just as Powell had sketched out for Bush in mid-August. The mid-January deadline for launching the war was fixed around when the offensive forces would be ready.[66] The air campaign was envisioned as running for just over a month, until the ground forces were fully in place, and it did. The ground forces were ready to move by late February, and that's when they were sent out.[67]

At any point along the way, things could have been thrown off track, either by an Iraqi withdrawal or some unexpected problem—but they weren't. And both the air war and ground war went incredibly smoothly. From August through February, accordingly, however exhausted and stressed and fearful American policymakers may have been, they were actually working in a relatively fixed and predictable environment. Once the shooting stopped, however, they were flying blind, and their actions showed it. This was when the most important drivers of American policy during the case—U.S. international standing and the lessons of the past—came back into the foreground.

The Gulf crisis occurred at a unique moment in America's relationship to the international system. On the one hand, the country was going through one of its periodic crises of self-confidence, symbolized by the recent popularity of Paul Kennedy's theories about American decline. U.S. relative strength vis-à-vis the system as a whole had dropped since the end of the last war; by 1990, the nation's share of world gross domestic product was down to just over a fifth, and thanks to a recession, during the war itself the American economy was actually shrinking. The United States had recently become the world's largest debtor, moreover, and found itself forced to ask its allies to underwrite the war's costs (which they did).

On the other hand, it was still the strongest power in the world and its rivals were on an even steeper downward trajectory, with the Soviet Union having just conceded the Cold War and heading for the dustbin of history itself. In retrospect, we know that war came at the start of an era of unprecedented American primacy. But at the time, decisionmakers were not feeling particularly confident. The great 1990s boom had not yet begun, and it would take the Gulf War itself to reveal just how dominant the U.S. armed forces had in fact become.

The result of this mixed picture was that officials in Washington recognized the need to provide the global public good of securing and stabilizing the Gulf, as well as their ability to do so. But they were leery about acting unilaterally, directly, or prospectively. Brzezinski had the Truman Doctrine in mind when he devised the Carter Doctrine—and just like their predecessors in the second half of the 1940s, officials in the Bush administration would at first try to cap their efforts abroad, agreeing to leave substantial American forces in place to protect a geopolitically crucial region only after the dangers in withdrawing became manifest.

Complicating matters further was a general failure to recognize and address the challenge of making force serve policy. Civilian officials had done a decent amount of planning for the postwar era in the Gulf, and even paid lip service publicly to the problems it would present.[68] Military commanders, however, had concentrated obsessively on the war itself and knew only that they wanted to bring their forces home as quickly as possible afterward.[69] It was only in March, as the complexities of the postwar situation sunk in, that the lack of coordination between these civilian and military perspectives emerged. The Third Army's official history of the war got to the heart of the problem:

> What was absent was a clear and common vision of how U.S. forces should be distributed on the ground to facilitate the inevitable transfer of the conflict's focus and energies back to the political arena. Also lacking was a common concept of what action to take regarding those Iraqi forces . . . that had been driven back into Basrah and its environs. All this was missing, in part, no doubt, because the end of offensive actions came sooner than anticipated. It also reflects a fundamental weakness in a traditional U.S. view that the military and political conduct of war are separable at all but the highest levels. In this concept of civil-military relations, the soldier is given a mission and fights the war according to what is militarily correct—albeit within the boundaries established by policy. He expects to be left alone to do his technical business of fighting until he has accomplished some gross military end that will enable the diplomats to arrive speedily at a resolution of the basic issues causing the war. The soldier then turns the conflict back to his political masters.[70]

This is indeed just how the Gulf War generals saw things. As Horner, the air commander, would put it later, "Quite frankly, I think we were preoccupied with planning the war, and we felt that somebody else was planning the peace. . . . [Regarding Safwan,] I think we were all surprised that there wasn't somebody ready to jump on a jet and fly over to do the negotiations with the Iraqis."[71] Boomer, the Marine commander, remains indignant: "I don't know why State Department people weren't on airplanes, flying out to take over this part of the campaign, or to move from the ending of the military campaign and take the next necessary step. No one has ever explained that and I've never heard, really, an apology for doing so."[72]

While military leaders were assuming that the civilians were going to be handling the transition from war to peace, the civilians were assuming that the military was thinking carefully about such matters. The ghost of Vietnam was whispering two messages into everyone's ears, both counterproductive: first, that the United States should avoid messy entanglements, and second, that politicians should back off and let the military do its job without interference. In mid-February, Bush noted in his diary: "I have no qualms now about ordering a ground war—none at all. . . . The reason is that the military are unanimous in recommending the course of action that Colin and Cheney outlined to me the other day. I have not second-guessed; I have not told them what targets to hit; I have not told them how much ordnance to use or not to use, or what weapons to use or not to use. I have learned from Vietnam. . . ."[73] In March, as he kept aloof from the Iraqi turmoil, he was thinking something similar: "Most compelling of all for Bush, officials said, was that his military advisers were demanding a definite military goal with a definite timetable, a demand that fit precisely with the president's passion to avoid another Vietnam."[74]

The problem, of course, was that Iraq was not Vietnam, and that Desert Storm was not a discrete, self-contained story but only one installment in what was bound to be a long-running serial. Some in the administration understood this, but they had a hard time convincing others of it or even, frankly, acknowledging to themselves what it really meant. Reflecting later on the difference between the fumbling NSC meeting on August 2 and the decisive one on August 3, Haass made a good point: "To put it bluntly, what we ultimately did—sending half a million people around the world and all that that entails—that was too big of a thought for people at the first meeting even to think about. So instead you had people talking . . . about how we could live with [the invasion]."[75] The exact same dynamic played itself out again the following spring, as it slowly dawned on administration officials just what providing for "the security and stability of the Gulf" was going to mean in practice.

A few days after the Safwan meeting, when the deputies realized that events were not playing out as they had expected, they tried to improvise, to call an audible. They started kicking around an interesting plan to retain U.S. forces on the strip of Iraqi territory that the coalition now controlled, playing with the idea of using an ongoing military presence to gain some leverage over the situation inside Iraq and shape it to Washington's advantage. But military leaders were hell-bent on getting home quickly and squashed the proposal with barely a glance. According to Michael Gordon and Bernard Trainor,

> It was Schwarzkopf himself who delivered the mortal blow to the plan for a security zone. Having promised the Iraqis that the allied forces would withdraw, which he wanted to do anyway as soon as possible, the Centcom commander was dead set against the demilitarized zone. When he met with Baker, Schwarzkopf argued that a security zone would have

> no military value and would delay the withdrawal of American forces from the region. After meeting with Schwarzkopf, Baker huddled with his team. Robert Kimmitt and Paul Wolfowitz disagreed with the commander's assessment, but the top generals had made their objections known and the civilians were reluctant to challenge them.[76]

Six weeks later, of course, as the consequences of letting Iraq fend for itself became increasingly clear, U.S. forces were indeed ordered back into the country, where they would garrison a de facto Kurdish protectorate as well as eventually patrol extensive aerial "no-fly zones" in the north and south. And by late May, after scores of thousands had been killed and the moment of greatest political fluidity had passed, the Bush team finally backed into its ultimate postwar stance. The United States would secure the Gulf by maintaining a major military presence in the region along with comprehensive sanctions on Iraq and covert actions to try to get rid of Saddam.

Belatedly assembled and agreed to, these policies would prove far more durable than anybody expected, lasting not for a few months or even a few years but for more than a decade—until they were scrapped by another Bush administration, which tired of containment and sought a more decisive answer to the underlying problem by going where its predecessors had feared to tread. Given the problems the later administration ran into, the first Bush team's reluctance to occupy the country is hard to mock. As Cheney put it in 1992,

> If we'd gone to Baghdad and got rid of Saddam Hussein—assuming we could have found him—we'd have had to put a lot of forces in and run him to ground some place. He would not have been easy to capture. Then you've got to put a new government in his place and then you're faced with the question of what kind of government are you going to establish in Iraq? Is it going to be a Kurdish government or a Shia government or a Sunni government? How many forces are you going to have to leave there to keep it propped up, how many casualties are you going to take through the course of this operation?[77]

Still, this hardly justifies the first Bush administration's actual handling of the end of the Gulf War. As a perceptive critic has written, "Defenders of the decision to halt the war after 100 hours of ground combat frequently posit a false choice between this and a march to Baghdad to overthrow Saddam Hussein. In fact, the United States possessed a range of options to pressure Saddam into leaving office, or at least admitting defeat. The real choice was between ending the war before coalition forces had completed their mission and pursuing options to compel Iraq to accept defeat. The time to do so was prior to the declaration of a ceasefire. Once the U.S. government announced a halt to military operations, its leverage over Saddam evaporated."[78]

Carelessly assuming that somebody else would solve the Saddam problem, the first Bush administration never forced itself to decide in advance just how much it wanted him gone. The administration's coyness about whether Saddam's ouster was a "stated" goal came back to haunt it when the time finally came to make a choice one way or the other. If Bush and his advisers believed that Saddam's continued leadership was indeed intolerable, then they should have marshaled the instruments of American power to remove him when they had the chance.[79] As a senior policymaker told me when asked about regrets,

> If I had known [then exactly how things were going to play out], I would have thought a lot harder about placing certain limits on what the Iraqis could do inside Iraq. . . . I might have continued the war several more days. I possibly would have done more to consider a symbolic humiliation of Saddam—essentially, I would have taken the risk of trying to engineer a succession. . . . [80]

On the other hand, some believed then—and some still believe now—that containment of a somewhat defanged Saddam was the least bad postwar outcome realistically available at the time, given all the constraints the administration faced. If *that* was what Bush and his advisers believed, however, then they could and should have gotten to that point more smoothly and efficiently than they ultimately did, with less chaos, suffering, and scrambling along the way, and in the process established the postwar containment regime on a less costly, more effective, and more sustainable basis.[81]

Another Asian war besides Vietnam sometimes crossed the minds of American policymakers during the crisis. Korea, several officials felt, offered a cautionary tale of what could happen when you escalated your goals in the flush of victory, without thinking through the full consequences of the decision. Realists who understood they were fighting a limited war, Bush and his advisers were determined not to repeat the mistake of driving recklessly across a 38th Parallel toward a Yalu of their own. There was some wisdom in the analogy, but it was a more cautionary tale than the administration chose to admit. For after all, the price of eschewing regime change and accepting half a loaf in Korea was that a large American force was left behind to garrison the peninsula—and does so to this day, more than half a century later, to protect a critical region from the dangers continuing to lurk in Pyongyang.

The Bush administration thought a full loaf in Iraq was too expensive to purchase, and many agreed. As the president was fond of saying, "not gonna do it—wouldn't be prudent." But in the unforgiving marketplace of geopolitics, buying only half a loaf didn't eliminate the costs. It just meant they would be paid in other ways, at other times, by other people.

8

THE IRAQ WAR

As the tanks and armored personnel carriers of the 2nd Brigade, 3rd Mechanized Infantry Division drove down Highway 8 into Baghdad on April 7, 2003, Colonel Dave Perkins kept his eyes peeled for trouble. When the invasion of Iraq had been launched three weeks earlier, the endgame had always been a bit unclear, with Baghdad in particular looming as a problem. Coalition forces needed to take the city in order to oust Saddam Hussein, but nobody wanted extended urban combat. So the plan was for the attackers to race to the outskirts of the city, establish a cordon around it, and then launch a series of probes to test Iraqi defenses. Two days earlier, Perkins had led the first such probe, called a "Thunder Run," successfully taking a battalion of Abrams tanks and Bradley fighting vehicles through western Baghdad and back out to Saddam International Airport. Now he was going in again, with a larger force and more ambition.

Major General Buford Blount, the 3rd ID's commander, and his boss, Lieutenant General William Scott Wallace, the commander of the V Corps, thought the second Thunder Run was going to be like the first—an armed reconnaissance raid into and out of the city. But Perkins wanted to do more if he could, and so when he met only moderate resistance, he kept moving forward. "When Col. Perkins got to the second intersection," Wallace later recalled, "he took a right turn and headed straight downtown. Now I don't think he was disobeying orders; I think he was taking advantage of the situation that was presented to him on the battlefield. . . . And Gen. Blount and I talked very shortly on the radio, and we said, 'Roger, let's let it go.' "[1] Braving intense fire, Perkins made it all the way to the center of the city, and soon images of American soldiers walking through Saddam's palaces in the heart of the Iraqi capital were being broadcast around the world on CNN.

When Perkins, Blount, and Wallace decided it would be no more difficult for the force to stay downtown than to go back to its base, the fight for the city took a great leap forward. Two days later, on April 9, helped by Marines from the 1st Marine Expeditionary Force, a crowd of Iraqis triumphantly pulled down a massive statue of Saddam in Firdos Square, hitting it with shoes and dragging its detached head through the streets. Sporadic fighting would continue for several more days, but to the world at large, Baghdad had fallen.

Saddam was a larger-than-life tyrant, a megalomaniac running a police state along the lines of Stalinist Russia. He had so dominated and brutalized his country that when his regime was finally toppled, waves of conflicting emotions—joy, grief, hope, fear—raced through the Iraqi population. "I'm 49, but I never lived a single day. Only now will I start living!" shouted one of the Iraqis pulling down the statue.[2] "Touch me, touch me, tell me that this is real," sobbed another man, standing outside the burning headquarters of Iraq's National Olympic Committee, a notorious torture chamber and charnel house run by Saddam's sadistic son Uday. "Tell me that the nightmare is really over."[3]

Thanks to careful and creative planning, the invasion had actually caused very little damage. The speed of the attackers and the rapid collapse of the defenders may have helped ensure that many potential problems, from the destruction of oil fields and civilian infrastructure to massive flows of refugees, did not arise.[4] But once the regime fell, swarms of human locusts proceeded to wreak the havoc that combat had not.

The coalition had invaded with a relatively small force, privileging speed over mass and precision over bluntness. Expecting to find a working state in place, the Americans had intended to remove its upper echelons while using the lower ones to run the country, turning control over to friendly Iraqis as soon as possible and leaving almost as fast as they had come. But with Saddam gone, the Iraqi state disintegrated and its personnel vanished into the heat and dust. Realizing that there was no one to stop them, the looters grew bolder by the hour, moving from Saddam's palaces and ministries to lucrative targets in the private sector to anything and everything at large.

When British forces liberated Basra on April 5, looters had followed in their wake. "No more Baath. No more Fedayeen. Just thieves, Ali Babas," locals proclaimed.[5] The same thing happened when U.S. forces liberated Baghdad and other cities across the country. Anarchy reigned: factories, offices, hospitals, museums, libraries, and private homes were sacked and burned, with even the plumbing and wiring stripped out to be sold as scrap.[6] There were far too few American soldiers around to maintain order, and those that were present mostly stood by and did nothing, lacking instructions to intervene. "Our job as U.S. Marines is not to act as a constabulary force," said a spokesman for the troops who had helped pull down Saddam's statue.[7] (Making matters worse—at least in terms of local perceptions of American intentions—the Marines did indeed secure and protect one local institution right from the start: the oil ministry.)

Back in Washington, Bush administration officials claimed media coverage of the chaos was overblown, even misguided. "The images you are seeing on television . . . over and over and over," Secretary of Defense Donald Rumsfeld told reporters on April 11,

> it's the same picture of some person walking out of some building with a vase, and you see it 20 times, and you think, "My goodness, were there that many vases? Is it possible there were that many vases in the whole country?" . . . I picked up a newspaper today and I couldn't believe it. I read eight headlines that talked about chaos, violence, unrest. And it just was Henny Penny—"the sky is falling." . . . Stuff happens. . . . Freedom's untidy, and free people are free to make mistakes and commit crimes and do bad things. They're also free to live their lives and do wonderful things, and that's what's going to happen here.[8]

Yet this was in fact the moment when the coalition began to lose Iraq. Occupation officials later calculated that the monetary cost of the looting came to several billion dollars, and the destruction crippled attempts to get the country up and running. "But the physical damage was less catastrophic than those effects that couldn't be quantified. Iraq's first experience of freedom was chaos and violence; the arrival of the Americans brought an end to the certainty of political terror and at the same time unleashed new, less certain fears."[9]

Summing up his feelings a week after Dave Perkins's second Thunder Run, one Shiite leader in Baghdad put it this way: "The situation of Iraqis is as if one eye is crying and one eye is laughing."[10] Another resident commented, "Saddam Hussein has ended, and he's gone. But nobody knows what's ahead. They just don't know. . . . We're like sheep. The shepherd's gone and everybody goes in their own direction." He thought for a moment, then added: "When will the Americans put an end to the looting?"[11]

A dozen years after trouncing the Iraqi army in battle only to stumble blindly into postwar turmoil, the United States did it again. The disorder that began in April 2003 continued; liberation turned into occupation; local uncertainty turned into insurgency and then civil war. Four long years after the fall of Saddam's statue in Firdos Square, a new and better-resourced American strategy managed to build on some positive local trends and stabilize the situation, so that by the end of the decade Iraq had pulled back from the brink and gained a chance at a better future. But even then nothing was guaranteed, as low-level violence and political turmoil continued.[12]

How could this happen? How could the strongest power in modern history, fighting a rematch against a much lesser opponent at a time and place of its own choosing, find itself yet again woefully unprepared for the aftermath?

The perversity of such an outcome belies simple explanations, which is why neither the George W. Bush administration's most passionate defenders nor its most passionate critics are good guides to the case. The problems that emerged after Saddam's ouster cannot be written off as random "acts of god." They were entirely predictable, and indeed were repeatedly predicted by many people inside and outside the government. This makes the failure to plan carefully for avoiding or at least mitigating them an act of gross negligence, whatever else about the war may have gone well.[13] Yet the Bush administration itself was one of the casualties of its blunders: the postwar mess in Iraq blackened the reputations of almost everybody involved, helped cost the president's party control of Congress in 2006, and contributed to Bush's leaving office with the lowest approval ratings in history. If it was all some nefarious self-interested conspiracy, it was a bafflingly inept one.

The true story is more complex, with several elements required to explain how events played out as they did. The decision to go to war was driven by the psychological impact of 9/11 on key administration officials, together with their preexisting beliefs about the dangers Saddam posed. The administration's scorn for "nation-building," meanwhile, led it to believe that postwar commitments could be kept limited without ill effect. A dysfunctional national security decisionmaking process allowed the operation to proceed without serious questioning of heroically optimistic assumptions or proper contingency planning. And the combination of American hegemony and the trauma of 9/11 removed any significant foreign or domestic check on the administration's actions.

With their tight focus on the views of senior administration officials, existing accounts of American policy have tended to ignore the interplay of active and permissive causes—of motivation and opportunity—that shaped U.S. behavior. Certainly the ideas and actions of a few individuals on the Bush team were crucial. Had the Florida vote count controversy gone the other way and Al Gore been named president instead of George W. Bush in 2000, the United States would not have gone to war against Iraq in 2003. And it might not have done so even with Bush as president, had senior posts in the administration been filled differently. That said, however, even the "actually existing" Bush team would not have been able to develop and execute the policies it did had it confronted more serious countervailing pressures.

Much has been made of the Bush administration's beliefs about Saddam's prohibited weapons programs, commitment to democracy promotion, and pursuit of "regime change" in Iraq. But all those were established U.S. policy, carried over whole from the Clinton administration before. What changed and made the Iraq War possible were not American goals or ideals themselves, but rather beliefs about how they should be pursued, along with the structural context within which policymakers acted. International primacy removed limits imposed by the world at large, and the 9/11 attacks swept away limits imposed by the domestic political system. The factor that allowed the Bush doctrine to pass from idea into policy, in other words, was lack of constraint. The administration's leading figures found themselves with extraordinary freedom of action and decided to use it to the fullest. Unfortunately, as the secretary of defense noted, free people are free to make mistakes—which Rumsfeld and his colleagues did in spades, with consequences that are still being paid for today.

THE ROAD TO WAR

During the decade following the liberation of Kuwait, a lot happened in the Persian Gulf but little changed.[14] As the presidency passed from Bush père to Bill Clinton to Bush fils, the United States retained the regional policies and posture that had been set in place after the liberation of Kuwait in 1991. Substantial U.S. forces stayed in the area, chiefly on remote bases in Saudi Arabia. They enforced no-fly zones and other restrictions on Saddam's Iraq, kept a wary eye on the Islamic Republic of Iran, and protected the oil-rich countries of the Gulf Cooperation Council from both of their menacing northern neighbors. The Clinton administration christened this approach "dual containment," and it was repeatedly attacked for its costs, risks, and general failure to do more than kick the can down the road. But the Gulf continued to be one of the world's most strategically important regions and all the other ways of securing it appeared even more problematic, so the policy continued.[15]

As the new millennium dawned, however, three separate trends began to gather steam. In the United States, hawks argued that a tyranny as terrible and dangerous as Saddam's called for a policy response more ambitious than mere containment. This view was enshrined in the 1998 Iraq Liberation Act (ILA), which declared, "It should be the policy of the United States to support efforts to remove the regime headed by Saddam Hussein from power in Iraq and to promote the emergence of a democratic government to replace that regime."[16]

In Iraq, meanwhile, Saddam was increasingly successful in slipping out of his shackles and evading the various sanctions and restrictions that had been placed on him following the Gulf War. He manipulated the United Nations' oil-for-food program to keep revenue flowing into his pockets, cut deals with friendly powers for a variety of prohibited items, and kicked U.N. weapons inspectors out of the country. These actions led even supporters of containment to worry that it would be increasingly difficult to keep Saddam "in his box" for long.[17]

And in the Middle East at large, finally, radical Sunni Islamism gained adherents and standing as a serious ideological alternative to the

American-sponsored regional order. Groups such as al Qaeda exhorted their followers to attack both the "near enemy" (secular authoritarian regimes in countries such as Egypt and Saudi Arabia) and the "far enemy" (the United States). The presence of infidel troops on the sacred soil of Saudi Arabia, the humanitarian disaster caused by the sanctions against Iraq, and continued American support for Israel fueled Islamist anger and made the United States an increasingly hated target—particularly as the "apostate" regimes in the Arab world proved more difficult to topple than expected.[18] These three trends converged in September 2001, setting the stage for the U.S. invasion of Iraq a year and a half later.

During the Clinton administration, both political appointees and members of the national security bureaucracies viewed Iraq and Islamist terrorism as largely distinct problems. Saddam's regime was indeed a state sponsor of terrorism, they reasoned, but terrorism was one of the lesser threats Iraq posed to U.S. interests—and Iraq was one of the lesser sources of international terrorism.[19] Despite a sense that containment was deteriorating, moreover, the Clinton team showed no real desire to change its fundamentally defensive and reactive Iraq policy. Clinton signed the ILA only because he felt it would be politically damaging not to, and throughout his term regime change in Iraq constituted a hope rather than a serious objective. In contrast, Clinton officials grew ever more worried about al Qaeda, to the point where they concentrated heavily on it in their transition briefings to the George W. Bush team in early 2001.[20]

But the incoming administration had those priorities reversed. Many of its officials believed Iraq was a serious problem that was getting worse, and many were less seized with the supposed dangers posed by al Qaeda—not least because they saw terrorism as driven by states rather than nonstate actors. During their first months in office, accordingly, senior Bush officials met several times to try to toughen Iraq policy while effectively putting the Islamist terrorist threat on a back burner.

The 9/11 attacks changed all that, yanking the fight against al Qaeda to the forefront of the administration's agenda. Once it was clear that al Qaeda had carried out the attacks and that the Taliban would not give the group up, the Bush administration launched an invasion of Afghanistan, increased its focus on homeland security, and stepped up diplomatic, intelligence, and military activities as part of a global campaign against violent radical Islamists. The administration also went beyond this, however, defining its "war on terror" expansively to include actors and issues unrelated to 9/11—with Iraq foremost among them.

In late November 2001, soon after the fall of Kabul, Bush told Rumsfeld to order Centcom commander General Tommy Franks to start preparing plans for a war with Iraq. Just after Christmas, Franks briefed Bush and the National Security Council on the war planning and was given instructions to continue. Over the next six months, the war plans were increasingly elaborated and other groundwork for a conflict laid. Senior administration officials never actually debated whether to go to war, and the president did not issue formal orders to do so until much later, but by midsummer 2002, U.S. policy had essentially shifted from "no war with Iraq unless Saddam provokes one" to "war with Iraq in early 2003 unless Saddam capitulates." As Richard Haass, then the State Department's director of policy planning, records,

> By late spring and summer 2002 . . . it was Iraq that was increasingly dominating interagency deliberations and the attention of senior officials. . . . I got the chance in early July to question Condi directly during one of our regular sessions in her West Wing office. . . . I told her I was worried [an] Iraq [war] would come to dominate the administration's foreign policy and that it would prove far more difficult to do and yield far less in the way of dividends than its advocates advertised. She brushed away my concerns, saying the president had made up his mind.[21]

Others with comparable access came to the same conclusion. On July 23, 2002, British prime minister Tony Blair, Bush's closest ally, discussed Iraq policy with his senior advisers. According to the minutes of the session (the so-called "Downing Street Memo"), the head of Britain's foreign intelligence service "reported on his recent talks in Washington. There was a perceptible shift in attitude. Military action was now seen as inevitable."[22]

During the first week of August 1990, George H. W. Bush had set in motion a policy that would lead to war unless Saddam abandoned his occupation of Kuwait. From that point on, a military conflict was the default outcome unless something came along to deflect it. During the first half of 2002, his son came to a comparable position, and from the summer on only a complete behavioral change on Saddam's part would have headed off a second U.S.-Iraq conflict.

As in the fall of 1990, however, in the fall of 2002 the White House felt obliged to seek formal domestic and international approval for the impending showdown. The administration would probably have gone ahead without such approval, but tried to get it for two reasons: there was an outside chance the efforts might head off war (by scaring Saddam straight), and even if they did not, they could increase support for the administration's policy at home and abroad.

When Congress returned from its summer recess, accordingly, the administration pressed for congressional backing for a hard line, and in early October the House and Senate duly passed a resolution authorizing the president "to use the Armed Forces of the United States as he determines to be necessary and appropriate" to "enforce all relevant UNSC resolutions" and "defend the national security of the United States against the continuing threat posed by Iraq."[23] Secretary of State Colin Powell, meanwhile, had convinced Bush to go through the United Nations rather than around it, and in early November, the administration was able to secure a fresh Security Council resolution declaring Iraq "in material breach" of previous resolutions and demanding new weapons inspections.[24]

As the public debate played out during the fall and winter, the administration finalized its plans for the war and aftermath. The deputies committee had been kicking around three postwar models—a quick transition to Iraqi control, a military administration run by Centcom, and some kind of civilian-led transitional authority—but during the fall, the administration opted for the first. In October, the NSC approved the idea of putting a single cabinet official—the secretary of defense—in charge of all postwar planning and operations, both military and civilian. Rumsfeld directed Undersecretary of Defense Douglas Feith to set up an office to handle the civilian efforts, but then canceled the instruction a few days later (apparently following instructions from Bush to make sure that postwar planning maintained a low profile and did not get in the way of the administration's diplomatic efforts).[25] On December 18, unsatisfied by the response the Iraqis had given the United Nations about their weapons programs, Bush told his top advisers, "I think war is inevitable."[26] At this point, Rumsfeld instructed Feith to set the civilian postwar planning office in motion, and the result was a formal presidential directive on January 20, 2003, establishing the Office of Reconstruction and Humanitarian Assistance, to be led by retired Lieutenant General Jay Garner.

On January 24, Franks delivered his final war plan to Rumsfeld, but the postwar pieces were still up in the air. Centcom was formally responsible for maintaining security in Iraq, but it continued to act as if somebody else were going to handle the job. Worried about Centcom's lack of planning, the Pentagon's Joint Staff had set up a special task force to assist it, but the late, unappreciated, and under-resourced initiative never got anywhere. And Garner's hastily thrown together ORHA team was scrambling to figure out what was going on.

In late February, Garner brought together officials from across the administration to run through how things would play out once the fighting stopped. For those with eyes to see, the exercise was sobering. Expectations of what officials would find waiting for them in terms of human and physical infrastructure were high and major issues were still unresolved. The official summary noted several "show-stoppers," problems that could spell mission failure if not resolved, including:

- Failure to obtain interagency agreement on role and mission of ORHA and other agencies.
- US/Coalition military does not act as police until relieved by competent indigenous civilian police.
- Key policy decisions not made, i.e., applicable law, size of U.S. "footprint" in justice sector, operations vs. development.
- Early reestablishment of public order under rule of law is critical to success but is achievable only if funds and staff are made available **now**.[27]

Despite lip service paid to the importance of such issues, however, little was actually done about them. Postwar security in particular was left an orphan, with nobody taking responsibility for providing it. Administration leaders apparently assumed that it would be a relatively small problem that could be handled by the remnants of the Iraqi state, newly available foreign forces, or some other deus ex machina. On March 10, the president approved plans for an Interim Iraqi Authority to take over from Centcom and ORHA soon after the war ended, but just what this would involve in practice—or how it would relate to the still-unresolved security problem—was never elaborated.[28] On March 17, Bush gave Saddam a final ultimatum: leave in forty-eight hours or else. And when Saddam stayed put, two days later the president made good on his threat.

ONCE MORE UNTO THE BREACH

Although the war was a rematch and might have been expected to follow a familiar script, the U.S. military was determined to fight differently this time around. Under intense pressure from Rumsfeld, Franks had developed a plan for attacking quickly, comprehensively, and decisively. There would be no slow buildup of large forces in theater; no lengthy preliminary aerial bombardment; and no deliberate set-piece battles. Instead, the air and ground attacks would start at the same time; operations would be truly joint, with all combat arms working together toward a common end; and a premium would be placed on speed. The objective was to deliver a knockout blow to Saddam's regime as quickly as possible, causing minimal damage along the way.

In the early morning of March 19, responding to what seemed reliable intelligence about Saddam's whereabouts, the United States launched a flurry of cruise missiles at a compound outside Baghdad. But the decapitation strike did not work, and the invasion began in earnest the following day. The ground offensive involved two lines of advance from the south converging on Baghdad. Army forces, led by the 3rd ID, attacked west of the Euphrates, while the 1st MEF moved up the Tigris to the east. A British division attacked northeast from Kuwait, taking Basra and securing the oil fields nearby. And U.S. and Australian Special Operations forces secured Iraq's western desert, suppressing Scud missile attacks on Israel and Jordan. (The 4th ID had been supposed to enter Iraq from the north, but was unable to when the Turkish parliament refused permission. It ended up being kept nearby as a decoy, and eventually deployed as a follow-on force in April.) The entire invading force—all arms and national contigents combined—totalled about 130,000 people.[29]

Franks's intention was that "our ground forces, supported by overwhelming air power, would move so fast and deep into the Iraqi rear that time-and-distance factors would preclude the enemy's defensive maneuver. And this slow-reacting enemy would be fixed in place by the combined effect of artillery, air support, and attack helicopters."[30] The campaign proceeded largely as planned, with one exception. Iraq's regular forces did not put up much of a fight, but irregular forces proved more troublesome than expected. Lightly armed paramilitary units loyal to the regime, primarily the Saddam Fedayeen, often came at coalition troops in a suicidal rush. They were annihilated in droves and did not seriously threaten the coalition's success, but the need to protect flanks and supply lines from such unexpected attacks raised questions about whether to slow down the advance. Matters were further complicated by the arrival of terrible sandstorms in late March. U.S. commanders decided to continue moving forward regardless, and their boldness was rewarded as coalition forces advanced quickly in following days, helped by the pounding that U.S. air forces delivered on Iraqi positions. By April 5, the 3rd ID had reached the outskirts of Baghdad and taken Saddam International Airport, setting up positions for the Thunder Runs that led to the fall of the capital four days later.

As described above, the days following the toppling of Saddam's statue in Firdos Square were filled with joy and release, confusion and chaos. Coalition forces continued to mop up pockets of opposition while looters rampaged and public services of all kinds remained shut down. Some of this was inevitable, but what was surprising was that as the days went by, the situation did not significantly improve. Centcom's failure to plan for maintaining postwar order came back to haunt it, as did its obsession with quick, light entry. The invading forces, it became clear, were not prepared to stabilize the country, and in any case there were far too few of them on the ground to do so. As the 3rd ID's after-action report noted (using military jargon for postcombat activities), "3ID (M) transitioned into Phase IV SASO [stability and support operations] with no plan from higher headquarters. There was no guidance for restoring order in Baghdad, creating an interim government, hiring government and essential services employees, and ensuring the judicial system was operational. . . . [The division] did not have sufficient forces or effective rules of engagement (ROE) to control civilian looting and rioting throughout the city."[31]

Franks's war plan envisioned the ORHA team arriving months after combat ended, but Garner could see that the situation was slipping out of control and pestered military commanders to let him deploy immediately from Kuwait.[32] Realizing that he had a point, they grudgingly complied, and Garner and a few of his colleagues got to Baghdad on April 21. But the ORHA team found a city in crisis and was unable to reverse the decline. Garner's demeanor, moreover, was not what the situation called for—less that of a bold leader than of a kindly yet ineffective substitute teacher. He frequently noted that he expected to leave soon. Asked whether he was the new ruler of Iraq, he said: "The new ruler of Iraq is going to be an Iraqi. I don't rule anything. I'm the coalition facilitator to establish a different environment where these people can pull things together themselves and begin a self-government process."[33]

Rumsfeld had always considered Garner the initial head of the civilian postwar reconstruction effort—someone appropriate to oversee the expected relief and humanitarian problems that would emerge after the shooting stopped, but not somebody to handle the political and administrative challenges that would follow later on. As it became increasingly clear during April that the administration's rosy expectations for the postwar period were being overtaken by events, a decision was made in Washington to put a more authoritative figure in place quickly. Rumsfeld told Garner himself of this decision on April 24, but neither of them nor anybody else said anything publicly about it for another two weeks. And if Rumsfeld was indeed troubled by the emerging problems, he was not so upset as to reverse his plans for pulling American forces out as quickly as possible. On April 16, as Baghdad was slipping deeper into pandemonium, he and Franks stopped the flow of U.S. troops into the theater, directed that the ones already there start moving out soon, and downgraded the status of the military headquarters running operations in Iraq.

The result of all this was that during the month after the fall of Baghdad, American policy toward Iraq proceeded on four separate tracks. Those troops actually on the ground were hastily pressed into civil affairs and constabulary duties, with varying success. At the same time, they were being readied for departure, with many of their potential replacements being stopped in their tracks. Garner, his colleague Zalmay Khalilzad, and their staffs continued with the original postwar plan, trying to restart public services and holding meetings with Iraqis as a prelude to setting up an indigenous government. And behind their backs, finally, senior officials in Washington were shifting to a hastily cobbled-together Plan B, a heavier-handed approach featuring more direct American control over the situation by a new special envoy.

As the troop drawdowns continued apace, on May 6 Bush announced the appointment of retired diplomat L. Paul "Jerry" Bremer III as the head of the Coalition Provisional Authority, an organization that would absorb ORHA and assume control over all nonsecurity aspects of Iraqi governance.[34] Bremer arrived in Baghdad on May 12, with a much different vision of his role than Garner. "My new assignment," he would write, "combine[d] some of the viceregal responsibilities of General Douglas MacArthur, de facto ruler of Imperial Japan after World War II, and of General Lucius Clay, who led the American occupation of defeated Germany. . . . I would be the only paramount authority figure—other than dictator Saddam Hussein—that most Iraqis had ever known."[35]

The conventional storyline on the CPA stresses its sharp break with previous policy, embodied in "three terrible mistakes" supposedly made unilaterally by Bremer in his first days on the job—the pursuit of extensive de-Baathification, the disbanding of the Iraqi army, and the imposition of direct and open-ended American rule.[36] But the actual situation was more complicated. De-Baathification—the purging of Saddam's loyalists from the Iraqi government—was part of Washington's original postwar vision. Plans for it had been formulated and approved at the highest levels of the administration weeks earlier, and Bremer's role was simply to announce and execute them.[37] The dissolution of the army and the rest of the Iraqi national security apparatus, meanwhile, did represent a shift in policy, but one that was approved by Washington as a legitimate response to changing facts on the ground, particularly the Iraqi army's spontaneous "self-demobilization."[38] The deferral of a transition to Iraqi sovereignty, finally, seems to have been due to a mixture of second thoughts in Washington, Bremer's own views, and deference to the new proconsul's judgment.

The course of administration decisionmaking during these weeks is shrouded in mystery, with very few records yet available and possibly few created in the first place. As a senior administration official close to events described them to me, after the fall of Baghdad, "Things are starting to go out of control. People are really very fearful at that point about what the hell is going to happen. Garner, for all of his virtues, is not conveying any authority. . . . [Because there had been] no decision ever made about what the source of political authority would be, the country is falling apart. Bremer is sent out there, he thinks, to provide a stronger hand, and no one ever tells him otherwise. And that's how we default into an occupation."[39]

The CPA, in short, was an improvisation. As Ali Allawi bitingly comments, it is "only explicable in terms of a cover for sorting out a post-war 'Iraq policy,' when none had existed prior to the invasion."[40] Nevertheless, for such an ill-starred, ad hoc, and perennially under-resourced operation, Bremer's outfit actually accomplished a decent amount during its brief life span. Despite all the mistakes it made and the bad press it received, it was in large part a well-intentioned, serious attempt to run the country, and a marked improvement on the administration's previous efforts in this regard.[41] But in the end, like ORHA before it, the CPA was set an impossible task. Bremer and his colleagues confronted vast problems, were given little support and resources, and ultimately saw their efforts come to naught primarily thanks to deficiencies in an area over which they had no control—security.[42] For as fast as Bremer's team tried the put the country back together, it was pulled apart even faster by crime and an insurgency—problems that flourished in the vacuum created by the military's failure to maintain public order.

As Major General William Webster, the deputy commander of coalition ground forces during the war, noted, "All along, General Franks said that the Secretary of Defense wanted us to quickly leave and turn over post-hostilities to international organizations and nongovernment organizations led by ORHA. That was the notion."[43] Those plans continued even though nobody emerged to take the baton. The mid-April order to stop flowing reinforcements and start sending U.S. troops home had set the U.S. military presence on a course to drop to thirty thousand by the end of the summer. "Franks explicitly stated that military leaders should take as much risk coming out of Iraq as we did going in—which meant that we were going to try to get by with the smallest number of ground troops possible," the newly appointed coalition military commander in Iraq, freshly minted Lieutenant General Ricardo Sanchez, would write later. Responding to Sanchez's pleas for more troops, Franks's Centcom successor General John Abizaid eventually halted the withdrawals, but was unable to get the Pentagon's military or civilian leadership to send additional forces. So Sanchez never had enough resources to control the country, and had to keep moving his limited forces from hot spot to hot spot. "In effect, I was told, 'Do the best you can with the resources available.' So that's what we did."[44]

After a fitful year, in the spring of 2004 the fires that had been smoldering in Iraq burst into flames. At the end of March, CPA officials began to crack down on a Shiite militia leader named Muqtada al-Sadr, bringing the young cleric and his Mahdi Army into open rebellion against the occupation. A few days later, four American contractors were ambushed and killed in Fallujah, leading to calls that the city be forcibly taken from the Sunni insurgents and radical Islamists who controlled it. Sanchez and Bremer did not have the strength or authority to deal with one serious challenge, let alone two. And when Washington realized just how much victory would cost, it backed down and accepted draws against both enemies, defusing the immediate crises but in the process revealing the limits of its power to all.

A few months earlier, the administration had pulled the plug on Bremer's plan for a multiyear occupation and shifted American strategy back toward a relatively quick political handover to an Iraqi government. The CPA transferred sovereignty to an Iraqi Interim Government at the end of June 2004, which passed it to an Iraqi Transitional Government at the beginning of May 2005, which passed it on to a permanent Iraqi government in early May 2006. Meanwhile, violence proliferated and public disorder continued to deteriorate.

Stuck in Iraq long after they had expected to go home, most American military forces retreated to large, secure, and well-equipped "forward operating bases," making occasional aggressive patrols outside to gather information, counter terrorism, and try to suppress the growing insurgency. Sunni Arabs felt disenfranchised by de-Baathification, the disbanding of the armed forces, and the empowerment of the country's Shiite Arab majority. The Shiites were angered by the Sunnis' past crimes and present insurgency. The Kurds jealously guarded their regional autonomy. And everybody felt threatened by the pervasive lack of personal and communal security. The center did not hold, and by the second half of 2006, more than three years after U.S. forces had conquered Baghdad, Iraq had for all practical purposes descended into civil war.

FROM 9/11 TO 4/9

The Bush administration's Iraq policy throughout these years puzzled even experienced observers. Three questions in particular call for analysis: Why did the administration choose to go to war against Iraq in 2003? Where did the notion of a light postwar footprint come from? And how did such a predictably self-defeating approach to the operation get enshrined as national policy? The answers to the first two questions lie in the ideas held by key policymakers in the White House and

Defense Department. Those ideas might have remained mere intellectual curiosities, however, if not for a uniquely permissive environment—bureaucratically, domestically, and internationally. So the answer to the third question lies not in motivation but in opportunity, in a context that allowed a handful of senior officials near total freedom to translate their unusual views directly into practice with no significant check or compromise.

Without the 9/11 attacks, there would have been no Iraq War, so the story starts there, with the administration's reaction to the catastrophe. Given the Bush team's desultory approach to the threat of radical Islamist terrorism during the spring and summer of 2001, its senior decisionmakers might have responded to the attacks with chagrin and self-recrimination, conceding (at least tacitly) that their initial national security priorities had been incorrect and embracing the arguments they had previously rejected. If they had responded this way, they would still have undertaken a military campaign against al Qaeda and the Taliban, strengthened global counterterrorist operations and intelligence gathering, and paid increased attention to homeland security. But they would not have gone to war with Iraq, because there was never any significant reason to believe that Iraq had been connected to 9/11 or would be connected to similar attacks in the future.

Instead, the Bush team responded by clinging to many of its earlier views, incorporating Iraq and other issues (such as defense transformation and revived presidential powers) into a new foreign policy framework. The crucial moment came when the administration's senior figures decided to define the post-9/11 challenge as not merely responding to the attack that had just occurred, but also as preventing any future attack as well, whether by al Qaeda or anybody else. This ambitious approach helpfully cast into shadow previous debates about which threats had deserved most attention beforehand. (As Rice would put it, "Your response isn't to go back and beat yourself up about 9/11. It's to try to never let it happen again.")[45] But just as important, it simultaneously grandfathered any official's pet concerns onto the new security agenda.

If the point was not retribution but prevention, then the response to 9/11 could be disconnected from the attack itself and directed at any target that appeared to represent a potential threat. In Feith's words, "identifying the perpetrators was not the same as deciding how to define the enemy. If the proper top priority of U.S. action was to prevent the next attack, after all, then the enemy was not just the particular group responsible for the 9/11 hijackings. It was the wider network of terrorists and their backers that might organize additional, large-scale strikes against the United States." Within a couple of hours of the attacks, Feith had prepared a memo for Rumsfeld making this point, arguing that "the U.S. government should not feel constrained to limit its response to seeking out the individuals who had planned the attack. Rather, the United States might want to direct blows against the broader network of terrorists. All organizations involved in international terrorism could be considered in partnership with others in that business and held accountable 'one for the other,' as are partners under the laws of many countries."[46] All three senior civilians at the Defense Department apparently felt this way, along with the vice president and senior members of his staff. And given their preexisting fixation with Iraq (something that to this day remains a bit mysterious), in practice it would be Saddam's regime that came to mind as a natural second target.[47]

On September 13, Bush led an NSC meeting to discuss how the United States should respond to the attacks. The president "wanted to know whether Saddam was implicated in the 9/11 attack or otherwise connected to al Qaeda." But the secretary of defense was less concerned about a direct connection: "Looking beyond bin Laden and Afghanistan, Rumsfeld mentioned Saddam Hussein's Iraq as a threat to both its region and to the United States. Iraq, he observed, was a state that supported terrorism, and that might someday offer terrorists weapons of mass destruction to use against us. Unlike Afghanistan, however, Iraq also had substantial infrastructure and military capability. In Iraq, he noted, we could inflict the kind of costly damage that could cause terrorist-supporting regimes around the world to rethink their policies."[48]

Two days later, Bush assembled his national security team at Camp David for a retreat to sort through strategy. It was in these meetings that the initial course of the war on terrorism was set, what one might call "al Qaeda and Afghanistan first." Much has been made of the fact that at these meetings, Rumsfeld and his deputy Paul Wolfowitz pushed hard for attacking Iraq as well as Afghanistan and were overruled. But as Wolfowitz pointed out later on, the president's actual decision was less definitive:

> There was a long discussion during the day about what place if any Iraq should have in a counterterrorism strategy. . . . The real issue was whether Iraq should be part of the strategy at all and whether we should have this large strategic objective, which is getting governments out of the business of supporting terrorism, or whether we should simply go after bin Laden and al Qaeda. To the extent it was a debate about tactics and timing, the President clearly came down on the side of Afghanistan first. To the extent it was a debate about strategy and what the larger goal was, it is at least clear with 20/20 hindsight that the President came down on the side of the larger goal.[49]

Because war planning was kept secret from late 2001 through the summer of 2002, many did not appreciate the true link the administration saw between 9/11 and Iraq. In retrospect, though, the president could hardly have been clearer about what he was actually thinking, and the best guide to administration policy during this period was its public rhetoric.

Bush's weekly radio address on September 15, taped in a break from the meetings at Camp David, set the stage: "Victory against terrorism will not take place in a single battle, but in a series of decisive actions against terrorist organizations and those who harbor and support them."[50] A few days later, in his speech to a joint session of Congress, he unpacked the point a bit: "Our enemy is a radical network of terrorists, and every government that supports them. Our war on terror begins with al Qaeda, but it does not end there. . . . We will pursue nations that provide aid or safe haven to terrorism."[51] Six weeks later, he picked up the theme again: "We are at the beginning of our efforts in Afghanistan, and Afghanistan is only the beginning of our efforts in the world."[52] And two days after that, he told the United Nations, "For every regime that sponsors terror, there is a price to be paid. And it will be paid."[53]

In his State of the Union address in January 2002, Bush began to fill in details. After a sentence each on North Korea and Iran, he devoted five to Iraq, followed immediately by a commitment to action:

> America will do what is necessary to ensure our nation's security. We'll be deliberate, but time is not on our side. I will not wait on events while dangers gather. I will not stand by as peril draws closer and closer. The

> United States of America will not permit the world's most dangerous regimes to threaten us with the world's most destructive weapons.[54]

Four months later, in a speech at West Point, he spelled out his rationale for preventive action:

> Containment is not possible when unbalanced dictators with weapons of mass destruction can deliver those weapons on missiles or secretly provide them to terrorist allies. We cannot defend America and our friends by hoping for the best. . . . If we wait for threats to fully materialize, we will have waited too long. . . . [T]he war on terror will not be won on the defensive. We must take the battle to the enemy, disrupt his plans and confront the worst threats before they emerge. In the world we have entered, the only path to safety is the path of action. And this nation will act.[55]

And in late August, finally, Vice President Dick Cheney picked up the baton and connected the dots unmistakably:

> Under the Bush doctrine, a regime that harbors or supports terrorists will be regarded as hostile to the United States. . . . Simply stated, there is no doubt that Saddam Hussein now has weapons of mass destruction; there is no doubt that he is amassing them to use against our friends, against our allies, and against us. And there is no doubt that his aggressive regional ambitions will lead him in to future confrontations. . . . We will not simply look away, hope for the best, and leave the matter for some future administration to resolve. As President Bush has said, 'Time is not on our side.' . . . The risks of inaction are far greater than the risk of action.[56]

At the time, Cheney's speech was widely regarded as a salvo in the administration's internal bureaucratic fight over Iraq policy. Powell, for example, was trying to convince the president to go slow on the issue, and had requested a special meeting with Bush and Rice three weeks earlier to lay out his concerns. He spoke at length about the costs and difficulties of the proposed war and the challenges of the postwar occupation. Ten days after the meeting, Brent Scowcroft, Rice's mentor and national security adviser to the president's father, published an op-ed bluntly titled, "Don't Attack Saddam."[57] Powell called him up to say, "Thanks, you gave me some running room."[58] When Powell heard about Cheney's speech, therefore, he was "dumbfounded" and "astonished"; after getting a clarification from Bush about the desirability of resuming U.N. weapons inspections, he felt that "Cheney's intervention . . . seemed to have been neutralized for the moment."[59]

In retrospect, however, it seems clear that Cheney was not freelancing or jockeying for position, but simply voicing the president's own thinking, which was already well on its way to being translated into administration policy. When Franks had briefed Bush and the NSC on Iraq plans in late December 2001, the president had laid down a clear marker at the end of the meeting. "We should remain optimistic that diplomacy and international pressure will succeed in disarming the regime," the president said. "But if this approach isn't successful, we have to have other options. That's why I asked Secretary Rumsfeld and Tommy to work on this concept. The worst thing that could happen to America would be a combination of WMD and terrorism. . . . I will not allow that to happen."[60] Seven months later—and one month before Cheney's speech—the British had gotten the message clearly: "Bush wanted to remove Saddam, through military action, justified by the conjunction of terrorism and WMD."[61]

During the fall of 2002, as the Bush administration sought to sell the coming Iraq War to Congress, the American public, and the world at large, it mounted a major public relations campaign that led many people to think war was necessary because the threat Saddam posed—whether of terrorism, WMD use, or a combination of the two—was urgent and growing. What the administration did not always admit, however, was that senior officials themselves had a lower bar for action. In the words of a sympathetic British official in March 2002, "The truth is that what has changed is not the pace of Saddam Hussein's WMD programmes, but our tolerance of them post-11 September."[62]

PLAN A

Just as the Bush administration could have responded aggressively to 9/11 without attacking Iraq, so it could have attacked Iraq without shortchanging the aftermath.[63] The administration chose to adopt a light footprint concept in its postwar planning, however, and that decision arguably paved the way for most of what followed. So what lay behind it? The lessons the administration drew from history and the last war.

Given that the Iraq War was a sequel, one might expect its endgame planning to have been driven by the memory of the Gulf War a dozen years earlier, and in one obvious way it was: this time around, the White House decided, the war would be fought to the finish and Saddam's regime would be toppled rather than simply forced back on its heels. But beyond that, the issue gets complicated.

The decision not to go to Baghdad in 1991, after all, had been made consciously and carefully, following a great deal of structured debate about the costs, risks, and potential benefits of alternative courses of action. Officials in the George H. W. Bush administration knew they could topple Saddam's regime fairly easily, but chose not to do so because they feared being stuck in a quagmire afterward. As then former secretary of defense Cheney had put it in 1992:

> If we'd gone to Baghdad and got rid of Saddam Hussein—assuming we could have found him—we'd have had to put a lot of forces in and run him to ground some place. He would not have been easy to capture. Then you've got to put a new government in his place and then you're faced with the question of what kind of government are you going to establish in Iraq? Is it going to be a Kurdish government or a Shia government or a Sunni government? How many forces are you going to have to leave there to keep it propped up, how many casualties are you going to take through the course of this operation?[64]

Even in retrospect, moreover, the former president and most of his senior national security team had few regrets about their decision—not because they liked seeing Saddam in power, but because they felt their original concerns remained valid. They saw no reason to fight the war a second time just to reverse the outcome.[65] (Cheney himself was the exception to this rule, changing his position over the course of the following decade for reasons that have never really been explained.)

When the later Bush administration decided to take the road less traveled, therefore, it might have been expected to do so on the basis of considered responses to its predecessor's concerns. But there is simply no evidence of this ever happening. What is striking is the reverse—just how *little* role the Gulf War analogy seems to have played in the later administration's thinking. Senior officials in 2001–2003 appear never to have engaged the experiences of 1991 seriously, asking themselves why the obstacles the earlier Bush administration raised were insignificant or how they would be overcome. The second Bush administration appears to have consigned the first to the dustbin of history, treating it less like a legitimate predecessor than like the supposedly contemptible Clinton administration in between—a source of policies so obviously wrongheaded as not to require serious consideration or refutation.[66]

The administration did rely on perceived lessons from the "last war"—but rather than the Gulf War, it was the post-9/11 Afghan campaign that filled this cognitive niche. Rumsfeld in particular had not been involved in the earlier conflict against Iraq and brought to his second turn as defense secretary (his first was under Ford) a strong conviction that the U.S. armed forces had become sluggish, hidebound, and excessively risk-averse in the years he had been out of government. He was insistent on promoting defense "transformation," which he saw as involving not only the adoption of new technology but also a new, more expeditionary approach to the use of force in general.

During the 1990s, many Republicans had excoriated the Clinton administration for getting bogged down in peacekeeping missions and humanitarian interventions from Somalia to Haiti to the Balkans. President Bush bought into this critique, and Rumsfeld did so even more.[67] He even added his own twist—a foreign policy version of the domestic policy argument that welfare creates a culture of dependency. The operations of the 1990s, Rumsfeld believed, were not just expensive but counterproductive. They were mistakes to avoid rather than lessons to follow. The use of force should be quick and decisive, with no lingering entanglements or cumbersome commitments in its wake. As far as Rumsfeld was concerned, the campaign in Afghanistan showcased just such qualities, and it could and should serve as a template for future campaigns in general—including the one on deck, which just so happened to be Iraq. As he put it a month before the invasion of Iraq began:

> From the outset of the war our guiding principle has been that Afghanistan belongs to the Afghans. The United States does not aspire to own it or run it. This shaped how we approached the military campaign. General Franks would not send a massive invasion and occupation force. . . . Instead he keeps the coalition footprint modest. . . . The objective is not to engage in what some call nation-building. Rather it's to try to help the Afghans so that they can build their own nation. This is an important

> distinction. In some nation-building exercises, well-intentioned foreigners arrive on the scene, look at the problems, and say let's fix it. This . . . can really be a disservice in some instances, because . . . they can create a dependency. . . . If the United States were to lead an international coalition in Iraq . . . it would be guided by two commitments: Stay as long as necessary, and to leave as soon as possible. . . . The goal would not be to impose an American-style template on Iraq, but rather to create conditions where Iraqis can form a government in their own unique way just as the Afghans did. . . .[68]

Seven months later, he proudly repeated the point, crowing over the "innovative and impressive plan to win the peace . . . in Iraq and in Afghanistan" and explaining how it was "different from some of the so-called nation building efforts of the past":

> Today in Iraq we're operating on the guiding principle that has brought success to our effort in Afghanistan. . . . [W]e did not flood the country with a half million U.S. troops; we kept our footprint modest, liberating Iraq with something slightly over 100,000 forces in the country, and when major combat ended we began working immediately to enlist Iraqis to take responsibility for governance and security of their own country. . . . [W]e are not in Iraq to engage in nation-building. . . . The foreign presence in any country is in my view unnatural, it's a lot like a broken bone, if a broken bone is not set properly in a relatively short period of time the tendons and the muscle and the skin grow around the break and the break becomes natural and eventually the body adjusts to what is an abnormal situation. If one then tries to refix it, to extract it, to mend that break after it's already healed wrong, there's a problem. And this is what's happened in some past nation-building exercises in my view. . . .[69]

The Bush administration knew it wanted to get rid of Saddam, and knew it wanted to avoid getting stuck in Iraq afterward, so it had to find a way of bypassing both of the obstacles its predecessors had bumped up against.[70] The solution came in the form of a conceptual differentiation between "occupation" and "liberation," based on the assumption that Iraqis would welcome rather than resist the overthrow of their regime, retain a functioning state apparatus, and cooperate easily with the invaders and each other afterward, rendering a full-scale occupation presence unnecessary and counterproductive. The correct historical precedent to rely on, the argument ran, was not post–World War II Germany or Japan, but post–World War II France, which had not required a lengthy or invasive foreign presence in order to flourish once the fighting stopped.[71]

There has been much discussion of the role of the exiled Iraqi opposition in the administration's Iraq policy, and critics have charged that Ahmed Chalabi in particular played a critical role in the drive to war and the shaping of initial postwar plans. Yet historians will probably accord the opposition a much less prominent role in events than contemporaries have. National security officials in the United States and other countries believed that Saddam had prohibited weapons programs for many reasons, not simply because they bought a bill of goods sold by Chalabi's opposition group, the Iraqi National Congress.[72] And while some on the Bush team did envision Chalabi as a future Iraqi leader, he and the other opposition figures were really convenient answers to a problem—who can we hand off postwar Iraq to?—rather than drivers of American policy. The fact that Chalabi presented himself as everything the administration wanted—pro-American, democratic, secular, even Zionist—is a testimony to his political savvy. But the real product he was selling was one that the administration's hawks had already decided to buy: a case for toppling Saddam and then walking away from postwar Iraq without feeling guilty.

The administration's decision to opt for a "zipless" approach to implementing regime change was not only consequential, but also radical—perhaps even more so than the war itself. The invasion of Iraq, after all, however controversial, could at least be said to have been launched in support of long-standing goals of great importance repeatedly endorsed in national and international policy. A quick-and-dirty approach to postwar security and reconstruction, in contrast, flew in the face of professional "best practices" and widely expressed conventional wisdom. As the first major independent case for the war, by Kenneth Pollack in *Foreign Affairs*, put it in early 2002,

> Using a standoff approach to regime change . . . would limit American ability to control events while opening the door to mischief-makers who would try to turn Saddam's fall to their own advantage. . . . The military aspects of an invasion, actually, are likely to be the easiest part of the deal. . . . The biggest headaches for the United States are likely to stem

> not from the invasion itself but from its aftermath. Once the country has been conquered and Saddam's regime driven from power, the United States would be left "owning" a country of 22 million people ravaged by more than two decades of war, totalitarian misrule, and severe deprivation. The invaders would get to decide the composition and form of a future Iraqi government—both an opportunity and a burden. . . . It would be up to the United States to make sure that a post-Saddam Iraq did not slip into chaos like Lebanon in the 1980s or Afghanistan in the 1990s, creating spillover effects in the region and raising the possibility of a new terrorist haven.[73]

Practically every aspect of the light footprint approach violated mainstream thinking among national security professionals. Prewar analyses by serious observers stressed the likely postwar problems the administration would face, the need to deploy U.S. forces capable of maintaining order, the importance of postwar security in determining the odds of a successful democratic transformation, and the need to plan the new regime's political arrangements carefully.[74] These points were so obvious they were even drilled home often in those bastions of Establishment consensus, the blue-ribbon panel report.[75]

Nor was it only outside experts who were making such points. The State Department's Policy Planning Staff did a careful study of what best practices in handling postwar issues would look like, and the department's "Future of Iraq Project" engaged large numbers of Iraqis in discussions of postwar problems.[76] The National Intelligence Council conducted a study that concluded, "Any new authority in Iraq would face a country with societal fractures and significant potential for violent conflict among domestic groups if not prevented by an occupying force."[77] And the U.S. Army War College's Strategic Studies Institute issued a particularly prescient study, the blunt conclusion of which is worth quoting in full:

> To be successful, an occupation such as that contemplated after any hostilities in Iraq requires much detailed interagency planning, many forces, multi-year military commitment, and a national commitment to nation-building. Recent American experiences with post-conflict operations have generally featured poor planning, problems with relevant military force structure, and difficulties with a handover from military to civilian responsibility. To conduct their share of the essential tasks that must

> be accomplished to reconstruct an Iraqi state, military forces will be severely taxed in military police, civil affairs, engineer, and transportation units, in addition to possible severe security difficulties. The administration of an Iraqi occupation will be complicated by deep religious, ethnic, and tribal differences which dominate Iraqi society. U.S. forces may have to manage and adjudicate conflicts among Iraqis that they can barely comprehend. An exit strategy will require the establishment of political stability, which will be difficult to achieve given Iraq's fragmented population, weak political institutions, and propensity for rule by violence.[78]

The senior civilian leadership of the Defense Department, of course, disagreed strongly with such thinking. When Army Chief of Staff General Eric Shinseki was asked at a congressional hearing a month before the war how many troops would be required for the postwar era, he answered, "something on the order of several hundred thousand soldiers. . . . We are talking about post-hostilities control over a piece of geography that is fairly significant with the ethnic tensions that could lead to other problems. It takes a significant ground force presence to maintain a safe and secure environment. . . ."[79] When they heard about Shinseki's remarks, Rumsfeld and his top aides were furious, and Wolfowitz was given authority to push back strongly. A couple of days later, Wolfowitz told another congressional committee that: "some of the higher-end predictions that we have been hearing recently, such as the notion that it will take several hundred thousand U.S. troops to provide stability in post-Saddam Iraq, are wildly off the mark. . . . It is hard to conceive that it would take more forces to provide stability in a post-Saddam Iraq than it would take to conduct the war itself and to secure the surrender of Saddam's security forces and his army—hard to imagine."[80]

It should not have been hard to imagine: Shinseki was not pulling his numbers out of thin air, and other experts were tossing around similar figures. But there is no reason to believe that Wolfowitz and his colleagues were being deceitful. They simply rejected the premises and reasoning on which mainstream professionals relied. At one point a worried NSC staffer took it upon himself to prepare a briefing for senior officials on the discrepancy between the scale of the postwar plans being prepared for Iraq and the scale of past such operations, but nobody batted an eyelash. "As far as the White House was concerned, the briefing largely spelled out how the Clinton administration and foreign governments had carried out nation-building and peacekeeping operations in the past. Afghanistan had been the Bush administration's first foreign intervention and it was charting a new course."[81]

FROM PLAN TO POLICY

Whatever one thinks about the merits of the light footprint approach, its outside-the-box nature means that accounting for its intellectual origins is only the beginning of the story—one must account as well for how it became the approved policy of the U.S. government as a whole and was then translated into action on the ground in Iraq. The answer lies in a highly unusual absence of checks and balances, both inside the administration and out. A combination of four separate factors—a dysfunctional national security decisionmaking process, an obedient and blinkered uniformed military, a trusting Congress and public, and global hegemony—removed all obstacles from the path of Rumsfeld and his allies, allowing their views to drive events following the fall of Baghdad. The first two were variants of bureaucratic politics, while the latter two were a function of 9/11 and American relative power in the international system.

"I'm not a textbook player. I'm a gut player," Bush told journalist Bob Woodward in 2002, and in retrospect this seems a crucial fact about the Bush presidency.[82] As one of his press secretaries would later put it, "President Bush has always been an instinctive leader more than an intellectual leader. He is not one to delve deeply into all the possible policy options—including sitting around engaging in extended debate about them—before making a choice. Rather, he chooses based on his gut and his most deeply held convictions. Such was the case with Iraq."[83] The problem was exacerbated by Bush's temperament, which prized certitude and resolve and scorned second-guessing and dissent of any kind. Throw in a penchant for bold, "consequential" decisions rather than "small ball," and the result was an accident waiting to happen.[84]

The risks inherent in such a situation could have been minimized by a decisionmaking process that supplied the analytical rigor and prudence the president himself lacked, but that was not to be. Bush chose three powerful, experienced figures for his initial national security team. To coordinate them and staff him personally, he chose someone with less stature but better chemistry. Bush must have known that Cheney, Powell, and Rumsfeld would disagree bitterly over key issues, and he must have known that Rice would have a difficult time herding them together. And yet his management approach was to instruct her to forge some sort of consensus, so that he would not have to resolve disputes himself.[85] Unsurprisingly, lacking the respect of all three of the cantankerous bulls and support from the president, Rice found it almost impossible to run a coherent interagency process.[86]

Rice made matters worse by catering to Bush's whims rather than challenging them. In the words of one colleague, Rice's "goal was to figure out where she thought the president was going to go and end up there about ten seconds before he got there."[87] Rice "defined her job as Bush's enabler and enforcer. This earned her the president's enduring trust, loyalty, and support—and ultimately a promotion to secretary of state. But it wasn't at all clear that seeing this job primarily as staffing the president rather than managing the policymaking process was what this president needed—even though, by all evidence, it was what he wanted."[88]

If the national security adviser could not bring herself to think differently from the president, meanwhile, the secretary of state could not bring himself to voice the different thoughts he did have. Never too upset about the conclusion of the Gulf War, even after 9/11 Powell thought that Saddam's regime was not a particularly urgent problem. "Iraq isn't going anywhere," he noted. "It's in a fairly weakened state. It's doing some things we don't like. We'll continue to contain it."[89] Nor did he see any way to avoid endless headaches once Saddam was toppled. When he began to realize just how serious the president was about going to war, he delivered an impassioned cri de coeur to Bush in private: "You are going to be the proud owner of 25 million people. You will own all their hopes, aspirations, and problems. It's going to suck the oxygen out of everything. *This will become the first term.*"[90] After the meeting, Powell "felt he had left nothing unsaid." Yet even in this, his most outspoken moment, he had pulled his punches so much that Rice, who was also there, thought a fitting headline for the meeting would be, "Powell Makes Case for Coalition as Only Way to Assure Success."[91]

Powell never told Bush he was opposed to war, and when asked to sign on to the operation two months before it was launched, he agreed.[92] (CIA director George Tenet also never told Bush he disagreed with the decision to go to war, although this is less significant because it is not the role of the CIA director to formally weigh in on policy issues.)[93] The result was that NSC debates "did not divide as prowar and antiwar. Rather, there were those (chiefly, the President, Cheney, Rumsfeld, and Rice) who developed the conviction that removing Saddam from power was necessary, even if it required war. And there were others (Powell first and foremost) who went along with the president's Iraq policy halfheartedly at most. Through comments and body language, the latter group signaled lack of commitment, but they did not champion an alternative strategy."[94]

After 9/11, the administration fell into a permanent crisis mode, with a dramatically heightened threat perception and a sense that desperate times called for desperate measures. Never wide to begin with, the president's circle of confidence narrowed further than ever, and he relied even more than before on the experienced and calmly decisive vice president. The White House slid into a hard-line course that was never formally vetted or weighed against alternatives, with policy formulation conducted by a few people at the top of the pyramid and execution delegated to carefully chosen junior officials in one of the line agencies.

Perhaps the best-known example of this was the legal side of the war on terror, where the chain of authority initially ran from the vice president's counsel, David Addington, through White House counsel Aberto Gonzales and senior layers of the Justice Department, down to the deputy in the Office of Legal Counsel, John Yoo, who provided the desired rationales for unfettered executive action.[95] There seem to have been echoes of such a pattern on Iraq policy as well, with strategy originating at the level of the president and vice president, passing lightly through Rice's NSC, and landing at Rumsfeld's office for elaboration and execution. Such a system had short-run benefits, allowing the president to get the policies he wanted without delay, deliberation, compromise, or confrontation. But it also had long-run costs, yielding policies that proved to be seriously flawed and unsustainable.

Thus when Iraq war planning moved from the administration's back rooms to its front rooms in August 2002, senior officials prepared a paper laying out the administration's "goals, objectives, and strategy for Iraq."[96] The goal was an Iraq that renounced weapons of mass destruction and support for terrorism, did not threaten its neighbors, remained unified, respected the rights of its people and the rule of law, and started moving toward democracy. The objective was to achieve such a goal without provoking the use of WMD or causing instability, and the strategy was to accomplish this by "employing all instruments of U.S. national power" and working with allies and compatible members of the Iraqi opposition (under Security Council approval "if possible"). After a conflict, the administration would set up

> an interim administration in Iraq that prepares for the transition to an elected Iraqi government as quickly as practical; immediately [help] provide for external and internal security; rapidly [start] the country's political, economic, and security reconstruction; [provide] immediate humanitarian assistance to those in need; substantially [preserve but reform] the current Iraqi bureaucracy; [bring] war criminals to justice; [and reform] the Iraqi military, security, and law enforcement institutions.

At the same time the administration was embracing this extremely ambitious agenda, however, it was also embracing extremely optimistic predictions about how little would need to be done to realize it. ("It turns out we had one erroneous assumption," Rice admitted a few years later: "that you could decapitate these ministries and that you'd have a civil service underneath that would actually take up the day-to-day running [of the country].")[97] And to top it off, the White House then conferred all responsibility for postwar planning and operations on the Defense Department, which was openly contemptuous of the entire nation-building concept. A better-structured decisionmaking process would have exposed and probed these inconsistencies, resolving them by either reducing the scale of U.S. objectives, increasing the efforts and resources devoted to achieving them, or reconsidering the operation altogether.[98] In the Bush administration, however, no one could tell the president that his idealistic goals were unlikely to be obtainable or tell Rumsfeld to do what was necessary to obtain them.

With the White House and other agencies providing little oversight or interference, Rumsfeld's main obstacle to putting the light footprint into practice was the uniformed military, some members of which were predisposed to be unsympathetic. The previous war against Iraq, after all, had involved half a million troops—and that was a force meant only to dislodge Saddam from Kuwait, not topple him and transform his country from the ground up. The Iraq war plans that Centcom had on the shelf when the Bush administration entered office were not that different, involving almost four hundred thousand troops and a long, slow buildup.

But if the model for civil-military relations during the Gulf War was Samuel Huntington's "objective civilian control"—that is, deference to the professional military on matters of strategy and tactics—the model during the Iraq War was its opposite.[99] Rumsfeld felt contempt rather than deference for the department's conventional wisdom, and calmly set about bending the military to his will. His first order of business was to eliminate the Joint Chiefs of Staff as an independent source of authority. Then he stocked the hierarchy with officers who would follow his lead. And finally he took personal charge of the war planning process, demanding endless drafts and relentlessly pushing Franks to deliver something that conformed to his specifications.

Few in the military were happy about all of this, particularly in the army (which bore the brunt of the secretary's ire). The mainstream view, in fact, might well have been summed up in the haiku one officer—the deputy intelligence officer for the invading forces—jotted down in late 2002:

Rumsfeld is a dick
Won't flow the forces we need
We will be too light.[100]

But the U.S. military is highly professional and deeply imbued with the tradition of civilian control, and it had no desire for occupation duties, either. So most officers simply shelved whatever disapproval they may have felt and gave their boss what he wanted. As Thomas White, the civilian army secretary during this period, put it: "If you grind away at the military guys long enough, they will finally say, 'Screw it, I'll do the best I can with what I have.' "[101]

Some in the military, moreover, had their own reasons for wanting a small presence. Abizaid, the Centcom deputy commander at the time of the invasion, believed that large numbers of American forces on the ground would make things worse rather than better. Discussing postwar issues in March 2003, he commented that "We must in all things be modest . . . [because] we are an antibody in their culture."[102]

The most important military figure involved in these matters was the theater commander, the senior officer squarely in the chain of command. It so happened, however, that Tommy Franks, the Centcom commander during the period in question, was just as uninterested in postwar Iraq as Rumsfeld, and just as determined to avoid anything resembling a large or protracted U.S. commitment there. So he not only failed to oppose Rumsfeld's light footprint vision, but actually encouraged it. Despite clear orders making him responsible for maintaining order in Iraq following the conflict, Franks ignored postwar planning almost entirely, seeing his mission in purely operational and negative terms—"removing Saddam from power."[103]

In April 2003, Franks expressed his true feelings about postwar duties during a discussion with staff about what to call the new, smaller military headquarters—a "combined joint task force"—that would manage the occupation. How about "CJTF-13," suggested one aide, poking fun at the misfortune of the officers who would be assigned there. "Let's make it CJTF-1369, unlucky cocksuckers," the Centcom commander cracked.[104] Soon afterward, he retired to write a memoir and go on the lecture circuit.

THE STRONG DO WHAT THEY CAN

The ideas and attitudes of senior officials obviously played a crucial role in shaping Iraq policy during the Bush years. But the common view that sees the administration's foreign policy as a quest for domination—of Iraq, the Middle East, or the world more generally—gets things backward. The administration's fundamental course, its unusually active role in world affairs, was less a pursuit of power than a reflection of it. The strong do what they can, Thucydides noted, and the relative strength of the United States had been growing for more than two centuries. By the turn of the millennium, the country was very strong indeed, and in such circumstances the surprise would have been not something resembling an American empire, but rather modesty, humility, or isolation. What the world saw after 9/11, in other words, was simply the latest chapter in a very familiar story—how the United States has used its power to try to shape the outside world in its image.

In the 1990s, following the collapse of the Soviet Union, American policymakers found themselves adrift in an unexpected and unfamiliar setting. Standing alone at the top of the international system, with no significant challengers to American primacy remaining, their reflexive instinct was to extend the liberal order of "the West" to the globe at large. Yet no one really knew how long the unipolar moment would last, and there seemed little interest at home in spending large amounts of blood and treasure on foreign adventures. The result was muddling through, as the country's foreign policy establishment tried to keep history rolling forward in its grooves without causing anybody, least of all Americans themselves, too much trouble.

And then came 9/11. In many ways, the debate over the war on terrorism was déjà vu all over again. Reprising the traditionalist interpretation of the origins of the Cold War, many observers saw the Bush administration's moves in Afghanistan, Iraq, and elsewhere as a reaction to a new set of pressing external threats. Others reprised the revisionist stance, arguing that the administration seized on the attacks as a pretext for doing what it wanted to do anyway, which was to expand its global writ at others' expense. As before, both of these perspectives caught part of the picture, but neither did justice to what actually happened—because neither adequately addressed the interaction between America's relative power, its ideals, and its behavior. What both omitted was the crucial fact that in the years between the collapse of the Soviet Union and the collapse of the twin towers, the United States pulled even further ahead of the rest of the pack, becoming in both economic and military terms not just the strongest power in the system but by some measures the strongest state in the modern history of international politics. This massive power potential was bound to express itself eventually in a comparably ambitious world role, although just when and how remained to be seen.

In retrospect, therefore, 9/11 may well take its place in the history books alongside the 1950 Communist invasion of South Korea, as a catalyst that intensified and militarized a new phase of international politics—this one characterized by American unipolarity. Just as the outbreak of the Korean War gave life and money to an American script for postwar order that had been largely written but not yet produced, so the attacks on New York and Washington galvanized Washington into fully accepting the leading role in post–Cold War international politics that it had previously viewed with ambivalence. The Bush administration's much-discussed 2002 National Security Strategy, from this perspective, was notable less for any intellectual innovation than for its open (and tactless) proclamation of this new state of affairs. It reflected the new ideological superstructure that followed naturally from the new material base.

The real story of the Bush doctrine in action is thus one of lack of constraints. Primacy removed constraints coming from the world at large, and the 9/11 attacks swept away constraints coming from the domestic political system. The administration's leading figures found themselves with extraordinary freedom of action, greater in some ways than that any of their predecessors had ever had, and the only question was how they would use it.[105]

The invasion of Afghanistan was reflexive, requiring no explanation more complicated than stimulus and response. After that, however, things started to get interesting. The administration still had unquestioned international and domestic power at its disposal, but there were several ways it could have put them to use. Some commentators suggested continuing to focus on al Qaeda and Afghanistan. Others pressed for a major initiative to reduce dependence on oil, or an attempt to restart the Middle East peace process, or a redoubling of efforts to corral loose nukes. The Bush team opted instead to go after Iraq.

No explanation relying only on structural variables can account for why, given all the options open to it, the eight-hundred-pound American gorilla decided to sit on Iraq (or why it did so clumsily). Yet no explanation relying only on agency can account for why a few officials with idiosyncratic views had the opportunity, during a brief moment in the sun, to seize the helm of American foreign policy and steer it wherever they wanted. With different decisionmakers in power in Washington in 2002–2003, there would not have been an invasion of Iraq (and if for some reason there had been, the aftermath would have been handled differently). Yet in a different structural context—such as the administration's first nine months or last four years—even the same decisionmakers would not have generated the same policies.

Primacy not only cleared the way for the administration to do what it wanted, but also helped the administration decide what it wanted to do. After all, the world is full of threats, of varying size and urgency. Weak countries can afford to deal with only the greatest or nearest of them, but strong countries can look further afield to head off dangers still aborning. George W. Bush sometimes compared himself to Harry S. Truman, and there were indeed some similarities between their situations. American policymakers during the Truman administration, for example, were truly worried about the Soviet Union, but those worries were themselves partly the product of America's extraordinary strength at the time—for what officials worried about was not an immediate military threat to American national security but some potential future challenge to America's broader environment. The same was true of the Bush administration half a century later. Policymakers were indeed worried about Iraq, but once again those worries were partly a product of extraordinary strength—for they were not about what Saddam was going to do tomorrow, but rather what he might do at some future point down the road. Only very strong powers can afford to indulge casually in such "anticipatory self-defense."[106] The differences in foreign policy activism between Bush the father and Bush the son, ironically, were due in significant part to the growth of American power during the Clinton interregnum.

EPILOGUE: THE SURGE AND WHAT MIGHT HAVE BEEN

For years after the invasion, Washington fiddled while Iraq burned. With the administration's course having been set, there was no real appetite or powerful constituency for changing it, especially when doing so would appear to validate the administration's growing number of critics. By the fall of 2006, however, as the country slipped ever deeper into open civil war, even the Bush team was forced to take notice, and the result was the most thorough debate on Iraq policy during the entire decade.[107]

Senior officials in the Defense Department, both civilian and military, wanted to continue the existing policy of transitioning responsibility to local Iraqi forces.[108] Others in the administration had come to the conclusion that such a middle course was no longer viable—not only because it was failing on the ground in Iraq, but also because that failure was leading to a loss of political support for the war at home in the United States. Representing this widespread popular dissatisfaction, a bipartisan panel of "wise men" had been appointed by Congress to conduct an independent review of the situation. This Iraq Study Group was set to report its findings by the end of the year, and it was an open secret that the group's general purpose was to chart a course for pulling back—for extrication rather than victory. The State Department's position was somewhat similar. Some staffers at the NSC, finally, along with a few outside experts and some dissident officers within the uniformed military, favored a third option, trying to stabilize the situation by throwing in more troops and adopting a different strategy.

In December, after a resounding Democratic victory in the midterm congressional elections and the firing of Rumsfeld, Bush opted for the third route. As he put it during one NSC meeting, " 'I want to make clear what I see as the options here. We can hold steady. None of you say it is working. We can redeploy for failure'—he looked over at Rice—'that's your option, Condi.' Or, he added, 'We can surge for success.' "[109] Bush announced the new policy in January 2007, and in February, David Petraeus replaced George Casey as the senior commander on the ground to implement it, supported by his pro-surge deputy (and later successor) Ray Odierno.

In many ways, the adoption of the "surge" (as the new policy became known) was the highlight of the Bush administration's dealings with Iraq—the result of a serious-minded exercise that considered a full range of options; assessed their potential costs, risks, and benefits; and backed up a clear choice with appropriate personnel and resources. In truth, though, the Washington drama of late 2006 was less about blazing a new path than about retracing steps and getting back on the road not taken. For the basic ideas of the surge—more U.S. troops rather than fewer, seeking to protect the population rather than kill enemies, making alliances with all local forces willing to cooperate, and in the process buying time for Iraqi politics to evolve peacefully—had been batted around for years.[110] They represented the course the Pentagon and administration in general had rejected in 2003 and later, as they tried to do the occupation on the cheap and be home by Christmas.

Listening to Bush discuss the details of the new approach, Rice thought to herself that the president "was aware that he had decided on too few troops for the initial invasion and occupation and was determined not to come up short again."[111] As one of its biographers has put it, "the new strategy was a plan for a 'long war.' First would come increased security. Then would come political progress, and with it, the building of a reliable army and police force. And all that—if it worked—would take many, many years. In sum, the short war approach that the United States had followed for years had been abandoned. The U.S. military had arrived in Baghdad in April 2003 with the expectation of largely leaving by that September. For three years after that, commanders had planned variations on that swift exit. Now the long war was about to begin."[112]

Even supporters of the surge were not sure whether it would end up being too little, too late, and it was not until the summer of 2007 that significant positive returns on the policy began to appear.[113] From that point on, however, the situation began to improve, and violence continued to decline in the years that followed. The progress was due partly to the new troops and the implementation of the military's new counterinsurgency doctrine, partly to continued and intensified efforts to bring Sunni tribal leaders in from the cold, and partly to a stand-down by Muqtada al-Sadr's Mahdi Army and other Shiite militias. None of the developments was decisive by itself, but together they created a virtuous circle of stabilization: the new U.S. military approach provided enough protection for secular Sunnis to break with the radical Islamists and survive; together, the U.S. and secular Sunni forces were strong enough to suppress the Sunni radicals; and all this helped coax the Shiite militias into cease-fires.

The result was neither total peace, nor true reconciliation, nor even a durable local political balance. Moreover, by strengthening peripheral forces at the expense of the central government, the surge and related policies may even have made long-term national stability harder to achieve. Yet as one official involved put it, "in order to have a long term, you had to have a short term." Petraeus was correct in telling his troops, when passing command to Odierno in September 2008, that with the surge they had "helped to reverse a downward spiral toward civil war and to wrest the initiative from the enemies of the new Iraq."[114]

The success of the surge, however partial or temporary, inevitably raises questions about what would have happened had similar policies been adopted in the immediate postwar period. Former U.S. ambassador to the United Nations John Bolton has argued that a neat division can be drawn between the administration's war and postwar Iraq policies, and that it is an "erroneous and pernicious view" to regard the failure of the latter as tarnishing the success of the former.[115] But this gets the matter precisely backward. Since the supposed threat posed by Saddam's unconventional weapons programs was the central casus belli, the war's legitimacy was inevitably undercut by the revelation of the true, relatively backward state of those programs. Yet a successful transition from Saddam's tyranny to a more benign political order might have given the operation some degree of retrospective legitimization, and so failure on that front was just as humiliating as the missing WMD and far more consequential. In fact, given the massive costs of the conflict and the lack of imminence of the threat, a hypothetically better postwar period would have been necessary to justify the war even if large WMD stockpiles had actually been found.

Some former Pentagon officials have argued that the real reason things went wrong in Iraq was that the original postwar plan for a quick transfer of sovereignty was jettisoned and replaced by an extended foreign occupation. Had the administration only continued on its original path, they suggest, all would have been fine.[116] But this claim glosses over the fact that the administration changed course only after, and because, it recognized that the original approach was in serious trouble and heading for more.[117]

The most interesting counterfactual to consider is how events might have played out if the administration had handled both the military and the political aspects of the postwar era differently from the start, planning properly to assume full control of Iraq after the fighting stopped and creating a stable and secure environment in which a new political order could emerge over time.[118] In that case, the argument runs, crime and violence might have been suppressed; foreign agitators kept at bay; basic services restored more quickly; political and social institutions designed to bridge sectarian cleavages and promote broad national interests; and efforts made to give all groups a stake in the new regime. Iraqis might not have felt so insecure and traumatized by their new circumstances and might have been less quick to take refuge in communal identities and counterproductive self-help behavior. Shiite militias might not have had free rein and the Sunni insurgency might have remained at the level of scattered banditry rather than a mortal threat to the occupation. Civil war might not have broken out and something closer to the Iraq of 2010 might have appeared several years earlier, without all the intervening turmoil.[119]

This more hopeful picture—with the chaos of 2003–2007 understood as a postoperative infection caused by the surgeon's malpractice—is less easy to dismiss than some might think. The chief argument against it is that Iraq's internal divisions essentially constituted a preexisting medical condition, one that the events of late spring 2003 revealed rather than caused. As Ali Allawi puts it:

> When the Coalition arrived in Baghdad on 9 April, 2003, it found a fractured and brutalized society, presided over by a fearful, heavily armed minority. . . . The terrible social legacy of the previous two decades

> was hardly recognized by American troops who entered Baghdad. . . . Neither did returning Iraqis fully fathom the changes that had taken place in their country, and the fundamental change that the Iraqi psyche had undergone over the decades of dictatorship, war, and sanctions. . . . Saddam had succeeded, to an extent that would only later become apparent, in instilling fear and anxiety as the governing, all-dominant, parameters in Iraqi society and politics. The raw and naked fissures inside Iraqi society became wider and deeper in the decades of Ba'athist rule, and with the removal of the heavy hand of the dictatorship they emerged into the light of day.[120]

A variant of this argument places greater blame on the invasion itself, but the thrust of the critique is similar:

> Seen in broadest perspective, the breaking of the state in effect destroyed Iraq's immune system, making it vulnerable to a host of ailments. Among these were criminal anarchy, the ease with which foreign terrorists set up shop on Iraqi territory, widespread access to arms and a protracted insurgency. These consequences followed from the act of war itself. They may have been mitigated by a fundamentally different war plan, but they were likely to ensue even if military plans had been informed by greater foresight and better calculated to meet the dangers presented.[121]

Yet as plausible as such analyses seem in light of what actually happened from 2003 to 2007, they are not the whole story. Dexter Filkins notes:

> Iraq might have been a traumatized country, it might have been broken, it might have been atomized—it might have been a mental hospital. But whenever the prospect of normalcy presented itself, a long line of Iraqis always stood up and reached for it. Thousands of them, seeing the opportunity in the events of April 2003, had set out to build an ordinary country with ordinary ways: newspaper editors, pamphleteers, judges, politicians and police officers. . . . And they went to the slaughter. Thousands and thousands of them. . . .

Nor was the carnage spontaneous or inexorable. "With all [its] brutality, you might conclude that the sectarian war that swept the mixed cities of Iraq was a collective fever, a psychosis of ancient hatreds. It certainly became that. But in the beginning, the sectarian violence and the ethnic cleansing were almost entirely calculated. They were planned and mapped like a military campaign."[122] A larger American presence that was trained, equipped, and directed toward the maintenance of public order might well have been able to keep Iraq's internal divisions in check long enough for a semblance of nonviolent political life to emerge—just as it did after the surge.

Still, whatever might have been, what actually happened was that Iraq fell into chaos after Saddam's regime collapsed and the Bush administration took several years to muster an appropriate response. In the end, the costs of the conflict would be huge: nearly five thousand coalition dead and over thirty thousand wounded, over a hundred thousand Iraqi dead, over three million Iraqi foreign or internal refugees, over a trillion dollars in direct U.S. expenditures.[123] Additional casualties of the fiasco included the U.S. reputation for credibility, competence, and moral superiority—as well as the very freedom of action that had enabled the administration to pursue the war unchecked in the first place.

The Bush team fully expected the war to be quick, cheap, and successful. In fact, one of the reasons officials were so cavalier about dismissing critics beforehand was their confidence that those same critics would sheepishly fall into line later, after victory was assured. But instead of being able to flip its investment quickly for a nice profit, parlaying the proceeds into new ventures elsewhere, the administration found itself trapped in a quagmire, hemorrhaging blood and treasure. The disposable capital it had previously been awash in—political, diplomatic, military, financial—was now suddenly tied up in a losing cause and being steadily frittered away. Reckless use of agency, in short, led to a shift in structure, which led to a corresponding curtailment of the administration's foreign policy choices across the board. Bush would continue in office for almost six years after the fall of Baghdad, but once postwar Iraq went south, his administration would never again carry out any truly major initiative abroad, not least because its hands were stuck fast to the Iraqi tar baby. Far from being complicated, therefore, the Iraq War ended up being one of the oldest and most straightforward stories in the book—a classic realist cautionary tale of unchecked power leading to hubris, then folly, then nemesis.

9

TO AFGHANISTAN AND BEYOND

In the fall of 2005, as the security situation in Iraq continued to spiral downward, Condoleezza Rice testified before the Senate Foreign Relations Committee. "Our strategy," she declared, "is to clear, hold, and build: clear areas from insurgent control, hold them securely, and build durable, national Iraqi institutions."[1]

When the secretary of defense heard what the secretary of state had said, he was furious. As far as Donald Rumsfeld was concerned, Rice's statement was both misleading and misguided, because the administration's real policy had always been to get the Iraqis to do those things for themselves. "Anyone who takes those three words and thinks it means the United States should clear and the United States should hold and the United States should build doesn't understand the situation," he ranted a few weeks later. "It is the Iraqis' country. They've got 28 million people there. They are clearing. They are holding. They are building. . . . The idea that we could do that is so far from reality. No one has any intention that we do that."[2]

This particular dispute was settled more than a year later, when the president finally abandoned the last vestiges of Rumsfeld's "go in light and get out quick" approach to Iraq and opted for a more hands-on, open-ended American intervention via the surge. The Rice-Rumsfeld exchange, however, symbolized more than the policy struggle during one phase of one war. It captured the essence of debate over American grand strategy in general throughout the country's history. For the fact is that over the centuries, despite the repeated objections of what one might call the Rumsfeldian camp, the United States has been engaged in nothing less than an ongoing campaign of global pacification—clearing, holding, and building in region after region around the world.

The campaign has unfolded in fits and starts, with pauses and occasional reverses along the way. Washington has not consciously sought such a role, and has usually backed into it reluctantly. The American public has no desire for the country to play the world's policeman, and does not respond well to such a characterization of its behavior. Yet that is what has been happening—from continental expansion and hemispheric dominance in the eighteenth and nineteenth centuries, through the world wars and Cold War in the twentieth, to much of the "war on terror" today.

One driver of this strategy has been military—a quest to eliminate security threats lying beyond American borders. Another has been economic—a quest to protect and acquire access to foreign resources and markets. Still another has been political—a quest to spread American ideals and institutions abroad. At base, though, what has been going on has been simply the natural behavior of a rising power doing what it can to control the chaos and disorder on its periphery.

Throughout history, states have responded to the uncertainties of international anarchy by seeking to shape their external environment. Whatever their individual characteristics and preferences, they have tended to seek more rather than less influence in the world at large and have exercised as much control as their capabilities have allowed. As the United States has grown from a small, weak set of federated colonies on the Atlantic seaboard to the world's dominant power, therefore, so have its leaders naturally sought to use the resources at their disposal to mold the world around them in ways consistent with American interests and values.[3]

The individual wars America has fought have constituted the "clearing" operations, defeating the nation's enemies and then destroying them or at least driving them back to whence they came. Wherever it has fought, however, the United States has eventually recognized that such battles by themselves cannot produce lasting results—because when U.S.

forces withdraw quickly from the field, defeated enemies recuperate or new ones rise to take their place. So the United States has taken on a variety of "holding" operations as well, protecting the cleared areas by garrisoning them with its own and friendly forces, so that the nation's enemies stay down or at least back. This tends to work well enough on a temporary basis, but it can be dangerous, costly, and politically problematic. So the only truly satisfactory long-term solution, policymakers have realized, is the "building" of stable, healthy, indigenous political orders in the areas in question, ones that allow local populations to thrive in harmony with each other and the world at large.

PEACE BE UPON US

As the country's relative material power has steadily increased, so has its ability to influence greater portions of the world—and so has its perceived need to do so. Over the last century, accordingly, the pacification pattern has played out in three strategically critical theaters, with Europe serving as the laboratory for East Asia and then the Middle East. Dragged into World War I against its will, the United States helped the Allies defeat the Central Powers in the hope that this would allow Americans to live in peace. Once Germany was beaten and democratized, the thinking went, American forces could come home and leave the Old World to its own devices. But this did not work out well, and a generation later the United States found itself once again dragged into battle against an aggressive German regime and its partners.

This time, U.S. policymakers decided, they would beat and democratize Germany even more thoroughly, so there would never have to be a third match. Looking up after the shooting stopped, however, they realized that even a complete transformation of Germany would not be sufficient to guarantee peace in Europe, since the continent's industrial heartland—one of the world's major power centers—now had to be protected against yet another threat, from the Soviet Union. So instead of going home, American forces stayed, and scores of thousands of them are still there today, helping to hold the ground their forebears cleared several generations ago. This task, however, is no longer particularly onerous, because the European Union—built up from the postwar regimes sponsored by the American liberators—now has the world's largest economy and stands as a model for regional peace and democratic political evolution.

Having been worked out in Europe, the approach was applied to Asia as well. After clearing the areas seized by Imperial Japan in World War II, the United States decided to stay there also in order to hold what had been taken. It incorporated some islands into American territory directly and made the rest of the Pacific theater, with its vital sea-lanes and world-class industrial potential, a de facto American protectorate. And additional scores of thousands of American forces remain there today also, guarding the flourishing democracies of the region, including the one built from the rubble of another former foe.

Policymakers initially thought this would be sufficient to escape further trouble in the region, but North Korea's attack across the 38th Parallel in 1950 made clear that true pacification of East Asia required something more—at the very least, a message that violent changes of strategically important borders would not be tolerated. So the United States intervened to push the invading forces back. When that was done, American leaders got cocky and tried to clear all of the Korean peninsula. That proved difficult, and so they ended up abandoning the North while holding the South—something the United States continues to do today, with the help of its strong, local democratic partner. A decade later, thinking it could replay this game in Vietnam, Washington stumbled into a tougher battle than it had expected and eventually withdrew completely, but kept to the larger regional mission nonetheless. Political development in Asia has played out more at the national than the international level, with regional integration progressing less far there than in Europe. So American military power continues to play an important role in keeping national rivalries at bay. But the basic pattern of events is familiar, and promising.[4]

As the century progressed, the Cold War gradually evolved into the "long peace" and the structures of the Pax Americana took root.[5] Through a quirk of geology, however, it turned out that the majority of the fossil fuel resources on which an ever-growing global economy depended lay beneath a particularly turbulent corner of the developing world. So preserving the stability of the Persian Gulf became yet another critical global public good—and after Britain withdrew from the region in 1971, the United States duly took over as the Gulf's principal foreign power.

At first Washington fulfilled this commitment indirectly, relying on Iran as a regional proxy. But that policy collapsed in 1979 with the Iranian Revolution, followed soon after by the Soviet invasion of Afghanistan. So the Carter administration formalized the American commitment to Gulf security and promised to back it up with direct intervention if necessary. A decade later Saddam Hussein called Washington's bluff by invading Kuwait, and George H. W. Bush made good on Carter's promise by pushing Saddam back. Once Kuwait had been cleared, however, the administration realized that it had to be held as well—and so a Korean-style settlement was followed by a Korean-style regional garrison.

A decade further on, the 9/11 attacks led another Bush administration to invade first Afghanistan and then Iraq, hoping to clear the broader Middle Eastern region of problems once and for all. But the second Bush team ignored many of the lessons of its predecessors' experiences and had to learn them all over again at great cost in blood, treasure, and reputation. The Obama administration thus inherited two ongoing wars, with one of them—Afghanistan—heading in the wrong direction.

Because the idea of pacifying the world piece by piece sounds so ridiculous and unattractive, American leaders have rarely described this grand strategy in so many words—perhaps not even to themselves. A host of critics would question the American right, need, or ability to accomplish such a grandiose mission. The contrary idea—that it is somebody else's job to clear, and somebody else's job to hold, and somebody else's job to build—has at least as distinguished a pedigree and far more popular backing.[6]

Yet so long as American relative power has grown and policymakers have focused on strategically critical areas, the grand strategy has had a compelling logic and its execution has been generally good for both the United States and the world at large. American leaders have used the country's power to carve out and protect an ever-larger "zone of peace" and create a mostly benign structural context in which local economic, social, and political development could proceed. As even the supposedly "antiwar" Barack Obama put it in his Nobel Peace Prize lecture, "it was not simply international institutions—not just treaties and declarations—that brought stability to a post–World War II world. Whatever mistakes we have made, the plain fact is this: The United States of America has helped underwrite global security for more than six decades with the blood of our citizens and the strength of our arms. The service and sacrifice of our men and women in uniform has promoted peace and prosperity from Germany to Korea, and enabled democracy to take hold in places like the Balkans."[7]

If global pacification has been the macronarrative of American foreign and security policy, individual wars have had their own micronarratives as well, as the forgoing chapters have described. For the United States, therefore, the Clausewitzian challenge—how to make force serve politics—has actually played out on two levels simultaneously, with policymakers needing to ensure the micro- and macronarratives fit together.

That is why the most successful war in modern American history was World War II—not only because victory in it rid the world of great evils, but because the war's ultimate settlement facilitated lasting peace and prosperity across large parts of the globe. The so-called "limited wars" in Korea and the Gulf were not very satisfying, but they too constituted modest successes, because their settlements left behind regional orders more stable than the prewar status quo. All three of these successes, nevertheless, would have benefited significantly from better preparation for the transition from war to peace. The outbreak of the Cold War probably could not have been prevented, but much of the hysteria surrounding it might have been. The Korean War could have ended almost a year and a half earlier on strategically comparable terms. And better planning during the Gulf War could have yielded a more sustainable and successful postwar containment of Saddam, or even his earlier demise.

World War I and the Iraq War, meanwhile, testify to how even decisive military victory can lead to problems if not harnessed to plans for a sustainable postwar political settlement. And Vietnam stands as a sobering reminder that an inability to chart a convincing course toward an eventual stable peace can be legitimate grounds for not entering a conflict in the first place.

As of this writing, the war in Afghanistan is hard to call. The United States entered the country in pursuit of the perpetrators of the 9/11 attacks, both for retribution and to prevent any future strikes. The Bush administration decided, sensibly, that in order to accomplish this mission it had to target not only al Qaeda but also Afghanistan's Taliban government (which was providing bin Laden's group with support and protection). But as would be true in Iraq later on, the administration paid little attention to what would happen after its enemies were defeated.[8] As a memo to Rumsfeld put it in the early stages of the war, in addition to "eliminat[ing]" al Qaeda, the "Goal is to terminate rule of current Taliban leadership to make an example of them (as State sponsor [of terrorism]) and to undercut al Qaeda. Creating a stable, post-Taliban Afghanistan is desirable but not necessarily within the power of the US. The USG should not allow concerns about stability to paralyze US efforts to oust the Taliban leadership. . . . Nation-building is *not* our key strategic goal."[9]

In Afghanistan as in Iraq, this approach worked well in the short term but poorly in the long term. The Bush administration designed the Afghan war and postwar effort around a small and light American footprint and after some creative military and diplomatic operations was able, by the end of 2001, to declare victory and establish a legitimate and reasonably attractive local government to run the country. Yet a few years later, in the absence of a well-considered and properly resourced plan to maintain public order, the situation on the ground began to deteriorate and hostile forces began to regroup. By the time the Obama administration took over in 2009, most experts were telling the new commander-in-chief that only a reinvigorated American effort could reverse the decline. So among its first major actions, the new administration agreed to send more troops and dispatched a new commander, General Stanley McChrystal, with a new approach to the war, along with instructions for him to report back on what else, if anything, needed to be done.

To the surprise and consternation of the White House, however, McChrystal's assessment—leaked to the *Washington Post* that September—was that the war was going quite badly and required far greater efforts in order to head off "mission failure."[10] This triggered a bitter, months-long debate over Afghan strategy inside the administration, as Obama and his team finally confronted the full extent of their dilemma. Some officials wanted to endorse an intensified and essentially open-ended counterinsurgency campaign comparable, in some ways, to the surge in Iraq (which had been cognitively transformed over the years from the "next" war to the "last" one). Others wanted to cap the American effort where it was or even move toward withdrawal. In the end, Obama decided to split the difference, announcing at West Point in December that he would send tens of thousands of new troops to Afghanistan to carry out expanded operations there, while at the same time seeming to declare that the United States would start withdrawing in the summer of 2011.[11]

Since there is little reason to believe that the situation in Afghanistan will improve dramatically and sustainably any time soon, the contradictions inherent in the West Point speech will likely come to a head as the withdrawal deadline approaches. The drama surrounding McChrystal's ouster in June 2010 and replacement by his former boss, Petraeus, did little to change this fundamental dilemma. Like the Nixon administration in Vietnam or the George W. Bush administration in Iraq, the Obama administration will eventually have to decide which goal in Afghanistan it cares about more—extricating the United States from a seemingly endless counterinsurgency or continuing to keep enemy forces at bay. Neither option is attractive. At best, Afghanistan could become another Iraq, with strong late innings gaining the United States the opportunity to draw down its forces gradually while leaving behind something better than the status quo ante. At worst, it could be a replay of Vietnam, with the White House deciding to pull the plug on a thankless struggle in a strategically marginal country, hoping that the dire predictions of postwithdrawal chaos (both at home and abroad) never materialize. Either way, however, the war will go down as one more operation crippled from birth by a failure to deploy military resources in support of a serious strategy for durable political success.

MAKING IT WORK

Since America's grand strategy of progressive global pacification has been underwritten by the country's steady rise in relative power, the future prospects of that strategy will inevitably be tied to the fortunes of the country's underlying material capabilities. Regardless of whether American hegemony declines or gains a second wind in decades to come, however, the United States will eventually find itself in new wars down the road. And when that happens, future policymakers in Washington will need to do a better job at handling the Clausewitzian challenge than their predecessors. The good news is that they can—so long as they pay more attention to the nature of the task at hand, approach it with the intellectual and moral seriousness it deserves, and absorb some straightforward lessons from past experience.

- *Plan ahead and work backward.* Given the terminology the U.S. military used during the Iraq War—labeling the creation and maintenance of the war's political settlement as mere "stability and support operations" and designating them "Phase IV" of the effort—it is not surprising that postwar planning for that conflict was the worst on record. It is only natural, after all, to think about Phase I before Phase IV. Numbering things that way predisposes people to start at the beginning and discuss so-called "kinetic" military operations on their own terms, without regard to politics—and to relegate the political items on the agenda to a back burner, something to be taken care of later on, by somebody else, as time permits and with whatever tools and resources happen to be available. Realizing its mistake, in the years since then the military has tried to correct this problem by extending the number of stages involved, emphasizing that the stages overlap, and mandating consideration of postwar issues from the start of the planning process. But a simpler and more effective way of driving the point home would be just to reverse the direction of the sequence. A stable postwar political situation, that is, should be considered Phase I, with the rest of the war being seen as a countdown to that blessed event. This easy fix would focus attention on the desired end result as the starting point for all war planning, with the earlier stages understood as having significance only as building blocks of or preparatory stages for the final outcome.[12]

- *Define goals precisely and check prices before buying.* One of the striking findings of this study is just how often leaders neglect Clausewitz's advice to think through clearly in advance just what a particular war is supposed to achieve. Rather than approach each new conflict with care and thoroughness, policymakers have tended to act as if following a script. Their thinking has been dominated by lessons drawn from the most recent war, whether or not those lessons were relevant or appropriate to the case at hand, and the deployment of resources has been driven more by availability than strategy. But this does not have to happen. Americans, and their leaders, need to learn that analogies usually confuse more than they clarify, and that abstract concepts such as "victory" or "democracy" are too vague to guide military planning. The political objective of any war should be framed clearly in practical terms directly relevant to the case at hand and defined in such a way as to fit comfortably within the country's broader grand strategy. Policymakers should have a clear sense of what will happen on the ground once military operations are finished—what local political and security arrangements will look like, who will maintain them and how. Forcing senior officials to define their objectives this way would serve as an excellent source of discipline, reminding them of the need to keep ends and means in balance and concentrating their minds on the Clausewitzian challenge from the start, so that the rest of the conflict can be planned and executed as effectively and efficiently as possible.

- *Pay attention to implementation and anticipate problems.* The formulation of clear practical objectives along with well-considered plans for achieving them constitutes the bulk of the strategic planning process. But Burns was obviously correct about what often happens to even the best-laid plans, so careful attention must be paid to implementation and potential contingencies as well. Any critical element of a strategy needs to be overseen from start to finish to make sure that it actually gets accomplished as intended. And any crucial assumptions underlying a plan need to be spelled out explicitly, with at least rudimentary backup plans prepared in advance for what to do if the assumptions prove invalid and things go better, worse, or differently than expected.[13]

Surely, you might say, all this is nothing but common sense. And you would be right. But in war, as in life more generally, common sense is actually quite uncommon. All of these seemingly obvious maxims have been violated in at least one of the wars discussed above, some in several of them. Woodrow Wilson fought a war to make the world safe for democracy, but never asked himself what democracy actually meant and whether, say, a constitutional monarchy in Germany would fit the bill. The Roosevelt administration never considered what would happen to its postwar arrangements if the Grand Alliance fell apart. Harry Truman and Dean Acheson made voluntary prisoner repatriation a key American war aim in Korea, but never asked how many prisoners might grab the option and whether it would block an armistice. The Kennedy and Johnson administrations dug themselves deeper and deeper into Vietnam without any plans for how to get out. George H. W. Bush assumed Saddam would fall as a result of defeat in the Gulf War, but did little planning for how to achieve that outcome or what would happen if it didn't occur. George W. Bush made sure Saddam's regime would be toppled, but didn't plan for what to do afterward.

Can it really be true that American leaders have repeatedly violated such basic rules of strategy? Sure. Study after study has shown that the keys to proper weight control are eating limited portions of healthy food while getting regular exercise. But every year tens of millions of people follow fad diets of one kind or another, popping pills or eating only grapefruit in a quest for some magic bullet to whisk the pounds away. And study after study has shown that practically anyone can achieve at least modest investing success over the long term by following a few simple rules about diversification, cost control, and perseverance. But most investors actually underperform the stock indexes most of the time because they lack the discipline to keep themselves from behaving stupidly out of fear and greed. So it is understandable that national security policymakers, who are after all only human, often ignore even the most rudimentary best practices in their field.

Understandable, perhaps—but still reprehensible. For the reality is that wartime leaders are not comparable to crash dieters trying to look good at the beach or ordinary plungers taking a flier on some stock tip they got from a chatroom or cable show. They're more like the surgeon general, or professional money managers with strict fiduciary responsibilities toward their clients. White House lingo might refer to senior officials as "principals," but they're not—they're really agents for 300 million others. For them, exercising prudence when deciding how to spend the blood and treasure of their fellow citizens is not an option; it's a moral obligation.

Clausewitz observed that war is a "paradoxical trinity—composed of primordial violence, hatred, and enmity, which are to be regarded as a blind natural force; of the play of chance and probability within which the creative spirit is free to roam; and of its element of subordination, as an instrument of policy, which makes it subject to reason alone."[14] The public at large, he wrote, gets trapped in its emotions and passion. Military officers, with their varying degrees of courage and talent and perception, work the odds on the battlefield. But it is the role of political leaders to be the voice of reason, seeing to it that wars are designed and prosecuted effectively so as to achieve some sensible political outcome. In the past, our leaders have not always done this. Maybe the next time they will.

ACKNOWLEDGMENTS

Only now do I realize how writing a book can be both an individual and a collective act. I started this project more than two decades ago—between the events discussed in chapters six and seven—and the (in)discipline involved in getting from there to here is mine alone. Whatever qualities the book may possess, however, are due to a host of others, for I am indeed a part of all that I have met.

Above all, I thank my parents, Daniel and Joanna S. Rose; my siblings, David, Joey, Emily; and our large and loving extended family. Like Obelix, I fell into the magic potion as a baby, and all the rest is commentary.

I have been blessed with an extraordinary run of teachers over the years, both in and out of school, all of whom contributed to this book whether they realize it or not, so I would like to thank the following: at Town, Margo Lion, John Newburger, Walter Birge, and their colleagues; at Horace Mann, Marty Sokolow, Tek Lin, Ion Theodore, and their colleagues; at Yale, Donald Kagan, Vasily Rudich, Paul Fry, and their colleagues; at Harvard, Eliot Cohen, Steve Rosen, Sam Huntington, Stanley Hoffmann, Joe Nye, Judith Shklar, Yuen Foon Khong, Steve Macedo, and their colleagues; at the *National Interest* and *Public Interest*, Owen Harries, Bob Tucker, Irving Kristol, Nat Glazer, and their colleagues; at the NSC, Martin Indyk, Ellen Laipson, David Satterfield, Mark Parris, and their colleagues; and at the CFR, Les Gelb, Richard Haass, Dick Betts, Jim Hoge, and their colleagues. Martin Indyk, Owen Harries, and Eliot Cohen are principally responsible for luring me into a career in policy-oriented security studies, and Steve Rosen, Sam Huntington, and Stanley Hoffmann served as unfailingly wise and supportive advisers for the dissertation that was the project's first incarnation.

My equally extraordinary friends believed in me more than I did myself; thanks go to Bart Aronson, Peter Babej, Gary Bass, Brad Berenson, Marvin and Shirley Berman, Andrew Berman and Danny Voloch, Michael and Sheila Berman, Steve Biddle, Max Boot, Ian Bremmer, Dan Byman, Bob Caro, Don Casse, Victor Cha, Art Chang and Allison Thrush, Tom Christensen, Mary Alice Cobb, Andrew Cortell, Consuelo Cruz, Mike Desch, Larry Diamond, Frank Dobbins and Michele Lamont, Mike Doran, Trish Dorff, Dan Drezner, Liz Economy, Irina Faskicnos, Peter Feaver, Adam Freedman and Kathleen Walsh, Neal Freeman and Kerry Griffin, Aaron Friedberg, David Fromkin, Sumit Ganguly, Alex Garvin, Greg Gause, John Gershman and Deborah Yashar, Paul Golob, Mark Goldman, Albert Goncalves, Phil Gordon, Steve Grand, Martin Grant, Joyce Hackett, Joan Hennessey, David Hermann, James Higgins, Jill Indyk, Beverly Jablons, Tonya Jenerette, Fred Kagan, Fred Kaplan, Ethan Kapstein, Zachary Karabell, Jeff Kopstein, Jessica Korn and Ron Liebowitz, Steve Kotkin, Andy Krepinevich, Regina Kulik, Charlie Kupchan, Judith Langis, Mel Leffler, Genevieve Lengard, Peter Liberman, Rob Lieberman and Lauren Osborne, Mark Lillan, Jim Lindsay, Shalom Lipner, Rob Long, Gloria Lopez, Marc Lynch, Sean Lynn-Jones, Sebastian Mallaby and Zanny Minton Beddoes, Michael Mandelbaum, Kate McNamara and Tomas Montgomery, Walter Russell Mead, Gil Merom, Worthy Monroe, Andy Moravcsik and Anne-Marie Slaughter, Glyn Morgan and Margarita Estévez-Abe, Tim Naftali, Claudia Nelson and Donald McNeil, Raymonde Nicholas, Mike O'Hanlon, John Owen, David Pearce, Ken Pollack, Josh Ramo, Marina Ramos, Sonya Rhodes, Frank Richardson, Inez Rodriguez, Janet Rogan, Gary Rosen and Leslie Kaufman, Rick and Nancy Rubens, Rozzie and Alan Schwartz, Steve Schwartzberg, Randy Schweller, Adam Segal, Anna Seleny, Lisa Shields, Jamie Shifren, Jan Shifren, Jonathan Shifren, Calvin Sims, Darlene Snyder, Jack Snyder, Allison Stanger, David Steiner, Kathryn Stoner-Weiss and Eric Weiss, Ray Takeyh, Ann Trotman, Catherine Waters, Jacob Weisberg, Bill Wohlforth, Alexi Worth and Erika Belsey Worth, Bobby Worth, Diane Vachon, David Victor, Alicia Villarosa, Enzo Viscusi, Arshad Zakaria, Fareed Zakaria and Paula Throckmorton Zakaria, Jonathan Zasloff, and Almaz Zelleke and Clay Shirky.

At *Foreign Affairs*, Jim Hoge was a wonderful and indulgent boss and mentor for more than a decade. The staff over the years didn't sign on to cover for and carry a distracted managing editor, but did so with good humor and put out a great magazine in the process; thanks on this front go to Katie Allawala, Nadine Apelian, Warren Bass, Ann Coleman, Chris Farah, David Feith, Helen Fessenden, Elisabeth Genn, Lynda Hammes, Rosemary Hartman, David Kellogg, Siddharth Mohandas, Ben Moxham, Paul Musgrave, Traci Nagle, Ib Ohlsson, Basharat Peer, Sasha Polakow-Suransky, Stuart Reid, Kamal Sidhu, Lorenz Skeeter, Ann Tappert, Alice Wang, Celia Whitaker, and Josh Yaffa—and especially Jonathan Tepperman, Stéphanie Giry, and Dan Kurtz-Phelan, who have taught me more than I ever taught them. In addition to her work at the magazine, Katie Allawala was also a perfect research assistant over the last two years of the project, serving as a constant sounding board, improving every chapter with multiple reads, and keeping the book and its author on track. I could never have done it without her.

For their willingness to answer endless queries and review parts of the manuscript, I am eternally grateful to Steve Biddle, Max Boot, Dan Byman, Steven Casey, Joe Collins, Larry Diamond, Mike Doran, Peter Feaver, Greg Gause, Richard Haass, Andy Krepinevich, Dan Kurtz-Phelan, Fred Logevall, Winston Lord, Greg Mitrovich, Ken Pollack, and Elihu Rose.

Fareed Zakaria has spent so much time with so many aspects of the project over so many years that it is as much his as mine (except for the war stuff). One of the innumerable things he gets credit for is connecting me with Tina Bennett, the world's best agent, who bet on me early with little reason to do so. Alice Mayhew, my fantastic editor, has been more enthusiastic than anybody else; her passion and wisdom kept me moving onward and upward. Jon Karp, Roger Labrie, Karen Thompson, Lisa Healy, Jackie Seow, Julia Prosser, and the rest of the gang at Simon & Schuster have masterfully turned a homely manuscript into a beautiful book. Jim Piereson and the Olin Foundation (via the Olin Institute for Strategic Studies at Harvard) and Arthur Ross (via the Council on Foreign Relations) generously provided crucial institutional support at different points over the life of the project. The CFR library staff did a great job of obtaining and processing a constant stream of materials, and the gang at 895 Park helped make my hours in the dungeons more bearable.

Many people close to events described in the book generously allowed me to interview them, often at length and sometimes repeatedly. Almost all of these discussions were off the record, so I want to thank the interviewees collectively here for their time and frankness. I do not expect all of you to agree with everything I ended up writing, but I hope you conclude that at least I tried hard to listen and learn. If there are deep insights in the book, meanwhile, they are rarely mine, or mine alone, and so I also want to thank all the authors listed in the notes—for doing the real work that someone like me could learn from and showcase.

At home, finally, Isaac and Lucy and Bilbo and Hjalmar and Smilla and Pogo and Domino and Checkers and their brethren have surrounded me with unconditional love and made my life joyous. The best part of finishing this is that I can now spend more time with them—and with Sheri Berman, my partner in life, my inspiration and role model, whose love means more to me than she can know. For two decades, she has tried to teach me that grownups eventually stop whining and making excuses and just do it. So I did.

ENDNOTES

1. THE CLAUSEWITZIAN CHALLENGE

1. "Dr. Condoleezza Rice Discusses Iraq Reconstruction," April 4, 2003, available at http://merln.ndu.edu/MERLN/PFIraq/archive/wh/20030404-12.pdf
2. Steven W. Peterson, "Central but Inadequate: The Application of Theory in Operation Iraqi Freedom," National War College (research paper, 2004), pp. 10–11, available at www.dtic.mil/cgi-bin/GetTRDoc?AD=ADA441663&Location=U2&doc=GetTRDoc.pdf. Peterson was "a member of the Coalition Forces Land Component Command (CFLCC) planning staff from November 2002 to June 2003, specifically . . . Chief of Intelligence Planning working within the C5."
3. James Conway, interview with *Frontline: Truth, War, and Consequences*, August 19, 2003, available at www.pbs.org/wgbh/pages/frontline/shows/truth/interviews/conway.html.
4. Carl von Clausewitz, *On War*, ed. and trans. by Michael Howard and Peter Paret (Princeton, N.J.: Princeton University Press, 1976), pp. 75, 87, 605.
5. Tommy Franks with Malcolm McConnell, *American Soldier* (New York: HarperCollins, 2004), p. 441 (emphasis in the original).
6. Clausewitz, *On War*, pp. 605, 111.
7. For surveys of the war termination literature, see Elizabeth A. Stanley, *Paths to Peace: Domestic Coalition Shifts, War Termination, and the Korean War* (Stanford, Calif: Stanford University Press, 2009); H. E. Goemans, *War & Punishment: The Causes of War Termination & the First World War* (Princeton, N.J.: Princeton University Press, 2000); and Gideon G. Rose, "Victory and Its Substitutes: Foreign Policy Decisionmaking at the Ends of Wars" (Ph.D. diss., Harvard University, 1994). An insightful book that covers some similar ground to this one is Michael D. Pearlman, *Warmaking and American Democracy: The Struggle Over Military Strategy, 1700 to the Present* (Lawrence: University of Kansas, 1999).
8. For fuller discussion of these theories and their application to military

endgames, see Rose, "Victory and Its Substitutes," chapter 2. On "neoclassical realism," see Gideon Rose, "Neoclassical Realism and Theories of Foreign Policy," *World Politics* 51 (October 1998), pp. 144–72.

2. WORLD WAR I

1. Klaus Epstein, *Matthias Erzberger and the Dilemma of German Democracy* (Princeton, N.J.: Princeton University Press, 1959), p. 275.
2. Harry R. Rudin, *Armistice 1918* (New Haven, Conn.: Yale University Press, 1944), pp. 349–51.
3. John Toland, *No Man's Land* (New York: Doubleday, 1980), pp. 558–59.
4. Rudin, *Armistice 1918*, pp. 364–65.
5. Maurice Baumont, *The Fall of the Kaiser* (New York: Knopf, 1931), p. 124.
6. Rudin, *Armistice 1918*, pp. 356–59. "A few minutes later, while Ebert and Scheidemann were finishing their luncheon, people rushed into the Reichstag and shouted that Scheidemann had proclaimed the Republic. Ebert turned red with rage and shouted at his companion, as he banged the table with his fist, 'Is that true?' Scheidemann answered that it was not only true—it was obvious. 'You have no right,' cried Ebert, 'to proclaim a republic! What Germany is to be, a republic or anything else, is for the Constituent Assembly to decide.' "
7. Baumont, *The Fall of the Kaiser* p. 179; Toland, *No Man's Land*, pp. 568–70. This logroll, in which the SPD agreed to maintain many of the privileges of the army and other elites in return for ostensible allegiance to the new regime, formalized the dysfunctional relationship behind what history would come to know as the Weimar Republic. For a discussion of the SPD's behavior throughout this period and how it lowered the prospects of a successful transition to democracy in Germany, see Sheri Berman, *The Social Democratic Moment* (Cambridge, Mass.: Harvard University Press, 1998).
8. Stephen Pichon to Jean Jules Jusserand, October 29, 1918, quoted in Klaus Schwabe, *Woodrow Wilson, Revolutionary Germany, and Peacemaking, 1918–1919: Missionary Diplomacy and the Realities of Power* (Chapel Hill: University of North Carolina Press, 1985), p. 432 fn. 61.
9. Ross Gregory writes: "Wilson and his advisers set out to press for two major American objects: maintenance of trade with Europe and preservation of neutrality, not fully conscious that these paths were not fully reconcilable, that action taken to promote one would jeopardize the other. . . . The only course that would have guaranteed peace for the United States was . . . severing all its European ties. . . . In 1914 that act would have placed serious strain on an economy that already showed signs of instability; by 1916 it would have been economically disastrous." *The Origins of American Intervention in the First World War* (New York: Norton, 1971), pp. 30, 133.
10. British foreign secretary Edward Grey made the point succinctly in his memoirs:

> [B]lockade of Germany was essential to the victory of the Allies, but the ill-will of the United States meant their certain defeat. After Paris had been saved by the battle of the Marne, the Allies could do no more than hold their own against Germany; sometimes they did not even do that. Germany and Austria were self-supporting in the huge supply of munitions. The Allies soon became dependent for an adequate supply on the United States. If we quarrelled with the United States we could not get that supply. It was better therefore to carry on the war without blockade, if need be, than to incur a break with the United States about contraband and thereby deprive the Allies of the resources necessary to carry on the war at all or with any chance of success. The object of diplomacy, therefore, was to secure the maximum of blockade that could be enforced without a rupture with the United States.

Viscount Grey of Fallodon, *Twenty-Five Years* (New York: Frederick A. Stokes, 1925), vol. 2, p. 107.

11. Consciousness of this factor made British diplomats simultaneously bold and wary. The British ambassador to the United States, for example, informed his government at one point:

> The reason why there has been no embargo on arms and ammunition is not sympathy with us, but the sense that the prosperity of the country on which the administration depends for its existence would be emperilled by such a measure. If there is a scarcity of material here, or any other reason why an embargo would pay, we should have an embargo. . . . Restraints on shipping may be ordered. Transport may be impeded. A loan may be made more difficult.

He echoed Grey's concerns: "The object [of British diplomacy] should be to ascertain when the [American] breaking point is near and where. There may be a breaking point. Do not deceive yourself as to that." Sir Cecil Spring Rice to Lord Robert Cecil, August 13, 1916, in Stephen Gwynn, ed., *The Letters and Friendships of Sir Cecil Spring Rice* (Boston: Houghton Mifflin, 1929), vol. 2, p. 345.

12. Sir Cecil Spring Rice to Lord Newton, October 21, 1914, in Gwynn, *Spring Rice*, vol. 2, p. 239.
13. A month into the war, the British ambassador in Washington reported to Grey: "The President said in the most solemn way that if [the German] cause succeeds in the present struggle the United States would have to give up its present ideals and devote all its energies to defence, which would mean the end of its present system of Government." Sir Cecil Spring Rice to Viscount Grey, September 8, 1914, in Gwynn, *Spring Rice*, vol. 2, p. 223. At the end of 1915 the American ambassador to Belgium,

visiting Wilson, promised to act impartially, but added, "I ought to tell you that in my heart there is no such thing as neutrality. I am heart and soul for the Allies." Wilson replied, "So am I. No decent man, knowing the situation and Germany, could be anything else. But that is only my personal opinion and there are many others in this country who do not hold that opinion." Quoted in Charles Segmour, *American Diplomacy During the World War* (London: Greenwood Press, 1975), p. 108.

14. For differing views of Wilhelmine Germany over time, see Ido Oren, "The Subjectivity of the 'Democratic' Peace: Changing U.S. Perceptions of Imperial Germany," *International Security* 20:2 (Autumn 1995).
15. "An Address to a Joint Session of Congress," April 2, 1917, in *The Papers of Woodrow Wilson*, vol. 41 (Princeton, N.J.: Princeton University Press, 1983), pp. 523–24 (hereafter *PWW*).
16. A. J. Balfour to Colonel House, June 29, 1917, in Charles Seymour, *The Intimate Papers of Colonel House*, vol. 3, *Into the World War* (Boston: Houghton Mifflin, 1928), p. 101.
17. Seymour, *Intimate Papers of Colonel House*, vol. 3, p. 105.
18. André Tardieu, *France and America* (Boston: Houghton Mifflin, 1927), p. 224.
19. Erich von Ludendorff, *Ludendorff's Own Story* (New York: Harper, 1919), vol. 2, p. 326.
20. "Conference at General Headquarters on August 14, 1918, Signed Protocol," in James Brown Scott, ed., *Preliminary History of the Armistice: Official Documents Published by the German National Chancellery by Order of the Ministry of State* (New York: Oxford University Press, 1924), pp. 18–19.
21. Arthur Rosenberg, *Imperial Germany: The Birth of the German Republic, 1871–1918* (Boston: Beacon, 1964), p. 117.
22. The Kaiser put it bluntly: "Dictatorship is nonsense." Charles F. Sidman, *The German Collapse in 1918* (Lawrence, Kans.: Coronado, 1972), pp. 81–82. As Rosenberg notes, "The parliamentarization of Germany was not fought for by the Reichstag; it was arranged by Ludendorff." *Imperial Germany*, p. 242.
23. "Tagebuchnotizen des Obersten von Thaer vom 1. Oktober 1918," in Gerhard A. Ritter and Susanne Miller, eds., *Die deutsche Revolution 1918–1918: Dokumente* (Hamburg: Hoffmann und Campe, 1975, Zweite Auflage), p. 27.
24. "The German Imperial Chancellor (Max of Baden) to President Wilson," in *Foreign Relations of the United States, 1918, Supplement 1: The World War*, vol. 1 (Washington, D.C.: U.S. Government Printing Office, 1933), p. 48 (hereafter *FRUS*).
25. "A Draft of a Note to the German Government," October 7, 1918, in *PWW*, vol. 51, pp. 255–57.
26. "The Secretary of State to the Swiss Chargé (Oederlin)," October 8, 1918, in *FRUS, 1918, Supp. 1*, vol. 1, p. 343.

27. "Max, Prince of Baden, to General Ludendorff," October 8, 1918, in *Preliminary History*, pp. 50–51.
28. "Conference at the Office of the Imperial Chancellor," October 9, 1918, in *Preliminary History*, p. 56.
29. "From the Diary of Colonel House," October 15, 1918, in *PWW*, vol. 51, p. 340.
30. "The Secretary of State to the Swiss Chargé (Oederlin)," October 14, 1918, in *FRUS, 1918, Supp. 1*, vol. 1, pp. 358–59.
31. "Conference of the Secretaries of State on October 17, 1918, at 5 pm," in *Preliminary History*, p. 102. As Hindenburg told Prince Max two days later, "The question must be asked: Will the German people fight for their honor, not only in words but with deeds, to the last man, and thereby assure themselves of the possibility of a new existence, or will they allow themselves to be forced to capitulate and thus delivered to destruction before making their last and final exertion?" "Telephone Message of October 20, 1918, 1 am," *Preliminary History*, p. 105. This was almost certainly a deliberate attempt to lay the groundwork for later charges that Germany had been defeated by a "stab in the back."
32. "Conference of October 17, 1918," in *Preliminary History*, pp. 78–99; exchange on p. 98. This meeting has been called "one of the most dramatic and moving events in Germany's history. The fate of a nation was being decided and the men who participated knew it. . . ." Rudin, *Armistice 1918*, p. 141. The "Questionnaire as a Basis for the Conference with General Ludendorff on October 17, 1918" (*Preliminary History*, pp. 76–77) demonstrates just how little information German political authorities had worked from in the past. That defeat took the people of Germany by surprise was due not only to the deceptions and propaganda of the high command, but also to the timidity of civilian politicians who had enabled the high command to pursue its own course without real obstruction or embarrassment.
33. Wilhelm himself "was at Potsdam when the note arrived. He summoned his aide, Major Niemann, showed him the despatch and exclaimed, 'Read it! It aims directly at the overthrow of my house, at the complete overthrow of monarchy.' " Rudin, *Armistice 1918*, p. 133. The government sought clarifications of Wilson's meaning from its contacts in neutral countries, who invariably confirmed this interpretation. The German ambassador in Belgium, for example, reported that "a reliable agent" interpreted Wilson's demand as: "Previous abdication of the throne by His Majesty the Emperor and the Crown Prince. Perhaps a regency would be possible by that brother of the Crown Prince who has been trained by the civil service." "Telegram, the Imperial Minister to the Foreign Office, October 17, 1918, 11.10 pm," in *Preliminary History*, p. 103. For the role played during this period by unofficial intermediaries, see Schwabe, *Woodrow Wilson*, and idem, "U.S. Secret War Diplomacy, Intelligence, and the Coming of the German Revolution in 1918: The Role

of Vice Consul James McNally," *Diplomatic History* 16:2 (Spring 1992), pp. 175–200.

34. "The German Secretary of State of the Foreign Office (Solf) to the Swiss Foreign Office for President Wilson," October 20, 1918," in *FRUS, 1918, Supp. 1*, vol. 1, pp. 380–81.
35. Entry from October 21, 1918, in E. David Cronon, ed., *The Cabinet Diaries of Josephus Daniels, 1913–1921* (Lincoln: University of Nebraska Press, 1963), p. 342.
36. "The Secretary of State to the Swiss Chargé (Oederlin)," in *FRUS, 1918, Supp. 1*, vol. 1, pp. 381–83. The Germans continued to probe as to Wilson's meaning, and continued to hear from their sources that the Kaiser's abdication was a prerequisite to peace. See *Preliminary History*, pp. 115ff., 132. A strikingly accurate analysis by Solf of Wilson's position, dated October 31, is on pp. 133–34.
37. Hindenburg submitted his resignation at the same time, but it was not accepted. On October 24, without consulting the political leadership, he had notified the German army that the "reply of Wilson demands military capitulation. Therefore it is unacceptable . . . for us soldiers Wilson's reply can only be a challenge to continue our resistance with might and main." This message caused a political firestorm and was quickly retracted. *U.S. Army in the World War, 1917–1919*, vol. 10, *The Armistice Agreement and Related Documents, Part 1* (Washington, D.C.: Center of Military History, U.S. Army, 1991), p. 19; see also Rudin, *Armistice 1918*, pp. 207ff.
38. "To Edward Mandell House," July 21, 1917, in *PWW*, vol. 43 (Princeton, N.J.: Princeton University Press, 1983), p. 238 (emphasis in the original). This attitude matched House's own, although House was more Anglophilic. Weeks after American entrance into the war he told the president, "I hope you will agree with me that the best policy now is to avoid a discussion of peace settlements. . . . If the Allies begin to discuss terms among themselves, they will soon hate one another worse than they do Germany. . . . If you have a tacit understanding . . . not to discuss peace terms with the other allies, later this country and England, will be able to dictate broad and generous terms—terms that will mean permanent peace." "From Edward Mandell House," April 22, 1917, in *PWW*, vol. 42 (Princeton, N.J.: Princeton University Press, 1983), p. 120.
39. "An Address to a Joint Session of Congress," January 8, 1918, in *PWW*, vol. 45, pp. 534–39. For issues surrounding the issuance of the Fourteen Points, see Walter Lippmann, *Public Opinion* (New York: Free Press, 1965), pp. 133–38; Lawrence W. Martin, *Peace Without Victory: Woodrow Wilson and the British Liberals* (New Haven, Conn.: Yale University Press, 1958); Arno J. Mayer, *Wilson vs. Lenin: Political Origins of the New Diplomacy* (Cleveland: World, 1964), pp. 329–67; John L. Snell, "Wilson's Peace Program and German Socialism, January–March 1918," *Missippi Valley Historical Review* 38, no. 2 (September 1951),

pp. 187–214, and "Wilsonian Rhetoric Goes to War," *Historian* 14:2 (Spring 1952), pp. 191–208; Schwabe, *Woodrow Wilson*, pp. 12ff; and Thomas J. Knock, *To End All Wars: Woodrow Wilson and the Quest for a New World Order* (New York: Oxford University Press, 1992).

40. "From Edward Mandell House," September 3, 1918, in *PWW*, vol. 49 (Princeton, N.J.: Princeton University Press, 1985), p. 428.
41. "An Address in the Metropolitan Opera House," September 27, 1918, in *PWW*, vol. 51, pp. 127–33. These were known as the "Five Particulars."
42. The prime minister wrote to one of his diplomats on October 12: "You should be careful to express no approval or disapproval of Wilson's attitude towards Prince Max's Note about which we were not even consulted. As you are aware we cannot accept his views about the Freedom of the Seas and our military advisers including Foch consider that the conditions he seems to contemplate for an Armistice [are] inadequate." "David Lloyd George to Sir Eric Geddes," October 12, 1918, in *PWW*, vol. 51, p. 313. Worried that they were being committed to the Fourteen Points by the correspondence, the British informed Wilson that "in framing the conditions of armistice care must be taken to prevent the Allies from being deprived of freedom of action in the settlement of the final terms in the Peace Conference and . . . steps should immediately be taken by the chief belligerent Powers to discuss the doubtful points and come to some agreement amongst themselves with regard to them." "Paraphrase of Telegram from Mr. Balfour to Mr. Barclay," October 13, 1918, in *PWW*, vol. 51, p. 336.
43. "To Edward Mandell House," October 28, 1918, in *PWW,* vol. 51, p. 473. This telegram was garbled in transmission, and the version House read placed less emphasis on keeping German power intact as a counterweight. See W. Stull Holt, "What Wilson Sent and What House Received," *American Historical Review* 65:3 (April 1960), pp. 569–71.
44. "To Edward Mandell House," October 29, 1918, in *PWW,* vol. 51, p. 505.
45. "To Edward Mandell House," October 30, 1918, in *PWW,* vol. 51, p. 513. In the end this telegram was not used, but House made a similar threat on his own during the discussions. See *PWW,* vol. 51, pp. 511–34.
46. Entry for November 6, 1918, in Cronon, ed., *Daniels Cabinet Diaries*, p. 343. This was not an isolated comment; three weeks earlier Daniels noted: "Discussing GB's selfish policy, WW said 'I want to go into the Peace Conference armed with as many weapons as my pockets will hold so as to compel justice.' " Entry for October 17, p. 342.
47. For overviews of the Wilson administration's behavior during the final phases of the war, see Schwabe, *Woodrow Wilson;* Knock, *To End All Wars;* and Gary Thomas Armstrong, "The Domestic Politics of War Termination: The Political Struggle in the United States Over the Armistice, 1918" (Ph.D. diss., Georgetown University, Washington, D.C., 1994).
48. "Memorandum of Interview with the President by Herbert Bruce

Brougham," December 14, 1914, in *PWW*, vol. 31 (Princeton, N.J.: Princeton University Press, 1979), p. 459.

49. Henry A. Kissinger, *A World Restored* (Gloucester, Mass.: Peter Smith, 1973), p. 33.
50. "An Unpublished Prolegomenon to a Peace Note," c. November 25, 1916, in *PWW*, vol. 40, p. 68.
51. Maurice Hankey to Herbert Asquith in 1916, quoted in John Milton Cooper, Jr., "The British Response to the House-Grey Memorandum," *Journal of American History* 59:4 (March 1973), p. 965.
52. "To Edward Mandell House," November 4, 1918, in *PWW*, vol. 51, p. 575.
53. Woodrow Wilson, *Robert E. Lee: An Interpretation* (Chapel Hill: University of North Carolina Press, 1924), pp. v, 9, 11–12, 28–29.
54. Woodrow Wilson, "The Reconstruction of the Southern States," *Atlantic*, January 1901, pp. 1, 11–12.
55. "A Preface to an Historical Encyclopedia," September 9, 1901, in *PWW*, vol. 12 (Princeton, N.J.: Princeton University Press, 1972), p. 184.
56. Sir William Wiseman, "The Attitude of the United States and of President Wilson Towards the Peace Conference," c. October 20, 1918, in W. B. Fowler, *British-American Relations 1918–1918: The Role of Sir William Wiseman* (Princeton, N.J.: Princeton University Press, 1969).
57. "An Address to the Senate," January 22, 1917, in *PWW*, vol. 40, p. 536.
58. "A Luncheon Address to Women in Cincinnati," October 26, 1916, in *PWW*, vol. 38 (Princeton, N.J.: Princeton University Press), p. 531.
59. Martin, *Peace Without Victory*, p. 161.
60. N. Gordon Levin, Jr., *Woodrow Wilson and World Politics: America's Response to War and Revolution* (New York: Oxford University Press, 1968), p. 5.
61. "The Secretary of State to Colonel E.M. House," April 8, 1918, in *FRUS, The Lansing Papers 1914–1920,* vol. 2 (Washington, D.C.: U.S. Government Printing Office, 1940), pp. 119–20. Lansing ended his missive as follows: "In reading over this letter it impresses me as a little too oratorical, but I am sure you will pardon that in view of the strong convictions which I have on the subject. I simply cannot think with complacency of temporizing or compromising with the ruffians who brought on this horror, because to do so will get us nowhere, and some future generation will have to complete the work which we leave unfinished." Compare Haig's comment of three months earlier to the British monarch: "Few of us feel that the 'democratising of Germany' is worth the loss of a single Englishman." Quoted in John Gooch, "Soldiers, Strategy and War Aims in Britain, 1914–1918," in Barry Hunt and Adrian Preston, eds., *War Aims and Strategic Policy in the Great War* (London: Croom Helm, 1977), p. 30.
62. "Notes on Interview with the President," April 1, 1918, in Fowler, *British-American Relations*, pp. 269–70.

63. Entry for October 21, 1918, in Cronon, ed., *Daniels Cabinet Diaries*, p. 343.
64. The governmental structure of Wilhelmine Germany included an executive branch—consisting of the emperor, the imperial chancellor, and their staffs—and a two-tiered legislative branch, consisting of a Parliament (Reichstag) and a Federal Council (Bundesrat). The emperor had broad authority over foreign policy, could appoint and dismiss the chancellor and other federal officials, and could "interpret" the constitution. The Reichstag had little voice on the formation of governments, but its assent was required for all legislation; while it could be dissolved by the emperor, it could not be prorogued indefinitely. Most matters affecting the daily life of German citizens, as well as the execution of federal laws, were left to state and local governments. The makeup of the Bundesrat assured that the Prussian aristocracy had a veto over constitutional revisions. See Gordon A. Craig, *Germany 1866–1945* (New York: Oxford University Press, 1978), pp. 38–60, and *Questions on German History: Ideas, Forces, Decisions from 1800 to the Present* (Bonn: German Bundestag Publications Section, 1992), pp. 209–13.
65. "From the Diary of Colonel House," October 9, 1918, *PWW*, vol. 51, p. 278. The secretary of the navy noted in *his* diary that "WW came into the cabinet room whistling . . . because he thought he had done right in answering Germans note. Only one thing troubled him. How could he have correspondence with Germany under autocracy?" October 8, 1918, in Cronon, ed., *Daniels Cabinet Diaries*, p. 339.
66. "Two letters from Joseph Patrick Tumulty," October 8, 1918, *PWW*, vol. 51, pp. 265–68.
67. "From David Lawrence," October 13, 1918, *PWW*, vol. 51, pp. 320–24.
68. Suggesting a further call for democratization, Tumulty told Wilson:

> See Springfield Republican editorial—The destruction of every arbitrary power, etc.
> See Borah's statement, New York Times
> See Bohn statement, especially with reference to Bismarck
> See article in New York Times entitled "Kaiser's Dynasty Shaken by Defeat."
> See Rabbi Wise interview; Poindexter, Senator Williams, Roosevelt.
> See The President's speech [on Sept. 27] . . . "They observe no covenants, etc."

He advised including the following section in Wilson's response:

> The present rulers of Germany must go. They are the enemies of democracy. They have sown the seeds of war. They shall not gather in the fruits of peace. . . . "Let us understand that the thing we

> are dealing with is a living, scheming, powerful agency, arbitrary, military, fanatical, bent upon the destruction of free governments." "We do not think the same thoughts, nor speak the same language of agreement." We cannot negotiate or come to terms with such a power, neither can we have any compassion with it. *This is not hate. It is simply the first step toward a permanent peace.*

"From Joseph Patrick Tumulty," October 14, 1918, in *PWW*, vol. 51, pp. 329–32 (emphasis in the original). The words in quotation marks come from earlier Wilson speeches.

69. "The Secretary of State to the Swiss Chargé (Oederlin)," October 14, 1918, in *FRUS, 1918, Supp. 1*, vol. 1, pp. 358–59.
70. Bullitt to Phillips, October 23, 1918, quoted in Schwabe, *Woodrow Wilson*, p. 433, fn. 76. Schwabe comments: "The so-called October constitution which Bullitt is referring to here and which was passed by the Reichstag on October 28, 1918 made the Chancellor's conduct of his office subject to the approval of the Reichstag. That is, it introduced parliamentary monarchy to Germany." He suggests a tantalizing counterfactual: "We cannot know whether Wilson would have accepted Bullitt's judgment here if the relevant information from Germany had arrived in Washington somewhat earlier" (p. 71).
71. "From the Diary of Colonel House," October 15, 1918, in *PWW*, vol. 51, p. 341.
72. "From Robert Wickliffe Woolley," October 22, 1918, in *PWW*, vol. 51, pp. 409–10. Wooley warned the president,

> I talked to no man or woman who did not condemn the latest note of the German government as a trick subtly phrased. . . . I was greatly angered by the sneeringly doubtful attitude of men who would gladly see you and all you stand for . . . butchered to make a Republican victory. . . . [T]hey gave your generous spirit another name—pacificism. . . . Some of your warm admirers expressed the gravest fears as to what the consequences of acceptance of this latest German proposal might be to your administration. . . .

73. "From Homer Stillé Cummings," October 22, 1918, in *PWW*, vol. 51, pp. 408–9. "I believe that the American people have already set a just value upon the German reply," Cummings wrote. "They see in it nowhere any assurance or guarantee that arbitrary and autocratic power has been destroyed . . . they see only evasions, temporary expedients and promises concerning things which have not as yet been done. They are uneasy in the belief that the note is a 'play for time' and part of the military program."
74. Entries for October 16, 21, and 23, 1918, in Cronon, ed., *Daniels Cabinet Diaries*, pp. 341–44.

75. Schwabe, *Woodrow Wilson*, pp. 71–72, and Schwabe, "U.S. Secret War Diplomacy, Intelligence, and the Coming of the German Revolution in 1918."
76. For the American domestic political environment during this period, see Armstrong, "The Domestic Politics of War Termination."
77. Senators Poindexter, Lodge, and McCumber, respectively, quoted in *PWW,* vol. 51, pp. 277–78, fn. 7.
78. "From the Diary of Colonel House," October 9, 1918, in *PWW,* vol. 51, p. 278.
79. "Tasker H. Bliss to the Adjutant General," October 7 and 8, 1918, in *U.S. Army in the World War,* vol. 10, Pt. 1, pp. 4–7.
80. "The Diplomatic Liaison Officer with the Supreme War Council (Frazier) to the Secretary of State," October 9, 1918, in *FRUS, 1918, Supp. 1,* part 1, p. 353.
81. "A Translation of a Letter from Jean Jules Jusserand to Colvine Adrian de Rune Barclay and Its Enclosure," October 11, 1918, in *PWW,* vol. 51, p. 308.
82. For the argument about the *Leinster*'s significance, see C. N. Barclay, *Armistice 1918* (London: J. M. Dent, 1968), p. 69, and Rudin, *Armistice 1918*, pp. 121ff. For Wilson's reaction, see "Two Telegrams from Sir Eric Geddes to David Lloyd George," October 13, 1918, in *PWW,* vol. 51, p. 326; for the German side of the story, see the documents in *Preliminary History*, pp. 109–12.
83. "Two Telegrams from Sir Eric Geddes to David Lloyd George," pp. 325–26. On October 16 Wilson told Wiseman: "It would be best for our Naval and Military experts to recommend terms for an armistice. The heads of governments will probably have to modify the terms because the soldiers and sailors will make them too severe." Quoted in Bullitt Lowry, "Pershing and the Armistice," *Journal of American History* 55:2 (September 1968), p. 283. For how the specific armistice terms emerged, see Lowry, *Armistice 1918* (Kent, Ohio: Kent State University Press, 1998).
84. The following clause was tacked on: "The Allies and the United States will concern themselves with the question of Germany's food supply during the Armistice to the degree considered necessary." In practice, little was done. The full armistice terms are in *U.S. Army in the World War,* vol. 10, part 1, pp. 52–60.
85. "Colonel Boyd for General Pershing," October 31, 1918, in *U.S. Army in the World War,* vol. 10, part 1, p. 31. Since only a few days earlier Pershing had taken a different position, the motives behind his "unconditional surrender" declaration are questionable; see Lowry, "Pershing and the Armistice."
86. "German Declaration at Signature of Armistice," in *U.S. Army in the World War,* vol. 10, part 1, p. 51.
87. Sir William Wiseman, "Notes on an Interview with the President," April

1, 1918, in Fowler, *British-American Relations*, p. 270. British leaders did not see the situation in precisely the same way. Throughout the war, Lloyd George, according to Maurice Hankey, secretary of the cabinet, "never lost sight of the advantages he might hope to derive at the eventual peace conference from the acquisition of the territory of our enemies." After hearing about the first German note, the prime minister sought to wrap up his territorial gains as quickly as possible so as to elude Wilson's scruples. Hankey noted in his diary on October 6: "Ll G . . . wanted us to go back on the Sykes-Picot agreement, so as to get Palestine for us and to bring Mosul into the British zone, and even to keep the French out of Syria. . . . He was also very contemptuous of President Wilson and anxious to arrange the division of Turkey between France, Italy, and G.B. before speaking to America. He also thought it would attract less attention to our enormous gains in the war if we swallowed our share of Turkey now, and the German colonies later." Quoted in David Fromkin, *A Peace to End All Peace: The Fall of the Ottoman Empire and the Creation of the Modern Middle East* (New York: Holt, 2001).

88. Wilson placed great faith in his influence over foreign opinion, and in the influence of that opinion on foreign governments. When warned during the summer of 1918 that the Entente leaders were unsympathetic to his vision, Wilson replied "Yes, I know that Europe is still governed by the same reactionary forces which controlled this country until a few years ago. But I am satisfied that if necessary I can reach the peoples of Europe over the heads of their leaders." Quoted in Ray Stannard Baker, *Woodrow Wilson: Life and Letters*, vol. 8, *Armistice* (New York: Doubleday, Doran, 1939), p. 253. He placed a similar faith in the powers of the presidency to dominate the political currents of the country. "His is the only national voice in affairs," he wrote years before being elected. "Let him once win the admiration and confidence of the country, and no other single force can withstand him, no combination of forces will easily overpower him. . . . If he rightly interpret the national thought and boldly insist upon it, he is irresistible. . . . A President whom [the country] trusts can not only lead it, but form it to his own views." "Constitutional Government in the United States," March 24, 1908, in *PWW*, vol. 18 (Princeton, N.J.: Princeton University Press, 1974), p. 114. The president, Wilson wrote in 1907, could also coerce the Senate: "The initiative in foreign affairs, which the President possesses without any restriction whatever, is virtually the power to control them absolutely. The President cannot conclude a treaty with a foreign power without the consent of the Senate, but he may guide every step of diplomacy, and to guide diplomacy is to determine what treaties must be made, if the faith and prestige of the government is to be maintained. He need disclose no step of negotiation until it is complete, and when in any critical matter it is completed the government is virtually committed. Whatever its disinclination, the

Senate may feel itself committed also." Quoted in Arthur S. Link, " 'Wilson the Diplomatist' in Retrospect," in *The Higher Realism of Woodrow Wilson and Other Essays* (Nashville, Tenn.: Vanderbilt University Press, 1971), pp. 82–83.

89. Specifically, he wrote, "We have to obtain vast loans, tonnage, supplies and munitions, food, oil, and other raw materials." "Memorandum on Anglo-American Relations," August 1917, in Fowler, *British-American Relations*, p. 250.
90. "Tasker Howard Bliss to Peyton Conway March," October 14, 1918, in *PWW,* vol. 51, p. 338.
91. "The language of the fourteen points and of the subsequent statements explaining or qualifying them," Roosevelt declared on October 24,

> is neither straightforward nor plain, but if construed in its probable sense many and possibly most of those fourteen points are thoroly mischievous and if made the basis of a peace, such peace would represent not the unconditional surrender of Germany but the unconditional surrender of the United States. Naturally they are entirely satisfactory to Germany and equally naturally they are in this country satisfactory to every pro-German and pacifist and socialist and anti-American so-called internationalist. . . . Moreover we should find out what the President means by continually referring to this country merely as an associate, instead of the ally of the nations with whose troops our own troops are actually brigaded in battle. If he means that we are something less than an ally of France, England, Italy, Belgium and Serbia, then he means that we are something less than an enemy of Germany and Austria. . . . Let us clearly show that we do not desire to pose as the umpire between our faithful and loyal friends and our treacherous and brutal enemies, but that we are the staunch ally of our friends and the staunch foe of our enemies.

Roosevelt to Lodge, in Elting E. Morison et al., eds., *The Letters of Theodore Roosevelt*, vol. 8, pp. 1380–81, quoted in *PWW,* vol. 51, pp. 455–56, fn. 1.

92. Quoted in Charles Seymour, *The Intimate Papers of Colonel House,* vol. 4 (Boston: Houghton Mifflin, 1928), p. 142.
93. "Two Telegrams from Edward Mandell House," November 5, 1918, in *PWW,* vol. 51, p. 594.
94. Quoted in Knock, *To End All Wars*, p. 198.
95. Knock, *To End All Wars*, p. 213.
96. Quoted in Paul Birdsall, "The Second Decade of Peace Conference History," *Journal of Modern History* 11:3 (September 1939), p. 373.
97. Harold Nicolson, *Peacemaking 1919* (New York: Harcourt, Brace, 1939), p. 41.

98. For contemporary analyses of the settlement, see Manfred F. Boemeke, Gerald D. Feldman, and Elisabeth Glaser, eds., *The Treaty of Versailles: A Reassessment After 75 Years* (Cambridge, England: German History Institute, Washington, and Cambridge University Press, 1998).
99. Reviewing the recent historiography of the armistice negotiations, David Stevenson comes to a similar conclusion: "The democrats who took power in Germany after the November Revolution were genuinely willing to accept a settlement based on the American programme, especially as they expected it to maintain their country's great-power status. The British, however, reconciled themselves to it only because of its vagueness, and the French reserved the right to apply the Fourteen Points one-sidedly and to demand much more, which at the 1919 peace conference they duly did, Wilson lacking the ruthlessness and perhaps the capacity to insist on Clemenceau yielding. To an extent, the Americans succeeded only by cultivating misunderstanding—or at least by papering over conflicting expectations. The bitterness and disillusionment that followed the Versailles Treaty were therefore predictable from the circumstances in which the war ended." "1918 Revisited," *Journal of Strategic Studies* 28:1 (February 2005), p. 129.

3. WORLD WAR II—EUROPE

1. Frédéric au marquis d'Argens (Breslau), January 18, 1762, in *Oeuvres de Frédéric le Grand*, vol. 19, p. 317, Digitale Ausgabe der Universitätsbibliothek Trier.
2. Thomas Carlyle, *History of Friedrich II of Prussia*, vol. 20, chapter 10, www.gutenberg.org/etext/2120.
3. Hugh Trevor-Roper, ed., *Final Entries 1945: The Diaries of Joseph Goebbels* (New York: G. P. Putnam's, 1978), p. 39.
4. Albert Speer, *Inside the Third Reich* (New York: Simon & Schuster, 1970), pp. 463–64.
5. Adam Tooze, *The Wages of Destruction: The Making and Breaking of the Nazi Economy* (New York: Viking, 2006), pp. 657–58.
6. General Karl Wolff quoting his conversations with Hitler, in John Toland, *The Last 100 Days* (New York: Random House, 1966), pp. 488–89. At that point Wolff was himself negotiating with the Americans and British over the surrender of German forces in Italy, an episode that fed Stalin's suspicion that the Western Allies might be seeking a separate peace.
7. Rudolf Semmler, *Goebbels—The Man Next to Hitler* (London: Westhouse, 1947), p. 193.
8. Pierre Galante and Eugène Silianoff, *Voices from the Bunker: Hitler's Personal Staff Tells the Story of the Führer's Last Days* (New York: Anchor, 1990), p. 19. A Graff portrait of Frederick can be seen at http://en.wikipedia.org/File: Friedrich_Zweite_Alt.jpg.
9. Winston S. Churchill, *The Second World War*, vol. 3, *The Grand Alliance* (London: Cassell, 1950), p. 539.

10. Warren F. Kimball, *The Juggler: Franklin Roosevelt as Wartime Statesman* (Princeton, N.J.: Princeton University Press, 1991), p. 17.
11. Charles Maier, "The Politics of Productivity: Foundations of American International Economic Policy After World War II," *International Organization* 31:4 (Autumn 1977), p. 630; Geir Lundestad, "Empire by Invitation? The United States and Western Europe, 1945–1952," *Journal of Peace Research* 23:3 (September 1986), pp. 263–77.
12. George Kennan, "Comment," *Survey* 21:1–2 (Winter/Spring 1975), p. 33.
13. Stephen E. Ambrose wrote: "What stands out [in the Western Allies' debates] is that until late 1943, Churchill got his way; from early 1944 to the end of the war, Eisenhower prevailed. This shift corresponds almost exactly with the change in the contribution to the whole force made by the UK and the USA. There were more British armed forces in the Mediterranean and European theatres than American until the end of 1943; after that, the Americans were the major partner." "Churchill and Eisenhower in the Second World War," in Robert Blake and William Roger Louis, eds., *Churchill: A Major New Assessment of his Life in Peace and War* (New York: Norton, 1993). p. 404. The extent to which British and American strategies differed has remained a controversial subject; it is fair to say, nonetheless, that "if it had depended on Churchill and the British chiefs of staff alone, they would not have invaded western Europe until after a collapse or drastic weakening of Germany." Tuvia Ben-Moshe, "Winston Churchill and the 'Second Front': A Reappraisal," *Journal of Modern History* 62:3 (September 1990), p. 528.
14. Quoted in Klemens von Klemperer, *German Resistance Against Hitler: The Search for Allies Abroad, 1938–1945* (Oxford, UK: Clarendon Press, 1993), p. 218.
15. Vojtech Mastny, "Stalin and the Prospects of a Separate Peace in World War II," *American Historical Review* 77:5 (December 1972), pp. 1365–88.
16. Churchill, in contrast, was briefed in the days following the attempt by John Wheeler-Bennett, who argued that Britain was "better off" with failure "than if the plot of July 20th had succeeded and Hitler had been assassinated." It was "to our advantage," he was told, that the purge of the Opposition should continue, "since the killing of Germans by Germans will save us from future embarrassments of many kinds." He delivered a speech in the House of Commons on August 2 crowing about how "the highest personalities in the Reich are murdering one another, or trying to, while the avenging armies of the Allies close upon the doomed and ever-narrowing circle of their power." See Klemperer, *German Resistance Against Hitler*, pp. 386–87.
17. As Max Hastings notes, "the German army was the outstanding fighting force of the Second World War, and . . . it could be defeated by Allied soldiers only under the most overwhelmingly favourable conditions."

OVERLORD: D-Day and the Battle for Normandy (New York: Simon & Schuster, 1984), p. 12. In retrospect, it can be said confidently that "an attempt to invade France in 1943, before the Luftwaffe had suffered crippling losses, and while the Germans still disposed large enough reserves to reinforce speedily in the west, would most probably have failed." Eliot A. Cohen, "Churchill and Coalition Strategy in World War II," in Paul Kennedy, ed., *Grand Strategies in War and Peace* (New Haven, Conn.: Yale University Press, 1991), p. 65.

18. Cordell Hull with Andrew Henry Thomas Berding, *The Memoirs of Cordell Hull* (New York: Macmillan, 1948), vol. 1, p. 81. "The basic approach to the problem of peace," Hull believed, "is the ordering of the world's economic life so that the masses of the people can work and live in reasonable comfort" (p. 364).
19. Quoted in Patrick J. Hearden, *Architects of Globalism: Building a New World Order During World War II* (Fayetteville: University of Arkansas Press, 2002). p. 41.
20. Hull, *Memoirs*, vol. 2, pp. 1736–37.
21. Harry Hopkins, who knew Roosevelt best, once felt it necessary to point this out to speechwriter Robert Sherwood when he questioned the president's convictions: "You and I are for Roosevelt because he's a great spiritual figure, because he's an idealist, like Wilson, and he's got the guts to drive through against any opposition to realize those ideals. Oh—he sometimes tries to appear tough and cynical and flippant, but that's an act he likes to put on, especially at press conferences. He wants to make the boys think he's hard-boiled. Maybe he fools some of them, now and then—but don't ever let him fool you, or you won't be any use to him. You can see the real Roosevelt when he comes out with something like the Four Freedoms. And don't get the idea that those are any catch phrases. *He believes them!* He believes they can be practically attained. . . . [H]e knows what he really is, even if he doesn't like to admit it to you or me or anybody." Robert E. Sherwood, *Roosevelt and Hopkins: An Intimate History* (New York: Harper, 1948). p. 266 (emphasis in the original).

    George Kennan agreed with Hopkins about FDR's aversion to Realpolitik, but viewed the prospect more glumly: "The truth is—there is no avoiding it—that Franklin Roosevelt, for all his charm and for all his skill as a political leader was, when it came to foreign policy, a very superficial man, ignorant, dilettantish, with a severely limited intellectual horizon. One has only to glance at the list of ideas he had in the thirties and then during the war for solving his various problems of external policy. . . . Either these schemes were cynically designed to appeal to a series of opinionated and unenlightened domestic lobbies, without serious regard to their external effect, or they bore witness to a very poor understanding of international affairs on the part of their author." "Comment," p. 31.
22. Perhaps the only thing missing was a new international security organiza-

tion, which was omitted for fear the American public was not yet ready for such a commitment. Two months earlier the president had written to Assistant Secretary of State Adolph Berle: "I have not the slightest objection towards your trying your hand at an outline of the post-war picture. But for Heavens' sake don't even let the columnists hear of it. . . . Don't forget that the elimination of costly armaments is still the keystone—for the security of all the little nations and economic solvency. Don't forget what I discovered—that over ninety percent of all national deficits from 1921 to 1939 were caused by payments for past, present and future wars." *Navigating the Rapids, 1918–1971* (New York: Harcourt Brace Jovanovich, 1973), p. 372. The text of the charter is in *Foreign Relations of the United States, 1941,* vol. 1 (Washington, D.C.: U.S. Government Printing Office, 1958), pp. 367–69, hereafter *FRUS*.

23. As Roosevelt wrote to Churchill three months after Pearl Harbor, "I know you will not mind my being brutally frank when I tell you that I think I can personally handle Stalin better than either your Foreign Office or my State Department. Stalin hates the guts of all your top people. He thinks he likes me better, and I hope he will continue to do so." Roosevelt to Churchill, March 18, 1942, in Francis L. Loewenheim, Harold D. Langley, and Manfred Jonas, eds., *Roosevelt and Churchill: Their Secret Wartime Correspondence* (New York: Da Capo, 1990), p. 196. After the war William Bullitt wrote that Roosevelt had responded to his warnings about Soviet intentions as follows: "I don't dispute the logic of your reasoning. I just have a hunch that Stalin is not that kind of a man. Harry [Hopkins] says he's not and that he doesn't want anything but security for his country, and I think that if I give him everything I possibly can and ask nothing from him in return, *noblesse oblige,* he won't try to annex anything and will work with me for a world of democracy and peace." "How We Won the War and Lost the Peace," *Life*, August 30, 1948, p. 94. Hopkins's own views were captured in a 1942 memo: ". . . it seems evident that Soviet relationships are the most important to us of all countries, excepting only the United Kingdom. It seems also evident that we must be so helpful and friendly to her that she will not only battle through to the defeat of Japan, but in addition willingly join with us in establishing a sound peace and mutually beneficial relations in the post-war world." Sherwood, *Roosevelt and Hopkins*, pp. 642–43. For a survey of the historiography on this issue, see Mark A. Stoler, "A Half Century of Conflict: Interpretations of U.S. World War II Diplomacy," *Diplomatic History* 18:3 (July 1994).

24. Hopkins told Sherwood months after the war ended: "We really believed in our hearts that [Yalta] was the dawn of the new day we had all been praying for and talking about for so many years. We were absolutely certain that we had won the first great victory of the peace—and, by 'we,' I mean *all* of us, the whole civilized human race. The Russians had proved that they could be reasonable and farseeing and there wasn't any doubt

in the minds of the President or any of us that we could live with them and get along with them peacefully for as far into the future as any of us could imagine. But I have to make one amendment to that—I think we all had in our minds the reservation that we could not foretell what the results would be if anything should happen to Stalin. We felt sure that we could count on him to be reasonable and sensible and understanding—but we never could be sure who or what might be in back of him there in the Kremlin." *Roosevelt and Hopkins*, p. 870. For Adolph Berle's picture of a bleaker Roosevelt toward the end, see *Navigating the Rapids*, pp. 527–28, 477.

25. *The War Messages of Franklin D. Roosevelt: December 8, 1941, to October 12, 1942* (Washington, D.C., 1943), p. 11.
26. The text of the declaration is in *FRUS, 1942*, vol. 1 (Washington, D.C.: U.S. Government Printing Office, 1960), pp. 25–26.
27. Harley Notter, *Postwar Foreign Policy Preparation, 1939–1945* (Washington, D.C.: U.S. Department of State, 1949)., p. 127.
28. Sherwood, *Roosevelt and Hopkins*, pp. 696–97.
29. John L. Chase, "Unconditional Surrender Reconsidered," *Political Science Quarterly* 70:2 (June 1955), p. 271.
30. John P. Glennon, " 'This Time Germany is a Defeated Nation': The Doctrine of Unconditional Surrender and Some Unsuccessful Attempts to Alter It, 1943–44," in Gerald N. Grob, ed., *Statesmen and Statecraft of the Modern West: Essays in Honor of Dwight E. Lee and H. Donaldson Jordan* (Barre, Mass.: Barre, 1967), p. 143.
31. For relations between the German Opposition and the West, see Klemperer, *German Resistance Against Hitler,* and Peter Hoffmann, *The History of the German Resistance, 1933–1945* (Cambridge, Mass.: MIT Press, 1977), pp. 205–48. For a good summary of what U.S. officials knew at the time, see "Overtures by German Generals and Civilian Opposition for a Separate Armistice," enclosed with "Memorandum by Brigadier General John Magruder, Deputy Director of Intelligence Services, Office of Strategic Services, to Mr. Fletcher Warren, Executive Assistant ot the Assistant Secretary of State (Berle)," May 17, 1944, in *FRUS, 1944, Vol. I,* (Washington, D.C.: U.S. Government Printing Office, 1966), pp. 510–13.
32. Donovan to Roosevelt, "Memorandum for the President," July 15, 1944, Franklin D. Roosevelt Library. See also Dulles's report on the attempt and its aftermath: "The developments did not come as a great surprise. . . . These persons hoped that they could make some sort of a deal with the West, along the lines of the Italian Pattern, and thus be in a better position to restrict the extent of Russian occupation of German territory." Donovan to Roosevelt, "Memorandum for the President," July 22, 1944. What would have happened had any of the attempts on Hitler's life succeeded must remain an open and fascinating question. From 1943 onward the Western Allies maintained contingency plans, under Operation

RANKIN, for dealing with a Nazi "collapse" by sending airborne troops to Berlin. These plans all envisioned imposing unconditional surrender by joint operations of the Allies; they ignored the possibility of a non-Nazi regime seeking a separate peace with the West. But that option might have had a greater attraction in 1944 than it did when Doenitz finally proposed it in late April 1945, and even if it had been rejected, the postwar era would have gotten off to quite a different start. See "Digest of Operation 'RANKIN,' " Memorandum by the Chief of Staff to the Supreme Allied Commander Delegate (Morgan), August 20, 1943, "Most Secret," in *FRUS, The Conferences at Washington and Quebec, 1943* (Washington, D.C.: U.S. Government Printing Office, 1970), pp. 1010–18. See also Kenneth O. McCreedy, "Planning the Peace: Operation Eclipse and the Occupation of Germany." *Journal of Military History* 65:3 (July 2001).

33. Winston S. Churchill, *The Second World War*, vol. 4, *The Hinge of Fate* (London: Cassell, 1951), p. 618. For other suggestions that Roosevelt publicly clarify his demands, see Berle, *Navigating the Rapids*, pp. 408–11, and *FRUS, 1944*, vol. 1, pp. 493, 501–5, 507–10, 513–21. A good summary of attempts to modify the policy is Glennon, " 'This Time Germany is a Defeated Nation.' "
34. Quoted in Hoffmann, *The History of the German Resistance*, p. 227.
35. George Frost Kennan, *Memoirs 1925–1950* (London: Hutchinson, 1968), p. 123.
36. Quotd in Michael Beschloss, *The Conquerors: Roosevelt, Truman and the Destruction of Hitler's Germany, 1941–45* (New York: Simon & Schuster, 2002), p. 11.
37. Roosevelt to Churchill, January 6, 1944, in Loewenheim et al., *Roosevelt and Churchill*, pp. 411–12. The president said the same thing publicly in a radio address two weeks earlier; see Hull, *Memoirs*, vol. 2, pp. 1572–73. Last quote in Daniel M. Smith, "Authoritarianism and American Policymakers in Two World Wars," *Pacific Historical Review* 47:3 (August 1974), p. 321.
38. Quoted in Raymond G. O'Connor, *Diplomacy for Victory: FDR and Unconditional Surrender* (New York: Norton, 1971), p. 38.
39. Entry for May 6, 1942, in Fred L. Israel, ed., *The War Diary of Breckinridge Long*, (Lincoln: University of Nebraska Press, 1966), pp. 264–65.
40. Stalin, displaying his customary cynicism, found the deal unremarkable: "It seems to me that the Americans used Darlan not badly in order to facilitate the occupation of Northern and Western Africa. The military diplomacy must be able to use for military purposes not only Darlan but, 'even the Devil himself and his grandma.' " See Sherwood, *Roosevelt and Hopkins*, p. 651ff.
41. Richard W. Steele, "American Popular Opinion and the War Against Germany: The Issue of Negotiated Peace, 1942," *Journal of American History*, 65:3 (December 1998), pp. 722–23.
42. See Stephen E. Ambrose, *Eisenhower and Berlin, 1945: The Decision*

to Halt at the Elbe (New York: Norton, 1967); Forrest C. Pogue, "The Decision to Halt at the Elbe," in Kent Roberts Greenfield, ed., *Command Decisions* (Washington, D.C.: Office of Military History, 1960), pp. 472–92; and Theodore Draper, "Eisenhower's War," in *A Present of Things Past: Selected Essays* (New York: Hill & Wang, 1990), pp. 32–66.

43. Stephen E. Ambrose, "Eisenhower as Commander: Single Thrust versus Broad Front," in *The Eisenhower Papers*, vol. V. p. 43. Ambrose continues: "Eisenhower's policy, like Grant's in 1864, would surely lead to victory. The only trouble was that if the Germans decided to fight on, victory would take time."
44. Michael Howard, "Montgomery," in *The Causes of War*, 2nd ed. (Cambridge, Mass.: Harvard University Press, 1984), p. 222. Montgomery's own chief of staff put it simply, both at the time and later: "Eisenhower was right." Francis de Guingand, *Operation Victory* (London: Hodder & Stoughton, 1947), p. 413.
45. See Harold Zink, *The United States in Germany, 1944–55* (Princeton, N.J.: D. Van Nostrand, 1957); James McAllister, *No Exit: America and the German Problem, 1943–1954* (Ithaca, N.Y.: Cornell University Press, 2002); Marc Trachtenberg, *A Constructed Peace: The Making of the European Settlement* (Princeton: Princeton University Press, 1999); Carolyn Woods Eisenberg, *Drawing the Line: The American Decision to Divide Germany, 1944–1949* (Cambridge: Cambridge UP, 1998); Philip E. Mosely, "Dismemberment of Germany: The Allied Negotiations from Yalta to Potsdam," *Foreign Affairs* 28:3 (April 1950); and McCreedy, "Planning the Peace."
46. Roosevelt quote in "Memorandum for the Secretary of State," October 20, 1944, Top Secret, in *FRUS: Malta and Yalta*, pp. 158–59. Kennan quote in *Memoirs, 1925–1950*, p. 166. The best analysis of the EAC's deliberations remains Daniel J. Nelson, *Wartime Origins of the Berlin Dilemma* (University: University of Alabama Press, 1978); see also William M. Franklin, "Zonal Boundaries and Access to Berlin," *World Politics* 16:1 (October 1963), pp. 1–31, and Philip E. Mosely, "The Occupation of Germany: New Light on How the Zones Were Drawn," *Foreign Affairs* 28:4 (July 1950), pp. 580–604.
47. Stephen Ambrose summarized this logic succinctly: "the British were in the northwest and the Americans in the south as a result of their respective positions in the proposed drive through France and into Germany, when the British would be on the left and the Americans on the right. This in turn resulted from the positions of the national forces in the initial landings on the Normandy beachhead, which in turn resulted from the position of American troops stationed in England. The Americans had been stationed in southwestern England, the area of the island closest to the United States and thus most easily reached by convoys; this positioning put them on the right flank in the Normandy landings." *Eisenhower and Berlin*, p. 38.

48. As he cabled Churchill on February 29, 1944: "I note that in the British proposal the territory of Germany is divided up in accordance with the British plan. 'Do please don't' ask me to keep any American forces in France! I just cannot do it. . . . I denounce and protest the paternity of Belgium, France, and Italy. You really ought to bring up and discipline your own children. In view of the fact that they may be your bulwark in future days, you should at least pay for their schooling now!" In Loewenheim et al., *Roosevelt and Churchill*, p. 457.
49. Churchill to Roosevelt, April 5, 1944, in Loewenheim et al., *Roosevelt and Churchill*, pp. 704–5.
50. As the British Official History notes, "It is perhaps easy, in view of developments in the following decade, to see in [the British attitude] the emergence of a policy which later became orthodox throughout the Western world. But attitudes and policy should not be confused. In the first place, even if the Prime Minister and the Foreign Secretary . . . had decided in the spring of 1945 that action should be taken on the assumption that Russia might be a potential enemy, there was no likelihood of such action being adopted by their country or in the United States. But secondly, they did not so decide. . . . The strategy they wished to adopt in Germany was designed, not for reasons of defence or attack against Russia . . . but with the object of negotiating from strength." John Ehrman, *Grand Strategy*, vol. 6, *October 1944–August 1945* (London: Her Majesty's Stationery Office, 1956), p. 150.
51. Alfred D. Chandler, Jr., ed., *The Papers of Dwight David Eisenhower, The War Years: IV* (Baltimore: Johns Hopkins University Press, 1970), p. 2593.
52. When Eisenhower inquired at the end of March about the cost of taking Berlin, Bradley guessed that it would involve one hundred thousand U.S. casualties. He offered his judgment to Eisenhower as well: "A pretty stiff price to pay for a prestige objective, especially when we've got to fall back and let the other fellow take over." Ambrose, *Eisenhower and Berlin*, p. 89.
53. "Personal from Eisenhower to General Marshall, eyes only," April 7, 1945; *The Papers of Dwight David Eisenhower, The War Years: IV*, p. 2592.
54. The chief reason Eisenhower's superiors did not overrule him was that they agreed with his analysis. As the British Chiefs of Staff were told on April 6: "The United States Chiefs of Staff continue to regard [Eisenhower's] plan as sound. . . . [They] believe that such psychological and political advantages as would result from a possible capture of Berlin ahead of the Russians should not override the imperative military consideration, which in their opinion is the destruction and dismemberment of the German Armed Forces. . . ." Quoted in Ehrman, *Grand Strategy*, p. 144.
55. "Prime Minister Churchill to President Truman," May 11, 1945, Top Se-

cret, in *FRUS, The Conference of Berlin (Potsdam)*, vol. 1 (Washington, D.C.: U.S. Government Printing Office, 1960), pp. 6–7.

56. Notes of the June 29 meeting between the Allied military commanders are in *FRUS, 1945*, vol. 3, pp. 353–61.

57. Truman wrote Churchill on June 11: "In consideration of the tripartite agreement as to zones of occupation in Germany approved by President Roosevelt after long consideration and detailed discussion with you, I am unable to delay the withdrawal of American troops from the Soviet zone in order to use pressure in the settlement of other problems. Advice of the highest reliability is received that the Allied Control Council cannot begin to function until Allied troops withdraw from the Russian zone. . . . I am advised that it would be highly disadvantageous to our relations with the Soviets to postpone action in this matter until our meeting in July." Churchill replied on June 14: "Obviously we are obliged to conform to your decision, and necessary instructions will be issued. . . . I sincerely hope that your action will in the long run make for a lasting peace in Europe." See *FRUS, 1945*, vol. 3 (Washington, D.C.: U.S. Government Printing Office, 1968), pp. 133–35.

58. The endgame regarding Prague was similar to that regarding Berlin: a Churchill challenge based on geopolitics, but couched less strongly; an Eisenhower refusal to direct forces for "political" ends without new authorization; a tacit decision by his superiors to support Eisenhower; occupation by the Soviets after American restraint. One difference was that Prague, unlike Berlin, could actually have been taken by the Americans without much difficulty. See Draper, *A Present of Things Past*, pp. 54–58.

59. When Harry Hopkins asked George Kennan in the spring of 1945 for concrete suggestions, the latter had little to offer: "[Hopkins] described to me Stalin's terms for a settlement of the Polish problem . . . and asked whether I thought we could do any better. I said I did not. Did I think, then, that we should accept these terms and come to an agreement on this basis? I did not; I thought we should accept no share of the responsibility for what the Russians proposed to do in Poland. 'Then you think it's just sin,' he said, 'and we should be agin it.' 'That's just about right,' I replied." *Memoirs, 1925–1950*, p. 213.

60. For the positive program, see Hearden, *Architects of Globalism*; Richard N. Gardner, *Sterling-Dollar Diplomacy in Current Perspective: The Origins and Prospects of Our International Economic Order*, expanded ed., (New York: Columbia University Press, 1980); and Stewart Patrick, *The Best Laid Plans: The Origins of American Multilateralism and the Dawn of the Cold War* (Lanham, MD: Bowman & Littlefield, 2009).

61. "Address to the Congress Reporting on the Yalta Conference," in Samuel I. Rosenman, ed., *The Public Papers and Addresses of Franklin D. Roosevelt*, vol. 13, *1944–45* (New York: Russell & Russell), p. 586. Cf. Hull's statement to a joint session of Congress upon his return from the Moscow Foreign Minister's Conference of October 1943: "As the provisions

of the Four-Nation Declaration are carried into effect, there will no longer be need for spheres of influence, for alliances, for balance of power, or any other of the special arrangements through which, in the unhappy past, the nations strove to safeguard their security or to promote their interests." Quoted in Herbert Feis, *Churchill, Roosevelt, Stalin: The War They Waged and the Peace They Sought* (Princeton, N.J.: Princeton University Press, 1957), p. 238.

62. From Stettinius's diary entry of March 17, 1944, quoted in Kimball, *The Juggler*, p. 66. Hopkins noted during Eden's March 1943 trip to the U.S., "The President has once or twice urged the British to give up Hong Kong as a gesture of 'good will.' In fact, the President had suggested a number of similar gestures on the part of the British and Eden dryly remarked that he had not heard the President suggest any similar gestures on our own part." Sherwood, *Roosevelt and Hopkins*, p. 719.
63. Maier, "The Politics of Productivity," p. 608.
64. Bruce R. Kuniholm, *The Origins of the Cold War in the Near East* (Princeton, N.J.: Princeton University Press, 1980), p. 204. "America's competitive superiority meant that countries accepting the principles of the Atlantic Charter, and the principle of equal trading opportunities for all, and which therefore were subject to the economic influence of the most able, often found themselves within what was tantamount to an American sphere of influence—a liberal capitalist international order dominated by the United States. Thus, while the United States could happily uphold the principles of the Charter and the United Nations, the Soviet Union was more chary of them" (p. 427).
65. Donald Cameron Watt, "Britain and the Historiography of the Yalta Conference and the Cold War," *Diplomatic History* 13:1 (Winter 1989), p. 91.
66. See J. Tillapaugh, "Closed Hemisphere and Open World? The Dispute Over Regional Security at the U.N. Conference, 1945," *Diplomatic History* 2:1 (Winter 1978).
67. "Memorandum by the Adviser on German Economic Affairs (Despres)," February 15, 1945, in *FRUS, 1945*, vol. 3, pp. 412, 413.
68. "Memorandum Prepared in the Department of State," March 16, 1945, in *FRUS, 1945*, vol. 3, p. 457.
69. Alexander George, *Presidential Decisionmaking in Foreign Policy: The Effective Use of Information and Advice* (Boulder, Colo.: Westview, 1980), p. 149. Cf. also Nelson, *Wartime Origins of the Berlin Dilemma*, pp. 143–48, 162–64; and A. E. Campbell, "Franklin Roosevelt and Unconditional Surrender," in Richard Langhorne, ed., *Diplomacy and Intelligence During the Second World War: Essays in Honor of F. H. Hinsley* (Cambridge, UK: Cambridge UP, 1985) pp. 237–38.
70. Quoted in Kimball, *The Juggler*, p. 7.
71. "Memorandum for the Secretary of State," October 20, 1944; see note 46 above. Hopkins noted after a lunch with Roosevelt, Eden, and Hull on March 22, 1943: "The President stated that he wanted no negotiated ar-

mistice after the collapse [of Germany]; that we should insist on total surrender with no commitments to the enemy as to what we would or would not do after this action." Quoted in Sherwood, *Roosevelt and Hopkins*, p. 715.

72. Robert Dallek, "Allied Leadership in the Second World War: Roosevelt," *Survey* 21:1–2 (Winter–Spring 1975), p. 2.
73. Quoted in Robert Dallek, *Franklin D. Roosevelt and American Foreign Policy, 1932–1945* (New York: Oxford University Press, 1978).
74. Quoted in James MacGregor Burns, *Roosevelt: The Soldier of Freedom* (New York: Harcourt Brace Jovanovich, 1970) p. 290.
75. Matthews Minutes of the Third Plenary Meeting, February 6, 1945; *FRUS: Malta and Yalta*, p. 667. Stalin obviously felt such comments were merely a feint. He responded: "But of your seven million Poles, only seven thousand vote," adding that he knew, because he had looked it up. Edward R. Stettinius, Jr., *Roosevelt and the Russians: The Yalta Conference* (Garden City, N.Y.: Doubleday, 1949), p. 113.
76. Bohlen Minutes of the Second Plenary Meeting, February 5, 1945; *FRUS: Malta and Yalta*, p. 617. He had written to Churchill a couple of months earlier: "You know, of course, that after Germany's collapse I must bring American troops home as rapidly as transportation problems will permit . . ." Roosevelt to Churchill, November 18, 1944, in *FRUS: Malta and Yalta*, p. 286.
77. Hastings Ismay, *The Memoirs of General Lord Ismay,* p. 392, quoted in Ambrose, *Eisenhower and Berlin*, p. 72.
78. Kennan to Bohlen, February 4, 1945, and Bohlen to Kennan, quoted in Charles E. Bohlen, *Witness to History: 1929–1969* (New York: Norton, 1973), pp. 174–77. On the debate in the U.S. government over whether to acquiesce in the division of Europe, see John Lewis Gaddis, *The Long Peace: Inquiries into the History of the Cold War* (New York: Oxford University Press, 1987), pp. 48–71.
79. Warren F. Kimball, "Wheel Within a Wheel: Churchill, Roosevelt, and the Special Relationship," in Blake and Louis, eds., *Churchill* p. 300. Official reports in April 1942, for example, told the Roosevelt administration that in answer to the question "Granting that it is important for us to fight the Axis every place we can, which do you think is more important for the United States to do right now: put most of our effort into fighting Japan or put most of our effort into fighting Germany?" 62 percent of the public chose Japan and only 21 percent chose Germany. Steele, "American Popular Opinion," p. 704, fn. 6.
80. See Levering, *American Opinion and the Russian Alliance*, pp. 94ff.
81. According to Thomas E. Lifka, "The bulk of the evidence suggests that American opinion of the U.S.S.R. during the war became fractured and fluid. Clearly, there was a transformation of the hostile consensus of the period 1939–1941, but that hostility had not been totally reversed by any means. The special ideological circumstances of the war merely cloaked

the deep distrust with a veil of cautious hope." *The Concept "Totalitarianism" and American Foreign Policy, 1933–1949* (New York: Garland, 1988), p. 258. See also Eduard Mark, "October or Thermidor? Interpretations of Stalinism and the Perception of Soviet Foreign Policy in the United States, 1927–1947," *American Historical Review* 94:4 (October 1989), pp. 937–62.

82. In 1943, for example, administration officials found that "by flattering his considerable personal and political ego through such consultations as those involving UNRRA [United Nations Relief and Rehabilitation Administration] . . . they could often get by with comparatively minor changes which Vandenberg would then defend to his colleagues as major ones wrung from the administration by his own hands." Richard E. Darilek, *A Loyal Opposition in Time of War: The Republican Party and the Politics of Foreign Policy from Pearl Harbor to Yalta* (Westport, Conn.: Greenwood, 1976), p. 80. But Vandenberg did make the administration chary of frankness regarding events in Eastern Europe by explicitly warning that he would not support American participation in a postwar United Nations if the Russians did not behave themselves: "with the greatest respect, I assert the view that our . . . [action] should be contingent upon whether the ultimate peace merits our support." Letter to Hull, May 3, 1944, in Arthur H. Vandenberg, Jr., ed., *The Private Papers of Senator Vandenberg* (Boston: Houghton Mifflin, 1952), pp. 97–98.

83. Levering, *American Opinion and the Russian Alliance, 1939–1945*, p. 204. On Roosevelt, public opinion, see Steven Casey, *Cautious Crusade: Franklin D. Roosevelt American Public Opinion, and the War Against Nazi Germany* (New York: Oxford, 2001).

84. For interesting discussions of this issue, see Ernest R. May, *"Lessons" of the Past: The Use and Misuse of History in American Foreign Policy* (London: Oxford University Press, 1973), pp. 3–18; John Lewis Gaddis, *The United States and the Origins of the Cold War, 1941–1946* (New York: Columbia University Press, 1973), pp. 1–31; and Herbert Feis, "Some Notes on Historical Record-keeping, the Role of Historians, and the Influence of Historical Memories During the Era of the Second World War," in Francis L. Loewenheim, ed., *The Historian and the Diplomat: The Role of History and Historians in American Foreign Policy* (New York: Harper & Row, 1967), pp. 91–121.

85. "Christmas Eve Fireside Chat on Teheran and Cairo Conferences," December 24, 1943, in Rosenman, ed., *Public Papers and Addresses, Vol. 12, 1943*, p. 559. Robert Sherwood testified that those "familiar with Roosevelt's real character . . . [knew] that the last thing he wanted to do was to repeat any of the history of the First World War or of the phony peace that followed it"; FDR was "haunted by the ghost of Woodrow Wilson." *Roosevelt and Hopkins*, pp. 263, 360.

86. Even secondary matters of wartime diplomacy were conceived of in relation to perceived errors of the past. Thus, in Roosevelt's 1944 State of the

Union address, he justified his summitry by saying that "in the last war such discussion, such meetings, did not even begin until the shooting had stopped and the delegates began to assemble at the peace table. There had been no previous opportunities for man-to-man discussions which lead to meetings of minds. The result was a peace which was not a peace." (Quoted in May, *"Lessons" of the Past*, p. 14.) And at the end of the previous conflict, war criminals had been turned over for judgment to new regimes in the former enemy nations, a policy that was considered a dramatic failure. This time, therefore, the victors would establish their own tribunal and exact punishment themselves.

87. Roosevelt to Stimson, August 26, 1944, copied to Hull, quoted in Hull, *Memoirs*, vol. 2, p. 1603. "We have got to be tough with Germany," the president told his Treasury secretary, "and I mean the German people not just the Nazis. We either have to castrate the German people or you have got to treat them in such manner so they can't just go on reproducing people who want to continue the way they have in the past." Quoted in Dallek, *Roosevelt and American Foreign Policy*, p. 472.
88. From his proclamation to the Wehrmacht on March 11, 1945, quoted in Ian Kershaw, *Hitler: 1936–1945, Nemesis* (New York: Norton, 2000), p. 783.
89. Donald W. White, "The Nature of World Power in American History: An Evaluation at the End of World War II," *Diplomatic History* 11:3 (Summer 1987), p. 191. Cf. also Lundestad, "Empire By Invitation?" p. 264.
90. Both quoted in White, "Nature of World Power," p. 182.
91. Quoted in Gaddis, *United States and the Origins of the Cold War*, p. 224.
92. White, "Nature of World Power," p. 190.
93. Christopher Thorne, *Allies of a Kind: The United States, Britain, and the War Against Japan, 1941–1945* (Oxford: Oxford University Press, 1978), p. 515. See also Geir Lundestad, "Moralism, Presentism, Exceptionalism, Provincialism, and Other Extravagances in American Writings on the Early Cold War Years," *Diplomatic History* 13:4 (Fall 1990), pp. 527–45.
94. Fala was Roosevelt's beloved Scottish terrier. Dallek, *Roosevelt and American Foreign Policy*, p. 470.
95. Quoted in Mark A. Stoler, "From Continentalism to Globalism: General Stanley D. Embick, the Joint Strategic Survey Committee, and the Military View of American National Policy during the Second World War," *Diplomatic History* 6:3 (Summer 1982), pp. 303–21. Embick's bureaucratic fiefdom was the Joint Strategic Survey Committee; his rivals operated out of the Strategy and Policy Group of the Operations Division. See also Stoler, *Allies and Adversaries: The Joint Chiefs of Staff, the Grand Alliance, and U.S. Strategy in World War II* (Chapel Hill: University of North Carolina Press, 2000).
96. Melvyn P. Leffler, *A Preponderance of Power: National Security, the Truman Administration, and the Cold War* (Stanford, Calif.: Stanford University Press, 1992), p. 16.

97. Ibid., p. 15.
98. Kuniholm, *The Origins of the Cold War in the Near East*, p. 129. As Hugh B. Hammett writes, "It was Roosevelt who originally made the bargain with the devil and then refused to pay the devil's price. . . . Roosevelt merely vacillated and delayed, hoping to avoid the hard decision that the American attitude made inevitable for his unfortunate successor." "America's Non-Policy in Eastern Europe and the Origins of the Cold War," *Survey* 19:4 (Autumn 1973), p. 161.
99. Quoted in Eduard Mark, "Charles E. Bohlen and the Acceptable Limits of Soviet Hegemony in Eastern Europe: A Memorandum of 18 October 1945," *Diplomatic History* 3:2 (Spring 1979), pp. 208–9. See also Eduard Mark, "American Policy toward Eastern Europe and the Origins of the Cold War, 1941–1946: An Alternative Interpretation," *Journal of American History* 68:2 (September 1981), pp. 313–36 (which maintains that the "open sphere" concept explains American policy during the war as well), as well as Berle's diary entry for February 5, 1942, and report of September 26, 1944, in *Navigating the Rapids*, pp. 401, 460–68. For the most up-to-date historiographical debate on these issues, see Marc Trachtenberg, "The United States and Eastern Europe in 1945: A Reassessment," *Journal of Cold War Studies* 10:4 (Fall 2008), and the H-Diplo Roundtable on it (10:12, May 2009), available at www.h-net.org/ndiplo/roundtables/PDF/Roundtable-X-12.pdf.
100. As Bohlen wrote in an influential memo:

> The United States is confronted with a condition in the world which is at direct variance with the assumptions upon which, during and directly after the war, major United States policies were predicated. Instead of unity among the Great Powers on the major issues of world reconstruction—both political and economic—after the war, there is complete disunity between the Soviet Union and the satellites on one side and the rest of the world on the other. There are, in short, two worlds instead of one. Faced with this disagreeable fact, however much we may deplore it, the United States in the interest of its own well-being and security and those of the free non-Soviet world must re-examine its major policy objectives. . . . The logic of the situation is that the non-Soviet world through such measures as are open to it would draw closer together politically, economically, financially, and, in the last analysis, militarily in order to be in a position to deal effectively with the consolidated Soviet area. . . . In these circumstances, all American policies should be related to this central fact.

"Memorandum by the Consular of the Department of State (Bohlen)," August 30, 1947, Top Secret, in *FRUS, 1947,* vol. 1 (Washington, D.C.: U.S. Government Printing Office, 1973), pp. 763–64.

101. John Lewis Gaddis, *The Cold War: A New History* (New York: Penguin, 2005), p. 26.
102. "A Security Policy for Post-War America," March 29, 1945, quoted in Stoler, *Allies and Adversaries*, p. 228. The paper was written by Frederick S. Dunn, William T. R. Fox, David Rowe, Arnold Wolfers, Grayson Kirk, Harold Sprout, and Edward Mead Earle.
103. Ironically, this was partly because the U.S.-British squabbling had exhausted everybody's time and patience. "One of the primary reasons . . . for the failure of the Western Powers to insist upon access rights to Berlin was the protracted struggle over transit rights through the British zone to the American zone. This dispute so occupied the energies of the Western negotiators and so distracted attention from so many other important issues that to have added another debate over transit rights through Soviet territory to Berlin would certainly have doomed the entire set of negotiations on Germany to breakdown and failure." Nelson, *Wartime Origins of the Berlin Dilemma*, p. 125.
104. Lucius D. Clay, *Decision in Germany* (Garden City, N.Y.: Doubleday, 1950), p. 26. As he arrived in Germany to take charge of the occupation, Clay wrote, "I was thinking of the task as an administrative problem and little did I realize what decisions would result from international differences and misunderstandings . . . (p. 7)."
105. Quoted in McAllister, *No Exit*, p. 62.
106. Harry S. Truman, *Memoirs of Harry S. Truman: Volume 1, Year of Decisions* (New York: Da Capo, 1955), p. 206.

4. WORLD WAR II—PACIFIC

1. Jerome Forrest, "The General Who Would Not Eat Grass," *Naval History* 9 (July/August 1995). This treatment of the final day also draws on the Pacific War Research Society, *Japan's Longest Day* (Tokyo: Kodansha International, 1968); Robert J. C. Butow, *Japan's Decision to Surrender* (Stanford, Calif.: Stanford University Press, 1954); Richard B. Frank, *Downfall* (New York: Random House, 1999); and Tsuyoshi Hasegawa, *Racing the Enemy: Stalin, Truman, and the Surrender of Japan* (Cambridge, Mass.: Harvard University Press, 2005).
2. Quoted in Herbert P. Bix, *Hirohito and the Making of Modern Japan* (New York: HarperCollins, 2000), pp. 751–2, fn. 79. "It was absolutely forbidden in the Japanese army to withdraw, surrender, or become a prisoner of war. The 1908 army criminal code contained the following provisions: 'A commander who allows his unit to surrender to the enemy without fighting to the last man or who concedes a strategic area to the enemy shall be punishable by death.' 'If a commander is leading troops in combat and they are captured by the enemy, even if the commander has performed his duty to the utmost, he shall be punishable by up to six months confinement.' The Field Service Code, issued in 1941 over Tojo Hideki's signature as army minister, contained the in-

junction 'Do not be taken prisoner alive.' . . . Even a lowly private who was captured but managed to return safely to his unit was expected to commit suicide." Saburo Ienaga, *The Pacific War: 1931–1945* (New York: Pantheon, 1978), pp. 49–50. On Japanese military attitudes and doctrine, see Edward J. Drea, *In the Service of the Emperor: Essays on the Imperial Japanese Army* (Lincoln: University of Nebraska Press, 1998).

3. Pacific War Research Society, *Japan's Longest Day*, pp. 112–13.
4. In Japan, the transition from the first to the second postwar vision was relatively smooth, because the occupation was a purely American concern. In places such as Korea, on the other hand, where responsibilities were shared with communists, the situation was messier and the result was a line of division similar to that which emerged in Europe.
5. Good guides to the English-language historiography can be found in J. Samuel Walker, "Recent Literature on Truman's Atomic Bomb Decision: A Search for Middle Ground," *Diplomatic History* 29:2 (April 2005); idem, "The Decision to Use the Bomb: A Historiographical Update," *Diplomatic History* 14 (Winter 1990); and Barton J. Bernstein, "The Atomic Bomb and American Foreign Policy, 1941–1945," *Peace and Change* 2 (Spring 1974). The current state of play is summarized well in Tsuyoshi Hasegawa, ed., *The End of the Pacific War: Reappraisals* (Stanford, Calif.: Stanford University Press, 2007), and the H-Diplo Roundtable on Hasegawa's *Racing the Enemy*, 7:2 (2006), available at www.h-net.org/~diplo/roundtables/. Crucial recent work includes Sadao Asada, "The Shock of the Atomic Bomb and Japan's Decision to Surrender: A Reconsideration," *Pacific Historical Review* 67:4 (November 1998); Frank, *Downfall;* Bix, *Hirohito;* and Barton Bernstein's various articles and book chapters over the last few decades. Other important book-length studies include Butow, *Japan's Decision to Surrender;* Leon V. Sigal, *Fighting to a Finish: The Politics of War Termination in the United States and Japan* (Ithaca, N.Y.: Cornell University Press, 1988); Hasegawa, *Racing the Enemy;* and Dale Hellegers, *We the Japanese People: World War II and the Origins of the Japanese Constitution* (Stanford, Calif.: Stanford University Press, 2001), vol. 1.
6. Japanese leaders saw this move as the least bad of the options facing them, offering not the certainty of victory but the possibility of escaping from various domestic and foreign troubles. "Ultimately it was always more advantageous for each of the . . . [factions in the Japanese leadership] to move to expand war rather than risk paralysis and complete breakdown of their system of rule. . . . Confronted with military strangulation by oil embargoes and the choice of admitting defeat in China, thereby abandoning a large part of his continental empire and probably destabilizing the monarchy he had inherited, Hirohito opted for . . . war against the United States and Britain. Like most of his top commanders he believed that Germany would triumph over Britain as it already had

over all of Europe. If certain strategic schedules were quickly achieved, Japan would be able to counter superior American productive capacity and force at least a standoff with the United States." Bix, *Hirohito*, pp. 429, 439.

7. The actual power and role of Hirohito, the Showa emperor who reigned throughout this era, is a matter of dispute. Traditional accounts such as Butow's see his role as primarily ceremonial, while recent accounts such as Bix's see him as the driving figure in events. The truth probably lies somewhere in between.
8. Bix writes: "Whether early Showa nationalism, grounded in emperor ideology and imperial myths and rituals, can properly be seen as part of a worldwide 'fascist' phenomenon remains contested among historians. Deification of the national racial community through its embodiment in a cult figure was a common element. Militarism, dictatorship, and the glorification of war, as well as youth, spirit, moral regeneration, and national mission, were certainly other common elements. . . . On balance, therefore, the ideological similarities among the leading revisionist fascist states during the 1930s, the similar psychological roles played by their cult leaders, as well as their historical trajectories of late development, all seem to be more important than their obvious differences." *Hirohito*, p. 203. Andrew Gordon agrees: "The cumulative weight of a politics of assassination, repression, and military-bureaucratic rule, a shrill cultural orthodoxy, and unilateral expansionism on the continent amounted to a sharp change in the character of Japan's modern experience. This change would have tragic consequence for millions. Should we sum this up by calling the 1930s the era of an emerging Japanese fascism? I would say yes, although other historians disagree. But in thinking about the history of these times, we should not be snarled by a definitional tangle. It is not that important whether one labels the Japanese political order of the 1930s 'fascist' or 'militarist.' It is more important to note that the dynamics and outcomes of political and cultural life in Japan shared much with the experience of the fascist states of Europe." *A Modern History of Japan* (New York: Oxford University Press, 2003), pp. 202–3.
9. "Operations for the Defeat of Japan," Memorandum by the United States Chiefs of Staff, January 22, 1945, C.C.S. 417/11, Top Secret, in *Foreign Relations of the United States: The Conferences at Malta and Yalta, 1945* (Washington, D.C.: U.S. Government Printing Office, 1955), p. 395, hereafter *FRUS*.
10. Because American casualty estimates for an invasion of the home islands were often cited afterward as justification for the dropping of the bomb, and because some of those retrospective citations were exaggerated, the issue has been a topic of bitter historiographical controversy. For a judicious discussion of the contemporaneous debate over casualty estimates, see Frank, *Downfall*, chapter 9 et seq.

11. Foreign Minister Shigenori Togo, quoted in Sigal, *Fighting to a Finish*, p. 52.
12. "The Japanese Minister of Foreign Affairs (Togo) to the Japanese Ambassador in the Soviet Union (Sato)," July 17, 1945, Secret, Urgent, in *FRUS: The Conference of Berlin (Potsdam)*, vol. 2, Washington, D.C., U.S. Government Printing office, 1960 p. 1249.
13. "The Japanese Minister of Foreign Affairs (Togo) to the Japanese Ambassador in the Soviet Union (Sato)," July 21, 1945, Secret, Urgent, in *FRUS: The Conference of Berlin (Potsdam)*, vol. 2, Washington, D.C., U.S. Government Printing office, 1960 p. 1258.
14. "The Japanese Minister of Foreign Affairs (Togo) to the Japanese Ambassador in the Soviet Union (Sato)," July 25, 1945, Secret, Urgent, in *FRUS: The Conference of Berlin (Potsdam)*, vol. 2, (Washington, D.C., U.S. Government Printing office, 1960) p. 1261.
15. Quoted in Frank, *Downfall*, p. 224.
16. Joseph C. Grew, "Memorandum of Conversation," May 28 1945, in *FRUS, 1945*, vol. 6, pp. 545–46; see also Joseph C. Grew, *Turbulent Era: A Diplomatic Record of Forty Years, 1904–1945, Vol. II* (Boston: Houghton Mifflin, 1952), pp. 1421ff. Grew also felt that the emperor would be useful after the war: "If, after final victory," he wrote in April 1944, "we wish to avail ourselves—as common sense would dictate—of any assets that we find in Japan which can be used for the maintenance of order as distinguished from the maintenance of the military cult, we would in my judgment, simply be handicapping the pursuit of our ultimate aims by any attempts to scrap or by-pass the institution of the Throne" (p. 1411). A good contemporary statement of his views is Joseph C. Grew, "War and Post-War Problems in the Far East," *Department of State Bulletin*, 10:236 (January 1, 1944), pp. 8–20. For the attitudes of Grew and his colleagues on postwar reforms in Japan, see Steven Schwartzberg, "The 'Soft Peace Boys': Presurrender Planning and Japanese Land Reform," *Journal of American-East Asian Relations* 2:2 (Summer 1993), pp. 185–216.
17. The text of various documents relating to the close of the war, including the relevant declarations, can be found in Butow, *Japan's Decision to Surrender*, pp. 241–50, and Raymond G. O'Connor, *Diplomacy for Victory: FDR and Unconditional Surrender* (New York: Norton 1971), pp. 118–27.
18. The exact sequence of events is unclear, and the record has been confused by later incorrect recollections from participants. The order to drop the bomb was sent just before the Potsdam Declaration was issued, coupled with what probably was "an informal but clearly understood arrangement" that Truman could override the order if he chose to in coming days. He did not so choose, and thus the order stood. See Barton J. Bernstein, "Writing, Righting, or Wronging the Historical Record: President

Truman's Letter on His Atomic-Bomb Decision," *Diplomatic History* 16:1 (Winter 1992), pp. 163–73.

19. Paul Kecskemeti, *Strategic Surrender: The Politics of Victory and Defeat* (Stanford, Calif.: Stanford University Press, 1958), p. 210.
20. This was partly because Japanese planners had not considered the psychological consequences of their surprise attack; in general, they "gave virtually no serious thought to how the conflict might be terminated. Somehow, before too long, they hoped, the Allies would tire of the struggle and agree to a compromise settlement which left the Co-Prosperity Sphere essentially intact." John W. Dower, *War Without Mercy: Race & Power in the Pacific War* (New York: Pantheon, 1986), p. 293.
21. Butow, *Japan's Decision to Surrender*, pp. 11, 12 (emphasis in the original).
22. United States Strategic Bombing Survey (Pacific), *Summary Report (Pacific War)*, Report No. 1 (Washington, D.C.: U.S. Government Printing Office, 1946), p. 28.
23. Quoted in Len Giovanitti and Fred Freed, *The Decision to Drop the Bomb* (New York: Coward McCann, 1965), p. 87 (emphasis in the original).
24. See Butow, *Japan's Decision to Surrender*, pp. 47–51, and John W. Dower, *Empire and Aftermath: Yoshida Shigeru and the Japanese Experience, 1878–1954* (Cambridge, Mass.: Harvard University Press, 1988), pp. 255–65.
25. Robert A. Pape argues that power calculations do in fact explain Japanese behavior. The key to capitulation, in his opinion, was "the ability of the United States to increase the military vulnerability of Japan's home islands, persuading Japanese leaders that the defense of the homeland was highly unlikely to succeed." This was indeed a major factor helping convince the Japanese military, finally, that the war was lost, but Pape's analysis is distorted by his view that the remarkable aspect of the case is "the fact that [Japan] surrendered without offering last-ditch resistance." Such a framing of the historical "puzzle" ignores the larger question of why the Japanese leadership waited until the summer of 1945, when they had no options left, to begin dealing with a situation which had been objectively hopeless for some time. "Why Japan Surrendered," *International Security* 18:2 (Fall 1993), pp. 154, 199.
26. Meeting of the Combined Chiefs of Staff with Roosevelt and Churchill, February 9, 1945, Noon, Livadia Palace, Combined Chiefs of Staff Minutes, "Report to the President and the Prime Minister," Top Secret, in *FRUS: The Conferences at Malta and Yalta, 1945*, p. 826.
27. Quoted in Frank, *Downfall*, p. 34.
28. U.S. Department of War, OPD, "Compilation of Subjects for Possible Discussion at Terminal," quoted in Sigal, *Fighting to a Finish*, p. 124.
29. "Memorandum by the Secretary of the Joint Chiefs of Staff (McFarland), Minutes of Meeting Held at the White House on Monday, 18 June

1945," Top Secret, in *FRUS: The Conference of Berlin (Postdam)* vol. 1, p. 909.

30. Robert E. Sherwood, *Roosevelt and Hopkins: An Intimate History* (New York: Harper, 1948), pp. 903–4.
31. Vladimir Dedijer, *Tito Speaks* (London: Weidenfeld & Nicolson, 1953), p. 234.
32. Winston S. Churchill, *The Second World War,* vol. 6, *Triumph and Tragedy* (Boston: Houghton Mifflin, 1985), p. 555. It should be noted, however, that constitutional monarchy was Churchill's political regime of choice, so he did not see a guarantee of some future role for the emperor simply as a concession. Consider, for example, his thoughts on Allied policy toward Germany at the end of the First World War: "The prejudice of the Americans against monarchy, which Mr. Lloyd George made no attempt to counteract, had made it clear to the beaten Empire that it would have better treatment from the Allies as a Republic than as a Monarchy. Wise policy would have crowned and fortified the Weimar Republic with a constitutional sovereign in the person of an infant grandson of the Kaiser, under a Council of Regency. Instead, a gaping void was opened in the national life of the German people. All the strong elements, military and feudal, which might have rallied to a constitutional monarchy and for its sake respected and sustained the new democratic and Parliamentary processes, were for the time being unhinged. The Weimar Republic, with all its liberal trappings and blessings, was regarded as an imposition of the enemy." *The Second World War,* vol. 1, *The Gathering Storm* (London: Cassell, 1948), p. 9.
33. Quoted in Bix, *Hirohito*, p. 503.
34. Cordell Hull, *The Memoirs of Cordell Hull, Volume II* (New York: Macmillan, 1948), p. 1594.
35. Dower, *War Without Mercy*, pp. 8, 52.
36. Ibid., pp. 53ff.
37. Sigal, *Fighting to a Finish*, p. 95.
38. Ibid., p. 95.
39. Barton J. Bernstein, "The Perils and Politics of Surrender: Ending the War with Japan and Avoiding the Third Atomic Bombing," *Pacific Historical Review* 46:1 (February 1997). 12, fn. 45.
40. Charles F. Brower IV, "Sophisticated Strategist: General George A. Lincoln and the Defeat of Japan, 1944–45," *Diplomatic History* 15:3 (Summer 1991), p. 327.
41. Sigal, *Fighting to a Finish*, p. 95.
42. Dean Acheson, *Present at the Creation: My Years in the State Department* (New York: Norton, 1969), p. 112.
43. "The Assistant Secretary of State (MacLeish) to the Secretary of State," "Interpretation of Japanese Unconditional Surrender," July 6, 1945, Top Secret, in *FRUS: The Conference of Berlin (Potsdam), Vol. I*, p. 895. At this point MacLeish was fighting against both the War Department (Stim-

son) and powerful figures at the State Department (Grew); his memo to Byrnes might profitably be viewed as a veiled threat to widen the scope of battle.

44. Briefing Book Paper, "The Position of the Emperor in Japan," July 3, 1945, Top Secret, in *FRUS: The Conference of Berlin (Potsdam)*, vol. 1, p. 887.
45. "The Acting Secretary of State to the Secretary of State," July 16, 1945, Top Secret, in *FRUS: The Conference of Berlin (Potsdam)*, vol. 2, p. 1267.
46. "Memorandum by the Secretary of the Joint Chiefs of Staff (McFarland), Minutes of Meeting Held at the White House on Monday, 18 June 1945," Top Secret, in *FRUS: The Conference of Berlin (Potsdam)*, vol. 1, p. 909.
47. Count von Bernstorff, quoted in Earl S. Pomeroy, "Sentiment for a Strong Peace, 1917–1919," *South Atlantic Quarterly* 43:4 (October 1944), p. 330.
48. Ernest R. May, *"Lessons" of the Past: The Use and Misuse of History in American Foreign Policy* (London: Oxford University Press, 1973), p. 8.
49. Press Conference, July 29, 1944, in Samuel I. Rosenman, ed., *The Public Papers and Addresses of Franklin D. Roosevelt*, vol. 13, *1944–45* (New York: Russell & Russell, 1950), p. 213.
50. Quoted in Schwartzberg, "The 'Soft Peace Boys,' " p. 198. All U.S. policymakers agreed on the need for fundamental social and political reforms in Japan after the war; disagreements arose over just how far-reaching these should be and what pillars of order and stability, if any, should be preserved.
51. "Message to Congress on the Progress of the War," September 17, 1943, in Samuel I. Rosenman, ed., *The Public Papers and Addresses of Franklin D. Roosevelt*, vol. 12, *1943* (New York: Russell & Russell, 1950), p. 391.
52. "Address to the Congress Reporting on the Yalta Conference," in Rosenman, ed., *Public Papers and Addresses*, vol. 13, *1944–45*, p. 584.
53. "The Assistant Secretary of State (MacLeish) to the Secretary of State," "Interpretation of Japanese Unconditional Surrender," July 6, 1945, Top Secret, in *FRUS: Conference of Berlin (Potsdam)*, vol. 1, p. 896.
54. John W. Dower, *Embracing Defeat: Japan in the Wake of World War II* (New York: Norton, 2000), pp. 77–83.
55. Gar Alperovitz, *Atomic Diplomacy: Hiroshima and Potsdam* (New York: Vintage, 1965), pp. 241–42.
56. Stimson Diary, July 22, 1945, quoted in *FRUS: The Conference of Berlin (Potsdam)*, vol. 2, p. 225.
57. Entry for July 18, 1945, quoted in Eduard Mark, " 'Today Has Been a Historical One': Harry S Truman's Diary of the Potsdam Conference," *Diplomatic History* 4:3 (Summer 1980), p. 322.
58. Churchill, *Triumph and Tragedy*, p. 553.

after repeated prodding by [U.S.] occupation authorities [in Japan], the U.S.S.R. announced that only ninety-five thousand prisoners remained, all of who would be returned by the end of the year. According to American and Japanese calculations, the actual number should have been around four hundred thousand." *Embracing Defeat*, pp. 51–52.

79. Frank's conclusion is compelling: "In summary, the Soviet intervention was a significant but not decisive reason for Japan's surrender. It was, at best, a reinforcing but not fundamental reason for the intervention by the Emperor. It shared with the atomic bombs a role in securing the compliance of the Imperial Army and Navy, but the atomic bomb played the more critical role because it undermined the fundamental premise that the United States would have to invade Japan to secure a decision." As for other potential factors, the impending destruction of the Japanese rail network by American air attacks would have brought the Japanese economy to a standstill and probably been decisive: "Such a catastrophe would likely have ruptured the key fault line between Japan's military and civilian decision makers. Imperial Army and Navy leaders as a group perceived foreign occupation as the sole lethal threat to the Imperial institution. What set the civilians, including Kido and the Emperor, apart from all but a few of the uniformed decision makers was the conviction that the Imperial institution could also perish by internal upheaval. This fear was a major factor in the Emperor's decision to end the war after Hiroshima, Soviet intervention, and Nagasaki, but before the destruction of the rail-transportation system. It is reasonable to assume that even without atomic bombs, the destruction of the rail-transportation system, coupled to the cumulative effects of the blockade-and-bombardment strategy, would have posed a severe threat to internal order and subsequently thus impelled the Emperor to seek to end the war." *Downfall*, pp. 348, 354. For informed counterfactual discussions of different war termination scenarios, see Richard B. Frank, "No Bomb: No End," in Robert Cowley, ed., *What If? 2* (New York: Putnam's, 2001); Hasegawa, *Racing With the Enemy, pp.* 290–98; Barton J. Bernstein, "Understanding the Atomic Bomb and the Japanese Surrender: Missed Opportunities, Little-Known Near Disasters, and Modern Memory," *International Security* 19:2 (Spring 1995), and "Compelling Japan's Surrender Without the A-Bomb, Soviet Entry, or Invasion," *Journal of Strategic Studies* 18:2 (June 1995); and Douglas J. MacEachin, *The Final Months of the War With Japan: Signals Intelligence, U.S. Invasion Planning, and the A-Bomb Decision* (Washington, D.C.: Central Intelligence Agency, Center for the Study of Intelligence, December 1998), pp. 33–38.

80. "This nebulous concept was never precisely defined until, facing the crisis brought on by the atomic bombing of Hiroshima and the Soviet entry into the war, Japanese policymakers were confronted with the issue of formulating concrete surrender terms." Tsuyoshi Hasegawa, "Introduction," in Hasegawa, ed., *The End of the Pacific War: Reappraisals*, p. 4.

81. Cf. Bix and Hasegawa: "Hirohito was not only a political and military leader, he was also his nation's highest spiritual authority. He headed a religiously charged monarchy that in times of crisis allowed the Japanese state to define itself as a theocracy. In a wooden building in the southwest corner of the palace compound, he regularly performed complicated rituals that clearly implied his faith in his mystical descent from the gods, and the sacred nature of the Japanese state and homeland. The fusion in one individual of religious, political, and military leadership complicates the study of the emperor." *Hirohito*, p. 16. "Japan's Meiji Consitution of 1889 defined the emperor as 'sacred and inviolable' and placed him at the pinnacle of all power: all legislative, executive, and judicial power emanated from his person. The emperor was also the supreme military commander, whose authority was beyond the reach of the cabinet. In addition, the emperor served as a symbol of the Japanese national community. . . . The emperor thus held absolute power in political, cultural, and religious terms. The *kokutai* was a symbolic expression of both the political and the spiritual essence of the imperial system." *Racing the Enemy*, pp. 3–4.
82. Tsuyoshi Hasegawa: "The number of victims and profound damage that the atomic bombs inflicted on the citizens of Hiroshima and Nagasaki, which the American policymakers had hoped would have a decisive influence on the Japanese government, were not among the top considerations of the Japanese ruling elite. The Japanese policymakers, from the emperor down to the military and civilian leaders . . . were prepared to sacrifice the lives of millions more Japanese to maintain the *kokutai* (national polity), however they interpreted this nebulous concept. If the effects of the bombs caused concern for the ruling elite—especially to Hirohito, Kido, Konoe, and others closest to the emperor—it was because the devastation caused by the bombs might lead to a popular revolt that could sweep away the emperor system." "The Atomic Bombs and the Soviet Invasion," in Hasegawa, ed., *The End of the Pacific War: Reappraisals*, pp. 120–21.
83. As Prince Konoye said to the emperor in a discussion following his presentation of the "Konoye Memorial" in February 1945, "I think there is no alternative to making peace with the United States. Even if we surrender unconditionally, I feel that in America's case she would not go so far as to reform Japan's *kokutai* or abolish the imperial house. Japan's territory might decrease to half of what it is at present, but even so, if we can extricate the people from the miserable ravages of war, preserve the *kokutai*, and plan for the security of the imperial house, then we should not avoid unconditional surrender." Dower, *Empire and Aftermath*, p. 265.
84. Quoted in Bix, *Hirohito*, p. 515. Cf. Hasegawa's judgment: "What motivated Hirohito was neither a pious wish to bring peace to humanity nor a sincere desire to save the people and the nation from destruction, as his imperial rescript stated and as the myth of the emperor's 'sacred deci-

sion' would have us believe. More than anything else, it was a sense of personal survival and deep responsibility to maintain the imperial house, which had lasted in unbroken lineage since the legendary Jinnu emperor." "The Atomic Bombs and the Soviet Invasion," in Hasegawa, ed., *The End of the Pacific War: Reappraisals*, p. 135.

85. Bix, *Hirohito*, pp. 521, 509.
86. Associated Press correspondent Louis Lochner tried to file an article on anti-Nazi Germans, only to find his dispatches censored. Pressing the issue, he discovered "that in addition to the regular censorship directives, there was a personal one from the President of the United States in his capacity as commander in chief, forbidding all mention of any German resistance. Stories of a resistance movement did not fit into the concept of Unconditional Surrender!" When Lochner tried to pass on messages from resistance groups to the White House, he got no reply; "but the Washington Bureau of the A.P. telephoned me that my insistence was viewed by official sources as 'most embarrassing,' and would I please desist?" Louis P. Lochner, *Always the Unexpected: A Book of Reminiscences* (New York: Macmillan, 1956), pp. 294–95.
87. "Radio Report to the American People on the Potsdam Conference," August 9, 1945, *Public Papers of the Presidents of the United States: Harry S. Truman, 1945* (Washington, D.C.: U.S. Government Printing Office, 1961), p. 212.
88. "Radio Address at Dinner of Foreign Policy Association," October 21, 1944, in Rosenman, ed., *Public Papers and Addresses*, vol. 12, *1944–45*, p. 349.

5. THE KOREAN WAR

1. Knowledgeable observers understood, or should have understood, that this was a real possibility. As the columnists Joseph and Stewart Alsop warned on June 12, "Hardly anyone is taking Syngman Rhee seriously enough, according to those who really know the old man and his people. It is rather generally assumed, both in this country and abroad, that Rhee's passionate rejection of the Korean truce terms has given rise to a mere teapot tempest, and that the American Government, on which Rhee is utterly dependent, will soon bring him to his senses. Yet for some days Rhee's defiance has occupied the almost exclusive attention of Secretary of State John Foster Dulles. Dulles and other presidential advisers have met repeatedly with President Eisenhower, and canvassed every possible way of dealing with the stubborn old Korean President. And the more they have examined the situation, the more obvious it has become that Syngman Rhee may be entirely willing to reject the Korean truce, and quite capable of doing so. . . . 'What the old man really wants,' remarked one worried policy-maker, 'is a green light to attack north, plus a promise to bail him out again if he gets into trouble.' " "Can the Tail Wag the Dog?" *Washington Post*, June 12, 1953, p. 25.

2. William S. White, "U.S. Sees Position in Korea as Grave," *New York Times*, June 20, 1953, p. 1. The idea of using the prisoners as the tool for "hindering the armistice" originated with the South Korean delegate at the armistice negotiations; see Choi Duk-Shin, *Panmunjom and After* (New York: Vantage, 1972), pp. 74ff.
3. "Text of Rhee Letter Rejecting Eisenhower Plan," *New York Times*, June 19, 1953, p. 4; Lindesay Parrott, "Korean Tanks Aid in New Breakout of War Prisoners," *New York Times*, June 21, 1953, p. 1; Clark letter to Roy W. Howard, July 7, 1953, quoted in William Stueck, *The Korean War: An International History* (Princeton, N.J.: Princeton University Press, 1995), p. 336.
4. "McCarthy applauds Rhee's POW Release," *Washington Post*, June 20, 1953, p. 9; "Knowland Asserts Rhee was Slighted," *New York Times*, July 6, 1953, p. 1.
5. Arthur Krock, " 'Mistakes' of Korea War Again a Political Issue," *New York Times*, June 28, 1953, p. E3; "Truce in Balance," *New York Times*, July 5, 1953, p. E1.
6. Jon Halliday and Bruce Cumings, *Korea: The Unknown War* (London: Penguin, 1990), p. 197; Barton J. Bernstein, "Syngman Rhee: The Pawn as Rock," "*Bulletin of Concerned Asian Scholars* 10:1 (1978), p. 44.
7. For details on the various U.S. plans to overthrow Rhee and why they were not adopted, see Bernstein, "Syngman Rhee," and Joseph C. Goulden, *Korea: The Untold Story of the War* (New York Times Books, 1982), pp. 617ff. and 635ff.
8. See I. F. Stone, *The Hidden History of the Korean War* (New York: Monthly Review Press, 1969 [1952]); Gabriel and Joyce Kolko, *The Limits of Power: The World and American Foreign Policy, 1945–1954* (New York: Harper & Row, 1972); Frank Baldwin, ed., *Without Parallel: The American-Korean Relationship Since 1945* (New York: Pantheon, 1974); and John Gittings, "Talks, Bombs and Germs: Another Look at the Korean War," *Journal of Contemporary Asia* 5:2 (1975), pp. 205–17.
9. Thomas J. McCormick, *America's Half-Century: United States Foreign Policy in the Cold War* (Baltimore: Johns Hopkins University Press, 1989), p. 104. Ironically, some far-right Republicans made similar arguments at the time. During the 1952 election, for example, Kansas senator Andrew Schoeppel charged that the Truman administration "was deliberately prolonging the Korean War so that it could sustain its 'much publicized prosperity'!" Ronald J. Caridi, *The Korean War and American Politics: The Republican Party as a Case Study* (Philadelphia: University of Pennsylvania Press, 1968), p. 206.
10. See Douglas MacArthur, *Reminiscences* (New York: McGraw-Hill, 1964), and Courtney Whitney, *MacArthur: His Rendezvous with History* (New York: Knopf, 1956).
11. The grounds for such an interpretation have been laid by the publication

of the relevant volumes of *Foreign Relations of the United States* and the archivally based "postrevisionist" scholarship on the war that started appearing during the 1980s, particularly Barton J. Bernstein, "The Struggle over the Korean Armistice: Prisoners of Repatriation?" in Bruce Cumings, ed., *Child of Conflict: The Korean-American Relationship, 1943–1953* (Seattle: University of Washington Press, 1983), pp. 261–308; Callum A. MacDonald, *Korea: The War Before Vietnam* (New York: Free Press, 1987); Burton I. Kaufman, *The Korean War: Challenges in Crisis, Credibility, and Command* (Philadelphia: Temple University Press, 1986); Rosemary Foot, *A Substitute for Victory: The Politics of Peacemaking at the Korean Armistice Talks* (Ithaca, N.Y.: Cornell University Press, 1990); Sergei N. Goncharov, John W. Lewis, and Xue Litai, *Uncertain Partners: Stalin, Mao, and the Korean War* (Stanford, Calif.: Stanford University Press, 1993); and Stueck, *The Korean War.* These supplement Walter G. Hermes, *Truce Tent and Fighting Front* (Washington, D.C.: Office of the Chief of Military History, United States Army, 1966), the final volume of the U.S. Army's thorough official history of the war. Newly available documents from Russian archives have shed light on lingering questions related to the origins of the war, Chinese entry, and the impact of Stalin's death on the armistice negotiations; these are collected in the *Cold War International History Project Bulletin* 3 (Fall 1993) and 6–7 (Winter 1995/1996) and summarized in Kathryn Weathersby, "Stalin, Mao, and the End of the Korean War," in Odd Arne Westad, ed., *Brothers in Arms: The Rise and Fall of the Sino-Soviet Alliance, 1945–1963* (Washington, D.C.: Woodrow Wilson Center Press, 1998), and Kathryn Weathersby, "The Soviet Role in the Korean War: The State of Historical Knowledge," in William Stueck, ed., *The Korean War in World History* (Lexington: University Press of Kentucky, 2004). The most thorough up-to-date analysis of the case is Elizabeth A Stanley, *Paths to Peace: Domestic Coalition Shifts, War Termination, and the Korean War* (Stanford, Calif: Stanford University Press, 2009).

12. Howard S. Levie, "Reminiscences of the Korean Armistice Negotiations," in Daniel J. Meador, ed., *The Korean War in Retrospect* (Lanham, Md.: University Press of America, 1998), p. 166; William Stueck, *Rethinking the Korean War* (Princeton, N.J.: Princeton University Press, 2002), p. 145; and David Rees, *Korea: The Limited War* (New York: St. Martin's, 1964), p. 285.
13. Allan E. Goodman, ed., *Negotiating While Fighting: The Diary of Admiral C. Turner Joy at the Korean Armistice Conference* (Stanford, Calif.: Hoover Institution Press, 1978), pp. 26, 6.
14. Memorandum by the Secretary of State to the President, February 8, 1952, Top Secret, *Foreign Relations of the United States, 1952–1954*, Vol. 15: *Korea, Part I* (Washington, D.C.: U.S. Government Printing Office, 1984), p. 44, hereafter *FRUS.*
15. Those potentially opposed to repatriation fell into several categories,

including former ROK soldiers who had been impressed into the North Korean army upon capture earlier in the war; North or South Korean citizens who had been similarly impressed; former Nationalist Chinese fighters who had been impressed into the Chinese Communist Forces after the Chinese civil war; and civilians, refugees, and straggling ROK troops who had gotten mixed in with the Communist prisoners (either voluntarily or by mistake). "Of the approximately 170,000 PW's in U.N. hands in early 1952, approximately 21,000 were Chinese and the remainder Korean. The Koreans included two distinct groups—about 100,000 soldiers of the North Korean Army whose homes were in North Korea, and about 49,000 persons whose homes were in South Korea. The South Korean prisoners were of three types: soldiers who had been captured and impressed into service by the North Koreans during its initial southward advance; civilians who had been impressed into North Korean army combat or labor units; and civilians rounded up by the U.N. forces, mainly in the fighting after the Inchon landings, on suspicion of being North Korean soldiers who were trying to avoid capture by changing clothes. North and South Koreans, indistinguishable at the time of capture, were initially interned together. Not until early 1951, when hope of a quick end to the conflict faded, was action begun to segregate them, and it was the summer of 1952 before 38,000 loyal South Koreans and civilian internees were released." Samuel M. Meyers and William C. Bradbury, "The Political Behavior of Korean and Chinese Prisoners of War in the Korean Conflict: A Historical Analysis," in Samuel M. Myers and Albert D. Biderman, eds., *Mass Behavior in Battle and Captivity: The Communist Soldier in the Korean War* (Chicago: University of Chicago Press, 1968), p. 225.

16. Report by the National Security Council to the President, NSC 81/1, "United States Courses of Action With Respect to Korea," September 9, 1950, Top Secret, *FRUS, 1950*, vol. 7, *Korea* (Washington, D.C.: U.S. Government Printing Office, 1976), p. 718.
17. "The special and frankly political objective of [this] program," a team of sociologists studying the prisoners later noted, became "a major focus of conflict in the PW camps." Meyers and Bradbury, "The Political Behavior of Korean and Chinese Prisoners of War," p. 219.
18. Violence and chaos in the UN camps will be discussed below. However much the conditions there diverged from the claims of Western propaganda, it should be pointed out that the treatment of prisoners by the United States was vastly better than that dispensed by all the Asian belligerents, even considering only those prisoners who made it to camps at all (the Communists routinely killed or impressed thousands upon capture). Writing about the Pusan camps, for example, an authoritative source notes that "although by U.S. standards the PW's were not well fed or adequately equipped, from January, 1951, they were relatively well off by their own standards and exceedingly so in comparison with both the

nearby civilian population and the South Korean soldiers who performed guard duty around the compounds." Meyers and Bradbury, "The Political Behavior of Korean and Chinese Prisoners of War," p. 237. This differential actually contributed, in some small measure, to later problems regarding repatriation, as some civilians and refugees had gotten themselves classified as POWs in order to receive food or medical treatment. See Stanley Weintraub, *War in the Wards: Korea's Unknown Battle in a Prisoner-of-War Hospital* (Garden City, NY: Doubleday, 1964).

19. For films shown in Communist camps, see Rees, *Korea: The Limited War*, p. 336. For a complete list of materials used in the American educational program directed at the prisoners, see Kenneth K. Hansen, *Heroes Behind Barbed Wire* (Princeton, N.J.: D. Van Nostrand, 1957), pp. 325–34. The reasoning behind showing prisoners films such as "Defensive Footwork in Basketball" or "Peanuts, a Valuable Crop" seems clear; it is harder to see the relevance of "Tanglewood Music School," "Western Stock Buyer," or "Meet Your Federal Government."
20. Joy, *Negotiating While Fighting*, p. 178.
21. Memorandum of Conversation, by the Deputy Assistant Secretary of State for Far Eastern Affairs (Johnson), "U.S. Position on Forcible Repatriation of Prisoners of War," February 27, 1952, Top Secret, *FRUS 1952–1954,* vol. 15, part 1, p. 69. Present at the meeting were the president, the secretaries of state, defense, and treasury, two of the Joint Chiefs, and three staff members from State and Defense.
22. See Bernstein, "The Struggle over the Korean Armistice," pp. 281–84.
23. Joy, *Negotiating While Fighting*, p. 368 (emphasis in the original).
24. Ostensibly this was a new and important gesture that traded UN concessions on some issues for Communist concessions on others in an attempt to reach a final armistice agreement. In fact, it was a ploy to disguise what was really going on: as the Joint Chiefs had cabled Ridgway on March 20, "If it becomes necessary to recognize that total impasse has been reached it would be to our advantage that Commies be forced to reject our proposals on several grounds and thereby emphasize their intransigence. . . . The package deal seems to us to have the advantage of having such recess occur with 3 items rather than merely the 1 issue of POWs." The Joint Chiefs of Staff to the Commander in Chief, Far East (Ridgway), JCS 904101, March 20, 1952, Top Secret, *FRUS, 1952–1954*, vol. 15, part 1, p. 107. " 'We all felt there would be a great uproar,' one senior State Department official privately noted, 'if [repatriation] was the only issue preventing the conclusion of an armistice and the return of our own prisoners.' To head off the domestic unrest that would probably ensue, the White House, State Department, and Pentagon all agreed that their information campaign would [thus] have to contain another essential ingredient: 'In the event that negotiations are to be broken off, every effort should be made to drive home the impression that *this was not the only issue* on which agreement could not be reached.' " Steven

Casey, *Selling the Korean War: Propaganda, Politics, and Public Opinion, 1950–1953* (Oxford: Oxford University Press, 2008), p. 287.

25. The Dulles quote is from "Second Restricted Tripartite Meeting of the Heads of Government, Mid Ocean Club, Bermuda, December 7, 1953," U.S. Delegation Minutes, Top Secret, in *FRUS, 1952–1954, vol. 5, part 2*, p. 1811. Dulles went on to note that "Rhee was a problem of considerable difficulty. This, added the Secretary was probably the understatement of the year. He did not think that any nation had ever exerted itself as fully with such a great combination of generosity on the one hand and threats on the other, as we had done to keep Rhee in line." The Eisenhower quote is from Notes by General Andrew Goodpaster of a meeting between Eisenhower and Johnson, February 17, 1965, quoted in Conrad C. Crane, "To Avert Impending Disaster: American Military Plans to Use Atomic Weapons During the Korean War," *Journal of Strategic Studies* 23:2 (June 2000), p. 72.
26. Quote in Caridi, *The Korean War and American Politics*, p. 267. Keefer's contention that as of December 1952, Eisenhower "had not yet decided on any specific plan to achieve peace in Korea," seems valid. "The clearest proof of Eisenhower's indecision was the ad hoc, even dilatory, manner in which his administration approached the problem once in office." Edward C. Keefer, "President Dwight D. Eisenhower and the End of the Korean War," *Diplomatic History* 10:3 (Summer 1986), p. 270.
27. Weathersby, "Stalin, Mao, and the End of the Korean War," p. 102.
28. Ibid., p. 108.
29. Hermes, *Truce Tent and Fighting Front*, p. 412.
30. Ibid., p. 427.
31. It was during this meeting, Eisenhower administration officials said later, that the nuclear threat was invoked; Dulles himself would claim that he had made known "our intention to wipe out the industrial complex in Manchuria if we did not get an armistice." His notes from the meeting, however, portray a less direct, nonnuclear threat: "I . . . stat[ed] that if the armistice negotiations collapsed, the United States would probably make a stronger rather than a lesser military exertion, and that this might well extend the area of conflict. (*Note*: I assumed this would be relayed.)" In a second meeting, "Mr. Nehru brought up the subject of the Korean armistice, referring particularly to my statement of the preceding day, that if there was no armistice hostilities might become more intense. . . . I made no comment and allowed the topic to drop." Memorandum of Conversation, by the Secretary of State, May 21, 1953, Secret, and Memorandum of Conversation, by the Secretary of State, May 22, 1953, Secret, *FRUS, 1952–1954*, vol. 15, part 1, pp. 1068, 1071. See also Richard K. Betts, *Nuclear Blackmail and Nuclear Balance* (Washington, D.C.: Brookings, 1987), pp. 42–43.
32. Bohlen wrote about his firm message to the Soviets that "I did not know that in a related action the U.S. was hinting to China through India that it

might use atomic weapons in Korea." Charles E. Bohlen, *Witness to History, 1929–1969* (New York: Norton, 1973), p. 351. He was not alone: "Neither the outgoing nor incoming army chiefs of staff, nor General Clark, were consulted about or knew of the atomic threat." Richard K. Betts, *Soldiers, Statesmen, and Cold War Crises* (Cambridge, Mass.: Harvard University Press, 1977), p. 106.

33. Rosemary J. Foot, "Nuclear Coercion and the Ending of the Korean Conflict," *International Security* 13:3 (Winter 1988–89) p. 99; see also MacDonald, *Korea: The War Before Vietnam*, pp. 186–9.
34. We know now that the Chinese had a pretty accurate take on what was happening. Li Kenong, the leader of the Communist delegation at the armistice negotiations, briefed Peng Dehuai, the commander of Chinese forces, about the situation on June 20, after Peng's return from a visit to Beijing. "Li said that the enemy was in a tight corner; Rhee and hawkish Americans did not have mass support. . . . Peng said, 'Rhee can't tell good from bad. It is definitely necessary to teach him another lesson.' . . . Peng drafted a telegram at Pyongyang and sent it to Mao Zedong. Peng suggested postponing the date for signing the truce in order to have time to punish Rhee and to inflict 15,000 more casualties on his troops. Mao agreed that signing the truce must be postponed. The right time to sign depended on the situation. It was extremely necessary to eliminate at least 10,000 more of Rhee's troops." Major General (Ret.) Chai Chengwen, "The Korean Truce Negotiations," in Xiaobing Li et al., eds., *Mao's Generals Remember Korea* (Lawrenceville: University Press of Kansas, 2001), p. 229.
35. Bradley's point was not that a larger anti-Communist war was necessarily to be avoided at all costs, but rather that "if the United States were forced to fight the Communists, the *right war* was a war against Russia itself, and the *right place* to fight it was not at the periphery, but at the heart of Soviet power. Most importantly, it implied that if it had to be fought at all (Bradley of course hoped it could be avoided), there was a *right time* for fighting it, namely, after American power had been built up." Marc Trachtenberg, "A 'Wasting Asset': American Strategy and the Shifting Nuclear Balance, 1949–1954," *International Security* 13:3 (Winter 1988–99), p. 27 (emphasis in the original).
36. Dean Acheson, *Present at the Creation: My Years in the State Department* (New York: Norton, 1969), p. 531.
37. The Secretary of State to the British Secretary of State for Foreign Affairs (Morrison), July 19, 1951, Top Secret, *FRUS, 1951*, vol. 7, *Korea and China*, part 1 (Washington, D.C.: U.S. Government Printing Office, 1983), pp. 699–700.
38. Hermes, *Truce Tent and Fighting Front*, pp. 136ff. For a full discussion of the World War II repatriation policy, see Mark R. Elliot, *Pawns of Yalta: Soviet Refugees and America's Role in their Repatriation* (Urbana: University of Illinois Press, 1982). For what happened to the prisoners once they returned home, see Aleksandr I. Solzhenitsyn, *The Gulag Archipel-*

ago, 1918–1956: An Experiment in Literary Investigation, Parts I & II (New York: Harper & Row, 1974), pp. 81ff., 243ff., and 259ff.

39. Memorandum by the Joint Chiefs of Staff to the Secretary of Defense (Marshall), "Policy on Repatriation of Chinese and North Korean Prisoners," August 8, 1951, Top Secret, *FRUS, 1951*, vol. 7, part 1, pp. 792–93.
40. He did suggest that removing potential nonrepatriates from the prisoner lists might be a way around the latter problem. The Secretary of State to the Secretary of Defense (Marshall), August 27, 1951, Top Secret, *FRUS, 1951,* vol. 7, part 1., pp. 857–58. For a different Acheson line later on, see "The Prisoner Question and Peace in Korea," *Department of State Bulletin* 27:698 (November 19, 1952), pp. 744–54.
41. Stueck, *The Korean War*, p. 260. Three days before Rhee let the prisoners loose in Korea in an attempt to block the armistice, the *Washington Post* ran a story whose lead sentence ran as follows: "Chancellor Konrad Adenauer today declared that if the Russians really mean to make peace in Germany they should release 300,000 German prisoners of war still held. . . ." "Adenauer Challenges Reds to Free POWs," *Washington Post,* June 15, 1953, p. 14.
42. The Commander in Chief, Far East (Ridgway) to the Joint Chiefs of Staff, CX-55993, October 27, 1951, Top Secret, *FRUS, 1951*, vol. 7, part 1, pp. 1068–70.
43. Elliott, *Pawns of Yalta*, pp. 45–46.
44. Memorandum by the Acting Secretary of State [Webb], "Meeting with the President, Monday, October 29, 1951," October 29, 1951, Confidential, *FRUS, 1951*, vol. 7, part 1, p. 1073.
45. *FRUS, 1951*, vol. 7, part 1, p. 1073, fn. 3.
46. Elliott, *Pawns of Yalta*, pp. 109ff.
47. In late January 1952, for example, he raged in private about how "prisoners of WWII to the number of some 3 million are still held [by the Soviets] at slave labor contrary to ceasefire terms," and vented his frustration by fantasizing about nuclear attacks on China and the U.S.S.R. See Barton J. Bernstein, "Truman's Secret Thoughts on Ending the Korean War," *Foreign Service Journal* 57:10 (November 1980), p. 33, and Cass Peterson, "Truman Idea: All-Out War Over Korea," *Washington Post,* August 3, 1980, pp. A1, 15.
48. Statement by the President on General Ridgway's Korean Armistice Proposal, May 7, 1952, *Public Papers of the Presidents of the United States: Harry S. Truman, 1952–1953* (Washington, D.C.: U.S. Government Printing Office, 1966), p. 321. Some scholars, such as Steven Casey, argue that this statement was critically important, because after it was made the political costs of backing away from the voluntary repatriation position were much higher than before.
49. Diary entry for May 18, 1952, in Harry S. Truman, *Off the Record: The Private Papers of Harry S. Truman,* ed. Robert H. Ferrell (New York: Penguin, 1982), pp. 250–51.

50. For example, U. Alexis Johnson, Oral History Interview, June 19, 1975, Harry S. Truman Library, pp. 71ff.
51. Memorandum of the Substance of Discussion at a Department of State–Joint Chiefs of Staff Meeting, March 19, 1952, Top Secret, *FRUS, 1952–1954*, vol. 15, part 1, pp. 103–4.
52. Bernstein, "Truman's Secret Thoughts," pp. 32–33.
53. MacDonald, *Korea: The War Before Vietnam*, p. 141.
54. Foot, *A Substitute for Victory*, p. 130.
55. Acheson, *Present at the Creation*, p. 653.
56. Memorandum of Conversation, by the Director of the Office of United Nations Political and Security Affairs (Wainhouse), "Korea," Top Secret, April 26, 1952, *FRUS, 1952–1954*, vol. 15, part 1, pp. 171–72.
57. MacDonald, *Korea: The War Before Vietnam*, pp. 134–35. The comment on the behavior of the ROK forces is from a publication of the U.S. Army's Office of Military History.
58. Max Hastings, *The Korean War* (New York: Simon & Schuster, 1987), p. 308.
59. Matthew B. Ridgway, *The Korean War* (Cambridge, Mass: DaCapo, 1986), p. 206.
60. Hastings, *The Korean War*, pp. 307–8.
61. MacDonald, *Korea: The War Before Vietnam*, p. 136.
62. Memorandum of the Substance of Discussion at a Department of State–Joint Chiefs of Staff Meeting, March 21, 1952, Top Secret, *FRUS, 1952–1954*, vol. 15, part 1, p. 113.
63. Memorandum by P. W. Manhard of the Political Section of the Embassy to the Ambassador in Korea (Muccio), Secret, March 14, 1952, *FRUS, 1952–1954*, vol. 15, part 1, pp. 98–99. Manhard's report was enclosed with a letter from Muccio to Johnson on March 19. As Muccio would put it later, "What went on within those compounds was *never* known or understood by the U.S. military. . . . I had on my staff Philip W. Manhard, a Chinese language officer and a Chinese specialist. Several times he made very disturbing reports of horrors being perpetuated in the prisoners camps . . . and Phil came to me several times about how horrible the situation in those Chinese cages were. . . . And what went on within those camps I don't think would stand very much—I don't know just how to put it, but there was a *terrific* ideological struggle in those cages that we were responsible for, but we were not aware what was going on in there." John J. Muccio, Oral History Interview, Harry S. Truman Library, February 10 and 18, 1971, pp. 100–1.
64. Johnson to Muccio, April 7, 1952, Secret, *FRUS, 1952–1954*, vol. 15, part 1, pp. 141–42.
65. Muccio to Secretary of State, May 12, 1952, Top Secret, *FRUS, 1952–1954*, vol. 15, part 1, p. 192.
66. The Ambassador in Korea (Muccio) to the Department of State, Top Secret, June 28, 1952, *FRUS, 1952–1954*, vol. 15, part 1, p. 360. See also

Muccio to Secretary of State, July 2, 1952, Top Secret, pp. 369–70, and Muccio to Secretary of State, July 5, 1952, Top Secret, p. 379.

67. "Estimate of Action Needed and Problems Involved in Negotiating and Implementing an Operation for the Re-Classification and Exchange of POWs," by A. S. Chase, Chief, Division of Research for Far East, Office of Intelligence Research, Department of State, July 7, 1952, Top Secret, National Archives, 693.95A24/7-752, pp. 3–4, 7. For pictures of such tattoos—which would make life problematic for the bearer if he were returned to the PRC—see Hansen, *Heroes Behind Barbed Wire*, pp. 23ff. Muccio had cabled in June the information that "approximately two-thirds pro-repatriation Chinese were tattooed against will," totalling 1,500 people at the least.
68. Joy, *Negotiating While Fighting*, p. 355.
69. Weintraub, *War in the Wards*, pp. 3–4. "Another Soviet cartoon depicted a gangster-like, helmeted GI with submachine gun, leading a group of burly soldiers over the bodies of prisoners to hold back others with their rifle butts. The caption depicted the gangster as scowling to the peace-loving, patriotic prisoners, 'Now, let's hear who else wants to be repatriated.' "
70. William H. Vatcher, Jr., *Panmunjom: The Story of the Korean Armistice Negotiations* (New York: Praeger, 1958), p. 154.
71. Menzies quoted in MacDonald, *Korea: The War Before Vietnam*, p. 145. The commander, General Haydon L. Boatner, agreed with Joy about the repatriation issue. As he wrote later, "Is there any reason why opportunities for negotiating a cease-fire might be missed, or why truce talks should be prolonged, while attempts are made to swap 'enemy' turncoats for American turncoats before the reasons for U.S. troop defections are known? Is it not crass hypocrisy for the U.S. to restrict immigration in times of peace when men are relatively free, yet take pride in the conversion of our erstwhile enemies to 'our side' by their 'free choice'? Especially when they were in fact in our prisons, subject to our indoctrination and therefore not free to make a 'free choice.' " Haydon L. Boatner, "Prisoners of War For Sale," *American Legion Magazine,* August 1962, p. 40.
72. Howland H. Sargeant to Secretary of State, "Steps to be Taken and Questions to be Considered Arising Out of POW and Related Issues," May 20, 1952, Secret, National Archives, 695A.0024/5-2052.
73. This adds a bittersweet note to U. Alexis Johnson's later comment: "Truman [decided] . . . that we were going to stand for voluntary repatriation, because that was the moral and the right thing to do. I have cited this sometimes as the greatest act of political courage by a President that I witnessed while I have been in the employ of the Government. And it's one thing above all for which I remember President Truman." Oral History Interview, June 19, 1975, Harry S. Truman Library, p. 79.
74. Rees, *Korea: The Limited War*, p. 325.

75. Commander in Chief, United Nations Command (Ridgway) to the Joint Chiefs of Staff, HNC-588, December 18, 1951, Top Secret, *FRUS, 1951*, vol. 7, part 1, p. 1371.
76. Memorandum for the Record, by the Deputy Assistant Secretary of State for Far Eastern Affairs (Johnson), "Position on POWs in Korean Armistice Negotiations," February 8, 1952, Top Secret, *FRUS, 1952–1954*, vol. 15, part 1, p. 41. The proposed resolution was not introduced after Secretary of Defense Lovett met with several senators. See also Memorandum for the Record, by the Deputy Assistant Secretary of State for Far Eastern Affairs (Johnson), "Consultation with Far East Subcommittees on Korea," April 26, 1952, Confidential, *FRUS, 1952–1954*, vol. 15, part 1, pp. 172–73.
77. Memorandum of the Substance of Discussion at a Department of State–Joint Chiefs of Staff Meeting, March 19, 1952, Top Secret, *FRUS, 1952–1954*, vol. 15, part 1, p. 100.
78. Casey, *Selling the Korean War*, p. 284.
79. "Public Comment on Airfield and Prisoner Issues at Panmunjom," March 3, 1952, National Archives, RG 59, Office of Public Opinion Studies, 1943–65, Public Opinion on Foreign Countries and Regions; Japan and Korea, 1945–54 (Box 39).
80. "American Opinion Trends on Korea," August 13, 1952 (emphasis in original).
81. "Public Opinion Factors Bearing on the Korean Truce," September 15, 1952, (same location as note 79)
82. Casey, *Selling the Korean War*, p. 286.
83. Memorandum of Discussion at the 139th Meeting of the National Security Council, Wednesday, April 8, 1953, Top Secret, *FRUS, 1952–1954*, vol. 15, part 1, pp. 893–94.
84. Keefer, "President Dwight D. Eisenhower and the End of the Korean War," p. 278. A poll at the time of the cease-fire showed that the public favored an armistice to continued fighting by 75 percent to 15 percent. John E. Mueller, "Trends in the Popular Support for the Wars in Korea and Vietnam," *American Political Science Review* 65:2 (June 1 1971), p. 374.
85. Paul Kennedy, *The Rise and Fall of the Great Powers: Economic Change and Military Conflict from 1500 to 2000* (New York: Vintage, 1987), p. 369. For the effects of the Truman administration's rearmament on U.S. confidence and strategic planning, see Marc Trachtenberg, *History and Strategy* (Princeton, N.J.: Princeton University Press, 1991).
86. Richard Whelan, *Drawing the Line: The Korean War, 1950–1953* (London: Faber & Faber, 1990), p. 322.
87. Joy, *Negotiating While Fighting*, p. 259. These are the words Joy used to U. Alexis Johnson during his trip to Korea in February 1952.
88. Joy to Ridgway, January 18, 1952, cited in Joy, *Negotiating While Fighting*, p. 203.

89. Hastings, *The Korean War*, p. 305.
90. The eventual fate of the repatriated Chinese prisoners, Pingchao Zhu writes,

> was disheartening. Upon crossing the border into Manchuria, . . . [they] were placed under the supervision of an office known as 'Returnees Administration' (Guiganchu). They were told that the government had already learned about their 'heroic deeds' in Korea, and now they must confess their 'disloyalty' during captivity. Almost overnight, they became turncoats, traitors, spies, cowards, and 'the most cursed.' In the years to come, their experience was comparable with those of the Soviet WWII repatriates. Many were deprived of Communist Party membership, expelled from the military . . . , stripped of the opportunity of education and employment, deported to remote areas to do hard labor, put in jail for the unwarranted charge of 'releasing military secrets to the enemy,' demoted, abandoned, divorced, and more. Some committed suicide, a few tried and failed miserably to appeal their case to the authorities. But a good many kept wondering how their POW experience made them enemies of the people.

Pingchao Zhu, *Americans and Chinese at the Korean War Cease-Fire Negotiations, 1950–1953, Studies in American History*, vol. 36 (Lewiston, Maine: Edwin Mellen, 2001), pp. 170–71.

91. For the fate of the nonrepatriated prisoners after the armistice, see Foot, *A Substitute for Victory*, pp. 190ff; Kaufman, *The Korean War*, pp. 343ff; and Sydney D. Bailey, *How Wars End: The United Nations and the Termination of Armed Conflict, 1946–1964* (Oxford: Clarendon, 1982), vol. 1, p. 314.
92. Official U.S. government sources recorded that in proportion to its total resources, North Korea suffered greater destruction than had Japan during World War II. For example, 635,000 tons of bombs were dropped (including 32,500 of napalm) during the Korean War, compared to 503,000 in the Pacific Theater. Foot, *A Substitute for Victory*, pp. 206–7.
93. Joy, *Negotiating While Fighting*, p. 436.
94. "The principle of voluntary repatriation, according to the Communist side, was in essence an open invitation to desertion and betrayal of Communist course, and therefore should never be permitted." Zhu, *Americans and Chinese at the Korean War Cease-Fire Negotiations*, p. 105.
95. Chai Chengwen, "The Korean Truce Negotiations," in Xiaobing Li, Allan R. Millett, and Binyu, eds., *Mao's Generals Remember Korea* (Lawrence: University Press of Kansas, 2001) pp. 225, 202. At the end of the day, it was just easier to give in: "America was the number one superpower, and it was unwilling to make any embarrassing compromises. . . . [W]e needed to give America more room for compromise by making adjust-

ments on the POW issue, which had blocked the negotiations for so long" (p. 228).

6. THE VIETNAM WAR

1. Henry Kissinger, *Ending the Vietnam War* (New York: Simon & Schuster, 2003), pp. 329–30. According to the North Vietnamese account of the negotiations, when the deal was first proposed, "joy appeared on the faces of Kissinger and all other members of the U.S. delegation." Luu Van Loi and Nguyen Anh Vu, *Le Duc Tho-Kissinger Negotiations in Paris* (Hanoi: The Gioi, 1996), p. 314.
2. H. R. Haldeman, *The Haldeman Diaries* (New York: Putnam's, 1994), pp. 516–17. Nixon's immediate response speaks volumes: "We then went into dinner in the outer office. The P told Manolo to bring the good wine, his '57 Lafite-Rothschild, or whatever it is, to be served to everyone. Usually it's just served to the P and the rest of us have some California Beaulieu Vineyard stuff."
3. Haldeman, *The Haldeman Diaries*, pp. 515–16.
4. Amazingly, Kissinger had described just such a scenario in *Foreign Affairs* in 1969: "When an issue is fairly abstract—before there is a prospect for agreement—our diplomats tend to present our view in a bland, relaxed fashion to the ally whose interests are involved but who is not present at the negotiations. The ally responds equally vaguely for three reasons: (a) he may be misled into believing that no decision is imminent and therefore sees no purpose in making an issue; (b) he is afraid that if he forces the issue the decision will go against him; (c) he hopes the problem will go away because agreement will prove impossible. When agreement seems imminent, American diplomats suddenly go into high gear to gain the acquiescence of the ally. He in turn feels tricked by the very intensity and suddenness of the pressure while we are outraged to learn of objections heretofore not made explicit." Henry Kissinger, "The Viet Nam Negotiations," *Foreign Affairs* 47:2 (January 1969), p. 225, fn. 4.
5. The transcript of the press conference can be found in Kissinger, *Ending the Vietnam War*, pp. 591–600.
6. The literature on Vietnam is vast and growing. The contours of the war's final years can be gleaned from Jeffrey Kimball, *Nixon's Vietnam War* (Lawrence: University Press of Kansas, 1998); idem, *The Vietnam War Files* (Lawrence: University Press of Kansas, 2004); Pierre Asselin, *A Bitter Peace* (Chapel Hill: University of North Carolina Press, 2002); Kissinger, *Ending the Vietnam War*; and Haldeman, *The Haldeman Diaries*. Recent books of note on the period include Lewis Sorley, *A Better War* (New York: Harcourt, 1999); Larry Berman, *No Peace, No Honor* (New York: Free Press, 2001); Ang Cheng Guan, *Ending the Vietnam War* (London: RoutledgeCurzon, 2004); Robert Dallek, *Nixon and Kissinger* (New York: HarperCollins, 2007); Stephen P. Randolph, *Powerful and Brutal Weapons* (Cambridge, Mass.: Harvard University Press, 2007);

and John Prados, *Vietnam* (Lawrence: University Press of Kansas, 2009). Older books worth noting include Roger Morris, *Uncertain Greatness* (New York: Harper & Row, 1977); Frank Snepp, *Decent Interval* (New York: Vintage, 1977); Leslie H. Gelb with Richard K. Betts, *The Irony of Vietnam: The System Worked* (Washington, D.C.: Brookings Institution, 1979); George C. Herring, *America's Longest War: The United States and Vietnam, 1950–1975*, 2nd ed. (New York: Knopf, 1986); Allan E. Goodman, *The Search for a Negotiated Settlement of the Vietnam War* (Berkeley: Institute of East Asian Studies, University of California, Berkeley, 1986); Nguyen Tien Hung and Jerrold L. Schechter, *The Palace File* (New York: Harper & Row, 1986); and Walter Isaacson, *Kissinger: A Biography* (New York: Simon & Schuster, 1992).

7. Appointed secretary of defense in early 1968, Clark Clifford supervised a review of the American war effort, emerging appalled: "I would ask the Joint Chiefs of Staff, 'If we sent another two hundred and six thousand [troops], is that enough?' They didn't know. 'Well, if we send that, will that end the war?' 'Well, nobody knows.' 'Well, is it possible that you might need even more?' 'That's possible.' 'Will bombing the North bring them to their knees?' 'No.' 'Is there any diminishing will on the part of the North to fight?' 'Well, we're not conscious of it.' Then finally, 'What is the plan?' There wasn't any. I said, 'There isn't any?' 'No. The plan is that we will just maintain the pressure on the enemy and ultimately we believe that the enemy will capitulate.' " Goodman, *The Search for a Negotiated Settlement of the Vietnam War*, p. 40.
8. Richard M. Nixon, "Asia After Vietnam," *Foreign Affairs* 46:1 (October 1967), pp. 111–25.
9. "Kissinger's Tribute to Nixon," *New York Times*, April 28, 1994, p. A20.
10. William Safire, *Before the Fall* (New York: Da Capo, 1975), p. 8. Safire also wrote: "Think of Nixon as a layer cake. The icing, the public face or crust, is conservative, stern, dignified, proper. . . . [U]nderneath that icing is a progressive politician, willing and even eager to surprise with liberal ideas, delighted with the Disraeli comparison. . . . Underneath *that* is an unnecessarily pugnacious man who had to scrape for everything he has in life and don't you forget it; self-made, self-pitying, but not self-centered; who regularly gets furious with what he considers to be loafers and bums who expect the world on a platter and think nothing of living off the sweat of hard-working people. . . . The next layer is a poker player with a long record of winning, the politician with a long record of losing, then winning, then losing again, but not quitting until he absolutely had to quit. . . . Under that is the hater, the impugner of motives . . . this is the contemptuous, contemptible layer that stimulated him to engage 'plumbers' to plug news leaks and to trample civil liberties in what he saw as a higher cause. . . . Another layer is the realist, the man who understands the motivation of nations and power groups, who senses weaknesses and opportunities in political alignments and in-

ternational affairs . . . and who could summon up the confidence to impose his presence and much of his idea of order on the rest of the world. Under that is the observer-participant, who is applauding or criticizing what he is doing while he is doing it. . . . Then there is the man of extraordinary courage, the calculating risk-taker whose refusal to bend to pressure on matters of foreign policy led to 'peace with honor,' diplomacy triangulated and linked, and summit triumphs unprecedented for an American president. . . . Underneath that is the loner, who identifies with 'the people' but hates to deal with more than a very few persons; the intellectual . . . who prefers the company of athletes to intellectuals, who dares to take the time to think things through alone, then wastes some of that precious time merely brooding . . . who dreams above all else that he is the one thrust into the times uniquely equipped to be the peacemaker, and who, in personal isolation and withdrawal, comes to the conclusion that America cannot indulge in isolation and must withdraw with care from unwise commitments. . . . When you take a bite of the cake that is Nixon, you must get a mouthful of all the layers; nibbling along one level is not permitted" (pp. 97–99).

11. "Address at the Gettysburg College Convocation," April 4, 1959, in *Public Papers of the Presidents of the United States: Dwight D. Eisenhower, 1959* (Washington, D.C.: U.S. Government Printing Office, 1960), pp. 311–13. See also David L. Anderson, "Dwight D. Eisenhower and Wholehearted Support of Ngo Dinh Diem," in David L. Anderson, *Shadow on the White House: Presidents and the Vietnam War, 1945–1975* (Lawrence: University Press of Kansas, 1993).
12. John F. Kennedy, "America's Stake in Vietnam," *Vital Speeches* 22:20 (August 1, 1956), p. 618.
13. Quoted in Larry Berman, *Planning a Tragedy: The Americanization of the War in Vietnam* (New York: Norton, 1982), p. 45.
14. See Berman, *Planning a Tragedy;* Yuen Foong Khong, *Analogies at War: Korea, Munich, Dien Bien Phu and the Vietnam Decisions of 1965* (Princeton, N.J.: Princeton University Press, 1992); and John P. Burke and Fred I. Greenstein (with Larry Berman and Richard Immerman), *How Presidents Test Reality: Decisions on Vietnam, 1954 and 1965* (New York: Russell Sage Foundation, 1989). For an argument that Johnson could have disengaged from Vietnam in the wake of Diem's assassination more easily than generally believed, see Fredrik Logevall, *Choosing War: The Lost Chance for Peace and the Escalation of War in Vietnam* (Berkeley: University of California Press, 2001).
15. Cable #4035, Taylor to Rusk, June 3, 1965, Top Secret, NSC History—Deployment in Vietnam.
16. On the role fears of Chinese intervention played in U.S. planning, see Khong, *Analogies at War*. For the positive rationale behind limiting the war, see Stephen Peter Rosen, "Vietnam and the American Theory of Limited War," *International Security* 7:2 (Fall 1982), pp. 83–113. The

war was kept limited in a third way as well, by not calling up the reserves and not whipping up passions at home. For the domestic political reasons behind these restrictions, see Berman, *Planning a Tragedy*, pp. 145–53, and Gelb and Betts, *The Irony of Vietnam.*

17. Quoted in Michael Maclear, *The Ten Thousand Day War: Vietnam, 1945–1975* (New York: St. Martin's, 1981), p. 417.
18. On the Saigon regime's relations with its society, see Jeffrey Race, *War Comes to Long An: Revolutionary Conflict in a Vietnamese Province* (Berkeley: University of California Press, 1972); Eric M. Bergerud, *The Dynamics of Defeat: The Vietnam War in Hau Nghia Province* (Boulder, Colo.: Westview, 1991); and Ronald Spector, *After Tet* (New York: Vintage, 1994).
19. In countries such as Vietnam, it has been noted, "The political function of communism [was] not to overthrow authority but to fill the vacuum of authority. . . . The difference in political experience between the northern and southern halves of [Vietnam and Korea] . . . was not the difference between dictatorship and democracy but rather the difference between well-organized, broadly based, complex political systems, on the one hand, and unstable, fractured, narrowly based personalistic regimes, on the other. It was a difference in political institutionalization." Samuel P. Huntington, *Political Order in Changing Societies* (New Haven, Conn.: Yale University Press, 1968), pp. 335, 343.
20. On the conduct of this war, see William C. Westmoreland, *A Soldier Reports* (Garden City, NY: Doubleday, 1976); Bruce Palmer, Jr., *The 25-Year War: America's Military Role in Vietnam* (Lexington: University Press of Kentucky, 1984); Guenter Lewy, *America in Vietnam* (Oxford: Oxford University Press, 1978); and Andrew F. Krepinevich, Jr., *The Army in Vietnam* (Baltimore: Johns Hopkins University Press, 1988). A typical operation is described in Jonathan Schell, *The Village of Ben Suc* (New York: Knopf, 1967).
21. The impact of Tet was much greater among elites than among the public at large. In this sense, Johnson's angry reaction to his March 1968 meeting with the "Wise Men"—"the establishment bastards have bailed out"—was accurate. He would say later that although while he was president he had been "screwed" by many, "the big-name foreign policy types did the royal job on me." See Morris, *Uncertain Greatness*, pp. 44–45, and Walter Isaacson and Evan Thomas, *The Wise Men: Six Friends and the World They Made* (New York: Simon & Schuster, 1986), pp. 672–703. The Tet Offensive's impact on public opinion trends is discussed in John E. Mueller, *War, Presidents, and Public Opinion* (Lanham, Md. University Press of America, 1973), pp. 57, 126ff.
22. Herring, *America's Longest War*, pp. 208, 203.
23. Much has been made of the "sabotage" of this peace move by Nixon and Kissinger. See, e.g., Seymour M. Hersh, *The Price of Power: Kissinger in the Nixon White House* (New York: Summit, 1983), pp. 16–24; Isaac-

son, *Kissinger*, pp. 129–32; and William Bundy, *A Tangled Web: The Making of Foreign Policy in the Nixon Presidency* (New York: Hillard Wang, 1998). Whatever secret contacts occurred, however, had little impact on the negotiations, although it is conceivable they might have had some on the American elections. See Safire, *Before the Fall*, pp. 84–91, 107, and Hung and Schechter, *The Palace File*, pp. 21ff. Thieu would undoubtedly have rejected what he saw as a bad deal without any external prompting—as indeed he did four years later, when the deal came from Nixon and Kissinger themselves.

24. Henry Kissinger, *White House Years* (Boston: Little, Brown, 1979), pp. 65ff, and Richard M. Nixon, *RN: The Memoirs of Richard Nixon* (New York: Simon & Schuster, 1990), pp. 340ff.
25. Kissinger, "The Viet Nam Negotiations," p. 230.
26. Kissinger, *White House Years*, p. 129.
27. H. R. Haldeman with Joseph DiMona, *The Ends of Power* (New York: Times Books, 1978), p. 83.
28. Quoted in Goodman, *The Search for a Negotiated Settlement,* p. 48. In an attempt to demonstrate its good intentions, the new administration changed the American negotiating position somewhat as well.
29. Haldeman, *The Haldeman Diaries*, pp. 69–70.
30. Morris, *Uncertain Greatness*, p. 164.
31. Thompson told the president in October 1969 "that, continuing the current U.S. policy and assuming South Vietnamese confidence that we would not pull out, victory could be won within two years." Nixon, *RN*, pp. 404–5, 413.
32. "I have become deeply concerned about our present course in Vietnam," he wrote Nixon in a memo on September 10. "While time acts against both us and our enemy, it runs more quickly against our strategy than against theirs. . . . Withdrawal of U.S. troops will become like salted peanuts to the American public: the more U.S. troops come home, the more will be demanded. This could eventually result, in effect, in demands for unilateral withdrawal—perhaps within a year. The more troops are withdrawn, the more Hanoi will be encouraged—they are the last people we will be able to fool about the ability of the South Vietnamese to take over from us. They have the option of attacking GVN forces to embarrass us throughout the process or of waiting until we have largely withdrawn before doing so. . . ." "Memorandum for the President," September 10, 1969, in Kissinger, *Ending the Vietnam War*, pp. 586–88.
33. Henry Kissinger, *Diplomacy* (New York: Simon & Schuster, 1994), p. 678.
34. Goodman, *The Search for a Negotiated Settlement*, pp. 59ff. Kissinger seems to have understood these implications. When the concession was made he spoke to some reporters off the record: "After we have put the South Vietnamese into the best possible shape that we can, and after we can tell ourselves in good conscience that we have done it in a way that is

not a cop-out, if then, after five years, it turns out that they can't make it anyway, I think we are facing different consequences than that of simply packing up and pulling out." Isaacson, *Kissinger*, p. 313.

35. Kissinger, *White House Years*, pp. 281, 979. At one point Le Duc Tho even suggested to Kissinger, "helpfully," that the United States could extricate itself by arranging Thieu's assassination. *Diplomacy*, p. 686.
36. Craig R. Whitney, "Speech in Saigon," *New York Times*, October 25, 1972, p. 1.
37. Kissinger and Nixon were clear and honest with Thieu about the declining political base in the United States for continuing the war, and explicit in arguing that the longer he dragged things out the more control his enemies in the U.S. Congress would have over his fate. As bad as the deal being offered to him was, therefore, Thieu should have realized that it was the best he was likely to get and tried to make it work rather than continuing to demand a change of heart from the White House. Apparently, if Washington never understood Saigon, Saigon never understood Washington, either: "Thieu's perceptions of the power of American public opinion and the relationship between Congress and the Executive were faulty and primitive. South Vietnam did nothing effective to make its case in America. Thieu continued to rely on Nixon, believing that as in South Vietnam the President could control the public and manipulate it at will." Hung and Schechter, *The Palace File*, p. 359.
38. A month later, another letter made the point even clearer: "I have therefore irrevocably decided to proceed to initial the agreement on January 23, 1973 and to sign it on January 27, 1973 in Paris. I will do so, if necessary, alone. In that case I shall have to explain publicly that your Government obstructs peace. The result will be an inevitable and immediate termination of U.S. economic and military assistance which cannot be forestalled by a change of personnel in your government. I hope, however, that after all our two countries have shared and suffered together in conflict, we will stay together to preserve peace and reap its benefits." Kissinger, *Ending the Vietnam War,* pp. 418, 427.
39. Hung and Schechter, *The Palace File*, p. 146.
40. Haldeman, *The Haldeman Diaries*, entry for June 29, 1971, p. 309.
41. Henry A. Kissinger, "Domestic Structure and Foreign Policy," 95:2 *Daedalus* (Spring 1966), p. 508. "The need to provide a memorandum," he noted, "may outweigh the imperatives of creative thought. The quest for objectivity creates a temptation to see in the future an updated version of the present. Yet true innovation is bound to run counter to prevailing standards. The dilemma of modern bureaucracy is that while every creative act is lonely, not every lonely act is creative."
42. Morris, *Uncertain Greatness*, p. 75.
43. Kissinger, "Domestic Structure and Foreign Policy," pp. 509–11.
44. The organizational scheme is set out in Morris, *Uncertain Greatness*, pp. 79–81. For descriptions of it in practice, see John P. Leacacos, "Kiss-

inger's Apparat," and I. M. Destler, "Can One Man Do?" *Foreign Policy* 5 (Winter 1971–72), pp. 3–40.

45. Peter Rodman, "Nixon's Policy," in Peter Braestrup, ed., *Vietnam as History: Ten Years After the Paris Peace Accords* (Washington, D.C.: University Press of America, 1984), p. 60.
46. See Isaacson, *Kissinger*, pp. 380–85. To be fair to Kissinger's rivals, he played the game as dirty as they did, if not more so—having the phones of the closest aides to the secretaries of state and defense tapped without their knowledge so he could "preview the opinions of their bosses" and gain a leg up in the bureaucratic rivalry. Safire, *Before the Fall*, p. 167. Laird now claims that he used the national security agency to secretly keep tabs on Kissinger's negotiations; Dale Van Atta, *With Honor: Melvin Laird in War, Peace, and Politics* (Madison: University of Wisconsin Press, 2008), p. 224.
47. Palmer, *The 25-Year War*, p. 107.
48. Haldeman, *The Haldeman Diaries*, entry for March 20, 1969, p. 42. Cf. entry for April 15, p. 50.
49. Quoted in Isaacson, *Kissinger*, p. 165.
50. Haldeman, *The Ends of Power*, pp. 82–83.
51. "What Dick Nixon Told Southern Delegates," *Miami Herald*, August 7, 1968, in Kimball, *The Vietnam War Files*, p. 64. See also Morton Halperin, "The Lessons Nixon Learned," in Anthony Lake, ed., *The Legacy of Vietnam: The War, American Society, and the Future of American Foreign Policy* (New York: New York University Press, 1975), pp. 414ff.
52. Henry A. Kissinger, *Nuclear Weapons and American Foreign Policy* (New York: Harper, 1957), pp. 50–51. Kissinger would return to this theme again and again in later writings. *White House Years* restates this passage almost verbatim (pp. 63–64), while *Diplomacy* (p. 489) contains the following comment: "American restraint [at the beginning of the Korean armistice negotiations] enabled China to end the process by which its army was being ground down by American technical and military superiority. Henceforth, and without significant risk, the Chinese could use military operations to inflict casualties and to magnify America's frustrations and domestic pressures to end the war."
53. Kissinger, "The Viet Nam Negotiations," p. 230.
54. Ibid., p. 226.
55. Gallup Poll, November 1967, cited in Mueller, *War, Presidents, and Public Opinion*, p. 90. For trends in public support for the war more generally, in addition to Mueller see William M. Lunch and Peter W. Sperlich, "American Public Opinion and the War in Vietnam," *Western Political Quarterly* 32:1 (March 1979), pp. 21–44; and Albert H. Cantril, *The American People, Viet-Nam and the Presidency* (Princeton, N.J.: Institute for International Social Research, 1970).
56. Twenty-six percent favored "withdraw completely" and 19 percent favored "continue present policy." An additional 19 percent favored an op-

tion described as "end as soon as possible"; this imprecise wording says nothing about what specific policies should be followed, but hints at the general level of frustration. Gallup poll, March 1969, cited in Mueller, *War, Presidents, and Public Opinion*, p. 92.

57. It fell to 7 percent in March 1970, rose to 13 percent in May (after the invasion of Cambodia), and dropped back to 10 percent in July. There seems to have been more support for escalation, however, if the phrase "send more troops" was not used. Thus in the fall of 1970, 24 percent chose "take a stronger stand even if it means invading North Vietnam." Gallup and University of Michigan Survey Research Center polls, cited in Mueller, *War, Presidents, and Public Opinion*, pp. 94–96.
58. Ibid., pp. 93, 94.
59. Kissinger, *White House Years*, p. 274. For various perspectives on the troop withdrawals, see the collection of articles in *Diplomatic History* 34:3 (June 2010).
60. Van Atta, *With Honor*, pp. 173, 202. As his official biographer comments, "Laird's mantra for the next four years [was] that the U.S. participation in the war was doomed because the folks at home were fed up with it. Kissinger, ever scornful of politics, never agreed. Nixon would come around only as the 1972 election drew closer. Until the president saw the light, Laird had to fight tooth and nail for each soldier he brought home" (p. 201). Laird would later claim that he was shocked at what happened to South Vietnam after American withdrew and he harshly criticized Kissinger and the Ford administration for letting Saigon fall to the Communists. "The shame of Vietnam," he wrote in 2005, "is not that we were there in the first place, but that we betrayed our ally in the end. It was Congress that turned its back on the promises of the Paris accord. The president, the secretary of state, and the secretary of defense must share the blame. In the end, they did not stand up for the commitments our nation had made to South Vietnam." Melvin R. Laird, "Iraq: Learning the Lessons of Vietnam," *Foreign Affairs* 84:6 (November/December 2005), p. 26. This is either disingenuous or naïve, since it was Laird who drove troop withdrawals forward relentlessly and displayed little contemporaneous concern for what the fate of South Vietnam would be once they were completed.
61. William Greider, "America and Defeat," in Allan R. Millett, ed., *A Short History of the Vietnam War* (Bloomington: Indiana University Press, 1978), p. 48. In September 1970 pollster Albert Cantril also reported on "the current state of ambivalence in American public opinion. . . . The public on balance has made up its mind that the war in Viet-Nam is too costly to sustain much longer. Yet even though it is generally agreed that the U.S. has no vital interests at stake in Viet-Nam, the people are troubled about the possibility of a Communist takeover. In short, they want to eat their cake and have it too." Cantril, *The American People*, p. 11.
62. Mueller, *War, Presidents, and Public Opinion*, pp. 94–96.

63. Quoted in Greider, "America and Defeat," p. 47.
64. "Unlike my contemporaries," Kissinger later remarked, "I had experienced the fragility of the fabric of modern society." Roger Morris commented that "Henry feared the Weimar thing in which he and the Jews would be accused of a bugout in Southeast Asia." Helmut Sonnenfeldt touched on a similar theme when he joked that "Kissinger the German-Jewish immigrant only kept on Haig, the all-American colonel from Philadelphia, to testify at some imagined right-wing trial, if Henry went too far with detente." See Isaacson, *Kissinger*, pp. 279–80, 761, and Morris, *Uncertain Greatness*, pp. 141–42, 170.
65. Haldeman, *Haldeman Diaries*, entry for December 15, 1970, p. 221. Cf. also the entries for December 21, 1970, and January 26, 1971, pp. 223, 239. For a heated exchange on this issue see Anthony Lewis, "Guilt For Vietnam," *New York Times,* May 30, 1994, p. A15; Henry Kissinger, "Hanoi, Not Nixon, Set Pace of Vietnam Peace," *New York Times*, June 3, 1994, p. A26; and Lewis, "The Lying Machine," *New York Times*, June 6, 1994, p. A15.
66. Kissinger, "The Viet Nam Negotiations," p. 218.
67. The realist objection to escalation, of course, would be prudential rather than moral, and thus could be withdrawn should a changed international environment seem to lower the risk—which is precisely what happened in the spring of 1972 and in the following winter.
68. Kissinger, *White House Years*, pp. 227–28.
69. Hans J. Morgenthau, "The Doctrine of War Without End," in *Truth and Power: Essays of A Decade, 1960–1970* (London: Pall Mall, 1970), p. 425.
70. "The Statement and Testimony of the Honorable George F. Kennan," in J. William Fulbright, *The Vietnam Hearings* (New York: Random House, 1966), pp. 108, 122, 147.
71. Kissinger, "The Viet Nam Negotiations," pp. 218–19, 234. The administration's constant invocations of "honor," he would write, were not "incompatible with a properly understood Realpolitik. For, in the end, a nation's reliability affects the steadiness of its allies and the calculations of its adversaries." Kissinger, *Ending the Vietnam War*, p. 537.
72. Isaacson, *Kissinger*, p. 461.
73. Robert E. Osgood, "The Nixon Doctrine and Strategy," in Robert E. Osgood, ed., *Retreat From Empire? The First Nixon Administration* (Baltimore, MD: Johns Hopkins JP, 1973) p. 8. To see how this played out across different issue areas, see Fredrik Logevall and Andrew Preston, *Nixon in the World* (New York: Oxford University Press, 2008).
74. John Lewis Gaddis, *Strategies of Containment: A Critical Appraisal of American National Security Policy During the Cold War* (New York: Oxford University Press, 2005), p. 320.
75. Tucker, "Change and Continuity," in Osgood, *Retreat From Empire?* pp. 47–48 (emphasis in the original).

76. George Ball memorandum for Rusk, McNamara, and Bundy, June 29, 1965, Top Secret, NSC History—Deployment in Vietnam.
77. Kissinger, *White House Years*, pp. 227–28.
78. Kissinger, *Diplomacy*, p. 680. He held this view at the time, not simply in retrospect. In a memorandum to Nixon dated September 18, 1971, for example, Kissinger wrote: "The underlying assumption remains what it has been from the outset of your administration: the manner in which we end the war, or at least our participation, is crucial both for America's global position and for the fabric of our society. A swift collapse in South Vietnam traced to precipitate American withdrawal would seriously endanger your effort to shape a new foreign-policy role for this country. The impact on friends, adversaries and our own people would be likely to swing us from post World War II predominance to post Vietnam abdication, instead of striking the balanced posture of the Nixon Doctrine." Kimball, *The Vietnam War Files*, p. 45. A few days after the Paris Accords were signed, Nixon met with former Japanese prime minister Eisaku Sato and said in private what he was saying in public: "The problem which many friends in the world did not recognize was that it was essential for the U.S. to end the war in an honorable way. Many in this country thought that when I came into office that I, as a political act, would let South Vietnam go down the drain, and blame Kennedy and Johnson, who started it." Although "peace elements" in other countries might have applauded such a move, Nixon continued, leaders like Sato "have seen that how the U.S. stood by a small ally would show the U.S. could be relied upon by a great ally, like Japan. . . . The people who had the greatest stake in the outcome were our allies in the world. If our allies saw we were undependable to a small ally, big allies would lose confidence in us. That is why it was essential that we show that strength and dependability." Berman, *No Peace, No Honor*, p. 237.
79. Lunch and Sperlich write: "Following the withdrawal of American combat troops from Vietnam, most Americans appear to have taken an attitude of studied indifference or even hostility to events in Southeast Asia. . . . [W]hen the Paris peace accords were signed, Gallup found widespread opposition to any continuing U.S. military role in South Vietnam. Later, as the American-backed regime in Saigon collapsed, more than three-quarters of the American people opposed sending it military aid, and a majority opposed even allowing the former U.S. clients to resettle in the United States." "American Public Opinion and the War in Vietnam," p. 32.
80. "The decrease in American aid," wrote the architect of the North's successful 1975 invasion, "had made it impossible for Saigon troops to carry out their combat and force-development plans. . . . Nguyen Van Thieu had to call on his troops to switch to a 'poor man's war.' . . . [They had] to change over from large-scale operations and deep-penetration helicopter and tank assaults to defense of their outposts, digging in and carrying out small search operations." Van Tien Dung, *Our Great Spring Victory:*

An Account of the Liberation of South Vietnam (New York: Monthly Review Press, 1977), pp. 17–18.

81. Herring, *America's Longest War*, pp. 262ff, and Lewy, *America in Vietnam*, pp. 207ff.
82. Dung, *Our Great Spring Victory*, pp. 18–20.
83. Quoted in Ron Nessen, *It Sure Looks Different From the Inside* (Chicago: Playboy Press, 1979), p. 108.
84. Letters from Nixon to Thieu, November 17, 1972, and January 5, 1973, in Gareth Porter, ed., *Vietnam: The Definitive Documentation of Human Decisions* (Stanfordville, NY: E.M. Coleman Enterprises, 1979), vol. 2, pp. 582, 592.
85. Kissinger, *White House Years*, p. 1373.
86. Nixon, *RN*, p. 889. Kissinger said at a press conference during the final collapse that the assumptions he had operated under during the negotiations "were later falsified by events that were beyond the control of, that indeed were unforeseeable by anybody who negotiated these agreements, including the disintegration of or the weakening of executive authority in the United States for reasons unconnected with foreign policy considerations." "Vietnam: The End of the War," *Survival* 17:4 (July/August 1975), p. 184.
87. Kissinger, *Ending the Vietnam War*, p. 428.
88. Kimball, *The Vietnam War Files*, p. 187. The words in italics were handwritten by Kissinger in the margin. The "political evolution" referred to meant internally driven changes in South Vietnam, not externally imposed ones.
89. Ibid., pp. 190–91.
90. Ibid., pp. 232–32.
91. "Memcon, Kissinger and Zhou Enlai, June 21, 1972," quoted in Jeffrey Kimball, "Decent Interval or Not?" *SHAFR Newsletter* (December 2003).
92. Zhou Enlai and Le Duc Tho meeting notes, Beijing, January 3, 1973, in Odd Arne Westad, Chen Jian, Stein Tonnesson, Nguyen Vu Tungand, and James G. Hershberg, eds., 77 *Conversations Between Chinese and Foreign Leaders on the Wars in Indochina, 1964–1977* (Washington, D.C.: Cold War International History Project, Working Paper No. 22, May 1998). A few days after the agreement was signed, Zhou commented: "It is good that the Vietnamese-American agreement lets the American troops leave Vietnam. This agreement is a success. After the withdrawal of American troops, including American naval, air, and land forces, and after the withdrawal of American military bases, it is easy to deal with Nguyen Van Thieu. . . ." Zhou Enlai and Pen Nouth meeting notes, Beijing, February 2, 1973. For evolving Chinese views on the war, see Qiang Zhai, *China & The Vietnam Wars, 1950–1975* (Chapel Hill: University of North Carolina Press, 2000).
93. Thomas Alan Schwartz, " 'Henry, . . . Winning an Election Is Terribly

Important': Partisan Politics in the History of U.S. Foreign Relations," *Diplomatic History* 33:2 (April 2009), pp. 173–74. A tape and transcript of the conversation is available at http://tapes.millercenter.virginia.edu/clips/1972_0803_vietnam/. For other transcripts from the tapes along similar lines, see Ken Hughes, "Fake Politics: Nixon's Political Timetable for Withdrawing from Vietnam, *Diplomatic History* 34:3 (June 2010). Of course, given how toxic the war had become at home, a lack of American popular interest in Vietnam could have worked to Saigon's benefit as well as loss. In March 1973, for example, Kissinger told South Vietnamese ambassador Tram Kin Phuong that "what we were trying to achieve was a situation where our people didn't give a damn any more about Vietnam. It would then allow the United States to be more effective in helping South Vietnam preserve its independence." Dallek, *Nixon and Kissinger*, p. 468.

94. Frank Snepp, a CIA officer on the ground during the final years, is worth hearing from on this point:

> As the Vietnam cease-fire gave way to renewed warfare, some of Kissinger's critics charged that he had never meant for the agreement to work anyway, but was merely trying through its convolutions and vagaries to assure a "decent interval" between the American withdrawal and a final fight to the death between the two Vietnamese sides. This judgment, however, hardly did justice to Kissinger himself. While he may not have put together a truly workable peace, he was most certainly concerned about preserving a non-Communist government in South Vietnam and the semblance of accommodation between Saigon and Hanoi. The essence of his "postwar" strategy was equilibrium. A rough parity, economic and military, he felt, must be established between the North and the South so that neither could impose a military solution on the other, and each would have an incentive to settle remaining differences peacefully. In part, this meant keeping Thieu strong enough to fend off the North Vietnamese troops on his doorstep. At the same time Kissinger hoped to moderate the aggressive tendencies of the North Vietnamese through various pressures and plums—by providing them with reconstruction aid, as called for in the Paris agreement, and by persuading the Soviets and the Chinese to reduce their support for the "revolution." Ideally, under these conditions Hanoi would be influenced to turn inward, eventually abandoning its crusade in the south.

Decent Interval, pp. 50–51. Kimball's assessment of the situation seems sound:

> Despite the continuing presence of PAVN and PLAF troops in South Vietnam, the decent-interval option did not absolutely guar-

antee Thieu's defeat. In theory his government might have been sustained by means of continued U.S. economic and military assistance, reforms in the Saigon government and in the countryside, successful pacification programs, the massive bombing of North Vietnam at the time American forces were leaving Vietnam, the collaboration of the USSR and the PRC in restraining the DRV, and the reintroduction of U.S. airpower in the event of renewed fighting after an American pullout. If, however, these measures could not sustain Saigon's government and army, Nixon and Kissinger believed that South Vietnam's defeat could then be blamed on Saigon's incompetence, Congress' obstructionism, the American public's irresolution, and historical fate.

The Vietnam War Files, p. 28.

95. Bui Tin, *From Enemy to Friend* (Annapolis, Md.: Naval Institute Press, 2002), p. 111. "At the beginning of 1975 not even the most optimistic person among us believed that the war would end in the same year with total victory on our side. . . . At a meeting of high-ranking cadres at the end of 1974 to discuss the military situation and missions, it was revealed that not even the Politburo expected victory before two more years of fighting. . . . No one predicted that we would have completely occupied the South by the end of 1976" (pp. 112–13). Cf. Guan, *Ending the Vietnam War*, pp. 127–65.
96. Bui Tin was a high-ranking North Vietnamese officer who played a key role in the war's final moments, before defecting to the West years later in revulsion at what the DRV had become. The North could never have been coerced into giving up its struggle, he argues, but it might have been kept at bay indefinitely. "Total, irretrievable defeat that brought with it the unconditional surrender of the South was not written in the stars. . . . [The United States] could have maintained a seesaw situation, one in which there could be no (clear) winners or losers, and perhaps have forced a compromise resulting in a fairer settlement—fairer because it was based on mutual concessions." Bui Tin, *From Enemy to Friend*, pp. 72–73.
97. *New York Times*, September 23, 1992, p. A5. The resulting exchange says much about the continuing American debate over the war: "Kissinger: Absolutely not. Kerry: Very close. Kissinger: Not even remotely. Kerry: Very close. . . ."
98. Sir Robert Thompson, *Peace Is Not at Hand* (London: Chatto & Windus, 1974), p. 126.

7. THE GULF WAR

1. This opening narrative draws on Richard M. Swain, *"Lucky War": Third Army in Desert Storm* (Fort Leavenworth, Kans.: U.S. Army Com-

mand and General Staff College Press, 1994); Stephen A. Bourque and John W. Burdan III, *The Road to Safwan* (Denton: University of North Texas Press, 2007); Michael R. Gordon and Bernard E. Trainor, *The Generals' War* (Boston: Little, Brown, 1995); Tom Clancy with Fred Franks, Jr., and Tony Koltz, *Into the Storm* (New York: Berkley, 1997); Rick Atkinson, *Crusade* (Boston: Houghton Mifflin, 1993); H. Norman Schwarzkopf with Peter Petre, *It Doesn't Take a Hero* (New York: Bantam, 1992); Kevin M. Woods, *The Mother of All Battles* (Annapolis, Md.: Naval Institute Press, 2008); Steve Coll, "Talks, Site, Remind Iraqis Who Won," *Washington Post*, March 4, 1991, p. A1; Steve Coll and Guy Gugliotta, "Iraq Accepts All Cease-Fire Terms, May Soon Release Some Prisoners," *Washington Post*, March 4, 1991, p. A1; Nora Boustany, "Violence Reported Spreading in Iraq," *Washington Post*, March 6, 1991, p. A1; Caryle Murphy, "Iraqi Troops Said to Quash Rebellion," *Washington Post*, March 7, 1991, p. A1; Lee Hockstader, "Baghdad Warns Insurrectionists 'They Will Pay,' " *Washington Post*, March 8, 1991, p. A1; and Elizabeth Neuffer, "Rebels 'Were Tied to Tanks and Shot' By Iraqi Troops," *Seattle Times*, March 8, 1991.

2. "Address to the Nation Announcing the Deployment of United States Armed Forces to Saudi Arabia," August 8, 1990, Public Papers of the President, George Bush Presidential Library. These principles would be enshrined almost verbatim in National Security Directives 45 and 54, which governed policy during Operations Desert Shield and Desert Storm, respectively.
3. Cf. Lawrence Freedman and Efraim Karsh, *The Gulf Conflict, 1990–1991* (Princeton, N.J.: Princeton University Press, 1993), pp. xxxii–xxxiii.
4. Zbigniew Brzezinski, *Power and Principle* (New York: Farrar, Straus & Giroux, 1983), p. 454.
5. Colin L. Powell with Joseph E. Persico, *My American Journey* (New York: Ballantine, 1995), p. 526.
6. The best general treatments of the case are Freedman and Karsh, *The Gulf Conflict, 1990–1991*; Gordon and Trainor, *The Generals' War;* Atkinson, *Crusade;* and Roland Dannreuther, *The Gulf Conflict*, Adelphi Paper 264 (London: IISS, Winter 1991/92). Important memoirs include George Bush and Brent Scowcroft, *A World Transformed* (New York: Vintage, 1998); James A. Baker, III, with Thomas M. DeFrank, *The Politics of Diplomacy: Revolution, War, and Peace, 1989–1992* (New York: Putnam, 1995); Richard N. Haass, *War of Necessity, War of Choice* (New York: Simon & Schuster, 2009); Powell with Persico, *My American Journey;* Schwarzkopf with Petre, *It Doesn't Take a Hero*; and Khaled bin Sultan, *Desert Warrior* (New York: HarperCollins, 1995), as well as the oral histories taken in conjunction with the 1996 *Frontline* documentary *The Gulf War.* On the Iraqi side of the story, see Woods, *The Mother of All Battles*. See also Kenneth M. Pollack, *The Threatening Storm* (New York: Random House, 2002); Michael Andrew Knights, *Cradle of Con-*

flict (Annapolis, Md.: Naval Institute Press, 2005); John T. Fishel, *Liberation, Occupation, and Rescue: War Termination and Desert Storm* (Carlyle Barracks, Pa.: U.S. Army War College, Strategic Studies Institute, 1992); Lawrence E. Cline, "Defending the End: Decision Making in Terminating the Persian Gulf War," *Comparative Strategy* 17:4 (1998); and Thomas G. Mahnken, "A Squandered Opportunity? The Decision to End the Gulf War," in Andrew J. Bacevich and Efraim Inbar, eds., *The Gulf War of 1991 Reconsidered* (London: Frank Cass, 2003). As of the time of this writing, a few documents from the NSC, CIA, and other parts of the U.S. government have been declassified, and some are cited in the notes below.

7. "I know he's a thug, but I never thought he was irrational," Soviet foreign minister Eduard Shevardnadze commented to U.S. secretary of state James Baker when they heard about the invasion. Christian Alfonsi, *Circle in the Sand* (New York: Doubleday, 2006), p. 57.
8. Brent Scowcroft, Oral History, *Frontline: The Gulf War* (1996), accessed at www.pbs.org/wgbh/pages/frontline/gulf/oral/. The U.S. intelligence community's contemporaneous portrait of Iraqi political culture and Saddam's place in it is worth noting:

> The Iraqis, like other nationalities, exhibit traits that reflect deeply imbedded cultural values and help explain how their leaders perceive the world. . . . Iraqis are generally regarded as self-confident and proud . . . direct . . . stubborn . . . suspicious . . . brutal . . . [and] persistent . . . Saddam Husayn makes all key policy decisions in Iraq. His sense of mission—to unite the Arab world and ultimately lead it to parity with the West—combined with his characteristically suspicious view of the world fuels much of his political behavior. He is a rational, calculating decisionmaker. Nevertheless, Saddam is a risk taker, and his xenophobic world view colors his judgment—factors that raise his chances of miscalculating. Over the past decade, we have found his leadership style to be characterized by several behavioral patterns, including: an unswerving commitment to his vision, along with an ability to rebound with vigor from temporary setbacks . . . ; a respect for strength, accompanied by a cold-blooded willingness to use any means necessary—including torture, mass murder, or assassination—to achieve his objectives and intimidate resistance; [and] the flexibility to make tactical retreats when confronted with overwhelming odds.

   Political and Personality Handbook of Iraq (CIA Directorate of Intelligence, January 1991, Secret), pp. 7, 10, accessible at www.foia.cia.gov/.
9. Baker with DeFrank, *The Politics of Diplomacy*, p. 271. This cable went out on July 19.
10. Critics would later argue, unfairly, that Glaspie had given some sort of green or at least yellow light for the invasion. Saddam did indeed doubt

that the United States would forcibly reverse his takeover of Kuwait, but that judgment stemmed from his broader negative assessment of American will and character, not from any specific last-minute moves by the Bush administration. There is little reason to think that any plausible U.S. course of action during the spring and summer—including a somewhat tougher warning—would have deterred an invasion. The transcript of Glaspie's meeting with Saddam can be found in Micah L. Sifry and Christopher Cerf, *The Gulf War Reader* (New York: Times Books, 1991), pp. 122ff.

11. Apparently expecting Kuwait's riches to heaped up somewhere like a pirate's treasure chest, the Iraqis were shocked and annoyed to find out that the hard assets they seized from Kuwait's central bank headquarters totaled only $2 billion. The Bush administration's quick thinking kept more than $200 billion in Kuwaiti foreign assets out of Saddam's reach. Phebe Marr, *The Modern History of Iraq*, 2nd ed. (Boulder, Colo.: Westview, 2004), 234.
12. United Nations Security Council Resolution 660. Yemen abstained. By declaring that the invasion constituted "a breach of international peace and security," the resolution established the predicate for later actions to reverse it, including the use of force. The incredibly swift and skilled moves by U.S. officials and their allies that night were critical in isolating and outmaneuvering Saddam. See David M. Malone, *The International Struggle Over Iraq: Politics in the UN Security Council, 1980–2005* (Oxford: Oxford University Press, 2006), p. 60; Bush and Scowcroft, *A World Transformed,* pp. 302ff; Haass, *War of Necessity, War of Choice*, pp. 60–61; and Freedman and Karsh, *The Gulf Conflict, 1990–1991*, pp. 80ff.
13. Bush and Scowcroft, *A World Transformed*, p. 318. On the way in to his first meeting with the principals, Bush was asked by a reporter, "Do you contemplate intervention as one of your options?" Trying to deflect the question, the president responded, "We're not discussing intervention. I would not discuss any military options even if we'd agreed upon them. . . . But I'm not contemplating such action." Because that offhand comment was followed by his tougher line after meeting Thatcher, a myth grew up that it was she who had changed his position—something reinforced by a well-publicized plea of hers a couple of weeks later for Bush not to "go wobbly." While Thatcher did indeed press a hard line throughout, it is clear that Bush's supposed earlier indecision was overplayed and that the president, encouraged by Scowcroft, was on the way to a hard line well before he met Thatcher in Aspen. "Remarks and an Exchange With Reporters on the Iraqi Invasion of Kuwait," August 2, 1990, Public Papers of the President, George Bush Presidential Library.
14. Minutes, "NSC Meeting on the Persian Gulf," August 3, 1990, George Bush Presidential Library. Haass, the notetaker for the meeting, comments in his memoirs that "all crises have a rhythm, and this was no ex-

ception. [Between the first and the second meetings with the principals,] people had had time to find their bearings and collect their thoughts. The president wanted to set a fundamentally different mood. . . . Again, there was no decision, but the future of U.S. policy was there for all to see." *War of Necessity, War of Choice*, pp. 62–63. In his memoirs, Powell notes that Cheney upbraided him later that day for going beyond his brief during the meeting: "You're Chairman of the Joint Chiefs. You're not Secretary of State. You're not the National Security Advisor anymore. And you're not Secretary of Defense. So stick to military matters." Powell, *My American Journey*, pp. 465–66.

15. In an unconscious echo of Woodrow Wilson's anger at learning the U.S. military had plans on file in case of a war with Germany, some in the State Department were horrified to learn that Centcom was even speculating about a possible war with Iraq. "Somehow [a visiting official from State] wandered into the tactical aspects of the [war game] planning," recalled Joseph Hoar, then Schwarzkopf's chief of staff and eventually his successor, "and went home and told his boss that Central Command was getting ready to go to war with Iraq. An assistant secretary called me and we had a long discussion about this. He wanted to point out to me that we were not at war with Iraq, that Iraq was not an enemy of ours, and that it was entirely inappropriate for Centcom or anybody else to be planning to fight a country with which we were not at war." Gordon and Trainor, *The Generals' War*, p. 45.
16. Schwarzkopf recalled: "I heard a few people around the table gasp. This was a much larger commitment of forces that they had ever imagined making in the Middle East. It was also much more time than they thought would be needed to solve the crisis by force." *It Doesn't Take a Hero*, pp. 301–2.
17. Many histories of the crisis place great importance on the August 6 meeting between Cheney's delegation and King Fahd, on the grounds that Saudi agreement on the nature of the Iraqi threat and the military measures required to counter it was a prerequisite for everything that happened later. It is true that the Saudi position was critical, but the meeting itself was less important than usually portrayed, since the agreement was largely worked out before the American delegation took off. As Scowcroft noted in the meeting on Sunday night, the Saudis "have accepted Cheney going over with the presumption that we are not talking about 'if' but 'how,' 'types,' etc. This was a major breakthrough if we can continue." "Minutes of NSC Meeting on Iraqi Invasion of Kuwait," August 5, 1990, George Bush Presidential Library. See Bush and Scowcroft, *A World Transformed*, p. 330, and Haass, *War of Necessity, War of Choice*, pp. 65ff. According to Khaled bin Sultan, Fahd was thinking on lines similar to the Bush administration from the beginning:

> the King's first instinct was to try to solve the Iraqi-Kuwaiti quarrel

> by mediation. But by Friday evening, after two days of telephoning and consultations with Arab and foreign leaders, he saw no use in pursuing the matter any further. He realized on that Friday that Saddam meant to stay in Kuwait and that no Arab force could expel him. . . . If Saddam were allowed to get away with the seizure of Kuwait, the independence of Saudi Arabia, and indeed of the whole Arab Gulf, would be threatened. . . . Once he had digested Kuwait, Saddam would become the undisputed master of the area—and Saudi Arabia would face pressure to bend to his will. From this perspective, whether or not Saddam attacked the Kingdom was in a sense irrelevant. On all important matters—particularly oil policy and foreign affairs—he would be in a position to dictate terms. . . . With the Kingdom in jeopardy, it was therefore more or less inevitable that the King should turn for help to the United States, the one power strong enough to evict Saddam from Kuwait and restore the status quo ante. . . .

Desert Warrior, pp. 18–21, 26.

18. "Remarks and an Exchange With Reporters on the Iraqi Invasion of Kuwait," August 5, 1990, Public Papers of the President, George Bush Presidential Library.
19. Wrote Baker: "From the start, I had viewed the Soviets as key. In every strategy calculation, I considered their support a prerequisite to a credible coalition. They had to be courted, nurtured, and included to a degree once unthinkable by American policymakers. . . . Their endorsement was so critical, and my relationship with Shevardnadze was sufficiently credible, that I was willing and able to go many an extra mile to keep them on board—even in the face of objections from time to time by some of my colleagues in the national security apparatus." *The Politics of Diplomacy*, p. 281.
20. Baker recalled: "The debate over whether to stop the tanker with military force was one of the few times I found myself completely isolated from my colleagues. Cheney, Powell, and Scowcroft all believed the ship should be promptly stopped, disabled, and boarded. There was even some sentiment for sinking the vessel if it ignored our warning shots. . . . I agreed that we had the right under Article 51 to stop the ship. But from conversations with Shevardnadze, I was sure that unilateral action at that point would be disastrous. . . . Without more explicit U.N. authorization, I was sure the Soviets would bolt from the coalition, a calamity that would surely threaten our entire strategy. . . . In retrospect, I believe that Soviet support for [Resolution 665, authorizing military enforcement of the sanctions] was the pivotal moment in the entire diplomatic process—a tougher vote for them, in my opinion, than the use of force resolution in November. If we had invoked Article 51 and boarded or sunk that ship, I believe we never would have gotten the Soviets to come with us on that

resolution . . . as well as subsequent ones that permitted military force to eject Iraq from Kuwait. The coalition might well have collapsed then and there." *The Politics of Diplomacy*, p. 287.

21. "Scowcroft: 'It was my impression that sometime in early to mid-October, President Bush came to the conclusion, consciously or unconsciously, that he had to do whatever was necessary to liberate Kuwait and the reality was that that meant using force. I began to detect in him a certain calmness. He seemed no longer wrestling with the issue of sending American boys to be killed—that awful decision that only a president can make. I think he had resolved that in his own mind and, therefore, the rest was general strategy and planning, not the terrible human decision he faced.' Bush: 'Brent is probably correct.' " As for "the problem of the time frame for war," Scowcroft noted later, "[w]e would not be militarily prepared for attack probably until early December, assuming we continued our buildup. The window for military action would close soon after that. Late February ushered in a period of frequent bad weather in the region, and then came the Muslim holy month of Ramadan (March 17–April 14), followed by the Haj pilgrimage to the holy sites in Saudi Arabia. While there were various views about the acceptability of conflict during Ramadan, we did not consider it wise to test Arab tolerance. Following the Haj, the heat would become so oppressive that military operations would be all but precluded. These factors together led us to concentrate on a period no later than January or February." *A World Transformed*, pp. 382, 385.
22. The "nightmare scenario" some in Washington worried about was a partial withdrawal in which Iraq retained enough fruits from its aggression to claim a victory. How events would have played out after that is unclear.
23. On the air campaign, see Thomas A. Keaney and Eliot A. Cohen, *Revolution in Warfare?* (Annapolis, Md.: Naval Institute Press, 1995), as well as the rest of the Gulf War Air Power Survey; Tom Clancy with Chuck Horner and Tony Koltz, *Every Man a Tiger* (New York: Berkley Books, 1999); John Andreas Olsen, *Strategic Air Power in Desert Storm* (London: Frank Cass, 2003); Stephen Biddle, "Victory Misunderstood: What the Gulf War Tells Us About the Future of Conflict," *International Security* 21:2 (Autumn 1996); and Daryl G. Press, "The Myth of Air Power in the Persian Gulf War and the Future of Warfare," *International Security* 26:2 (Autumn 2001).
24. Interestingly, Saddam seems to have thought his negotiations with the Soviets were going well and that the crisis was almost over. Kevin Woods writes: "It is clear from Saddam's discussion of the diplomatic situation early on the morning of the 24th that the Iraqi leadership was stunned [by the coalition attack]. The recordings of that morning capture the great frustration that last-minute negotiations through the Soviet Union over Kuwait's final status were not going to preclude the actual ground war. . . . From Saddam's point of the view the 'mediations' under way by

the Soviet Union were making great progress. . . . [Tariq] Aziz announced in Moscow on the 22nd that Iraq would agree to an immediate cease-fire and Iraqi forces would withdraw from Kuwait over a three-week period if the international community would lift sanctions within forty-eight hours. From Saddam's point of view this was the final act of the war that began with international sanctions after the 'liberation' of Kuwait and had continued under more than forty days of air attacks. All that remained were 'technical details.' This was likely the status of the war as Saddam saw it just as coalition forces crossed the barriers into Kuwait and Iraq early on the 24th." *The Mother of All Battles*, pp. 213–14.

25. As Powell noted during the air war, "Our strategy to go after this army is very, very simple. First we're going to cut it off, and then we're going to kill it." Another Defense Department official explained the idea of the ground campaign even more precisely and colorfully: "What we want to do is put them in a bag, tie the top of the bag, seal it, and then punch the bag." Dan Balz and Rick Atkinson, "Powell Vows to Isolate Iraqi Army and 'Kill It,' " *Washington Post*, January 24, 1991, p. A1; R. Jeffrey Smith, "U.S. Aims to Destroy Core of Iraq's Military," *New York Times*, February 25, 1991, p. A1.

26. "Disagreement within the Coalition and in the UNSC over the extent to which Iraq should be reduced could well become acute if conflict is protracted," Freeman continued, "e.g., in an extended air campaign directed primarily against Iraq and Iraqi forces outside Kuwait prior to a ground assault on Iraqi positions inside Kuwait. . . . It follows that attacks on military infrastructure, units and lines of communication in Iraq must be justified as paving the way for the liberation of Kuwait by Arab forces in the Coalition, rather than as an end in themselves. . . . The destruction of Iraq's CBW capabilities and missile forces should likewise be justified in terms of the need to protect Saudi Arabia and other GCC members from the immediate threat of Iraqi attack on their population centers and economic infrastructure, rather than as serving a long-term U.S. objective." Freeman noted presciently that "the crafting of a diplomatic mechanism to accept Iraqi capitulation to the terms set by the UNSC and to arrange a cease-fire must be accomplished before an offensive is begun. Knowing how we will end the conflict is as important as defining how we will conduct it. Achieving the earliest possible surrender of Iraqi forces is vital to preserving Iraq's role in the post-crisis regional balance. This cannot be achieved without a clear statement of the terms we are asking Iraq to accept and an efficient and cohesive mechanism for negotiating their acceptance by Iraq." "U.S. and Coalition War Aims: Sacked Out on the Same Sand Dunes, Dreaming Different Dreams?" Cable 11439, Riyadh to Washington, 12/30/90, in "Iraq—December 1990 [4]," Richard N. Haass Files, National Security Council Collection, Bush Presidential Records, George Bush Presidential Library.

27. These missions were to be carried out while taking every effort to "a.

minimize U.S. and coalition casualties and b. reduce collateral damage incident to military attacks." The document also included a threat that had been conveyed directly from Baker to Aziz at their meeting in Geneva a few days before: "Should Iraq resort to using chemical, biological, or nuclear weapons, be found supporting terrorist acts against U.S. or coalition partners anywhere in the world, or destroy Kuwait's oil fields, it shall become an explicit objective of the United States to replace the current leadership of Iraq." National Security Directive 54, January 15, 1991, George Bush Presidential Library.

28. "Post Crisis Gulf Security Structures," undated paper, "Iraq—January 1991 [5]," Richard N. Haass Files, National Security Council Collection, Bush Presidential Records, George Bush Presidential Library. Cf. Alfonsi, *Circle in the Sand*, pp. 149ff.
29. *This Week with David Brinkley*, ABC News, February 24, 1991.
30. Baker with DeFrank, *The Politics of Diplomacy*, p. 435. Cf. Powell's formula: "We hoped that Saddam would not survive the coming fury. But his elimination was not a stated objective. What we hoped for, frankly, in a postwar Gulf region was an Iraq still standing, with Saddam overthrown." Powell, *My American Journey*, p. 490.
31. James Baker, Oral History, *Frontline: The Gulf War* (1996), accessed at www.pbs.org/wgbh/pages/frontline/gulf/oral/.
32. Atkinson, *Crusade*, p. 59. This reluctance to speak forthrightly about the topic in public was reinforced when Cheney fired Air Force chief of staff Michael Dugan in September for doing so. Scowcroft later conceded, "We don't do assassinations, but yes, we targeted all the places where Saddam might have been." "So you deliberately set out to kill him if you possibly could?" "Yes, that's fair enough." Andrew Cockburn and Patrick Cockburn, *Out of the Ashes: The Resurrection of Saddam Hussein* (New York: HarperCollins, 2000), p. 34. The Gulf War Air Power Survey's comment is straightforward: "Though senior officials and planners both hoped for the demise of Saddam Hussein, all were wary of making that an express aim of Desert Storm. Soon after the air campaign began, Bush said publicly that, 'We are not targeting any individual.' Powell and Schwarzkopf also announced publicly that Saddam Hussein was not specifically targeted. There seem to have been at least three reasons for this reluctance. First, prior to the war, some were concerned that targeting Hussein might be contrary to Executive Order 12333, which prohibits U.S. Government involvement in 'assassination.' . . . Second, planners were aware that the United Nations resolutions around which the coalition coalesced said nothing about eliminating Saddam Hussein. They appeared to realize that setting goals that went beyond those of the UN would necessitate complex and possibly counterproductive negotiations with the allies. Third, and perhaps more important, they were conscious that they could not guarantee strikes aimed at killing Hussein would have their intended effect. . . . Adopting the physical demise of Hussein as a

stated objective and then failing to meet that objective would mar the military as well as the political success of Desert Storm. . . . The president and his advisers were less hesitant about authorizing actions intended to bring about Saddam Hussein's political demise, which, Iraqi politics being what it was, would have brought about his physical demise as well. . . . *Despite somewhat ambiguous policy guidance, the chief architects of the air campaign targeted Saddam Hussein and planned air operations meant to create conditions conducive to his overthrow.*" *Gulf War Air Power Survey*, vol. 1, *Planning and Command and Control* (Washington, D.C.: U.S. Government Printing Office, 1993), pp. 97–99 (emphasis added).

33. "Iraq: Saddam Husayn's Prospects for Survival Over the Next Year," Special National Intelligence Estimate, September 1991, p. 11, accessible at www.foia.cia.gov/.
34. Bush and Scowcroft, *A World Transformed*, pp. 432–33.
35. Swain, "*Lucky War*," pp. xxvi–xxvii. See George C. Herring, "Preparing *Not* to Refight the Last War: The Impact of the Vietnam War on the U.S. Military," in Charles E. Neu, ed., *After Vietnam: Legacies of a Lost War* (Baltimore: The Johns Hopkins University Press, 2000).
36. Colin Powell, Oral History, *Frontline: The Gulf War* (1996), accessed at www.pbs.org/wgbh/pages/frontline/gulf/oral/.
37. Frederick Franks, Oral History, *Frontline: The Gulf War* (1996), accessed at www.pbs.org/wgbh/pages/frontline/gulf/oral/.
38. Walt Boomer, Oral History, *Frontline: The Gulf War* (1996), accessed at www.pbs.org/wgbh/pages/frontline/gulf/oral/.
39. Bush and Scowcroft, *A World Transformed*, p. 354. Cf. these comments by Baker and Gates: "I think the president was aware of the experience of Vietnam consistently through this episode, he knew that the politicians had dictated the war, that it was a limited war, the military had never been able to fight the war they thought they needed to fight to win it, and he was determined to let the military call the shots . . . about how it was conducted, about when it was ended and all the rest and that's exactly what he did and he bent over backwards to give them everything in the world that they might need, so there really couldn't be any suggestion that the civilians were going to try and run the war." Baker, Oral History, *Frontline: The Gulf War* (1996), accessed at www.pbs.org/wgbh/pages/frontline/gulf/oral/. "President Bush was especially good, as was President Reagan, at giving the military their mission, their orders, and staying the hell out of the way. And not trying to micro-manage the conflicts, so you don't have a Lyndon Johnson going down to the Situation Room picking targets as he did in Vietnam. Bush and Reagan stayed out of the way, so when the land war started we were basically in receive mode, just waiting for information to be passed . . . about how things were going." Robert Gates, Oral History, *Frontline: The Gulf War* (1996), accessed at www.pbs.org/wgbh/pages/frontline/gulf/oral/.

40. Samuel P. Huntington, *The Soldier and the State* (Cambridge, Mass.: Harvard University Press, 1957).
41. Powell, *My American Journey*, p. 526.
42. Bush and Scowcroft, *A World Transformed*, p. 471.
43. George Bush, *All the Best, George Bush* (New York: Scribner, 1999), p. 511.
44. Patrick E. Tyler, "After the War; Powell Says U.S. Will Stay in Iraq 'For Some Months,' " *New York Times*, March 23, 1991, p. A1.
45. Bush and Scowcroft, *A World Transformed*, p. 464.
46. "Needless to say, Michael Gordon had a sumptuous dinner at the expense of Dick Cheney." Bernard Trainor, "Analyzing Desert Storm: Observations and Criticisms," in *In the Wake of the Storm* (Wheaton, Ill.: Cantigny First Division Foundation, 2000), p. 6. The conclusion of one prewar report from the intelligence community was typical: "If military action is necessary to force Iraq out of Kuwait, it will likely require a major U.S. military effort and lead to the fall of Saddam Husayn. . . . The military's role in future Iraqi regimes will likely remain central even if Saddam is no longer in power. A successor to Saddam would most likely be a Baath party official, probably from Saddam's Tikriti clan, who would govern with heavy military involvement, or a military officer who would probably also be a Baath party official." "Iraq's Armed Forces After the Gulf Crisis: Implications of a Major Conflict," Defense Intelligence Memorandum, Secret, January 1991, p. 2, in "Iraq—January 1991 [11]," Richard N. Haass Files, National Security Council Collection, Bush Presidential Records, George Bush Presidential Library. Baker writes, "We never embraced as a war aim or a political aim the replacement of the Iraqi regime. We did, however, hope and believe that Saddam Hussein would not survive in power after such a crushing defeat." *The Politics of Diplomacy*, p. 435.
47. On Powell's distribution of passages from Fred Ikle's *Every War Must End*, see *My American Journey*, p. 519. On the Haass memo, see Alfonsi, *Circle in the Sand*, pp. 154 ff.
48. Schwarzkopf briefing, February 27, 1991, in Harry G. Summers, Jr., *On Strategy II: A Critical Analysis of the Gulf War* (New York: Dell, 1992), pp. 27, 280–81, 292.
49. Powell, *My American Journey*, p. 520; Schwarzkopf, *It Takes a Hero*, p. 469. Some have pointed to this exchange as evidence of the army-centric perspective of Schwarzkopf and Powell, since of course it was only the ground campaign that had lasted five days, not the whole conflict.
50. George Bush, "Address to the Nation on the Suspension of Allied Offensive Combat Operations in the Persian Gulf," February 27, 1991, George Bush Presidential Library. The requirements for a permanent cease-fire, Bush noted, included the following: "Iraq must release immediately all coalition prisoners of war, third country nationals, and the remains of all who have fallen. Iraq must release all Kuwaiti detainees. Iraq also must

inform Kuwaiti authorities of the location and nature of all land and sea mines. Iraq must comply fully with all relevant United Nations Security Council resolutions. This includes a rescinding of Iraq's August decision to annex Kuwait and acceptance in principle of Iraq's responsibility to pay compensation for the loss, damage, and injury its aggression has caused. . . . This suspension of offensive combat operations is contingent upon Iraq's not firing upon any coalition forces and not launching Scud missiles against any other country. If Iraq violates these terms, coalition forces will be free to resume military operations."

51. Barry D. Watts writes: "Scrutiny of Operation Desert Storm reveals that Clausewitzian friction persisted at every level of the campaign. . . . Key individuals in the chain of command had had little sleep since the ground campaign started, and many were approaching physical and mental exhaustion; gaps had begun to open up between where friendly units actually were on the ground and where higher echelons though they were; and the clarity of communications, up as well as down the chain of command, had begun to deteriorate in the press of events. . . . The cumulative weight of friction appears more than adequate to explain how and why coalition commanders failed to achieve their operational objective of destroying the Republican Guard." *Clausewitzian Friction and Future War*, rev. ed., McNair Paper 68 (Washington, D.C.: National Defense University, Institute for National Strategic Studies, 2004), pp. 31, 51. Regarding the state of Iraqi forces at the end of the war, Kenneth Pollack writes:

> Of the eight Republican Guard divisions deployed to the Kuwaiti Theater, only three had been destroyed, and a fourth had lost about half its strength. Centcom actually did not know where many American units were, believing them to be farther forward than was actually the case. Nor were the exits from the Kuwaiti Theater cut off. Even the reported "slaughter" on what was becoming called the "Highway of Death" turned out to have been wrong: in fact, the vast majority of the Iraqis fled their vehicles when the first aircraft appeared, and only a few dozen bodies were found among the hundreds of wrecked vehicles. As a result, it was a rude surprise for the administration in the first days of March when we at the CIA began to write about the 842 Iraqi tanks that had survived Desert Storm (about 400 of which were Republican Guard T-72s) and the steps that the surviving Republican Guard divisions were taking to put down the revolts against Saddam's regime.

Pollack, *The Threatening Storm*, pp. 45–46.

52. Calvin Waller, Schwarzkopf's deputy, described feelings that were shared by many at the second tier of decisionmaking, both civilian and military:

"So [Schwarzkopf] gets up in this briefing and he says, 'the gates are closed,' and I look at him and I look at the other people who are around him and my immediate first sensation is, I don't think so, that may be bullshit, that the gates are closed. But I must confess, I didn't . . . I didn't do anything about it. In hindsight, I wish I had said no, we ought to recon[noiter] with this, we should go on, we should do . . . but I didn't." "Why not?" he was asked. "Because at the time I really believed that we had done enough to cause Saddam Hussein to be put out of office, to be run out of Baghdad on a rail, to be hung from the nearest yardarm or what have you. I just did not believe that Saddam Hussein could have survived that sort of defeat and still be in power, and I was wrong." Calvin Waller, Oral History, *Frontline: The Gulf War* (1996), accessed at www.pbs.org/wgbh/pages/frontline/gulf/oral/.

53. Kenneth Pollack writes: "Despite the enormity of Iraq's military defeat, the manner in which Baghdad's military leadership was able to conduct the retreat from the KTO enabled them to snatch a small victory from the jaws of total defeat. Despite all of their mistaken assumptions about the war, at the crucial moment, the Iraqi General Staff quickly put together an effective operation to save as much of their military as was possible. The determined stand by several Iraqi units—mostly RGFC divisions—on 26 and 27 February allowed a larger number of other—albeit, mostly inferior—Iraqi units to escape destruction. The sacrifice of the Tawakalnah, Adnan, and Nebuchadnezzar Divisions, the 2nd Armored Brigade of the Madinah Division, and a handful of other units allowed the survival of the forces Baghdad relied on to suppress the Shi'ah and the Kurds when they revolted against Saddam's rule after the war. Moreover, the escape of other Republican Guard units left Saddam with a core of competent, relatively powerful, formations to spearhead the campaigns against the internal insurrection. To some extent, then, Baghdad's victory over the Iraqi intifadah of 1991 can be said to have been won on the battlefields of the Wadi al-Batin and Madinah Ridge." *Arabs at War* (Lincoln: University of Nebraska Press, 2002), p. 263.
54. It is worth noting that the uprisings seem to have taken Saddam by surprise, too; see Cockburn and Cockburn, *Out of the Ashes*, pp. 15, 21.
55. Bush and Scowcroft, *A World Transformed*, pp. 486–87.
56. Bush and Scowcroft: "We discussed at length the idea of forcing Saddam personally to accept the terms of Iraqi defeat at Safwan . . . and thus the responsibility and political consequences for the humiliation of such a devastating defeat. In the end, we asked ourselves what we would do if he refused. We concluded that we would be left with two options: continue the conflict until he backed down, or retreat from our demands. The latter would have sent a disastrous signal. The former would have split our Arab colleagues from the coalition and, de facto, forced us to change our objectives. Given those unpalatable choices, we allowed Saddam to avoid personal surrender and permitted him to send one of his generals. Per-

haps we could have devised a system of selected punishment, such as air strikes on different military units, which have proved a viable third option, but we had fulfilled our well-defined mission; Safwan was waiting." *A World Transformed*, p. 490.

57. On the postwar uprisings in Iraq and the responses to them, see *Endless Torment: The 1991 Uprising in Iraq and its Aftermath* (New York: Middle East Watch, June 1992); Faleh Abd al-Jabbar, "Why the Uprisings Failed," *Middle East Report 176* (May–June 1992); Cockburn and Cockburn, *Out of the Ashes;* Jonathan C. Randal, *After Such Knowledge, What Forgiveness?* (New York: Farrar, Straus & Giroux, 1997); Kanan Makiya, *Cruelty and Silence* (New York: Norton, 1993); Robert C. DiPrizio, *Armed Humanitarians* (Baltimore: Johns Hopkins University Press, 2002); and Gordon William Rudd, "Operation Provide Comfort" (Ph.D. diss., Duke University, 1993).
58. Ann Devroy, " 'Wait and See' on Iraq," *Washington Post*, March 29, 1991, p. A1. The policy was formalized at a White House meeting on March 26. "We don't want Iraq dismembered, since that would go counter to the reason we fought the war," said one policymaker. "Let Hussein deal with this, then the dust will settle and he's going to have to pay the piper for the war over Kuwait. Or at least, that is what we are counting on." Andrew Rosenthal, "After the War; U.S., Fearing Iraqi Breakup, Is Termed Ready to Accept a Hussein Defeat of Rebels," *New York Times*, March 27, 1991, p. A1.
59. Ann Devroy and Al Kamen, "Bush, Aides Keep Quiet on Rebels," *Washington Post*, April 3, 1991, p. A1.
60. DiPrizio writes: "A close analysis of available evidence suggests that the Bush administration's decision to launch Operation Provide Comfort was motivated by two primary factors. Probably the most important was the desire to assist an important U.S. ally in a strategically sensitive area in managing what both states understood to be a security threat that might lead to further regional instability. The administration was also greatly influenced by pressure from its European allies to act, especially since the United States and its Gulf War coalition were partly to blame for the situation. Two other factors should be noted but considered secondary factors at best. The administration claims that the humanitarian impulse was a driving factor in its decisions and that OPC was consistent with such a purported motivation. But since the intervention can adequately be explained without reference to the humanitarian impulse, and evidence in support of this motivation is less than overwhelming, one should consider it a secondary motivating factor. Finally, widespread media coverage and its likely effects on public opinion should also be considered of secondary importance." *Armed Humanitarians*, pp. 42–43.
61. Stanley Meisler, "U.S. Sanctions Threat Takes U.N. By Surprise," *Los Angeles Times*, May 9, 1991, p. A10.
62. Cockburn and Cockburn, *Out of the Ashes*, p. 31

63. Bush recalled: "I felt the heavy weight that I might be faced with impeachment lifted from my shoulders as I heard the results [of the vote authorizing the war]. In truth, even had Congress not passed the resolutions I would have acted and ordered our troops into combat. I know it would have caused an outcry, but it was the right thing to do. I was comfortable in my own mind that I had the constitutional authority. It had to be done." Bush and Scowcroft, *A World Transformed*, p. 446. The best study of the domestic sphere is John Mueller, *Policy and Opinion in the Gulf War* (Chicago: University of Chicago Press, 1994). He concludes that public opinion affected how policy was articulated far more than how it was formulated: "Bush was able to get the country into war without increasingly bringing the public or Congress around to his view that war was necessary to resolve the conflict. And he carried the venture off in major part through unilateral presidential actions that committed the country to a course of action that in turn increasingly caused people to become fatalistic about it" (p. 138).
64. Bush and Scowcroft, *A World Transformed*, pp. 399–400. Concerned about the possible adverse consequences of the president's passionate obiter dicta, the national security adviser tried to make sure his boss had a handler to enforce message discipline. "It was clear that the President was becoming emotionally involved in the treatment of Kuwait. He was deeply sincere, but the impact of some of his rhetoric seemed a bit counterproductive. . . . [So in late October] Bob Gates and I began the practice of one of us traveling with him on campaign trips. The primary purpose was to have someone at his side were a sudden crisis to arise in the Gulf or elsewhere. But, secondarily, it was to remind him about the occasional flights of rhetoric, which were getting him into trouble." Ibid., p. 389.
65. This was not true on the tactical level, however. Decisionmakers throughout the administration demonstrated a sincere concern for legality and even humanitarianism, often working hard to minimize the war's death and destruction. The differences between these tactical and strategic attitudes resulted in some striking paradoxes. On the one hand, the U.S. military took great pains to spare unnecessary civilian casualties and the destruction of cultural and religious targets. That is why, despite the extraordinary scale of the coalition's effort, there were fewer than 2,300 Iraqi civilians killed and 6,000 wounded during the war itself. On the other hand, the destruction of Iraqi infrastructure during the air war had massive unintended indirect consequences on Iraqi civilians after the fact, as did Washington's decision to stand back and permit Saddam's forces to wipe out the postwar rebellions. Thus American officials were extremely careful to limit the damage they themselves caused to, say, the shrine cities of Najaf and Karbala—only to watch passively as those towns were nearly leveled by somebody else less than a month later. An ordinary Iraqi might be forgiven for failing to see the difference. Cf. Freedman and Karsh, *The Gulf Conflict*, pp. 329, 318, 419.

66. Cf. Bush and Scowcroft, *A World Transformed*, pp. 395, 414.
67. Gordon and Trainor: "In the final analysis, Schwarzkopf acknowledged later, the selection of the ground-war date was determined more by Army and Marine logistics than by a sense that the air war had exhausted its potential. Late February was the earliest possible date that the Army would be ready to attack, and attack it would." *The Generals' War*, p. 307.
68. As Baker told David Brinkley on February 24, "I don't think we ought to underestimate the difficulty that will be involved in securing the peace in the aftermath of winning the war. There will be different viewpoints with respect to what sort of regional security arrangements there should be, with respect to how the Arab-Israeli conflict should be solved, with respect to whether there should be arms control and proliferation regimes, with respect to questions of economic reconstruction." *This Week with David Brinkley*, ABC News, February 24, 1991. Cf. Haass, *War of Necessity, War of Choice*, ch. 4.
69. As Schwarzkopf wrote in his after-action report to Powell, "The rapid success of the ground campaign and our subsequent occupation of Iraq were not fully anticipated. Thus, some of the necessary follow-on actions were not ready for implementation." Gordon and Trainor, *The Generals' War*, p. 515, fn. 12. Cf. Franks' view: "If students of military history and operations want to learn the major lesson the Gulf War teaches, they should look at the war's end state. It was a significant challenge, no doubt about it, to orchestrate the end of a campaign of lightning swiftness that had been conducted by a thirty-five-nation coalition in a region of the world with many opportunities and pitfalls. Nonetheless, it seemed that we gave a lot more thought (at least in the theater) to how to get in and get started than how to conclude it. The intellectual focus seemed to be in inverse proportion. The closer we got to the end, the less we focused." Clancy with Franks and Koltz, *Into the Storm*, pp. 468–69. John Yeosock agrees: "Everyone had a great picture of the tactical-operational aspects of Desert Storm, of how to fight and win the war, but no one had given very much thought to the difficulties and exigencies of conflict termination. There just was not much foresight in this regard." "What We Should Have Done Differently," in *In the Wake of the Storm*, pp. 19–20. Gordon Brown, the foreign service officer who served as Schwarzkopf's chief foreign policy adviser at Centcom, put it simply: "We never did have a plan to terminate the war." Gordon and Trainor, *The Generals' War*, p. 461.
70. Swain, "*Lucky War*," p. 280.
71. Charles Horner, "What We Should Have Done Differently," in *In the Wake of the Storm*, p. 28.
72. Walter E. Boomer, "What We Should Have Done Differently," in *In the Wake of the Storm*, p. 29.
73. February 14, 1991, diary entry, *All the Best, George Bush*, p. 511.
74. Ann Devroy and Molly Moore, "Winning the War and Struggling with the Peace," *Washington Post*, April 14, 1991, p. A1.

75. Richard Haass, Oral History, *Frontline: The Gulf War* (1996), accessed at www.pbs.org/wgbh/pages/frontline/gulf/oral/.
76. Gordon and Trainor, *The Generals' War*, pp. 451–52. "The proposal found no favor in Schwarzkopf's headquarters. 'What the hell is it for?' Cal Waller fumed. 'It serves no useful purpose. How are you going to man the thing? We don't want another Korea, do we?' " Atkinson, *Crusade*, p. 490.
77. Freedman and Karsh, *The Gulf Conflict*, p. 413.
78. Mahnken, "A Squandered Opportunity?" p. 122.
79. As Wafic al Samarrai, the former head of Iraqi military intelligence, would later note: "Before the ceasefire, [Saddam] felt that his doom was very close by. . . . He sat before me and he was almost in tears, not crying, but almost in tears. . . . He said, 'We do not know what God will bring upon us tomorrow.' This shows that he was virtually collapsing. So, he was at his lowest. . . . Within two hours of [Bush's announcement of the ceasefire], Saddam came with his escort and media people to our headquarters and started to issue orders by phone. He became a hero and he felt that everything was now subdued and there is no more danger, and well, we have this legend in our history. He was feeling himself as a great, great hero. He started to go like, 'We won, we won!' His morale was boosted from zero to one hundred." Oral History, *Frontline: The Gulf War* (1996), accessed at www.pbs.org/wgbh/pages/frontline/gulf/oral/.
80. Interview with author, July 20, 2009.
81. Kenneth Pollack writes: "When [Saddam] did not fall, it was left up to a group of working-level officials in Washington to cobble together a containment strategy to keep Iraq under control and apply enough pressure to topple him. . . . When he defied the odds and stayed in power, the United States was left with an unstable containment regime that would require great skill and attention, and the repeated application of military force, to keep in place. The sanctions could have been better designed so that they focused more on Saddam and his military and had less of an impact on the Iraqi people. The United States could have built in elements that could have made it easier to employ limited military operations against Iraq when it reneged on its commitments to the United Nations. Likewise, the inspection regime could have been set up to ensure greater Security Council unity over the long term and make it harder for Iraq to exploit ambiguities in U.N. resolutions and differences among the five permanent members." *Threatening Storm*, pp. 53–54. Some Bush administration officials, it is worth noting, do not fault the design of the containment regime erected in the spring of 1991 so much as what they see as halfhearted implementation of it.

8. THE IRAQ WAR

1. William Scott Wallace interview, *Frontline: The Invasion of Iraq*, available at www.pbs.org/wgbh/pages/frontline/shows/invasion/interviews/wallace.html
2. Anthony Shadid, "Iraqis Now Feel Free to Disagree," *Washington Post*, April 10, 2003, p. A1.
3. John F. Burns, "Cheers, Tears, and Looting in Capital's Streets," *New York Times*, April 10, 2003, p. A1. "Watching [the looting of the Olympic headquarters] from a few paces away was a platoon of American marines. A young lieutenant stood with his men, looking on with a troubled expression. I asked him why he was letting the Iraqis destroy the building, destroy the city. 'I don't have orders,' he said, shaking his head. 'No orders.' " Dexter Filkins, *The Forever War* (New York: Vintage, 2008), p. 98.
4. The claims of Bush administration officials on this point have been disputed. See Stephen Biddle, "Speed Kills: Reevaluating the Role of Speed, Precision, and Situation Awareness in the fall of Saddam," *Journal of Strategic Studies* 30:1 (February 2007).
5. Keith B. Richburg, "British Forces Enter Basra As Residents Loot City," *Washington Post*, April 7, 2003, p. A1.
6. "From government offices, state-owned companies and U.N. buildings came computers, appliances, bookshelves, overhead fans, tables and chairs. From military bases came new Toyota pickups, without license plates, that were careering through Baghdad by afternoon [on April 9]. An elderly woman made her way down Saadoun Street, her back sagging from a mattress she was carrying. Others rode on top of white freezers they wheeled down the road. Throughout the day, trucks piled high with booty roamed the capital." Shadid, "Iraqis Now Feel Free to Disagree."
7. Mary Beth Sheridan, "Beseeching the Conqueror for Aid, Protection," *Washington Post*, April 15, 2003, p. A1. "The problem is, the people doing the looting are not threatening our forces," said one official. "So the right of self-defense to justify the use of force doesn't apply." Vernon Loeb and Bradley Graham, "Group Says U.S. Lags on Restoring Order," *Washington Post*, April 12, 2003, p. A1.
8. "DoD News Briefing, Secretary Rumsfeld and Gen. Myers," April 11, 2003, available at www.defense.gov/Transcripts/Transcript.aspx?TranscriptID=2367.
9. George Packer, *The Assassins' Gate: America in Iraq* (New York: Farrar, Straus & Giroux, 2005), p. 139.
10. Ian Fisher and John Kifner, "G.I.'s and Iraqis Patrol Together to Bring Order," *New York Times*, April 15, 2003, p. A1.
11. Anthony Shadid, "A City Freed From Tyranny Descends Into Lawlessness," *Washington Post*, April 11, 2003, p. A1.
12. Since few actual records of U.S. decisionmaking on Iraq have yet been

made public, any treatment of the case must be considered provisional. Early general accounts of the period include Bob Woodward's books *Bush at War, Plan of Attack, State of Denial*, and *The War Within* (New York: Simon & Schuster, 2002, 2004, 2006, and 2008, respectively); Packer, *The Assassins' Gate*; Michael R. Gordon and Bernard E. Trainor, *Cobra II: The Inside Story of the Invasion and Occupation of Iraq* (New York: Pantheon, 2006), and Thomas E. Ricks's books *Fiasco* and *The Gamble* (New York: Penguin, 2006 and 2009, respectively). Important memoirs and biographies include Douglas J. Feith, *War and Decision* (New York: HarperCollins, 2008); Richard N. Haass, *War of Necessity, War of Choice* (New York: Simon & Schuster, 2009); Tommy Franks with Malcolm McConnell, *American Soldier* (New York: HarperCollins, 2004); Ricardo S. Sanchez with Donald T. Phillips, *Wiser in Battle: A Soldier's Story* (New York: HarperCollins, 2008); L. Paul Bremer III with Malcolm McConnell, *My Year in Iraq* (New York: Simon & Schuster, 2006); Larry Diamond, *Squandered Victory: The American Occupation and the Bungled Effort to Bring Democracy to Iraq* (New York: Henry Holt, 2006); Bradley Graham, *By His Own Rules: The Ambitions, Successes, and Ultimate Failures of Donald Rumsfeld* (New York: PublicAffairs, 2009); Barton Gellman, *Angler: The Cheney Vice Presidency* (New York: Penguin, 2008); Joseph J. Collins, *Choosing War: The Decision to Invade Iraq and Its Aftermath* (Washington, D.C.: Institute for National Strategic Studies, National Defense University, April 2008); and the various oral histories collected by the *Frontline* team (available at www.pbs.org/wgbh/pages/frontline/terror/). Important studies of the occupation include James Dobbins et al., *Occupying Iraq: A History of the Coalition Provisional Authority* (Santa Monica, Calif.: Rand, 2009); *Hard Lessons: The Iraq Reconstruction Experience*, Report from the Special Inspector General for Iraq Reconstruction (Washington, D.C.: U.S. Government Printing Office, 2009); Nora Bensahel et al., *After Saddam: Prewar Planning and the Occupation of Iraq* (Santa Monica, Calif.: Rand, 2008); Ali A. Allawi, *The Occupation of Iraq* (New Haven, Conn.: Yale University Press, 2007); and Robert M. Perito, *The Coalition Provisional Authority's Experience with Public Security in Iraq* (USIP Special Report 137, Washington, D.C., April 2005). Important combat studies include Anthony H. Cordesman, *The Iraq War: Strategy, Tactics, and Military Lessons* (Westport, Conn.: Praeger, 2003); Kevin M. Woods et al., *Iraqi Perspectives Project: A View of Operation Iraqi Freedom from Saddam's Senior Leadership* (U.S. Joint Forces Command, 2006); and the U.S. Army's two official histories of the conflict, Gregory Fontenot et al., *On Point: The United States Army in Operation Iraqi Freedom* (Annapolis, Md.: Naval Institute Press, 2005), and Donald P. Wright and Timothy R. Reese, *On Point II: Transition to the New Campaign* (Fort Leavenworth, Kans.: Combat Studies Institute Press, 2008). The second volume opens with an extraordinary statement: "In many ways, [this] is a book the Army did not expect to write because numerous observers, military leaders, and government officials believed, in the euphoria of April 2003, that US objectives had been achieved and military forces could quickly redeploy out of Iraq. Clearly those hopes were premature."

13. Larry Diamond, one of the country's leading experts on democracy promotion and an adviser to the Coalition Provisional Authority, goes further:

> I opposed going to war in Iraq when we did. The largely unilateral rush to war created predictable problems from the outset. But I now believe that the truly cardinal sin was going to war so unprepared for the postwar—despite all the detailed warnings to which the administration had access. To my mind, this was negligence on a monumental scale, what is called in the law "gross negligence" or "criminal negligence." I do not use the terms lightly. . . . What do we tell the families of the more than one thousand [now more than four thousand] Americans who have lost their lives *since the end of the war*, and the families of the many thousands [now tens of thousands] of Iraqis, Americans, and other foreigners who have been injured grievously or killed in the postwar chaos? There are laws against individuals and corporations who take grossly negligent actions. There are no laws—and there probably cannot be—against negligence, however gross, on the part of government officials at the highest levels. But in the broader calculus of moral responsibility, which is the greater offense?

Squandered Victory, pp. 292–94 (emphasis in the original).

14. For a survey of Gulf politics over the last several decades, see F. Gregory Gause, III, *The International Relations of the Persian Gulf* (Cambridge, England: Cambridge University Press, 2010).
15. For the original articulation of dual containment, see Martin Indyk, "The Clinton Administration's Approach to the Middle East," Washington Institute Soref Symposium, May 18, 1993, available at www.thewashington institute.org/templateC07.php?CID=61. For an overview of U.S. Iraq policy debates during the 1990s, see Patrick Clawson, ed., *Iraq Strategy Review: Options for U.S. Policy* (Washington, D.C.: Washington Institute for Near East Policy, 1998).
16. 1998 Iraq Liberation Act, Public Law 105–338, HR4655 (1998), available at http://thomas.loc.gov/cgi-bin/query/z?c105:H.R.4655.ENR. The bill passed 360–38 in the House and unanimously in the Senate.
17. For an assessment of what seemed to be the parlous state of containment a decade after the end of the Gulf War, see Kenneth M. Pollack, *The Threatening Storm* (New York: Random House, 2002). For the less-dire-but-still-worrying true state of affairs as revealed in retrospect, see the *Comprehensive Report of the Special Adviser to the DCI on Iraqi*

WMD (a.k.a. "the Duelfer Report"), December 20, 2004, and its addenda, available at www.cia.gov/library/reports/general-reports-1/iraq_wmd_2004/index.html).

18. On the rise of radical Islamism, see Daniel Benjamin and Steven Simon, *The Age of Sacred Terror* (New York: Random House, 2003); Steve Coll, *Ghost Wars* (New York: Penguin, 2004); and Lawrence Wright, *The Looming Tower* (New York: Knopf, 2006).
19. Cf. Pollack's assessment: "If the only problem the United States had with Saddam Hussein's regime were its involvement in terrorism, our problems would be relatively mild. On the grand list of state sponsors of terrorism, Iraq is pretty far down—well below Iran, Syria, Pakistan, and others. Similarly, if one were to make a list of all of Saddam Hussein's crimes against humanity, his support for international terrorism would be far down the list, and almost beside the point when compared to his mass murders, horrific torture, use of WMD against civilians, and other atrocities." *Threatening Storm*, p. 153.
20. Bob Woodward writes: "About a week before Bush's inauguration, [incoming national security adviser Condoleezza] Rice attended a meeting at Blair House, across from the White House, with President-elect Bush and Vice President-elect Cheney. . . . For two and one half hours, [CIA director George] Tenet and [Deputy Director for Operations James] Pavitt had run through the good, the bad and the ugly about the CIA to a fascinated president-elect. They told him that bin Laden and his network were a 'tremendous threat' which was 'immediate.' There was no doubt that bin Laden was coming after the United States again, they said, but it was not clear when, where or how. . . . Tenet and Pavitt presented bin Laden as one of the three top threats facing the United States. The other two were the increasing availability of weapons of mass destruction . . . and the rise of Chinese power." *Bush at War*, pp. 34–35. This was not what the new team wanted to hear: "In early January 2001, before George W. Bush was inaugurated, Vice President-elect Dick Cheney passed a message to the outgoing secretary of defense, William S. Cohen. . . . 'We really need to get the president elect briefed up on some things,' Cheney said, adding that he wanted a serious 'discussion about Iraq and different options.' The president-elect should not be given the routine, canned, round-the-world tour normally given incoming presidents. Topic A should be Iraq." Woodward, *Plan of Attack*, p. 9.
21. Haass, *War of Necessity, War of Choice*, p. 213. "It is important to be clear about the significance of my conversation," he continues. "The suggestion is not that a formal decision to go to war had been made in the summer of 2002 and was kept secret. Rather, by July the president had reached the conclusion that it was both necessary and desirable that Saddam should be ousted, and that he was prepared to do what was necessary to bring it about. That this would almost certainly require the use of military force by the United States was not an obstacle. Getting Congress

and the U.N. on board was judged to be desirable but not essential. Although the formal decision to go to war would not be made for six more months, by mid-2002 the president and his inner circle had crossed the political and psychological Rubicon" (p. 216).

22. "Iraq: Prime Minister's Meeting, 23 July," Matthew Rycroft to David Manning, July 23, 2002, available at www.timesonline.co.uk/tol/news/uk/article387374.ece.
23. "Authorization for Use of Military Force Against Iraq Resolution of 2002," Public Law 107-243, October 16, 2002, available at www.gpo.gov/fdsys/pkg/PLAW-107publ243/content-detail.html.
24. UNSC Resolution 1441, November 8, 2002, available at http://daccess-dds-ny.un.org/doc/UNDOC/GEN/N02/682/26/PDF/N0268226.pdf?OpenElement.
25. Feith, *War and Decision*, pp. 316–17.
26. Ibid., pp. 339–43.
27. ORHA Briefing, "Inter-Agency Rehearsal and Planning Conference," February 21–22, 2003, available at www.waranddecision.com/docLib/20080404_ORHAConferencebriefing.pdf, pp. 14, 31 (emphasis in the original). The briefing notes: "Facilities and infrastructure we hope will be intact following hostilities to facilitate our work: Entire oil infrastructure from wells to refineries to export facilities; facilities associated with local, civilian police; court and prison facilities associated with ordinary law enforcement; banks; electrical grid; radio and TV stations; also, all key buildings/facilities of the ministries and agencies for which CIVAD [civil administration] is responsible" (p. 10).
28. Feith, *War and Decision*, pp. 402–3; *Hard Lessons* report, p. 71. For contemporaneous views of how ORHA and the IIA were supposed to work, see Douglas J. Feith, "Post-War Planning," testimony before the Senate Committee on Foreign Relations, February 11, 2003; "Background Briefing on Reconstruction and Humanitarian Assistance in Post-War Iraq" (Jay Garner), March 11, 2003, available at www.globalsecurity.org/wmd/library/news/iraq/2003/iraq-030311-dod01.htm; and "Dr. Condoleezza Rice Discusses Iraq Reconstruction," April 4, 2003, available at http://merln.ndu.edu/MERLN/PFIraq/archive/wh/20030404-12.pdf.
29. Personal communication with former CFLCC planner, May 2010.
30. Franks, *American Soldier*, p. 415
31. Third Infantry Division (Mechanized) After Action Report, Operation Iraqi Freedom (July 2003), available at www.globalsecurity.org/military/library/report/2003/3id-aar-jul03.pdf, pp. 281, 18.
32. At a meeting during the second week of March, Garner learned for the first time that the war plan was designed to bypass Iraqi cities other than Baghdad rather than secure them in detail, forcing him to change his plans for an immediate, rolling transition to postwar reconstruction. He also discovered that his team was not supposed to arrive in the Iraqi capital for a long time after its capture: "The Phase IV plan envisaged ORHA

entering Baghdad after 120 days, by which time most of the country would be pacified and the military would have the necessary resources available to support this civilian organization. This came as quite a shock to ORHA, especially just a few days before the onset of major combat operations. Garner had briefed his concept of operations to senior civilian and military officials for several weeks, without ever being informed that the warplans might require him to operate differently." Bensahel et al., *After Saddam*, p. 67. "CENTCOM wasn't going to let us go in until they felt that the environment was permissive enough for us to get in there. I mean, they didn't want to put the ORHA team in there and get them all shot up on the first day. . . . I went to see Tommy Franks on the 17th in Qatar, and said, 'You got to get me into Baghdad.' He said, 'You know, it's really hot there right now, it's really going to be hard to protect you.' I said, 'I think we'll take our chance.' He said, 'Well, let me talk to the military commanders.' It was either the night of the 17th, the night of the 18th, he called and said, 'Go ahead, and we'll give you all the support we can.' " Jay Garner, interview for *Frontline: Truth, War, and Consequences*, July 17, 2003, available at www.pbs.org/wgbh/pages/frontline/shows/truth/interviews/garner.html.

33. Monte Reel, "Garner Arrives in Iraq to Begin Reconstruction," *Washington Post*, April 22, 2003, p. A1. The *Post* also reported: "Garner constantly lectures his staff, several officials said, on the limited nature of their mission, telling them they must be prepared to 'work their way out of a job' within 90 days. On his first visit to the southern Iraqi port of Um Qasr today, Garner made that point publicly. 'We're here to do the job of liberating them, of providing them with a form of government that represents the freely elected will of the people. We'll do it as fast as we can, and once we've done it, we'll turn everything over to them. We'll being turning things over right away, and we'll make this a better place for everybody,' he said." Susan B. Glasser and Rajiv Chandrasekaran, "Reconstruction Planners Worry, Wait, and Reevaluate," *Washington Post*, April 2, 2003

34. Bremer was often seen as Garner's successor, and in some ways he was, but the actual situation was a bit more complicated. "Garner's job had been to create and run ORHA, which became an office within Centcom, under Franks. Garner was never the head of the CPA; Franks was. Garner's role was to assist Franks in performing the CPA job. . . . When asked to serve as the new civilian administrator in Iraq, Bremer insisted that the job be elevated. He was not interested in stepping into Garner's shoes as head of ORHA. Accordingly, Bremer was hired to replace Franks at the top of the CPA. It was a different and much bigger job that was designed to report directly to Rumsfeld. Bremer's appointment meant that the occupation government of Iraq was now passing from military to civilian hands." Feith, *War and Decision*, p. 422. As for Khalilzad, his departure may not have been premeditated: "Plans had called for Bremer to share

responsibilities with Khalilzad, who on the ground in Iraq was still spearheading political arrangements for a new government. But in a meeting with Bush, Bremer insisted that Khalilzad be removed from the Iraq account, telling the president that he needed 'full authority.' In Bremer's view, it made simple sense that there be only one presidential envoy in a country. Bush agreed. Khalilzad learned his mission had been canceled just minutes before Bremer's appointment was announced on May 6." Graham, *By His Own Rules*, p. 401.

35. Bremer, *My Year in Iraq*, pp. 36, 4.
36. Woodward, *State of Denial*, p. 219.
37. Feith, *War and Decision*, pp. 426–28; Bremer, *My Year in Iraq*, pp. 39–42. Part of the problem on this issue stemmed from faulty assumptions and poor planning. Everyone inside and outside the administration agreed that Saddam's key henchmen should be purged, so the real question was not whether there should be de-Baathification but how deep it should go. Officials in Washington thought they were authorizing a moderate version, because theirs was far less extensive than de-Nazification in post–World War II Germany. In the Iraq context, however, what they had approved was perceived by many as quite extensive.
38. On May 9, Feith writes,

    > Bremer and Slocombe told me of their plan to dissolve the Iraqi army. . . . Before the war, I had presented to President Bush a plan to use the Iraqi army for reconstruction and then to reform and "downsize" it. That plan, developed by General Garner, assumed that the army would remain largely intact—that we could readily employ its human and material assets, including organization, discipline, technical skills, buildings and facilities, trucks, and other equipment. Given that assumption, the case for Garner's plan was reasonably strong. . . . At my March 10 briefing to the President, following Rumsfeld's direction, I had endorsed Garner's plan to use the Iraqi army, reasoning that the pros somewhat outweighed the cons. Now, two months later, the coalition had toppled Saddam's regime—and the Iraqi army had scattered. . . . Under these circumstances, many of the key reasons to preserve the army no longer applied, while the arguments for dissolving it were still relevant. The March analysis that had supported Garner's plan to use the Iraqi military was now, in May, yielding the opposite conclusion, because the facts on the ground had changed.

    Feith, *War and Decision*, pp. 431–34. The plan was authorized by Rumsfeld and briefed to the president and the NSC on May 22. Bremer, *My Year in Iraq*, pp. 53–58.
39. Interview, January 2010. Bremer's and Feith's accounts of the period are instructive. Bremer notes, "In my first meeting with the president, on May 6, 2003, he made clear that his policy was to take the time neces-

sary to create a stable political environment in Iraq. Secretary of State Colin Powell repeated this guidance at a meeting of the NSC principals two days later. . . . The vice president added that 'we are not at the point where people we want to emerge can yet emerge.' The next day, at a full NSC meeting, after a discussion of the political process, the president said his message was 'that this will take a long time." Bremer took all this as license and guidance to adopt a significantly different approach than the one that Garner and Khalilzad had been implementing. L. Paul Bremer III, "Facts for Feith," March 19, 2008, *National Review Online*, available at http://article.nationalreview.com/351979/facts-for-feith/l-paul-bremer-iii. Feith's account has a somewhat different spin. By May 5, he notes, both "Powell and Rumsfeld were talking of slowing down the IIA process, but for different reasons. Powell did so because he opposed setting up an Iraqi government in the coming months. Rumsfeld did so mainly because he didn't want to limit Bremer's flexibility to manage the CPA's relationship with the Iraqi leaders. . . . Bremer could have heard. . . . encouragement to go slow in setting up an IIA [during the meetings he had over the next few days]. . . . At the time, I did not interpret [the various] signals as a reversal or an undoing of the IIA policy. . . . Bremer was processing those comments through a different filter. Although my office had given him the lengthy written record of the government's IIA policy, his understanding developed not from that written record but from what he chose to call the 'clear' guidance he received straight from the mouths of the President and the principals." *War and Decision*, pp. 437–40.

40. Allawi, *The Occupation of Iraq*, p. 110.
41. As one authoritative study generously notes, grading on a curve, "Senior levels of the CPA staff were generally competent and experienced. Everyone worked very hard. . . . Most CPA policies were consistent with best practices that had emerged in the conduct of postconflict reconstruction missions over previous decades. The results in most spheres . . . bear comparison—in some cases, quite favorable comparison—with the record of earlier such operations." Dobbins et al., *Occupying Iraq*, p. xlii. One administration colleague's blunt assessment seems apt: "Jerry held that fucking place together when it was at risk of really flying apart." Interview with the author, January 2010.
42. During its short life, the Rand study notes, the CPA

> restored Iraq's essential public services to near or beyond their prewar level, instituted reforms in the Iraqi judiciary and penal systems, dramatically reduced inflation, promoted rapid economic growth, put in place barriers to corruption, began reform of the civil service, promoted the development of the most liberal constitution in the Middle East, and set the stage for a series of free elections. All this was accomplished without the benefit of prior planning or major infusions of U.S. aid. Measured against progress

> registered over a similar period in more than 20 other American-, Nato-, and UN-led postconflict reconstruction missions, these accomplishments rank quite high. But the CPA could not halt Iraq's descent into civil war. . . . With respect to security, arguably the most important aspect of any postconflict mission, Iraq comes near the bottom in any rankings of postwar reconstruction efforts. The CPA thus largely succeeded in the areas where it had the lead responsibility but failed in the most important task, for which did not. . . . Principal responsibility for rising insecurity must be attributed to the U.S. administration's failure to prepare its forces to assume responsibility for public safety after the collapse of Saddam's regime, to deploy an adequate number of troops for that purpose, and to institute appropriate counterinsurgency measures when widespread violence and resistance emerged. These omissions cannot be laid solely, or even principally, at the CPA's door.

Dobbins et al., *Occupying Iraq*, pp. xxxviii–xxxix.

Diamond's assessment of the CPA chief could stand for his organization as well: "Bremer represented the best and worst of the United States. He was brilliant and yet had only a limited understanding of Iraq. He was alternately (and at times simultaneously) engaging and domineering, charming and patronizing, informal and imperial, practical and inflexible, impressive in his grasp of detail and yet incessantly micromanaging." *Squandered Victory*, p. 299.

43. Wright and Reese, *On Point II*, p. 141
44. Sanchez with Phillips, *Wiser in Battle*, pp. 168, 208. Abizaid took over from Franks on July 8, and reversed the drawdown order three days later. He also extended deployments of the forces in theater.

> Abizaid had obtained the reluctant approval of Donald Rumsfeld beforehand, but the Secretary really had no choice by then. It was either that or total chaos in a couple of months. . . . Abizaid's insistence that nobody could leave without a replacement sent shockwaves through the Pentagon. Everything simply stopped—all the withdrawal plans, all the forces moving out of Iraq—everything just came to a screeching halt. . . . When reality set in, shock turned to anger. . . . By the latter part of July, the Army staff continued to exert tremendous pressure on us to downsize the overall force. "What you want us to do is impossible," they said. "You've got to get your requirements down to a level that we can sustain over time." After some intense conversations about this issue, it became painfully clear to me that the Army did not have the forces available to meet our requirements. . . . [W]e had more than half of the Army's entire combat force already on the ground in Iraq. How

could the Army sustain these numbers? It *was* impossible. Accordingly, Abizaid and I agreed to a sustainable force of 138,000 (pp. 227–30).

45. Elisabeth Bumiller, *Condoleezza Rice: An American Life* (New York: Random House, 2009), p. 169.
46. Feith, *War and Decision*, pp. 6, 4.
47. Some have argued that the key to understanding the decision to go to war against Iraq was the heightened post-9/11 threat environment in which decisionmakers found themselves, bombarded daily with endless and almost unfiltered reports of potential new attacks—including the actual anthrax letters that started being sent in the second half of September. (See, e.g., Goldsmith, *The Terror Presidency;* and Weisberg, *The Bush Tragedy*) This state of seemingly justified near-paranoia, it is claimed, naturally led officials to take a hair-trigger approach to all threats. While accurately describing what Bush administration officials experienced, though, such concerns must have been at most an intensifying factor rather than a generative one, because the Iraq-as-broad-war-on-terror-target meme was conceived and elaborated right after the twin towers collapsed, before information about possible additional attacks was gathered or disseminated.
48. Feith, *War and Decision*, pp. 14–15. The precise views, at precise moments, of senior administration officials about connections between Iraq and 9/11 itself remain murky. Apparently those at the CIA and State Department never believed Iraq was involved, while some at the Defense Department and White House initially thought it was a possibility. Woodward reports that on September 17, the president said, "I believe Iraq was involved, but . . . I don't have the evidence at this point" (*Bush at War*, p. 99). Over time, the weight of evidence seems to have convinced most of the administration that Iraq was not directly involved, but some officials (including the vice president) seem to have continued to regard Iraqi involvement as an open question. For many administration insiders, in any case, the decision to focus on the next attack rather than the last one made the question of a direct connection to 9/11 less relevant than many outsiders believed. As Feith put it in one memo justifying the war, "Don't we need a link to 9/11? No: This isn't about revenge or retaliation, but about self-defense. A link to 9/11 would just emphasize what we already know—that the current Iraqi regime is extremely hostile to us and is willing to cooperate with international terrorism." "Presentation—The Case for Action," September 12, 2002, p. 10, available at http://waranddecision.com/docLib/20080403_TheCaseforAction.pdf.
49. "Deputy Secretary Wolfowitz Interview with Sam Tannenhaus, *Vanity Fair*," May 9, 2003, available at www.defense.gov/transcripts/transcript.aspx?transcriptid=2594.

50. George W. Bush, "Radio Address of the President to the Nation," September 15, 2001, available at http://georgewbush-whitehouse.archives.gov/news/releases/2001/09/20010915.html.
51. George W. Bush, "Address to a Joint Session of Congress and the American People," September 20, 2001, available at http://georgewbush-whitehouse.archives.gov/news/releases/2001/09/20010920-8.html.
52. George W. Bush, "President Discusses War on Terrorism," November 8, 2001, available at http://georgewbush-whitehouse.archives.gov/news/releases/2001/11/20011108-13.html.
53. George W. Bush, "President Bush Speaks to United Nations," November 10, 2001, available at http://georgewbush-whitehouse.archives.gov/news/releases/2001/11/20011110-3.html.
54. George W. Bush, "President Delivers State of the Union Address," January 29, 2002, available at http://georgewbush-whitehouse.archives.gov/news/releases/2002/01/20020129-11.html.
55. George W. Bush, "President Bush Delivers Graduation Speech at West Point," June 1, 2002, available at http://georgewbush-whitehouse.archives.gov/news/releases/2002/06/20020601-3.html.
56. Richard B. Cheney, "Vice President Speaks at VFW 103rd National Convention," August 26, 2002, available at http://georgewbush-whitehouse.archives.gov/news/releases/2002/08/20020826.html.
57. Brent Scowcroft, "Don't Attack Saddam," *Wall Street Journal,* August 15, 2002, available at www.opinionjournal.com/editorial/feature.html?id=110002133.
58. Woodward, *Plan of Attack*, p. 160.
59. Ibid., p. 167.
60. Franks, *American Soldier*, pp. 315, 356–57.
61. "Iraq: Prime Minister's Meeting, 23 July," Matthew Rycroft to David Manning.
62. "Iraq: Advice for the Prime Minister," March 22, 2002, memo from Peter Ricketts (political director, U.K. Foreign and Commonwealth Office) to Jack Straw (U.K. foreign secretary), available at http://downingstreetmemo.com/memos.html. Senior Bush administration officials generally agree on what lay behind the decision, whether or not they agreed with it. Compare Feith's and Haass's conclusions: "Weighing America's vulnerabilities against Saddam's record of aggression, [President Bush] decided that it would be too dangerous to allow Saddam to choose the time and place of his next war with us. . . . War would be risky; leaving Saddam in power would be risky, too. Reasonable people differed then, and differ now, on whether war was the right choice." Feith, *War and Decision*, p. 224. "The arguments for going to war, whether you approve of them, whether you agreed with them or not, were sufficiently broad. It wasn't because of any one individual. It was really based upon a calculation of, 'Could we live with this situation, with an Iraq in possession of chemical and biological weapons, given its history? Could we live with that for

months or years to come?' Some people felt yes, we could. Others clearly felt no. Those who felt no decided—ultimately the president decided—to go to war." Richard Haass, interview for *Frontline: Truth, War, and Consequences,* September 15, 2003, available at www.pbs.org/wgbh/pages/frontline/shows/truth/interviews/haass.html.

63. The most prominent Iraq hawk outside the administration, Kenneth Pollack, made this case extensively in his widely read brief for war; see *The Threatening Storm*, ch. 12. For his and others' mystification over why this path was not followed, see Pollack, "Mourning After: How They Screwed It Up," *New Republic*, June 28, 2004; Eliot Cohen, "A Hawk Questions Himself as His Son Goes to War," *Washington Post*, July 10, 2005; and James Dobbins, interview with *Frontline: The Lost Year in Iraq,* June 27, 2006, available at www.pbs.org/wgbh/pages/frontline/yeariniraq/interviews/dobbins.html.
64. Lawrence Freedman and Efraim Karsh, *The Gulf Conflict, 1990–1991* (Princeton, N.J.: Princeton University Press, 1992), p. 413.
65. Scowcroft, the elder Bush's national security adviser, openly opposed the Iraq War. James Baker, the former secretary of state, opposed it procedurally (in what most took to be a watered-down version of the Scowcroft position). Powell, former chairman of the joint chiefs of staff, did not favor the war but went along with it as a loyal administration official. The former president himself never took a position, but was widely believed to have been in synch with Scowcroft. (Cf. Haass, *War of Necessity War of Choice,* p. 217.) Cheney was the only Gulf War principal to enthusiastically support the Iraq War.
66. One possible reason for this was the president's insistence on viewing Iraq through the prism of 9/11 and the war on terror. In late 2003, he told Bob Woodward that he had never spoken to his father about Iraq because the situation during his presidency had nothing to do with the situation during his father's. "This is part of a large and a different kind of war. It's like a front." "Did you say to him, 'Dad, how do I do this right? What should I think about?' " Woodward asked. "I don't think I did," Bush replied. "It's a different war. See, it's a different war." *Plan of Attack*, p. 421. Another possible reason has to do with Bush family psychodynamics. Although I began research unsympathetic to such interpretations, I now find it plausible that these might have played some conscious or unconscious role in the younger Bush's decisionmaking, and by extension in the views of his followers. Cheney aside, the clear disdain senior Bush 43 officials displayed for senior Bush 41 officials and their views is puzzling and hard to account for otherwise. The single most important player in postwar planning the second time around, moreover—Rumsfeld—was widely known to be a long-standing enemy of the former president. For the argument that familial relationships explain a great deal about the younger Bush's presidency, see Weisberg, *The Bush Tragedy*.
67. In NSC meetings during the Afghan campaign, Bush would repeatedly de-

clare his opposition to using the military for nation building. Cf. Woodward, *Bush at War*, pp. 237, 241.

68. Donald Rumsfeld, "Beyond Nation Building," February 14, 2003, available at www.defense.gov/speeches/speech.aspx?speechid=337.

69. Donald Rumsfeld, "Secretary Rumsfeld Remarks at the Eisenhower National Security Conference," September 25, 2003, available at www.defense.gov/transcripts/transcript.aspx?transcriptid=3189.

70. Weisberg writes: "Covering the 2000 campaign, I found that if you didn't know Bush's position on an issue, you could hazard a fairly accurate guess by figuring out what he *wouldn't* think. George W. didn't want to agree with his father, but he didn't want to agree with Bill Clinton either. So he performed what we learned in the Clinton era to call 'triangulation.' " *The Bush Tragedy*, pp. 64–65 (emphasis in the original).

71. Assistant Secretary of Defense Peter Rodman articulated the point in August 2002:

> The State Department has proposed a Transitional Civil Authority (TCA) led by the United States to govern Iraq once Saddam is gone. . . . My concern is that this occupation government may unintentionally prolong the vacuum in Iraq and enable the wrong people to fill it. . . . While Iraq has no de Gaulle, the [post–World War II] French experience seems to me more instructive than that of [post–World War II] Germany and Japan:
>
> - There are bad guys all over Iraq—radical Shia, Communists, Wahhabis, al-Qaeda—who will strive to fill the political vacuum.
> - An occupation government will only delay the process of unifying the moderate forces.
> - The best hope for filling the vacuum is to prepare the Iraqis to do it.
>
> Thus, I see Afghanistan as the model to be emulated, even if the Iraqis are not yet ready for their Bonn process.

"Who Will Govern Iraq?" Rodman to Rumsfeld, August 15, 2002, in Feith, *War and Decision*, pp. 546–48.

72. See *The Report of the Commission on the Intelligence Capabilities of the United States Regarding Weapons of Mass Destruction*, March 31, 2005, available at www.gpoaccess.gov/wmd/index.html, and *The Report of the Select Committee on Intelligence on the U.S. Intelligence Community's Prewar Intelligence Assessments on Iraq*, July 9, 2004, available at www.gpoaccess.gov/serialset/creports/Iraq.html. Reviewing all the evidence, as well as all the problems and failures and contributing factors to the WMD intelligence debacle, Robert Jervis's conclusion seems the most judicious available:

> The fundamental reason for the intelligence failures in Iraq was that the assumptions and inferences were reasonable, much more so than the alternatives. . . . Saddam had vigorously pursued WMD in the past (and had used chemical weapons to good effect), had major incentives to rebuild his programs, had funds, skilled technicians, and a good procurement network at his disposal, and had no other apparent reason to deceive and hinder the inspectors. In fact, even if there had been no errors in analytic tradecraft I believe that the best-supported conclusion was that Saddam was actively pursuing all kinds of WMD, and probably had some on hand. The judgment should have been expressed with much less certainty, the limitations on direct evidence should have been stressed, and the grounds for reaching the assessments should have been explicated. But while it would be nice to believe that better analysis would have led to a fundamentally different conclusion, I do not think this is the case. If before the war someone had produced the post-war Duelfer Report, I am sure that she would have been praised for her imagination, but would not have come close to persuading. Even now, the report is hard to believe.

"Reports, Politics, and Intelligence Failures: The Case of Iraq," *Journal of Strategic Studies*, 29:1 (February 2006), p. 42. Weapons inspector David Kay offers the most succinct summary of what happened: "We missed it because the Iraqis actually behaved like they had weapons and we weren't smart enough to understand that the hardest thing in intelligence is when behavior remains consistent but underlying reasons change." Woodward, *State of Denial*, p. 278.

73. Kenneth M. Pollack, "Next Stop Baghdad?" *Foreign Affairs* 81:2 (March/April 2002), pp. 42–45. For Pollack's retrospective take on his prewar analyses, see Kenneth M. Pollack, "Spies, Lies, and Weapons: What Went Wrong," *Atlantic* 293:1, January/February 2004, and "Mourning After: How They Screwed It Up."
74. James Fallows, "The Fifty-First State?" *Atlantic*, November 2002; Rachel Bronson, "When Soldiers Become Cops," *Foreign Affairs* 81:6 (November/December 2002); Daniel Byman, "Constructing a Democratic Iraq," *International Security* 28:1 (Summer 2003); Aideed I. Dawisha and Karen Dawisha, "How to Build a Democratic Iraq," *Foreign Affairs* 82:3 (May/June 2003); and James Dobbins et al., *America's Role in Nation-Building from Germany to Iraq* (Santa Monica, Calif.: Rand, 2003).
75. Cf. *Guiding Principles for U.S. Post-Conflict Policy In Iraq* (New York: Council on Foreign Relations and the James A. Baker III Institute for Public Policy of Rice University, 2003); *Iraq: The Day After* (New York: Council on Foreign Relations, 2003); and *A Wiser Peace: An Action Strategy for a Post-Conflict Iraq* (Washington, D.C.: Center for Strategic and International Studies, 2003).

76. See "Reconstruction in Iraq—Lessons of the Past," Haass to Powell, September 26, 2002, in Haass, *War of Necessity, War of Choice*, pp. 279–93. Powell "read [this memo] carefully and agreed with most of it. He also sent it around to his counterparts, including the secretary of defense, the national security adviser (for herself and the president), and the vice president" (p. 228). The fruits of the State Department's "Future of Iraq Project" are available at www.gwu.edu/~nsarchiv/NSAEBB/NSAEBB198/index.htm.
77. *Principal Challenges in Post-Saddam Iraq* (National Intelligence Council, ICA 2003–004, January 2003), p. 19, published as Appendix B to the Senate Intelligence Committee's "Report on Prewar Intelligence Assessments about Postwar Iraq," May 2007, available at www.intelligence.senate.gov/prewar.pdf.
78. Conrad C. Crane and Andrew W. Terrill, *Reconstructing Iraq: Insights, Challenges, and Missions for Military Forces in a Post-Conflict Scenario* (Carlisle, Pa.: U.S. Army War College, Strategic Studies Institute, 2003), p. 1.
79. "Hearings Before the Committee on Armed Services, United States Senate," February 25, 2003. "We concluded that General Shinseki's opinions about the number of US troops it was going to take to occupy Iraq were shaped, to some extent, by the study [*Reconstructing Iraq*]. Because we think he read it." "Question and Answer with Conrad C. Crane," in Brian M. De Toy, ed., *Turning Victory Into Success: Military Operations After the Campaign* (Fort Leavenworth, Kans.: Combat Studies Institute Press, 2004), p. 27.
80. "Hearing Before the Committee on the Budget, House of Representatives," February 27, 2003.
81. Gordon and Trainor, *Cobra II*, p. 104.
82. Woodward, *Bush at War*, p. 137.
83. Scott McClellan, *What Happened* (New York: PublicAffairs, 2008), p. 127.
84. For administration loyalists, of course, this was a feature, not a bug. As second-term national security adviser Stephen Hadley put it to Woodward, "The guy's really a visionary. . . . He defies the conventional wisdom by his boldness. He's unapologetic. He sits there and reaffirms it, and clearly almost relishes it. And, you know, it traumatizes people. And they think, 'What's he doing . . . this cowboy?' . . . Those of us who are here [in the White House] believe in him. Believe in him and believe he has greatness in him." Hadley "said there was a style of discourse at Cornell and Yale Law School, from which he had graduated in 1972, that was academic, long-winded and analytical, but Bush had 'rejected all of that.' Bush had adopted the style of Midland, Texas, and many people think 'it's simplistic, it's two-dimensional, it's not subtle.' " Woodward, *The War Within*, p. 27.
85. This approach puzzled and frustrated nearly all senior members of the

administration, who often initially attributed it to Rice before concluding that she was only carrying out the president's wishes. The president expressed his vision himself near the beginning of the administration: "When [the members of my national security team] give advice, I trust their judgment. Now sometimes the advice isn't always the same, in which case my job—the job is to grind through these problems, and grind through scenarios, and hopefully reach a consensus of six or seven smart people, which makes my job easy." Note the crucial shift from "my job" to "the job," which accurately signaled how Bush would seek to avoid deciding among competing options and push onto Rice the burden of trying to get the principals to sign off on a single, lowest-common-denominator position. Woodward, *Bush at War*, p. 74. As one of Rice's biographers would put it, "Bush was uninterested in having Rice haul his senior advisers into the Oval Office to adjudicate their disputes. 'His close friends agree that Bush likes comfort and serenity; he does not like dissonance,' *Newsweek* would report in 2005." Marcus Mabry, *Twice as Good: Condoleezza Rice and Her Path to Power* (New York: Modern Times, 2007), p. 202. On the Bush administration's national security decisionmaking process, see Peter W. Rodman, *Presidential Command* (New York: Knopf, 2009), ch. 9, and Ivo H. Daalder and I. M. Destler, *In the Shadow of the Oval Office* (New York: Simon & Schuster, 2009), ch. 8.

86. Rumsfeld was openly dismissive and insubordinate, treating her as a functionary who did not have to be answered or even listened to. "A little more than a year into the administration, the secretary of defense was doing nothing to hide his lack of regard for the national security adviser, at least when the president was not around. . . . In meetings Rumsfeld would read while Rice spoke, or he would be so dismissive of her comments that he made other senior officials in the room uncomfortable." A year and a half later, it was "clear not only to Bremer but everyone at the White House [that] Rice and Rumsfeld were settling into a relationship of mutual loathing." Bumiller, *Condoleezza Rice*, pp. 178, 225. Rumsfeld also played games with Powell. As retired four-star general Wayne Downing, who served as deputy national security adviser for combating terrorism, put it, "Before a meeting, . . . Rumsfeld might say or do something to get Powell rattled or angry. 'He'd talk about something that he knew was a hot button for Colin,' Downing recounted. 'It might be about voting rights or immigration or education or abortion—just something to get Colin pissed off. Then the meeting would start, and Colin, who is usually a cool head, would lose his cool. And I'd think to myself, Wow, Rumsfeld is screwing with his head. That's when I decided he was a very dangerous man.' " Graham, *By His Own Rules*, pp. 341–42. In contrast, Cheney—Rumsfeld's close friend and usual policy ally—was a gentleman to his colleagues, but never felt constrained to channel his influence on the president's decisions through interagency meetings or procedures.

87. Interview with author, January 2010. Cf. Woodward's observation: "She felt comfortable when she knew precisely what the president was thinking." *Bush at War*, p. 258.
88. Daalder and Destler, *In the Shadow of the Oval Office*, p. 252.
89. Bill Keller, "The World According to Powell," *New York Times Magazine*, November 25, 2001 p. 60. As this profile was published, Rumsfeld, on Bush's orders, was telling Franks to begin planning seriously for an Iraq campaign.
90. Woodward, *Plan of Attack*, p. 150 (emphasis in the original).
91. Ibid., p. 151.
92. At the August 2002 meeting, Powell "had not said, Don't do it. Taken together the points of his argument could have been mustered to reach that conclusion. Powell half felt that, but he had learned during 35 years in the Army, and elsewhere, that he had to play to the boss and talk about method. It was paramount to talk only within the confines of the preliminary goals set by the boss. Perhaps he had been too timid." On January 23, 2003, Bush asked Powell: "Are you with me on this? I think I have to do this. I want you with me." Powell replied, "I'll do the best I can. Yes, sir, I will support you. I'm with you, Mr. President." Woodward, *Plan of Attack*, pp. 151, 271.
93. In the fall of 2002, "Tenet told [his aide John O.] Brennan that in his gut he didn't think invading Iraq was the right thing to do. Bush and the others were just really naïve, thinking they would just be able to go into Iraq and overturn the government. 'This is a mistake,' Tenet finally told Brennan. But Tenet never conveyed these misgivings to the president. . . . Tenet could have said, "No, this is crazy, this won't work, you shouldn't do this.' But Tenet never said it." Woodward, *State of Denial*, p. 90.
94. Feith, *War and Decision*, pp. 245–46.
95. See Goldsmith, *The Terror Presidency*, and Gellman, *Angler*.
96. "Iraq: Goals, Objectives, Strategy," signed by Bush on August 29. The quotations in the text are from a later version of this document dated October 29, available at www.waranddecision.com/docLib/20080402_IraqGoalsStrategy.pdf.
97. "You can have all the planning you want," she continued, but "if you've got that wrong assumption, then [it's] going to fall apart." Mabry, *Twice as Good*, p. 193.
98. As Dobbins and his coauthors write: "The United States went into Iraq with a maximalist agenda—standing up a model democracy that would serve as a beacon to the entire region—and a minimalist application of money and manpower. . . . The subsequent difficulties encountered owe much to the disjunction between the scope of America's ambitions and the scale of its initial commitment. . . . Had the administration recognized that it was taking on tasks comparable to those Nato had assumed only a few years earlier in Bosnia and Kosovo, but in a society ten times bigger, it might have scaled up its initial military and monetary commitments

and scaled back its soaring rhetoric. (Alternatively, of course, such a realization might have caused the administration to reconsider the entire enterprise.)" *Occupying Iraq*, pp. xxix, xli.

99. Some controversy exists over how to characterize the George W. Bush administration's approach to civil-military relations. Certainly the civilians rather than the military dominated decisionmaking, but whether their dominance was exercised appropriately is disputed. In his 2002 book *Supreme Command*, Eliot Cohen argued for an alternative to Huntington's "objective control" that he called the "unequal dialogue," in which civilian leaders aggressively engaged their military commanders throughout all stages of a conflict. In the unequal dialogue, civilian authorities are supposed to study matters carefully, ask questions, probe relentlessly, and get different opinions, while military authorities are supposed to candidly deliver their own views up the chain of command and then ultimately follow the orders they are given. In a postscript to a 2003 edition of the book, Cohen wrote that "the planning and conduct of the Iraqi war of 2003 followed the model of the unequal dialogue." (*Supreme Command* [New York: Anchor, 2003], p. 240). It would seem, however, that the "surge" decisionmaking process of 2006–2007—which essentially reversed the administration's earlier approach to the war—was a better, or at least more successful, example of the unequal dialogue in action. In addition to Cohen, *Supreme Command*, see the exchanges over these topics in Michael C. Desch, "Bush and the Generals," *Foreign Affairs* 86:3 (May/June 2007) and Desch, et al., "Salute and Disobey" *Foreign Affairs* 86:5 (September/October).
100. Woodward, *State of Denial*, p. 98. For military grumbling about the war planning, see Ricks, *Fiasco*, pp. 40ff.
101. Gordon and Trainor, *Cobra II*, p. 461. White was fired by Rumsfeld in April 2003 for being insufficiently enthusiastic about defense transformation.
102. Michael R. Gordon, "The Conflict in Iraq: Winning the Peace: Debate Lingering on Decision to Dissolve the Iraqi Military," *New York Times*, October 21, 2004.
103. Franks, *American Soldier*, pp. 338. Trying to show how seriously "Phase IV" was taken by the administration, Franks recounts in his memoir that its problems "commanded hours and days of discussion and debate among Centcom planners and Washington officials" (p. 421). He seems not to recognize what a damning admission this constitutes, in light of the year and a half the same planners and officials devoted to getting Phases I–III right.
104. Gordon and Trainor, *Cobra II*, p. 486. The final name decided upon for Sanchez's command was CJTF-7.
105. See Stephen G. Brooks and William C. Wohlforth, "American Primacy in Perspective," *Foreign Affairs* 81:4 (July/August 2002).
106. However Orwellian it might sound, this term is a more accurate de-

scription of Bush's policy than the "preemption" label the administration adopted. See "Sovereignty and Anticipatory Self-Defense," OUSDP memo, August 24, 2002, available at www.waranddecision.com/docLib/20080402_SovereigntyDefense.pdf. On the relation of power, threat perception, and policy in the Truman and Bush administrations, see Melvyn P. Leffler, *A Preponderance of Power: National Security, the Truman Administration, and the Cold War* (Stanford, Calif.: Stanford University Press, 1992), and idem, "9/11 and American Foreign Policy," *Diplomatic History* 29:3 (June 2005), pp. 395–413.

107. See Michael R. Gordon, "Troop 'Surge' in Iraq Took Place Amid Doubt and Intense Debate," *New York Times*, Aug. 31, 2008 p. 41; Ricks, *The Gamble;* and Woodward, *The War Within.*
108. On October 20, for example, Rumsfeld repeated his standard mantra at a press conference: "The biggest mistake would be to not pass things over to the Iraqis, create a dependency on their part, instead of developing strength and capacity and competence. . . . It's their country. They're going to have to govern it, they're going to have to provide security for it, and they're going to have to do it sooner rather than later." "DoD News Briefing with Secretary Rumsfeld and South Korean Minister of National Defense Yoon Kwang-Ung at the Pentagon," October 20, 2006, available at www.defense.gov/transcripts/transcript.aspx?transcriptid=3763. The commanding general in Iraq, George W. Casey, agreed, reporting in mid-November, "We are in a position in the campaign where accelerating and completing the transition of security responsibility to capable Iraqi security forces is both strategically appropriate and feasible." Woodward, *The War Within*, p. 231.
109. Woodward, *The War Within*, p. 292.
110. See Kenneth M. Pollack, *After Saddam: Assessing the Reconstruction of Iraq* (Washington, D.C.: Brookings Institution, 2004); Andrew F. Krepinevich, "How to Win in Iraq," *Foreign Affairs* 84:5 (September/October 2005); and Kenneth M. Pollack, *A Switch in Time: A New Strategy for America in Iraq* (Washington, D.C.: Brookings Institution, 2006).
111. Woodward, *The War Within*, p. 306.
112. Ricks, *The Gamble*, p. 124.
113. Ricks writes: "One of the few relative optimists around Petraeus was a senior intelligence official who would be interviewed only on condition that he not be identified by name. 'I thought we had a real chance of making it work,' he remembered. At the American military headquarters in Iraq, he said, 'A lot of people were thinking ten percent, fifteen percent.' He was at 40 percent, he said. Despite the odds, they were going to try, especially because they didn't see a lot of good alternatives. Just because the odds were bad didn't mean there was a better choice available. . . . Even the principals harbored profound doubts. 'I didn't know,' said Ambassador [Ryan] Crocker. 'I thought it could work. If I had thought it absolutely would not I would be insane to come out here. . . . I will not be one of

those who said I saw this all along. I thought probably it was a long shot, given the levels of violence that had prevailed and the damage they had done to the political and social fabric.' " It was not until "early August [2007], just weeks before he would have to return to Congress to deliver his assessment of the state of the war, [that] Petraeus began to think the surge was working." *The Gamble*, pp. 152, 241.

114. Petraeus's letter, dated September 15, 2008, is available at http://graphics8.nytimes.com/images/2008/09/15/world/20080915petraeus-letter.pdf. On the connections between the surge, the Sunni realignment, and the future of Iraq, see Stephen Biddle, "Seeing Baghdad, Thinking Saigon," *Foreign Affairs* 85:2 (March/April 2006); Austin Long, "The Anbar Awakening," *Survival* 50:2 (April–May 2008); Steven Simon, "The Price of the Surge," *Foreign Affairs* 87:3 (May/June 2008); Colin H. Kahl, "When to Leave Iraq: Walk Before Running," *Foreign Affairs* 87:4 (July/August 2008); Stephen Biddle, Michael E. O'Hanlon, and Kenneth M. Pollack, "How to Leave a Stable Iraq," *Foreign Affairs* 87:5 (September/October 2008); and Marc Lynch, "Politics First," *Foreign Affairs* 87:6 (November/December 2008).
115. John Bolton, *Surrender is Not an Option* (New York: Simon & Schuster, 2007), p. 438.
116. Cf. Feith, *War and Decision*, pp. 496ff.; Rumsfeld, in Graham, *By His Own Rules*, p. 406; and Peter Rodman's comments at a panel discussion on Feith's book held at the Hudson Institute, Washington, D.C., on April 28, 2008, available at www.hudson.org/files/documents/feith%20transcript%20final.pdf.
117. Dobbins and his coauthors again: "It is impossible to know what would have happened if the United States had empowered an unelected Iraqi government in the spring of 2003. Perhaps the Iraqi leaders would have risen to the challenge. It seems equally possible, however, that the sectarian fighting that erupted in 2005–6 would still have come, and at a time when Iraqi institutions would have been even less able to cope than they proved to be a couple of years later. Certainly an Iraqi government formed in the spring of 2003 would have enjoyed an even narrower political base than the one empowered a year later, would have been more dominated by émigré leaders long absent from the country, and would have faced all the challenges that the CPA encountered." *Occupying Iraq*, pp. 48–49.
118. For various perspectives on this topic, see Daniel Byman, "An Autopsy of the Iraq Debacle: Policy Failure or Bridge Too Far?" *Security Studies* 17:4 (October 2008); Kenneth M. Pollack, "The Seven Deadly Sins of Failure in Iraq: A Retrospective Analysis of the Reconstruction," *Middle East Review of International Affairs* 10:4 (December 2006); David C. Hendrickson and Robert W. Tucker, "Revisions in Need of Revising: What Went Wrong in the Iraq War," *Survival* 47:2 (Summer 2205); Bensahel et al., *After Saddam*, p. xxvii; and Wright and Reese, *On Point II*, p. 183.

119. Larry Diamond's version of this counterfactual runs as follows:

> Consider an alternative historical scenario, with the following steps:
>
> 1. Anticipating the chaos and looting that might transpire after the war, the United States deploys an invasion force of 250,000 to 300,000 troops.
> 2. Immediately on taking Baghdad, Coalition troops surround major public buildings, infrastructure, and cultural and historical sites with thousands of troops, armed not only with heavy weapons but with tear gas and other means of crowd control, and with orders to protect the structures from looting and sabotage. Public order is then reestablished relatively rapidly, with only moderate damage and loss of life.
> 3. Tens of thousands of Coalition troops and supporting aircraft are deployed along Iraq's borders to prevent the incursion of foreign fighters—and the exit of Saddam loyalists.
> 4. The Iraqi police are called back to duty, with promises of retention, increased pay, and professional retraining for all those who pass an extended vetting process.
> 5. All soldiers and officers (up to a certain level) in the Iraqi Army are told to report to regional centers, where they are processed to receive continuing pay and then considered for readmission to duty.
> 6. A policy is announced that bans a few thousand top Baath Party and government officials from public life, while subjecting the other top tiers of party membership to a vetting process that retains them in their public sector jobs, and their right to run for office, if they are not found guilty of serious abuses under the old order. The Baath Party itself is allowed to reemerge under a new leadership.
> 7. Immediately on establishing authority in Baghdad, the United States proposes to transfer to the United Nations the primary authority for constituting, within three months, an Iraqi interim government, beginning with the selection of national conference delegates from communities around the country and ending with the conference choosing the members of an interim government.
> 8. In the emerging political processes, Iraqi exile groups must compete for standing with leaders and social forces that remained in the country and the resulting national conference runs the gamut of political tendencies. . . .
> 9. During the first six months after the war, local elections are conducted, to the extent possible, in communities across the country.

10. The United Nations and the United States ask the interim government, in interaction with the national conference delegates, to draw up a timetable for the election of a constitutional convention, the drafting of a constitution, and the election of a permanent government.

There is no guarantee that such a scenario would have been successful. But it might have taken the steam out of the resistance and focused Iraqis on peacefully reorganizing and rebuilding the country. The other cleavages—ethnic, regional, sectarian—would have asserted themselves, as they inevitably do. Even so, the country might have been able to get on with the political challenges it faced. Diamond, *Squandered Victory*, pp. 303–5.

120. Allawi, *The Occupation of Iraq*, pp. 16, 130, 133. American diplomat David Satterfield captured the idea simply: Iraq was like "a tank of 'mutually carnivorous fish.' " Woodward, *State of Denial*, p. 402.
121. Hendrickson and Tucker, "Revisions in Need of Revising," p. 17.
122. Filkins, *The Forever War*, pp. 82, 319.
123. Cost estimates for the war are highly disputed. These rough figures are based on Amy Belasco, *The Cost of Iraq, Afghanistan, and Other Global War on Terror Operations Since 9/11* (Washington, D.C.: Congressional Research Service, 2009), and the Brookings Institution's *Iraq Index*, available at www.brookings.edu/saban/iraq-index.aspx. See also the *Hard Lessons* report, p. 319.

9. TO AFGHANISTAN AND BEYOND

1. Condoleezza Rice, "Iraq and U.S. Policy," Senate Committee on Foreign Relations October 19, 2005, p. 1, http://foreign.senate.gov/testimony/2005/RiceTestimony051019.pdf.
2. Donald Rumsfeld on CNN's *Live From,* November 29, 2005, transcript available at http://transcripts.cnn.com/TRANSCRIPTS/0511/29/lol.01.html.
3. See Gideon Rose, "Neoclassical Realism and Theories of American Foreign Policy," *World Politics* 51:1 (1998), pp. 144–72; Fareed Zakaria, *From Wealth to Power: The Unusual Origins of America's World Role* (Princeton, N.J.; Princeton University Press, 1998); and Michael Mandelbaum, *The Fates of Nations: The Search for National Security in the Nineteenth and Twentieth Centuries* (Cambridge, England: Cambridge University Press, 1988).
4. On Asian regional institutions, see Aaron L. Friedberg, "Ripe for Rivalry: Prospects for Peace in a Multipolar Asia," *International Security* 18:3 (Winter 1993–94), pp. 5–33, and Kent E. Calder and Francis Fukuyama, eds., *East Asian Multilateralism: Prospects for Regional Stability* (Baltimore: Johns Hopkins University Press, 2008). How the rise of China in coming decades will affect the region remains to be seen; for one sobering

forecast, see Robert D. Kaplan, "The Geography of Chinese Power," *Foreign Affairs* 89:3 (May/June 2010), pp. 22–41.

5. John Lewis Gaddis, "The Long Peace: Elements of Stability in the Postwar International System," *International Security* 10:4 (Spring 1986), pp. 99–142.
6. For recent statements of the critics' case, see Andrew Bacevich, *Washington Rules: America's Path to Permanent War* (New York: Metropolitan, 2010) and other offerings from the American Empire Project, www.americanempireproject.com/index.html. For a sketch of what a true pacification strategy toward the Middle East might look like, see Kenneth M. Pollack, *A Path out of the Desert: A Grand Strategy for America in the Middle East* (New York: Random House, 2008).
7. Barack Obama, "A Just and Lasting Peace," Nobel Lecture, Oslo, December 10, 2009, http://nobelprize.org/nobel_prizes/peace/laureates/2009/obama-lecture_en.html.
8. See James F. Dobbins, *After the Taliban: Nation-Building in Afghanistan* (Dulles, VA: Potomac Books, 2008); Ahmed Rashid, *Descent into Chaos: The United States and the Failure of Nation Building in Pakistan, Afghanistan, and Central Asia* (New York: Viking, 2008); and Seth G. Jones, *In the Graveyard of Empires: America's War in Afghanistan* (New York: W. W. Norton, 2009).
9. "Afghanistan Strategy," Douglas Feith to Donald Rumsfeld, October 11, 2001 (emphasis in original); available at www.waranddecision.com/docLib/20080420_AfghanistanStrategy.pdf.

10 Bob Woodward, "McChrystal: More Forces or 'Mission Failure,' " Washington Post, September 21, 2009, p. A1. The commander's assessment can be found at http://media.washingtonpost.com/wp-srv/politics/documents/Assessment_Redacted_092109.pdf?sid=ST2009092003140.

11. "Remarks by the President in Address to the Nation on the Way Forward in Afghanistan and Pakistan," December 1, 2009, available at www.whitehouse.gov/the-press-office/remarks-president-address-nation-way-forward-afghanistan-and-pakistan.
12. The Iraq War was such a complete fiasco in this regard that it has prompted several people to make a similar point. Cf. Nora Bensahel et al., *After Saddam: Prewar Planning and the Occupation of Iraq* (Santa Monica, Calif.: Rand, 2008), p. xxix, and Frederick W. Kagan, "War and Aftermath," in Brian M. De Toy, ed., *Turning Victory into Success: Military Operations After the Campaign* (Fort Leavenworth, Kans.: Combat Studies Institute Press, 2004).
13. For further discussion of contingency planning, see Gideon Rose, "The Exit Strategy Delusion," *Foreign Affairs* 77:1 (January/February 1998), pp. 56–67.
14. Carl von Clausewitz, *On War*, ed. and trans. by Michael Howard and Peter Paret (Princeton, N.J.: Princeton University Press, 1976), p. 89.

INDEX

Page numbers beginning with 293 refer to endnotes.

ABOUT THE AUTHOR

Gideon Rose is the Editor of *Foreign Affairs*. Before serving as Managing Editor of the magazine, he served as Associate Director for Near East and South Asian Affairs on the staff of the National Security Council and as Olin Senior Fellow and Deputy Director of National Security Studies at the Council on Foreign Relations. After studying classics at Yale, he received a Ph.D. in government from Harvard and has taught American foreign policy at Princeton and Columbia.